Books by EDWIN O'CONNOR

THE ORACLE

THE LAST HURRAH
(*Atlantic Prize Novel,* 1955)

BENJY

THE EDGE OF SADNESS

THE EDGE
OF
SADNESS

THE EDGE OF SADNESS

BY

EDWIN O'CONNOR

An Atlantic Monthly Press Book

LITTLE, BROWN AND COMPANY
BOSTON   TORONTO

FIRST EDITION

ATLANTIC–LITTLE, BROWN BOOKS
ARE PUBLISHED BY
LITTLE, BROWN AND COMPANY
IN ASSOCIATION WITH
THE ATLANTIC MONTHLY PRESS

Published simultaneously in Canada
by Little, Brown & Company (Canada) Limited

PRINTED IN THE UNITED STATES OF AMERICA

For
Frank O'Malley

I

I

THIS STORY at no point becomes my own. I am in it — good heavens, I'm in it to the point of almost never being out of it! — but the story belongs, all of it, to the Carmodys, and my own part, while substantial enough, was never really of any great significance at all. I don't think this is modesty; it seems to me a simple fact. Because now that it's all over, and I can look back on all those weeks and months — not with detachment, of course, but with a somewhat colder eye than before, I have the feeling that whatever happened would have happened whether I had been on hand or not, whether I had spoken or been still, whether I had known the Carmodys all the days of my life or had met them for the first time one sunlit afternoon in the middle of last week.

Still, there is this: I was at least there. The friend of the family, the invited intruder, the small necessary neutral cushion against which all belligerents might bank their shots in turn — I was there, as I say, and there I stayed. I stayed with the Carmodys and their story from the first — from that Sunday in June when old Charlie Carmody, saluting the one day of the year which could be counted on to move him deeply, gave himself a birthday party. . . .

The story begins, really, some days before that Sunday: it begins with an early morning telephone call. Even now, months later, I can recall that morning with a special vividness, for it was the first such morning in a long time. There had been a heat wave, a severe one and the first of the summer, and on this morning I woke to find that it had broken at last. The wind was sweeping in from the sea, and even here — here, in this old rectory, set in this soiled and airless slum — it was possible to smell and feel the morning, the sunlight and salt air. It was the start of one of the great dazzling days that sometimes break unannounced over this city, cool and shining and full of light, and I knew that if I got up and walked to the rectory roof and looked out through the scoured and cloudless morning I could see for miles and miles to the muted bluish outlines of the hills far to the north. . . .

Which, I should say at once, I did not intend to do. I was in bed and fully awake: I had awakened shortly after six o'clock. In recent months I've been saying the seven o'clock Mass, and I wake at this same hour each morning, usually without the alarm. Which is fine, but is only half the battle, for to wake up is one thing, and to get up quite another. And this, for me, is one of the old, long-standing problems; I can remember, years ago in the seminary, speaking of it to old Father Condon. Overscrupulous, to be sure, but there it was and there *he* was, my spiritual counselor: a marvelously serene old man with the face of a happy rabbit and almost no voice at all. It was said that he had worn it out, giving advice.

"Oh my goodness," he whispered, his upper lip twitching away at some invisible carrot. "Oh my goodness me. Why, that is a very slight problem, my dear boy. It is almost not a problem at all. It is a mountain made out of a molehill: perhaps you know the expression? A little discipline, a little self-sacrifice, a little remembering each day of just what it is we get up *for*. We are doing God's work, are we not, and Satan does not sleep till noon. That is a good thought, my dear boy: *Satan does not sleep till noon.* No no no. Keep that uppermost in your mind before retiring each night and you will find that in a surprisingly short time you will be *bounding* out of bed in the morning. Rising will become, not a chore, but a positive joy. Oh yes yes yes. I have lived a very long time and I have seen it happen again and again. Why, I recall that once, many many years ago now, of course, I. . . ."

And then his voice, as it had a habit of doing, faded off entirely, and he, poor simple kindly old man, all unconscious of this, kept on talking for some time, smiling all the while, his lips moving rhythmically, his long old hands feathering the air, presumably pointing up inaudible anecdotes. I stayed for the pantomime — young seminarians are not encouraged to walk out on the performances of their superiors — and considered the advice. I found that I had listened dutifully but had not believed. Seminaries are peppered with occasional doubts, but mine were secular rather than theological: I could not believe in the joyous morning bound. It was disbelief well-founded: thirty-five years between then and now, and while I rise punctually I do so grudgingly; each morning brings its own renewal of the battle. . . .

All of which has nothing whatever to do with the problems of the Carmodys, into which I was brought suddenly as the telephone by my bed rang, at six-fifteen in the morning, and surprisingly the caller was old Charlie Carmody.

"Well, well, Father," he said, "good mornin' to you." He had a queer, old man's voice: strong enough, yet every word came out wrapped in some sort of powdery cocoon, as if he had a permanent dustbin in his throat. "I hope, now, I didn't get you up out of bed, Father? It's not too early for you?"

The question was solicitous enough, but then I had been brought up on Charlie Carmody; I thought I knew what he was really saying. My father had been a great expert on Charlie. They had been boys together, and my father — who never became successful in business — seemed to spend most of his time studying Charlie — who became very successful indeed — watching him with incredulity, some amusement, a certain

[5]

amount of rather reluctant admiration, and a somewhat larger amount of positive dislike. He had collected hundreds of stories about Charlie and told them all; sometimes his analysis of Charlie's character took the form of a curious defense.

"The man is misunderstood," he would say. "There are people in this city who think that Charlie's the meanest man that ever drew on a pair of trousers. He's no such thing. In his whole life he never did anything mean just for the sake of being mean. One, there's no money in it. Two, it's not his style at all. Charlie's not the lad to jab his thumb in your eye just so's your eye will sting. But say you went into his real estate office one day to buy a little piece of land worth maybe ten dollars, and Charlie was good enough — you being an old friend — to sell it to you for a hundred. And say you went to go out of the door with your little bargain under your arm, and Charlie ran around from behind his desk to help you on with your hat — just to keep on being friendly. And say just at the moment he had your hat in the air, ready to slip it on your head, you twisted your head around of a sudden and got his thumb smack dab in your eye — well now, that's the sort of thing that makes the day for Charlie. He's not only cheated you deaf and dumb, but you almost go blind in the bargain! What sensible man could ask for more? I tell you, it's the little bonuses that count the most with Charlie. They go to prove, don't you see, that God's on the right side. That He's up there smiling away in Heaven, whipping up the frosting to put on the cakes that his partner Charlie bakes!"

This was my father on the subject of his boyhood chum. Not a calm and measured judgment, exactly, but not without its truth, either; I discovered that as over the years, and from one source and another, I came to know a good deal about Charlie. Enough, for example, to know that while he would never have called me simply to wake me — a practical joke which put no money in your pocket was, to Charlie, simply not practical — still, if he could have wakened me en route, so to speak, to his main purpose, why, so much the better! Just one more little bonus. And so, still lying on my bed, I said, "No, no, I've been up for some time, Mr. Carmody."

But Charlie was a veteran campaigner; his disappointment, if there, did not show.

"Ain't that grand!" he said instantly. "Is that a fact, now? Well well. Up for some time. I tell you, Father, nothin' does me more good than to hear a thing like that. Nothin' makes me feel better than to know there's somebody besides myself ain't afraid to get up in the mornin'. Specially when he's a young feller like yourself."

This was Charlie's brand of flattery. Or else it was simply that to the really old all others are young. In any case, on my last birthday I was fifty-five.

Charlie went on to pay his tribute to youth.

"Mostly," he said, "they're a bunch of bums. You have to club them to get them up out of bed, and then when you do they can't do nothin'. It was different in my day, Father. D'ye know what time I got up when I was a young feller? I'll tell you: *four o'clock*. How's that for gettin' up in the mornin', Father? And d'ye know what time I get up today, old as I am? D'ye know that, Father?"

"You've always been an early riser, Mr. Carmody. . . ."

"Four o'clock!" he cried. "The same as always. Old as I am I'm on my own two feet and downstairs in the kitchen gettin' my own breakfast every blessed mornin' of my life. Would you believe that, Father?"

I would indeed, for his son John, who had been in the seminary with me, had often spoken of this habit of his father's. He had spoken of it without enthusiasm.

"It doesn't make any sense," he had said, frowning. In those days, John — fresh out of boyhood, towheaded, with large light serious eyes, and already regarded, even in the seminary, as pretty much of a lone wolf — still thought of his father, not so much with irritation (although there was plenty of that) as with a puzzled incomprehension — as someone who by right

[7]

of position deserved respect and affection and love, but whose every baffling action threw one more block across the path. "You see, when he gets up everyone else has to get up too. Oh, you don't actually *have* to, but you might just as well: I can tell you that after four o'clock there's no sleep for anybody in that house. There are all those noises in the kitchen, for one thing, and then when he finishes there he can always find something else to do. Something that's *noisy*. He'll water the lawn, for instance. Have you any idea how much noise that can make? At five in the morning when it's pitch-black outside? And when it's Dad who's doing the watering? With his own special early-morning technique? Of course you can always complain but when you do he always says the same thing. He says we're the last people who should be complaining because he's only doing it for us. For *us!*"

He had shaken his head, badly perplexed, and somewhere in the distance I had seemed to hear my father's cough of knowing laughter. Here was corroboration indeed!

"Yes," Charlie was saying now, "I get up nice and early before the sun and do the little things that need doin' around the house. And then what d'ye think I do, Father? You'd never guess. Not in a million years you wouldn't. I'll tell you what I do: *I go out in the yard and have a grand look at all the birds.* Ain't birds lovely, Father?"

This was the softer side of Charlie: rarely visible, like the other side of the moon. I said, "Are you a bird watcher, then, Mr. Carmody? That's something I wouldn't have guessed."

"Ah well, I ain't a loony about it, Father. I don't go crawlin' around on my belly through the wet grass lookin' for the golden-headed hoohoo. That's nut stuff. But the fact of the matter is that nothin' makes me feel better than comin' down and findin' the whole place littered with birds, all kinds, singin' and chirpin' away all around me. I tell you, Father, there's days I might be Saint Francis himself!"

I said, "Aha." It was a pale acknowledgment, unworthy of

[8]

such an announcement, but the truth is that I had nothing better to offer. Thirty years as a priest and still unable to make the appropriate small talk with the living duplicates of the sanctified! Who, by the way, are more numerous than you might imagine. With Charlie, however, it seemed safe enough to stick to the birds, and so I said, "I suppose they come around because you're good to them; you probably put out a little seed for them every once in a while.

There was a pause.

"Ah well," he said slowly. "I don't exactly do that now, Father. No no. I'm a great man for the birds, none greater, but the way I do is this: they can damn well feed themselves. And they do! I'm here to tell you they do. *On my grass seed.*" The old voice had suddenly become louder; there was a new note, unmistakably grim. "Grass seed is sellin' for two dollars the pound," he said, "and every robin on the place is gettin' big as a hen. Oh, I tell you, Father, a man has to look sharp or they'll eat him out of house and home. What I do, sometimes, is I sit around waitin' for them with a few little stones in my pocket." A dusty reminiscent chuckle came over the telephone. "I pegged one at this big black devil of a starlin' the other day," Saint Francis said gleefully, "and damn near took his head off. Well, well, we mustn't complain, Father. That's the way life goes."

I agreed that it was, it was indeed, and took a look at my watch. It was getting late, and the question was: Why? Why, that is, this telephone call? Because nothing was clearer than that old Charlie had not called to discuss birds with a parish priest. Especially this parish priest: in all his life Charlie had never telephoned to me before. There was no reason why he should have. We were hardly old friends; he had of course known my father well, but me he knew chiefly as a boy who occasionally used to be seen about his house in the company of his son John. And although I knew all the Carmodys, it was only Helen and John to whom I was at all close, and in recent years I had seen John only half a dozen times, while Helen I

[9]

had not seen at all. So that to hear from any Carmody was rare enough, but to hear from old Charlie was unprecedented. It is a tribute to my father's schooling that I knew at once that Charlie wanted something, that he wanted it badly, and that he wanted it from me. But exactly what he could want — or, for that matter, what I had to give — was beyond me. Meanwhile, there was the hour, and Mass was to be said; the problem was to get Charlie to the point and get him there quickly.

But Charlie came to the point by himself and almost at once. Apparently tiring of preliminaries, he said with a sudden briskness, "Well now, Father, I didn't call you up to talk about the robin redbreast, did I? I wouldn't waste the time of a man like yourself on that. The thing is this: will you come to dinner? On Sunday next?"

And this completely surprised me: so completely that I could manage only the simple-minded echo: "Sunday?"

"My birthday," he said matter-of-factly. In just such a tone might another man have said, "Thanksgiving" or "Christmas." He added, "Eighty-two years old, Father. Eighty-two this Sunday, that's what I am. And not an ache or pain in my body or a doctor's bill in sight. How many d'ye know can say the same?"

"Not many," I said absently, and wondered: Is *this* what Charlie wanted? My presence at his birthday dinner? Was this probable? No. Yet all the same. . . .

"Not many," he repeated. Clearly, the answer did not satisfy. "I don't know *none*," he said. "Except myself. They're droppin' like flies around me but I feel grand. I might live to be as old as Methuselah's Uncle Jack. So we'll have a little celebration on Sunday, Father. John'll be there, of course, now he's back in the city, and I know he'd like to see you. As would we all, Father. As would we all. Will you come along?"

There was the possible answer: John. Was it he, back again in his home city after so many years away, the pastor now of the very church in which he had been baptized, who was behind the invitation? In a way this made sense, yet in another way it did not, for Charlie had never been known to bend to the wishes of any member of his family. Was it at all in character for him to invite his son's friend to dinner — to his own birthday dinner? Simply to oblige his son? Once again I seemed to hear my father sounding his notes of polite derision. Still — and here is the really curious thing — almost instantly, and without the faintest reasonable motive (for was it possible that I could have wanted to go and watch Charlie cheer the fact of his own survival?) I said, "I'd like very much to come, Mr. Carmody. It's good of you to think of me."

"That's grand," he said. "Ah, that's grand, Father. We won't have nothin' fancy. Just the family and a few old pals. It'll be like old times."

Old pals? Old times? Was this the explanation: had Charlie, subject to the confusions of old age, taken me for his own contemporary? But he had done nothing of the kind; clarification came with his most surprising statement yet. He said, "Seein' you there will remind me of your pa. Oh yes, Father, your pa and I were great pals in the old days. Did you know that, I wonder?"

I thought of what my father would have said to this; I said only, "I knew you were boys together."

"Boys and *pals*," he corrected me. "Born on the same block, not fifty feet from each other. And in the same year. Ah, those were the great days, Father." He sighed. "Beefsteak," he said emotionally. "D'ye know what beefsteak was sellin' for then, Father? I'll tell you: ten cents the pound. And liver was nothin' at all. Oh yes yes, Father, there's not a day goes by I don't think of your poor pa. He's dead now . . . how long? Ten years, would it be?"

"Nine."

"Nine years. Well well. And here I am, fit as a fiddle." He sighed and said, "Well well. But that's the way life goes, Father. We mustn't complain."

This was a curious kind of resignation, to be recalled, apparently, only in connection with particular triumphs: the near-beheading of the starling with the stone, the outliving of my father by almost a decade. In view of the way life was going for Charlie, there did not seem too much reason for complaint.

"Well," he said, "we'll see you on Sunday, then, Father." And then, as an afterthought, he said suddenly, "Ah, I'll tell you what I'll do: I'll have John stop by to pick you up."

"No no," I said quickly, for John's parish, in which his father lived, was at the farthest point of the city from mine; the trip would have taken him miles out of his way. "It's not necessary, Mr. Carmody. I have my car."

"Not another word, Father!" he cried happily, for he had seen the possibility and was on it like a cat: here, in this needless errand for his son, lay the seeds of another little bonus. "He'll be there for you with bells on. A nice drive in the open air of a Sunday: there's nothin' the boy likes better!"

I thought of the "boy" — who was my own age, almost to the day — wheeling his car through the open air of a large city on a steaming Sunday afternoon in summer; I said, "But Mr. Carmody —"

"Goodbye, Father!" he cried. "And don't forget old Charlie at the altar now and again. Don't forget the odd prayer. A man needs all the prayers he can get!" The dusty old voice stopped abruptly; there was a click; old Charlie was gone.

So it was all arranged: I was going to a birthday party. And all the while, as I rose, as I bathed, shaved, dressed, even as I prayed, the question returned, over and over again, drifting in like the soft flow of the morning itself — the question which still was: Why? Not so much why I had been invited — although, the peculiarities of my host considered, that was mysterious enough — but much more to the point, why I had agreed to go. Because these days I was hardly a birthday party man; also, I was not particularly a Charlie man. And, even leaving this to one side, there was the fact that any party of Charlie's would be, for me, more than a party, a simple family get-together. The familiar setting, the old faces, the old themes, the memories, one after another: for me, it would be nothing less than a trip to the past. And in view of all that's happened, is such a trip really necessary? Is it even advisable? For now, here in Saint Paul's at least — and at last — I seem to be doing well enough: then why not let well enough alone . . . ?

Saint Paul's: what a strange parish it is, really. Days, even weeks go by, and I don't even think of this; then, without preparation of any kind, there comes a moment — such as this one, at the beginning of a glorious day — when suddenly all the lights seem to be turned on at once, piercing the comfortable protection of routine, and I am confronted with the cold fact of Saint Paul's. It is called Old Saint Paul's, but there is no New Saint Paul's — the adjective refers only to the age of the parish. The church itself is the perfect mirror of the district: once, three generations ago, active, prosperous, in a way even noble; today, a derelict, full of dust and flaking paint and muttering, homeless, vague-eyed men. This section of the city is dying and so is Old Saint Paul's. In a sense it is hardly a parish at all any more, but a kind of spiritual waterhole: a halting place for transients in despair. Still, we have our permanent families, those who live and stay here: Syrians, Greeks, some Italians, a few Chinese, the advance guard of the Puerto Ricans — a racial spectrum whose pastor I am. Here the pastor cuts quite a different figure than he does in one of the old, compact, all-Irish parishes. I know those parishes well. I was raised in one; I have in fact been pastor of one. Now I am here — and it should be said that this is hardly regarded as a promotion. Yet I have no complaints, not a single one, for this parish has come to mean something so special to me that I can't begin to say or explain. . . .

Well, my point is that in those other parishes there does exist, invariably, this peculiar rapport between the priest and the people, and I suppose it springs largely from their knowledge that he is one of them — that he is from their own particular branch of the tree. The result is that whether they love him or fear him or respect him or admire him or distrust him, they are aware of him, he does enter their daily lives, he is a part of them.

In Old Saint Paul's, not so. These people are good people — at least I think they are: after almost a year here, I know them scarcely at all. I say Mass for them (and they come: in fair numbers on a Sunday, very few if any on a weekday); I hear their confessions (despite certain obvious difficulties, for I am no linguist); sometimes I baptize them, marry them, bury them; occasionally I go to their homes on sick calls. There are the formal, necessary points of contact between the shepherd and his flock — beyond them we do not go. They accept me as their priest, but after that they keep their distance — and I must admit (and this is perhaps my fault, my dereliction) that I keep mine. And I must admit this too: that sometimes, in the rectory, at night, I think with a little longing of the old days and the old ways — because, after all, a man may turn his back on something and still remember it. But these are thoughts that come and go, and not too often at that; for the most part, day in and day out, I know the truth: that this way, the present way, is for me the best way. The work gets done, I don't neglect my people, and I can truly say this: that here, in this shabby corner, in what is undoubtedly the backwater of the diocese, I am happy. Or, if not happy — what a word that is! — at least content and secure in the pattern of my days. Which is more, far more, than once, not so long ago, I would have thought possible.

So then, why revisit the old days? Why go to see Charlie whooping it up for himself? Why even go to see John and Helen? Nostalgia? Curiosity? Even loneliness? Possibly; probably. Is there any harm in it? No. Is there any point to it? No. Yet all the same, on Sunday I am going to Charlie's birthday party. . . .

And now I am going to my Mass. . . .

[14]

2

SUNDAY was a day of double significance: it was the birthday of old Charlie; it was the feast day of Saint Paul. Charlie Carmody and the Apostle of Charity: it was a strange coupling. I wondered if Charlie was aware of it. Probably. I wondered if he approved of it. Probably not. Saint Paul was Saint Paul, to be sure, but Charlie's birthday was Charlie's birthday, and he was a jealous guardian of his own. So it was more than likely that if he thought at all of Saint Paul this morning, he did so with some truculence, regarding him as something of an intruder, a kind of heavenly poacher.

But Saint Paul is the patron saint of my parish, and at both the seven o'clock and the eight-thirty Masses — Father Danowski, my curate, said the ten and the eleven — he was the subject of my sermon. I talked a little longer than usual — for a total of perhaps ten minutes. Which I suppose is really not very long at all, but fashions in sermons have changed: the full-fledged oration of today would have been no more than a warmup a generation ago. When I was a boy in Saint Raymond's — the same parish where John Carmody is pastor now — old Monsignor Degnan thought nothing, absolutely nothing, of climbing the steps Sunday after Sunday and settling down for a solid minimum of thirty minutes. And thirty violent,

[15]

storm-tossed minutes at that, for the Monsignor rarely whispered when a shout would do.

What an extraordinary man he was, really. And what an extraordinary voice: a great, soaring roar that clearly had been meant for vast cathedrals, but had somehow wound up in small, neat Saint Raymond's. ("Like a war whoop in a telephone booth," my father once said.) It was also a voice that came oddly from this little bald man who looked so frail — the Monsignor's appearance was of the kind that breeds pious legends. It was said, for instance, that he was engaged in a perpetual fast, eating nothing but a thin soup and unbuttered bread. The fact was that he had an enormous appetite: once when I was a young priest in his rectory, I watched him eat a breakfast of fruit, oatmeal, fried eggs, fried ham, fried potatoes, several cups of tea, and a quarter of an apple pie.

"A man should eat food that sticks to the ribs," he had declared. He had never looked more drawn or insubstantial than at that very moment.

There was also the rumor that he was ill, desperately so, and that he had come to Saint Raymond's to die — although exactly why this should have been the ideal parish for such a purpose was never explained. The rumor survived for fifty years and so did the Monsignor. He lived to be ninety, dying only last year, an eccentric, despotic, devout old man who, like so many of the old-time pastors, seemed to have won from his people something which was not love, exactly, but a peculiar kind of exasperated idolatry. . . .

Those famous Sunday sermons! It seems to me now that I remember them all, and this is surprising because I never listened to one. Really *listened*, I mean. I don't think many people did. The Monsignor, roaring away through the complicated underbrush of his discourse, defied all pursuit. His successor, on the other hand, is at the opposite end of the stick: lucidity itself. With John Carmody there is no underbrush at all. The level of the sermons at Saint Raymond's, then, unquestionably has gone up; the question is: Has the number of listeners gone up too? And the answer to that is — No. Which is not necessarily John's fault: like all of us in the pulpit today, he has problems of which the Monsignor did not even dream. For when the Monsignor spoke to his flock of fifty years ago, he spoke always to the same solid, homogeneous band — that is, to men and women who worked harder with their hands, who had little education (in almost all cases far less than the Monsignor himself), and whose wants and needs and thoughts were fairly uniform and simple. But the laity of today is a far different matter, and now John Carmody, as he looks down each Sunday from his pulpit in Saint Raymond's, knows that ideally every sermon, in order to be effective, must be comprehensible to a congregation composed of lawyers, stevedores, educators, doctors, scrubwomen, politicians, bankers and baby-sitters — in short, to an incredible layer cake of intellect and imagination. And when you talk about what matters most — that is, when you talk about Almighty God — how do you talk to a layer cake? With the simplicity of genius? Exactly — except that in the diocese at the moment the genius-priest is in relatively short supply. And so John Carmody does the best he can, talking away each Sunday, occasionally looking down at all the familiar faces, searching for signs of interest or at least attention, and finding all too often the vacant eye and the drooping head. Which, even on the most superficial level, is not pleasant: no man particularly enjoys being a bore. . . . . .

My own problem is the same, and yet slightly different. I too talk away and look down at all the faces, but here in Saint Paul's they're faces which are still strange to me, and in which I can read — nothing. Not interest or attention or boredom or discontent — just polite, neutral nothing. In the whole church only Mr. Yee supplies the break in the pattern. Mr. Yee is Chinese: a round soft man who sells herbs in a small dark shop a few blocks from the church. (Most of the city's China-town is within my parish, although few of the Chinese are

Catholics: Mr. Yee is the most visible exception.) He sits in the same spot every Sunday at the seven o'clock Mass, and when I begin to speak I see him lean forward eagerly, as if he'd been waiting all week long for just this moment. Throughout the sermon he sits in this same position, wolfing down every phrase. So this is gratifying, flattering, a boost to the ego. Or, rather, it would be if it were not for a discovery I made some weeks ago. Mr. Yee understands no English. Not a single blessed word. . . .

And yet the saving thing is that it all couldn't matter less. The sermons, I mean. Granted that a good sermon is better than a bad one, what really counts — what *only* counts — is of course the Mass itself, and the people do come to that. As for the effectiveness or ineffectiveness of the sermon — well, who can measure these things? I know priests who are counted immensely successful in the pulpit: vibrant, eloquent men who capture a throng with a word. I don't for a moment doubt that they do good work, but at the same time I always wonder how deep down the word really goes, and if it does go down, does it stay awhile, or is it gone overnight, like some bubble of a child's happy dream? One never knows. . . .

At least *I* never know, and in any case it has little enough reference to my own situation: very few throngs have been captured with a word from the present pastor of Old Saint Paul's. The most I can say for my sermons is that they're short, they're simple, and I'm reasonably sure they do no harm.

They certainly do none to Mr. Yee. . . .

But I mentioned the seven o'clock Mass this morning: a curious thing happened. I had finished the sermon and was going back to the altar for the *Credo*; as I turned to walk across the sanctuary I thought I saw Helen Carmody. She — if it *was* she — was seated at the side of the church, towards the back, but since the lighting is bad and I had only the one quick glimpse, I could not be sure. After Mass, when I looked out from the sacristy, she had gone. Was it Helen? The more I wondered, the more I realized how unlikely it was: that she would have come all the way across the city to Mass, and more, that she would have come at this hour of the morning. For she had none of her father's passion for getting up before the birds: as a rule, the later the Mass, the better for Helen. And so most probably I had been mistaken, although the mistake did serve to point out rather clearly the extent to which the Carmodys, one by one and after so long a time, had suddenly begun to pop up in my mind. . . .

I had called John the day before, simply to tell him that there was no need to pick me up, and to make it quite clear that the suggestion had come, not from me, but from old Charlie.

"Yes, I recognized the touch," he had said. "The thumbprints of the master were all over that one." Even in his voice there was a little of his father: he was high and clear, and spoke with a sardonic, rushing impatience which became somewhat more pronounced whenever his subject was old Charlie. The years had sharpened his attitude towards his father; the bafflement of boyhood had been succeeded by less indulgent emotions. "Characteristically, I disappointed him," he said. "I told him that I'd be delighted to pick you up, that it wouldn't inconvenience me in the least. He hadn't counted on that at all; naturally it upset him. So I'm coming."

"John, it's silly. I really can drive. . . ."

"I'm coming," he repeated emphatically. "I want to see you, I want to see your place. So don't argue. I'll be there."

And so he came. He came just as I was having one of my little talks with Father Danowski. Father Danowski was disturbed: the collections, always small, had been smaller than usual this Sunday. For this Father Danowski was disposed to blame the man who had passed the collection basket at the eleven o'clock Mass. It seemed that he had been late, that he had not begun to pass the basket until Mass was nearly over, that the people, already congratulating themselves upon the

[19]

supposed oversight, had resented the last-minute attempt at recovery and had given grudgingly, if at all. Father Danowski had had to take steps.

"I was forced to give him a reprimand," he said. "A severe reproach."

A severe reproach! I could see it all: Father Danowski, solemn, chunky, broad-faced, butter-haired, and twenty-five, looking like some impossibly grave fullback, elaborately explaining to the old Portuguese collector — who is well past twice his age — that he has done wrong. Very wrong. And does the collector get the point? No. Does he get Father Danowski? Again, no. For which I can hardly blame him: my curate is a strange lad. I don't think I've ever seen a priest quite like him; there are times when he reminds me of nothing so much as a child who has sneaked into a full-dress suit, just to startle the grownups. Because he's just a boy, really, and yet somehow he's managed to pick up this extraordinary manner which comes out of him like steam; a queer, comic, old-fashioned, slightly foreign ornateness which, I suppose, is intended to suggest age, cosmopolitan experience. It's in his movements, his walk, his talk — in the pulpit on Sundays, for example, he's quite likely to use words and phrases that haven't been heard for decades: "Beware!" or "I beg of you, desist!" That sort of thing. It's almost as though he'd landed on the shore and discovered the language the day before yesterday — yet he was born here and raised here; I doubt if he's left the city five times in his life. . . .

Of course part of it is that he's so young and wants to prove that he isn't. Saint Paul's is his first assignment; curiously enough, he seems to enjoy it. I think he regards the parish as a challenge. I think he regards me the same way. He hasn't a grain of humor, but he's full of zeal, and he's obviously determined to make poor old Saint Paul's once more a going concern. I think he sees a future of shining Gothic and stained-glass windows and a great swell of Gregorian positively shaking the stones. I haven't the heart to destroy this innocent vision, and it's not my place to do so; young dreams like this need no outside push to help them perish. Meanwhile, it can be a little hard on delinquent volunteer collectors, who of course must be reproached for postponing all that new stained glass.

But my curate is better than this: there are depths here that are seldom seen. For instance, there is the matter of my story — he must know it; the diocesan grapevine is no less efficient than any other. But if so, he's never once given the slightest sign of knowing — which is not so easy for a boy just out of the seminary, and which argues a tact and a thoughtfulness I wouldn't have suspected in him. I suppose in a way I don't understand him at all: he's like the rest of the mysterious facts that make up Old Saint Paul's. But we get along well, I like him, and there are those moments when he forgets to be impressive — sometimes I see his face as he says his Mass, or when he baptizes a child — and then I know that underneath all this elaborate, faintly pompous, faintly absurd surface is a very decent lad who will one day make a fine priest.

In the meantime, however, there *is* that surface. . . .

"I impressed it on him most firmly," he said. "I said to him: 'Reflect, Manuel: when you do not pass your collection basket promptly, as you promised you would do, do you know what you are being? You are being a laborer who is not worthy of his hire! That is what you are being!' "

"Yes. Although his hire isn't much, is it? He isn't paid anything for passing the basket."

"A metaphor, Father," Father Danowski said sternly. His reproaches were by no means confined to collectors. "A metaphor which I am sure struck home. I said to him: 'You must not break a promise to God, my son!' "

My son . . . !

We talked for some moments about the collector, then passed on to other subjects. There was the immediate matter of Sunday dinner and the fact that I would not be there to eat it. This astonished Father Danowski: in the six months he had been with me, I don't think I had left the rectory once for a purely social occasion. So now I was revealing an unfamiliar side: the pastor in his butterfly aspect. His round young blue eyes grew rounder; rounder still when he learned the identity of my host.

"Charles Carmody!" he exclaimed. "The celebrated miser?"

Father Danowski is full of surprises. I said only, "Well, he has money, a lot of it, and I've never heard that he threw any of it away. But I've never heard that he was regarded as a miser. Much less that he was celebrated as one."

"Oh yes, Father," he said knowingly. "By many people. I can tell you of this from my own personal experience. You see, my family once lived in a house of which Mr. Carmody was the owner. A large apartment house. This was many years ago when I was a small boy in what I believe was generally termed Polish Town. You're familiar with that section of our community, Father?"

"Yes. Yes, indeed." Although in fact the general term had been somewhat less kind: the section had in fact never been called anything but Polocks' Town. Father Danowski's suave alteration was understandable. I said, "At one time, I know, he owned a good deal of property over there. I suppose he still does."

"How thrifty he was!" said Father Danowski. "He would come around *in person* on the first day of each month to collect his rents. He would come in person and on foot, Father, and he would be wearing old garments, despite his great wealth. One could not help thinking that he was like some person from the pages of the great English novelist, Charles Dickens." He paused, and for just a moment I was absolutely certain that he would next ask me if I were familiar with the great English novelist, Charles Dickens. But he did not; he continued with Charlie's rent gathering.

"We were always prepared for him. Of course it would be

foolish to pretend that we were highly prosperous at the time. That was quite impossible, as my father was then employed as a school custodian. That is somewhat like a janitor, Father."

"Yes, yes, I know. . . ."

"At the Harold E. Babson Elementary School, to be precise. A very modern, well-constructed building, but the pay was low. However, no matter how reduced our circumstances, we were always most prompt with our rent. That is something my father insisted upon. How well I recall his saying to me: 'Stanley, you must always remember this: *Be on time with your rent, and keep up the payments on your car.* That way they can never get you.' My father is an extremely shrewd person, Father. Despite his lack of formal education."

I nodded. Respectfully, I hope. I had never met Father Danowski's father, but it made no difference: by now he had emerged from our conversations as a vivid figure, larger than life, and I felt that I had known him forever. Apparently he was a man of great strength and independent spirit who had worked at many jobs, remaining at each only long enough to confirm his contempt for his employer. From his varied experiences he had drawn a set of maxims, all geared to the practical aspects of everyday living: how to cure a cold at home, how to sleep soundly and on which side, when to borrow and when to lend, how to get ahead in the Park Department, how to make dogs like you, what to say when you are invited to a picnic. Father Danowski remembers these maxims, all of them; he quotes them reverently and very often. And in the face of this I find myself peculiarly helpless, for when it comes to someone quoting his father, am I of all people in any position to object . . . ?

"How ironical it is," Father Danowski said now. "By that I mean, Father, that here on the one hand we have the Church, with her needs which are so many and so great. And here on the other hand we have Mr. Carmody, an aging person, with his great funds and his saving ways. How good it would be,

[23]

Father, if through some old friend he could at last be made to see that it is truly more blessed to give than to receive!"

His words were enthusiastic; he looked at me significantly. And I knew that, for him, I had suddenly acquired new meaning: I had become the possible shortcut to the bigger, better Saint Paul's. His eyes were bright; I think that already a vision was forming of the aging person, persuaded of the error of his saving ways, slowly untwisting the clasp of some mammoth leather purse and releasing an endless fluttering flood of dollar bills which spilled out like flags from a magician's hat. . . .

Poor Father Danowski!

I said, "It would be good indeed. The only trouble is that for years any number of old friends have been trying to tell Mr. Carmody about the blessings of giving. And with no success: he just doesn't find the idea congenial."

"But," said Father Danowski, "if perhaps it were put to him in the correct way? As, for example, in the light of the ultimate rewards to be gained? 'A cup of cold water given in my name . . . ?'"

"Yes. Of course men like Mr. Carmody haven't the slightest objection to giving you a cup of cold water. The danger is that they're likely to stop right there."

"But," said Father Danowski, "but. . . ."

But it was at this point that John came in, and Father Danowski was forced to abandon the attack, at least for the moment. And when I introduced him to John, his face fell; clearly, he had forgotten — if indeed he had ever known — that old Charlie had a son in the Church. I have an idea that as soon as he saw John he saw also the demolition of his hopes; in any case, he said only a few words — although these were delivered in his glossiest, most elaborate manner — and then withdrew. John watched him go with curious eyes; he said, "What's that supposed to be?"

"My new curate."

"Why does he talk like that?"

"It lends him authority. Or at least he thinks it does, which is pretty much the same thing. Don't judge him by that; he's not bad at all."

But the words were automatic; I was not really thinking of Father Danowski or his hidden merits. I was looking at John — I suppose with the usual speculative look of appraisal with which most men who are getting along regard their contemporaries. Every meeting becomes a comparison test. In this instance, the comparison was hardly to my advantage; I said admiringly, "You don't change much, do you? You seem in great shape."

And he did: a tall man with the spare body of a boy, who (like myself) was fifty-five, and who (unlike myself) looked years younger. I think it was impatience that kept him trim; it was surely not exercise — even as a boy he had hated all forms of athletics. But now well into his middle years, he had not an extra sag or pouch or fold; there was still a kind of adolescent boniness about him which the years and his own temperament had not been able to conceal. His face was long, alert and almost without lines; his hair, though gray, had been gray for thirty years; and in the end, it was only the eyes — pale-blue, rather distant, occasionally washed with fatigue or, more probably, exasperation — which gave the clue to age.

He shrugged. "I'm all right. I stay about the same." Then, perhaps feeling that something in the way of reciprocity was called for, he said hurriedly, "You're not looking so bad." This may have been less than a handsome compliment, but it was quite good enough, considering the facts — and also considering John. For he was not at his best with the little courtesies usual at such moments, probably because he didn't think of them as courtesies at all. He thought of them as traps, dangerous traps, and he avoided them whenever possible.

"I've given up saying 'How are you?' to people," he had announced to me one day, some years before this, "because everybody I meet has a kidney stone. Or a spot on his lungs. Or a boy in college who wants to give up medicine and become an orchestra leader. I swear I don't know a single soul who can just say 'Fine!' and keep on walking!"

I knew what he meant. A priest — any priest — is especially vulnerable here. Every parish has its core of hardy conversationalists who are always on the prowl, day and night, carrying with them a little invisible knapsack of treasured complaints; at the sight of the first Roman collar, the eyes brighten and the knapsack opens. Not only in the parish, but anywhere; walking along an unfamiliar street, riding on a train, a priest will suddenly find beside him a stranger who, given the faintest encouragement, or even given no encouragement at all, will obligingly and at once reveal the sum total of his private woes. Not, certainly, that these are always trivial. Sometimes — not often, but sometimes — what comes out is so personal and so loaded with pain that it becomes almost unbearable even to listen. But you do listen, of course. You listen; then you say something, anything; then you hope for the mercy of God. This is what you do, and — not being God — this is all you can do. . . .

But, as I say, revelations of such gravity and sadness are not the common run, and for the most part these confidences have no great seriousness. Unfortunately, they have no great variety, either. I've often thought, as I've stood where I've been stopped, listening, nodding, every now and then making my own invaluable contribution to the occasion — "Yes, yes," "I see," and "Of course you did!" — that each of these impromptu monologues was remarkably like the one before it, and that all the words taken from all of them together might easily have been compressed into one of two short sentences:

(1) *I've given them everything, Father, and what do I get in return?*

(2) *I'm no good to anyone, Father, not even to myself!*

The spirit of the second sentence is humbler. It's also usually the result of a rather full evening's drinking.

All of which is natural enough. There are few who are per-

[26]

petually on the crest of the wave; most of us can get lonely or miserable and then, suddenly, feel the urge to get outside family and friends and talk to someone who doesn't know us too well — someone, in short, to whom we may complain that we have no one to complain to. For this role, the priest is an obvious choice. And if this occasionally has its annoying side, it also — particularly in the case of John — has a comic one as well. For no one could have been a more reluctant confidant than he — this withdrawn man, whose years with so meddlesome a parent as old Charlie had hardly made him more outgoing; yet almost from the day of his ordination he seemed to become a marked man, a hitching post for minor complaints. Nuisances, even celebrated nuisances, sought him out and found him; he must have given them slim comfort, but they came back for more. Why this should have been I have no idea — possibly for the same mysterious reason that a man who dislikes dogs is invariably the one at whom the puppy leaps. Be that as it may, one of the earliest and most typical recollections I have of John as a priest is that of a tall young figure hurrying down Cathedral Avenue on an autumn afternoon, his normally long stride lengthening in desperation, while behind him, half a block away but coming on strong, sprinted a gray little wisp of a woman with a face of eager woe, crying, "Ooo-hoo! Father! I got another letter from Tim today!"

I wondered, now, how much of this had gone on in recent years. It was hard to say, for he had been away, stationed in the western part of the diocese, but I was sure that a good bit of it continued — and sure, too, that he received it no less fretfully. Once or twice, in our rare meetings, he had spoken of it, and I gathered that he had begun to think longingly of some ideal pastorate in the future: one in which, say, he would at last find himself surrounded by suitable parishioners — those whom he had once so wistfully described to me, those who could be relied upon to ". . . just say 'Fine!' and keep on walking!"

If anything like this had been his goal — a curious goal, ad-

[27]

mittedly, for a priest — he must have been cruelly disappointed. For of all the parishes in the diocese he might have been given, he had in fact been given Saint Raymond's — busy, gossipy, preternaturally inquisitive Saint Raymond's, where he had been a boy, where he had grown up, where everyone knew everyone else, and where almost no one kept on walking. And where, finally, old Charlie sat — dominant, vigorous, and waiting for his son.

It could not have been at all what John had planned.

But he seemed in good spirits now; looking about him, examining his surroundings, he said, "It must be twenty years since I've been over here. Not since Dan Leahy was pastor. Come on, take me on the grand tour."

And so I took him around my place, so different from his own. We went first through the short passage which led from the rectory into the church. Outside, it was a bright afternoon of full summer sunlight, but here, before the main altar, it could easily have been the middle of the night. The architect responsible for Saint Paul's so many years ago — just who he was doesn't seem to be in the parish records — clearly had not foreseen the day when the outdoors would be welcomed into church; his church had been built like an armory, and the heavy blocks of stone were almost proof against all light and sound. We could hear nothing, and for the first few moments all we could see were dim outlines, the dull red glow of the sanctuary lamp, and, spearing its way across the nave, one single thin shoot of sunlight which came in through a broken stained-glass pane.

We stood there awhile in the darkness and the silence. Old churches like Saint Paul's — old churches, that is, which are not merely old, but whose best days are obviously over, and whose slow quiet fade has long ago begun — have an atmosphere all their own. The air is heavy and still — as if to announce that no crowds now pass through to stir or change it — and there is always a particular smell: a smell of dust, and incense, and coats

[28]

of varnish on old wooden pews, and the burned wax of endless votive candles. And in such an atmosphere there is always a certain sadness, but there is always too a feeling of calm and timelessness which is not at all unpleasant. . . .

We stood there; from the back of the church came a series of shuffling noises. I looked around, and through the dimness I could make out a man pushing himself up from his knees. I recognized him as an old man who comes here every afternoon and stays for a long time, perhaps praying, perhaps resting, perhaps just coming in because he has no place else to go. He's been doing this for possibly three weeks now: I have no idea if he belongs to the parish, or where he comes from, or who he is. He makes no attempt to come up to me or to speak to me; the answer probably is that he prefers to be let alone. Which is reasonable enough, certainly. . . .

We went back to the rectory, and because John had been here many years ago, I took him through the entire building — a trip I seldom make myself. For the rectory is really huge: built in a day when wood was cheap, even the long hallways were heavily paneled in a gloomy oak; I once had the feeling that I was walking about inside a giant's coffin. The rooms were also paneled, and there were many of them; in its heyday, the rectory could accommodate perhaps a dozen priests. But now, with only Father Danowski and myself, I had closed most of it off, and we used only our two bedrooms on the second floor, and a kitchen, dining room, and combination office-reception room on the first. This half-rectory was hardly splendid, but it was comfortable and it was neat — this, thanks to an elderly Italian woman who came in each day to cook and to clean. It was also in some need of repairs — this, thanks to our janitor-handyman: a queer, unreliable, almost-unemployable named Roy, who often disappeared for days at a time, and then returned, mumbling evasively of improbable misadventures. I think he very rarely told the truth: his stories about himself, his parents, his nationality, his schooling, his previous experience were usually in wild conflict with one another. Father Danowski disliked him — largely, I suppose, because Roy (who is fairly dark and almost certainly part Negro) once or twice has claimed Polish descent. However, when he does work he works reasonably well, and in any case we are in no position to be choosers. . . .

As we walked around, I told John something about the parish. He said very little, but he had a sharp eye in these matters — surprisingly enough, for someone who had no taste for business details, he was an excellent administrator; in the astute regulation of his own parish there was the reminder that he was, after all, old Charlie's son — and I suspected that he was missing nothing. When we came back to our starting point he shrugged and said abruptly, "Just as I thought: it hasn't changed a bit. All right, you've roped off half your rectory, which doesn't solve anything. You ought to put a rope around the whole business and then pull. Hard."

I smiled. "You're not impressed with Old Saint Paul's?"

"I am not. Today it's an absurdity, and no one knows that any better than you. The only really sensible answer is the bull-dozer. Or possibly you might turn it over to the Franciscans: they like to run around in these antique beehives. But as a practical, workable church for this part of the city, in this day and age — it's simply crazy, Hugh. For one thing it can't even begin to pay its way."

"No. But then, I don't think anyone expects it to. The Bishop is willing to carry us along."

"I'll bet he is. Out of the goodness of his well-known heart," he said sardonically. He had never been one of the Bishop's greatest supporters. Now, I suppose, he was less so than ever — for of course it was the Bishop who had brought him back to Saint Raymond's, two months before. He said now, "One more brilliant episcopal stroke."

This was a small challenge thrown out to me, an invitation to debate: we had argued before about the Bishop. For where

[30]

John certainly felt nothing remotely like gratitude towards the Bishop, I, on the other hand. . . .

But there was no point in arguing now; I said, "Brilliant or not, it worked out well enough. At least it did for me."

He waved an impatient hand. "Ah," he said. "You give him too much credit. All right: he did you a favor. Was it really such an enormous favor? It's as if you had a cold and he lent you a cotton handkerchief. That's really not the same thing as giving you a ton of penicillin and a cashmere coat to keep you warm. Anyway, it's impossible to talk to you on that score." His tone suddenly shifted and he said, "You're getting along all right, then?"

For with all the years he had spent in devising various brakes to prevent him from slipping down the chute into the great swamp of other peoples' lives, when it came to me the brakes were no good: he could not bring himself to use them. He felt for me not only friendship, but what, I suppose, was a kind of protective concern, and although we seldom saw each other these days I knew from different sources that he had been greatly worried about me, and I think he may have worried about me still. He added, "Everything's going well? No problems?"

It was the most general of questions, but we both knew that it had a most particular meaning. And, knowing this, I could answer truthfully, "No, John. Not a one."

"Really? *No fooling, now!*"

This solicitude came galloping across the room like a threat, and I thought of what my father had once said of a man he knew: "He's a grand friend to have. Tell him your troubles or he'll beat your brains out!" Which was a little like John, although here the belligerent kindness owed something to inexperience: after all, to *volunteer* as a dumping ground for burdens was hardly his usual practice. I said, "No fooling at all. Everything's fine."

He seemed reassured. "Well," he said, "that's good to hear, at any rate." He looked around him and said, "It even puts this lovely establishment in a better light."

"It's by no means the worst," I said, and added, without really thinking, "After all, you're spoiled: you've got Saint Raymond's."

"The plum of the diocese?" he said, with a fierce politeness. "The old and handsome church that time has treated well? The modern parish school, the splendid renovated rectory with not one, but *two*, television sets, the four sturdy curates to lend supporting hands, the satisfying surplus in the bank? It's enough to spoil any man, isn't it? Not to mention the congregation. It's a friendly, helpful congregation, Hugh. Do you know what they do? They come to the rectory at all hours — day, night, any time — just to see me. Do you know why they want to see me? They want to tell me that they knew me when I was a little boy. And then when they've finished telling me that — which often takes rather a long time — do you know what they do? They tell me about someone named, say, Aunt Gert — there's always an Aunt Gert — who also knew me when I was a little boy but who unfortunately died in the hospital the Monday before last. She had a very expensive room, but thank God she had the Blue Cross. Then they tell me about her son, Bad Eddie. Bad Eddie is a man of fifty, and incredible as it may seem, he did *not* know me when I was a little boy. Possibly as a consequence of this he has not turned out well: he plays the horses and has been seen with a toe-dancer. Well, it's suggested that someone should go to see Bad Eddie, to talk to him. Someone who's a priest. And not just *any* priest: some priest who, you might say, is virtually a member of the family. Some priest whom Bad Eddie's mother knew when that priest was a little boy. Of course there is the fact that for years Bad Eddie has refused to go within ten miles of a priest, but that, I gather, is no difficulty at all. Presumably the priest just puts on a pair of sneakers and scales Bad Eddie's wall, shouting, 'Your mother knew me when I was small!' Then, with the subject of Bad Eddie out of the way, they go on to tell me about my predecessor, the Monsignor. You remember the Monsignor, Hugh?"

"Vividly." He was rolling along full tilt now, in familiar style; I saw him as the central figure in a siege, embattled, exasperated, and alone, the walls of the splendid renovated rectory a frail protection against the mighty fusillade of words.

"They talk about him a lot. Helpfully, of course: they want to make quite sure that I really understand just how the Monsignor used to do things. Isn't that kind of them, Hugh? It's kind — but it's also unnecessary, because the Monsignor took good care of that himself. He turns out to have been a man of astonishing foresight. He left a full set of instructions for his successor — and do you know how he left them? On little slips of paper, hundreds of them, secreted all over the rectory — in drawers, between the pages of books, under blotters. I find a new one every day: a stern reminder of how to wear the mantle I have so fortunately inherited. So that even in death the Monsignor is available. You might almost say he's unavoidable. And that's the way I find things today. Thanks to your friend His Excellency the Bishop not only have I got Saint Raymond's, but I've got everything that goes with it. While you've got only this." One hand shot out and around, indicating the few sticks of hand-me-down furniture in the old room. "It's dreadful, Hugh. You've got nothing at all. Worse than nothing. And," he said, "I'll tell you this: if I could I'd trade with you in a minute! And feel that I'd made the deal of my life!"

So much for Saint Raymond's. And all this without even mentioning old Charlie, who surely must have ranked high among the "everything" that went with the parish. . . .

He did not, in fact, refer to his father until we were in the car, on our way to the birthday dinner. Then he said, "This expedition has its peculiar side, hasn't it? I mean, my father's sudden hospitality to you: what's behind it, do you know?"

"No, I have no idea. I thought at first you might have been."

He shook his head. "I'm delighted you're coming; you know that. But it wouldn't have occurred to me to suggest it, for reasons that are all too obvious. No, it was his own idea: another of the famous mysterious schemes. We'll undoubtedly find out about it before the afternoon is over. Although," he said, a little grimly, "not *all* about it — you can depend on that. He's not giving anything away. Even at eighty-one."

"Eighty-one? I thought he said he was eighty-two today?"

"Yes, I know. That's another thing he does: he pretends to be a year older than he is. For no reason, except possibly to annoy us. Although why that should annoy us I don't know. But for some reason it does. At least it does me." He drove on, and in a few moments said, "At any rate it will be an experience for you. My father's birthday dinners aren't much like most others."

This was a point on which I had some curiosity; I said, "Just what *are* they like, John?"

"Like nothing on this earth," he said glumly. Then he shrugged. "The family is there. And my father's friends — or those of them who are still alive. As far as I can see, all of them are. And the conversation has a tendency to become rather specialized." He added drily, "My father's name comes up from time to time. As you can imagine. Although to tell the truth I really shouldn't be talking as an expert. I haven't been to the dinners in recent years. All the time I was out in Deerford I managed to miss them all. But now, of course, that's all over. I won't miss any more. I'm back home. To stay."

This apparently was the gloomiest thought yet; so gloomy that it left him in silence for the rest of the ride. It was in this party spirit that we drove up, at last, to old Charlie's house.

3

OLD CHARLIE lived in a large, squarish, old-fashioned wooden house, complete with tower rooms, deeply sloping roofs, and Victorian gingerbread. Over the years this house had often changed its color: it had been dark brown, battleship gray, white, lemon, light blue — all depending, as John once explained to me, on whatever bargain his father had managed to strike in the matter of surplus paints. It was at present the color of mustard. Around it on all sides was a large and level lawn, enclosed by an old and patchy barberry hedge. Two huge elms, splotched with creosote and filled with cement, still survived on the front lawn, while in back there were a number of smaller trees: maples, hawthorns, a crabapple. It was under these, presumably, that the birds which gave old Charlie such delight came each morning to sing, to eat, and to be stoned.

Charlie had bought this house when he was a very young man on the rise; he had lived here for more than fifty years, and it was here that his children had been born and raised. He took an enormous pride in this property, and there were those who suggested that he considered it to be something more than the mere dwelling place of a private citizen. My father had been among these; he had always called old Charlie's house The Shrine.

"I wonder will he run pilgrimages out there one day?" he

had said thoughtfully. "I don't know why not: it's the next step. It's well known the man has miraculous powers. I hear now that if you go out there with a dime in your hand and wave at him while he's sitting on the front stoop in the sunshine, it cures cuts. And the beauty of it is a thing like that can go on forever. Even when Charlie dies — always supposing he *does* die, of course — they can keep it going by sticking a little relic up on the porch with a thumb tack. His wallet, say. I tell you, there are thousands would come to see that. Let alone touch it. They could never get near it while the man was alive!"

Be that as it may, old Charlie was very far from the relic stage at the moment. He had come to the front door to greet us, and as we approached I noticed once again that the difference between father and son was as astonishing physically as in every other way. For Charlie was a small man, on the stout side, with a great head of white hair and little snub features all gathered together in a bunch. It was a strange combination: the majestic flow of hair, the kewpie-doll face. But his skin was marvelous — the clear, polished skin that old men sometimes have — and his eyes were deep blue and very bright, somehow managing to suggest that, in spite of everything you might have heard from every other living man, the man who stood before you was open, straight, and candid. However misleading this may have been, it was undoubtedly true — and, to me, almost incredibly so — that at the age of eighty-one he was alert and vigorous and bouncing up and down.

Whether John had hung back purposely or not I don't know, but in any case it was I who reached old Charlie first; I said, "Happy birthday, Mr. Carmody."

"Well well!" he said, grabbing my hand. "Well well, Father. It's grand to see you. And grand to see you here in the house again. It's been a long time between drinks, as the poet says." He had no sooner said this than a slight but curious change came over his face. I had the extraordinary feeling that I was caught up in a rare moment, that I was seeing Charlie actually embarrassed. Did he suspect that his convivial poet's phrase had a peculiar inappropriateness when addressed to me? But the look passed in an instant, and he said loudly, "Yes, it's grand to hear nice words like that 'Happy birthday!' from a young feller like yourself. There's nothin' makes me feel better than to know there's still young fellers in the world today that ain't afraid to get up off their behinds and come all the way across the city to say hello to an old man on his birthday. I tell you, Father, a man like me appreciates that. Hello John."

This was abrupt enough, but John was well accustomed to just such shifts. "Hello, Dad," he said, and, bending forward, he barely brushed the old man's cheek with his lips; just as quickly he said, "Happy birthday."

"Welcome to the house!" old Charlie said jubilantly. "Family and friends! Oh yes, that's what a man likes to have around him on the great days! Come in, come in. All the others are here." Then followed an authentic Charlie touch; he said, "It don't matter that you're a bit late."

John said swiftly, "We're not at all late. There was no exact time set. . . ."

"Don't apologize!" cried Charlie. "No no! There's no need for that on this day of days. Not at all. You're here and that's what matters. Come in, come in!"

John looked at me and shrugged; we followed his father into the house. I had not been here in years, and yet as soon as I stepped inside the door I had the feeling that I might have been here only yesterday, and that nothing had really changed at all. The truth was, of course, that nearly everything had changed, very much and for us all, but here in this deep, familiar, somber front hall, this was a truth it was easy to forget. For not a single remembered object seemed to have been displaced, altered, or moved an inch; although Charlie's wife had died some years before, his oldest daughter Mary, who had not married and who had remained at home with him, had evi-

[37]

dently held to her mother's housekeeping arrangements with the most scrupulous fidelity. Even the rug on the hall floor was the same old, tough, dull maroon covering which had been woven, apparently, from indestructible fibers, and on which, long ago, as a schoolboy, I had upset a bottle of ink — the stain, I saw now, was still dimly visible. (Did Charlie, I wondered, remember today the cause of that stain? I thought it quite likely that he did.)

Just behind the door was the long umbrella stand. Curiously enough, it was still jammed with its full cargo, although now, in the diminished household, with only old Charlie and Mary at home, who could possibly have used all those umbrellas? There was the huge antlered hatrack at its position by the foot of the front stairs; against the left wall stood the massive mahogany table, supporting its company of knickknacks: the squat, unchanged vases sprouting blooms of purple paper; the dish of wax fruit; the tray of unopened letters (not the same unopened letters, to be sure, but like their predecessors in at least one respect: I noted in passing that all seemed to be from charitable organizations — one more proof of the boundless optimism of man). Above the table, hanging side by side on the wall, were a framed sampler and a copy of "The Horse Fair." Finally, just before the entrance to the living room, there was the large bust of Daniel O'Connell. I remember having been puzzled by this at one time, largely because I could think of no reason for its being there. Charlie was articulate enough on the subject of Ireland and her troubles — as was my father and, indeed, as was every man of that generation and of that special world — but his words always seemed to me to lack any great conviction. In fact, whenever I heard Charlie on Ireland I felt that he was merely going through the motions, like an acrobat performing some sort of standard, universal handspring which had come to be expected of all acrobats everywhere, but which he did with neither pride nor interest. I think he was far too hardheaded and preoccupied

[38]

with his own affairs to waste much time or thought — let alone money — on the problems of a distant land where he owned ancestral ties, to be sure, but not one blade of grass. So then, why this enormous bust of The Liberator? Once again, it was John who had come up with an explanation.

"Somebody gave it to him," he had said.

It was a simple explanation: was it enough? Yes.

We passed the gift now, on our way to the "family and friends," and as we reached the living room door, but before we could actually look into the room itself, there was a quick rise of laughter, and I could hear several voices, all talking at once. And I think I may have stopped still; I know that at that precise instant I was suddenly yanked from the past into the fact of the present, and now, for the first time since my arrival, I felt a spasm of apprehension, and a regret that I had come. For this was a moment I had postponed for a long time, and one I had never dreamed would finally take place on a summer afternoon at an old man's birthday party. Unlike John, I had come back, not to stay, but only for an hour or so — long enough to see and to savor again, for the first time in nearly five years, that small and surprisingly unchanged part of the city where I was born and had spent so much of my life, where I knew every building and back alley as well as I knew my own front yard, where I had been a young priest, where I had had my own parish, and where, as in no place else, I had belonged, I had been at home. I suppose it's the mark of the provincial man, but in any case I find that I have a special and lasting love for this place which is so obviously just a place, which has no particular beauty or grace or grandeur of scene, but which is, quite simply, a neighborhood, *my* neighborhood, a compound of sights and smells and sounds that have furnished all my years. What kind of man is it who, after almost fifty years, can still spend half his time remembering the cry of the chestnut man, as it came floating down the street on a winter night . . . ?

[39]

And the people, all the people, the people one knew and understood almost by instinct, who had warmth and wit and kindness and an astonishing cascading rush of words — and who also had long and unforgiving memories, and tongues that cut like knives. . . .

And so now, as I went with Charlie and John into the living room, and realized that in the next second I would see again, not the comfortable strangers of Old Saint Paul's, but some of these very people whom I knew and had known all my life, and who of course knew me and all about me, I had a strange and absurd feeling of last-minute panic, like some child who has suddenly forgotten his lines in the school play, and the only thing in the world I could think of was: *What will I say to them? How will I begin . . . ?*

But there proved to be no problem of beginning at all; Charlie saw to that.

"Here we are!" he cried, bursting into the room ahead of us: a bounding, exuberant little figure, waving his arms, compelling attention. "Hail, hail, the gang's all here! Here's the last of the party, just arrived! And d'ye see who it is? Not only John, but Father Hugh Kennedy himself, come back to us just to say hooray to an old man on his birthday! Ain't that lovely? Ain't that grand? Oh, I tell you it is! The son of my old pal, God rest his soul! Like father, like son, as the poet says! Well well well! Come in, come in, Father Hugh! You don't want to stand back there like a stranger! Come in here and say a grand hello to all the old friends! Look at them: they're leapin' around like salmon at the sight of you!"

And of course there was no one leaping but Charlie himself. His performance was an astonishing one: it was hard to believe that a simply birthday could have lifted this seldom hospitable man to such cordial — if embarrassing — heights. He was literally whirling in high spirits: all during this spout of words he had been on the move, circling about like an old and extremely skilled sheepdog, rounding up his guests from different corners of the room and forcing them in towards me in a single central bunch. In a way it was ridiculous — this group of elderly, middle-aged and young adults being spun about in some sort of crazy parlor game — but it was also impossible to resist: Charlie's churning excitement was contagious. Before I knew it we were all together, shaking hands, greeting each other, while in the background Charlie continued to send up his urgent and enthusiastic cries.

And in this way the moment that I had been dreading passed — swiftly, almost without my realizing that it had come and gone, and with none of the expected awkwardness at all. A miracle? No: just Charlie. Unused to the strange climate of geniality, he seemed to have run amok, converting his living room into a kind of gymnasium of good will, knocking us all together so suddenly and with such violence that we were simply too startled to be constrained. Had Charlie intended this? Or was it more or less accidental? I didn't know: I don't think I cared, really. The important thing was that somehow it had happened, and suddenly I felt enormously relieved: at least the first hurdle had been taken, and there were no broken bones. . . .

4

ONE THING was clear from the start: Charlie was giving himself a party of at least respectable size. When we entered, there were probably fifteen people already in the room, and as we came together I saw that they represented four generations. There were the very old: Charlie's widowed sister, Julia Burke; Bucky Heffernan; and, surprisingly — for I thought he had died years ago — old P. J. Mulcahy. There was the next generation, my own, the generation of Charlie's children: his daughter Mary; Helen's husband, Frank O'Donnell; and Dan Carmody, who had the reputation of being the black sheep of the family, and who was here with his wife, a stout, gay-faced woman whom I didn't know. As a matter of fact I knew Dan only slightly, and so I was a little startled when he presented me to his wife as if we had been inseparable friends forever.

"Will you ever forget the football games, Hugh?" he said. He was a small, dapper man with sharply pointed shoes: a sprucer, sportier edition of old Charlie. "Every Saturday morning? On the vacant lot, next to old man Cassidy's? Talk about your rough-and-tumble: no shoulder pads, no protection, nothing. Just a bunch of football-crazy kids who played the game because they loved it." He turned to his wife and said, "Believe it or not, Flo, this was one of the greatest natural ends I ever saw. I think he could have been a professional if he'd stayed with it."

I had never played football particularly well. I had never played football with Dan. I had never played anything with Dan. And yet as I looked at him now, smiling reminiscently, recalling each detail of those famous games that had never been played, it occurred to me that he might at this moment actually believe that they had. The Carmodys were not an unimaginative family.

His wife laughed gaily and said, "I can believe it. Father looks as though he might have been very athletic."

Dan's face grew grave. "And yet," he said, "he went into the priesthood. That didn't surprise anyone, Flo; we always knew he would. Kids are funny that way. They have a way of knowing. Everybody always said that Hugh was bound for the seminary, just as they all said that I was bound for the stage. Well, as things worked out, they were wrong about me, but they certainly weren't about Hugh. No, there was something about him right from the beginning!"

This had gone far enough; I said quickly, "I'm a little out of touch, Dan: what are you doing these days?"

"Wool," he said promptly. "I'm in wool."

I remembered that years ago I had asked him the same question. "Securities," he had said then. "I'm in securities." And, then as now, his deep blue eyes — old Charlie's eyes — had been open and candid, the guarantee of sterling worth. But the eyes which had helped to work such wonders for the father had not done so well for the son; something had been lacking; Dan had not been a success. All along the line things had suddenly "gone wrong"; he had lived a life of great mobility, changing residence hurriedly and often; there had been stories of near-disasters and of angry, last-minute rescues engineered by old Charlie; and I remembered that five years ago, just before I had left the city, I had heard that this long-time bachelor had presented his family with still another of his uncomfortable surprises: he had announced his marriage, somewhere in the Middle West, to a widow whom none of the Carmodys had met, and who was apparently some years Dan's senior. This was Flo.

"Wool," said Dan, with a sagacious nod. "You can't beat wool in the long pull, Hugh."

Flo laughed happily. "There'll always be sheep," she said.

I wondered what Charlie thought of this on his birthday . . . ?

We went, now, one more step down the ladder to another generation, to Helen's son Ted, and to the improbable fact that the eager gawky boy I had known was now this well turned out young man in his late twenties, with his air of quiet confidence, with his Uncle John's long good looks, and with a wife and two solemn little pale-haired children whom I had never seen until this afternoon. And it was this, I think — this sight of Ted, complete with family — which more than anything else showed me just how far away I'd been from this closely knit world which I once knew in every last detail. . . .

I talked only briefly with Ted: long enough to see that he was as agreeable as ever and, I think, genuinely pleased to see me. And then he introduced me to Anne, his wife: a trim, handsome green-eyed girl, with dark hair pulled back over her ears into a single braid at the back of her head. Even this early in the season she was deeply tanned, and she was dressed in something cool and white and sleeveless; as I looked at her there jumped into my mind pictures I had seen in the society sections of Sunday papers, those pictures which seem always to be there, the pictures of swiftly graceful young women standing at the ready beside country club tennis courts. And, seeing her standing by her husband's side, I realized suddenly how much they resembled each other. Not facially, that is, but in a certain *style:* both had a quiet, neat, expensive, well-cut air which was almost like a uniform — a uniform worn by no one else in this room.

Certainly not by old Charlie. It was astonishing to transfer from grandson to grandfather — as I did now, automatically — and to realize, in this fantastic familiar contrast, the sheer *speed* of the polishing process: that two generations, plus the money, plus the schooling (which was not only better but of an entirely different kind), plus the new and now permissible associations, had ground down all the bumps and smoothed off all the edges. And I suddenly wondered, as I looked back and forth, from one to the other — all in a split second — what on earth the two talked about when — and if — they found themselves alone together. Because even under the best of circumstances there are few enough bridges over which the young can cross into the queer, half-lit landscape of the really old. And when the circumstances were not the best, when the "really old" was someone like old Charlie, and the normal gulf had been so quickly and dramatically widened, could young Ted even begin to get across? Or, in other words, how did this new, improved Carmody regard the old model, fifty years away from him in time, immeasurably farther in so many other ways?

Which was purest speculation, of course: for all I knew Charlie and his grandson might have been in touch on a hundred different levels. All the same. . . .

All the same, right at the moment Anne O'Donnell was talking to me, saying something swift and pleasant in a young, agreeable voice. I listened; I answered; and I would have said more, except that now the fourth and last generation came over to me, and this consisted of Ted's two children. They came over, led not by their mother or their father, but by their grandmother. Who was, of course, Helen. And for just an instant, when I saw her stepping lightly across the room, smiling, as slender as ever, her hair still the same soft gold that caught the sunlight, I'm ashamed to say that I felt, not joy at seeing how well she looked or how little time had changed her, but a quick and foolish spasm of sadness, as if in seeing

[45]

her coming towards me with two unwilling tots in tow I realized for the first time that she was a *grandmother*, and that this, far more forcefully than Charlie's white hairs or the little puckered trot of Bucky Heffernan, brought home to me the blunt truth that she and John and all of us who had been young together were young no longer, and that we moved steadily, day by day, to the once distant world of the old. . . .

Which, as I say, is a foolish way to feel: obviously no one ever grows closer to the cradle. But getting old is a strange business. It's happening to you every minute of every day, and you almost never give it a thought; then, one day, you catch a glimpse of an old friend, or you hear a phrase from an old song, or your eye falls on a solitary sentence in the daily paper, and suddenly, without being able to do a thing in the world about it, you seem to be for a moment outside your own skin, taking one good long look at yourself, exactly as you stand, exactly as you are. And at this point, no matter who you are, or what you believe, or what you may be, it sometimes becomes a little hard to give three cheers for the inevitable. . . .

Happy thoughts on Charlie's happy birthday!

"Hugh," Helen said, coming up, putting out her hands, taking mine. "Hugh, Hugh, Hugh. Welcome home!"

And it was grand, really grand, to see her again. She was a year younger than John, and looked very much like him — both were fortunate enough to resemble their mother, although with Helen the clear, alert face was softer, more responsive, without the edges of impatience. She introduced her son's children to me: they were twins, a boy and a girl, age three, who looked at me with frankly inquisitive eyes, exchanged glances in the silent conspiracy of childhood, and then fidgeted until, obviously relieved, they were led off by their parents. It was the end of the parade; the introductions and greetings were over. After this there was some general conversation, the kind of conversation in which everyone more or less marks time, and then, slowly, we began to split up into

[46]

smaller groups. Charlie himself led the way: his role of master of ceremonies temporarily over, he hustled over to the garden windows, followed by several of the older guests. Helen and I walked over by the doorway.

"A long time," she said, with a smile. "Too long. Listen, Hugh, how are you, anyway? You look absolutely fine!"

She had such a warm and convincing way of breaking into something like this that I came close to believing her; in any case I thanked her and managed a few words about the grandmothers of today being younger and prettier than grandmothers used to be. I think it was a clumsy compliment; I've grown a little out of the habit of small gallantries.

"It takes work," she said. "Slave labor, practically. Hours spent in beauty parlors, slenderizing salons . . . all sorts of places you don't know anything about, Hugh. It's not important . . . did you know, by the way, that this is the second time I've seen you today?"

Then it had not been a mistake; she had been at Saint Paul's this morning. "The seven o'clock Mass?" I said. "I thought I saw you, but then I thought the hour was against it. Not to mention the place."

"Oh, the hour," she sighed. "I've changed, Hugh. I really have. I get up with the sun these mornings. I don't know that I really want to, but I do. I think it must be something connected with age, and I can't go to the beauty parlor for *that*. And as for the place, well, I thought I ought to see you at least once on your home grounds before you came over here. You see, it wasn't until the day before yesterday that I learned you were coming today. When Daddy told me he'd invited you I was just about bowled over. You can understand why; you know Daddy. Normally, he's just not that . . . expansive. So I thought the least I could do was to go and just look in on you this morning. And so I did." She paused and said, "Do you like it, Hugh?"

"I'm afraid I do. Surprised?"

"No," she said, "not really. I'm not much good at gauging these things: you like Saint Paul's, John dislikes Saint Raymond's, and in both cases I suspect it hasn't too much to do with the place itself. Anyway, over I went this morning, and there you were, looking fine. And in very good voice, I must say. Did you know you were holding your audience, Hugh? One little Chinese near me was sitting there positively spellbound."

We all have our vanity; I decided not to explain about Mr. Yee. Instead I said, "Why didn't you come back after Mass and say hello?"

"I was going to, and then I thought I wouldn't. You might have been busy, for one thing, and also, I hadn't been over before, and it had been a long time. I think I felt a little guilty. Were you ever angry, Hugh, that we never went over to Saint Paul's to see you? John or myself, I mean?"

"No."

"Honestly?"

It was a softer version of John's "*No fooling!*" I said, "Honestly, Helen. I was never angry; you know that. There would have been no reason."

"I'm glad. I didn't think you'd be, but you never know. We were going to go over; we talked about it. Many times. And I often thought that some afternoon I might drop in on you without even saying I was coming, just to see how you were getting along. I wasn't going to bring you anything: no knitted socks, no fruit cake, no pretty curtains to brighten up the rectory. I was just going to bring me. But I never even did that. It wasn't that I didn't want to: it was just that I felt — *we* felt — that you'd rather we didn't. You know, that you wanted to take your own good time, and that you'd come back whenever you got ready. And now you have. I can't tell you how happy we are!"

I knew she meant it, every word. And while it was good to hear — it's never exactly painful to discover that you've been missed — all the same, it did suggest a difficulty. For the truth was that I had not "come back" — not, that is, in Helen's sense of the word. In her voice, in the kind and generous welcome, there seemed to be the assumption that I had now re-entered the world of the Carmodys and the old association, that by coming here this afternoon I had already begun to pick up and hold firm the strings that had been dropped five years before. And I knew, of course, that this could not be done, that — wisely or unwisely — I had come to Charlie's party on an impulse that even now I did not fully understand, and that this was a single visit, nothing more. Surely, then, I should have explained something of this to Helen, and maybe I would have done so, but I suddenly felt a touch, a hard touch, on my elbow. It was Agnes, the Carmody maid, an ancient, privileged, contemptuous woman, surely as old as Charlie himself.

"Aha, Father," she said, giving me a tough old wink of welcome. "Ain't it nice to see you back."

"Hello, Agnes. You get younger by the year."

"Aha," she said scornfully. And properly enough: she had had a lifetime of the little clerical jocosities. She held out her tray of glasses. Helen took one and Agnes said to me, "Have a glass of sherry-wine, Father. It builds up the blood."

Was it my imagination, or had the room suddenly become quieter? I said, "Thanks, Agnes. I don't think so."

But she persisted. "Ah, there's nothin' to this stuff, Father," she said, looking down with disdain at Charlie's sherry. "A little sherry-wine never hurt no one. It's no more than milk, hardly. They give it to babies to settle their stomachs."

Are there such things as Firm Phrases for the New Teetotaler? Convincing variations on the prim "No-thank-you"? Undoubtedly; but I didn't know them. I said only, "I'll pass it up this time, Agnes."

She shifted her feet and I recognized the maneuver: she was digging in for battle. These hardy old household dragons are

[49]

great battlers. But fortunately Helen intervened, saying, "Perhaps later, Agnes. I think you might take the tray over to my father now. I saw him looking for you a moment ago."

Agnes gave her a look of frank and total disbelief; to me, she gave the same look she had given Charlie's sherry. Then, muttering, she moved off, and the moment was over. I looked around the room and everything seemed normal: Charlie was springing up and down, people were chatting easily with each other, no one was paying the slightest attention to me. And yet I knew that just a few seconds ago a tension, watchfulness had been there — and indeed, how could it not have been? For after all, the irresistible attraction had been on hand: The Temptation of Father Kennedy. . . .

Which is bitter, which is self-pitying, and which is also foolish. Because, given the fact of me — and, of course, of that tray — how else could they have behaved? What else could they have done? Politely drifted out of the room en masse? Looked up at the ceiling and whistled loudly, to show that they really weren't watching at all? You can't stop peoples' memories — especially when they're the iron memories that everyone over here seems to have from birth — and in the light of what had happened, any such guarded, expectant scrutiny was normal enough, was only human. Which nevertheless didn't make it a thing of joy; it still stung. . . .

But it's possible to give too much to such a moment, and the plain truth is that a sting is not a mortal wound. I looked at Helen and saw the concern in her eyes; I smiled and said, "I'll live. I give you my word."

She said quietly, "Ah, Hugh, we're not doing very well by you, are we? I'm sorry. Is it bad?"

"Not that bad," I said. "Nothing is. Come on, Helen, cheer up: remember it's a happy birthday. And I'm glad I'm here. So now you can do me a favor and tell me something. About your father. John didn't know why he asked me over today; do you?"

She did not. She answered abstractedly, plainly unwilling to change the subject so easily; my switch to old Charlie had been something less than graceful. But as I pushed on, and as Charlie was one of those people who were born to be discussed, gradually she began to speak with greater interest. I remembered something John had said and, curious, I asked Helen now how old her father really was.

"Eighty-one. Yes, I know," she said, "he told you he was eighty-two. He did, didn't he?" I nodded and she said, "He tells everyone that. *He* knows he's eighty-one, and he knows *they* know he's eighty-one, but he's discovered that for some reason it seems to upset them if he pretends to be eighty-two. So of course he does. You know how Daddy is."

I did indeed. I said, "If the aim is to upset, he's fairly successful with John."

"Yes. Well," she said, "he's not entirely unsuccessful with me."

Her eyes moved away from me, and I saw that she was looking out into the room in the direction of her father; apparently the simple recollection of his tactics inspired a kind of uneasy, periodic inspection. He was standing in the center of a small group, still talking away, but now talking chiefly, it seemed, to Helen's husband. This gave the scene a certain comic-strip quality, for Frank O'Donnell was a large, impressive man, and every now and then Charlie would shoot up like some spry, white-crowned jumping jack, as if to boost his words up the steep ascent to the full Roman face. Frank was a doctor and a successful one; it was with something of the professional manner that he stood listening to Charlie now, his head bent slightly forward, nodding with a grave regularity. If he had suddenly produced a stethoscope I would have felt no great surprise.

Helen sighed. "Poor Daddy. I'm not very nice to him on his birthday, am I? But he's such a strange man, really."

Which was a restrained enough comment, surely. . . .

[51]

We had much more to talk about: I wanted to ask her about Mary, about John, about her husband, about Ted and his family, and most of all I wanted to ask her about herself. But we were at a party, after all, and two people could hardly stand together in private conversation forever. The interruption came when Mary, Bucky Heffernan, and P. J. Mulcahy joined us. Helen stayed only long enough to say a few words to them, then went back to her grandchildren, and I was left with Mary and the two old men.

"Did you notice any changes, Father?" Mary said, a trifle anxiously. "In the house, I mean? Or do you think it looks about the same? About the way it always did?"

"Just the same, Mary. Exactly the way it always did."

Mary beamed. I think it was the greatest compliment I could have paid her. She was the oldest of the Carmody children, and I sometimes found it hard to believe that she was really one of them, that any member of any family could be so unlike the others. Mary resembled no one. Now nearly sixty, she was large and plump, although with none of the high color and bustling bounce that such women often have; instead, she was a docile, good-hearted, great gray dumpling of a woman, a slow stout shadow who silently appeared in old Charlie's train, who was seen, was recognized, was spoken to, and was promptly forgotten as soon as she moved out of sight. Most people, when addressing Mary, instinctively shifted into a simpler speech, although this was unnecessary, for she was not at all simple-minded. She had gone to good and extremely expensive schools, and she had passed through them, if not with distinction, at least without failure. What it all amounted to, I suppose, was this: that there was something in Mary, some passive element missing in the other children, which allowed her to accept, with an almost stupefying readiness, the single role in life for which her father had cast her: his humble servant.

It was the kind of development that had infuriated John.

"It's right out of *Gulliver's Travels*," he had once said to me. "They ought to sell tickets: Watch a Girl Become a Yahoo. After a lifetime with my father, this good, agreeable, even intelligent girl can now converse freely on the following subjects: cheap margarine, good drying days, how to patch underwear. Isn't that encouraging?"

But Mary showed no signs of discouragement; it was with a certain enthusiasm that she said to me now, "Of course you haven't been upstairs yet. But it's all the same up there, too."

"You're doing a difficult thing, Mary: preserving the status quo in a changing world."

"Except for the electric blankets," she said. "We have them now. Do you have electric blankets over where you are, Father?"

"No, I'm afraid not. . . ."

"They're nice," she said fondly. "Warmth without weight."

This was Mary; this was our conversation. Could we have gone further along these lines? In any case, we did not, because now P. J. Mulcahy put in a word.

"You're back in the city again, Father," he stated softly. He was a tall, calm, unwrinkled old man with gray eyes so light as to be almost without color, and a remarkably gentle voice. I had seen him around this part of the city all my life — he was one of those men you can never recall as being anything but very old, and who never seem to grow any older — and I had heard my father speak of him often, yet at this moment all I could remember about him was a single detail, and this an odd one: that he had been at one time in the hay and grain business, and then, at some later date, he had become an undertaker.

"I am, Mr. Mulcahy," I said.

He studied me with some care. "Well," he said finally, "you look the same as always. Your father all over again and no mistake. The spittin' image and no mistake. Specially up round the eyes."

"Would you say the eyes, P. J.?" said Bucky instantly, squinting critically at me. "Would you say the eyes? Be precise there, P. J. The eyes in a way, yes. I don't deny you could say the blue eyes were like the Dad's. That I admit. That I grant you. But let me ask you this, P. J.: *What about the nose?*" He looked about him with an air of triumphant finality, as if this question were one he had at long last succeeded in placing before some vast, invisible deliberative body. He was a few years younger than P. J. and looked older: a wrinkled, inquisitive little stump who was reputed to be a great talker, of the kind fond of "examining the issues." He said now, "Isn't that what you might call the family nose, P. J.? Take a real good look at it, the way it crooks down there, a little lopsided, like. What man in the city had a nose like that only Dave Kennedy?"

It was an odd compliment, but a compliment nevertheless. And one delivered with an extraordinary detachment, as if I were not really there in front of them, or as if I had been a statue or a plastic dummy. . . .

"Your father to the life," P. J. said. "If I was to meet you on the main street of the moon, Father, I'd say, 'There goes Dave Kennedy's lad.'"

"You knew my father well, Mr. Mulcahy?"

"I did," he said. "A lovely man. With the pipe and the smile. And never too busy for the nice long chat. He died too young, poor man. You were still over this way at the time?"

I said only, "Yes. Yes, I was."

"And then you went away," he said reflectively, "and now you're back." He nodded, as if he had now straightened out all details. He added courteously, "Well, it's good to see you, Father."

It was a simple enough welcome, but one which I found strangely moving, coming as it did from this old man whom I knew so slightly. I thanked him, and then Bucky chimed in.

"Home sweet home," he said. "That's the place to be. All the big world travelers come to that in the end. Back to the fireplace and the slippers and the pills. There's no place like home." Then he said quickly, "You were a good while away, Father. Out to the West, was it?"

I saw that two red-veined, watery old eyes were now focused on me with a surprising sharpness; clearly, inquisition was about to begin. I said, "For a good part of the time, yes."

"The West," he said. "I never was out to the West. I remember one time I went to Georgia. Down to the South. The whole place was a swamp and the people ate pies made of nuts. A very poor piece of country. The consensus is agreed on that." With a return to sharpness he said, "I s'pose there's a good many things a priest can do out West, Father?"

"A good many things, as you say, Mr. Heffernan."

"Parish work, say," he said. "There's parishes all over the place. East or West, North or South, it makes no difference, there's parishes. The heart of the Church is the parish. As we all know. Was it mostly parish work you were in out there, Father?"

"I wouldn't say mostly, Mr. Heffernan. Although I did some, of course."

"Ah." Disappointment shaded the old, inquisitive face; he tried again. "Or there's the missions," he said. "Oh, they're the boys that do the great job. Out there in the missions I'm told the priests live like cowboys. Up on a horse all day long, out baptizing Indians, getting bit by rattlesnakes. We know from the books that some very high-class martyrs died out there. Man, woman, and child, we all praise the missions. Did you enjoy that class of work, Father?"

"I did very little, Mr. Heffernan. I didn't happen to be assigned to any of the mission bands."

He frowned, and I could tell that I was letting him down badly. I had never baptized an Indian; I had not been bitten by a snake; but worse, I was making a mystery of things. He was having to work hard. And the odd thing was that, although this was just what I had been dreading most — this probing, this tireless rooting around which was the great specialty over

[55]

in this district — somehow Bucky managed to give it the dimension of a comic game. I felt it would be almost unfair not to play.

He shook his head and said doggedly, "Then there's *chaplains*. . . ."

But this, too, came to nothing, for now P. J. broke in, saying with a slight smile, "Ah, you could of done a hundred things out West, it's that big a place. But I tell you one thing you couldn't of done out there, Father. You couldn't of gone to Charlie's birthday party!"

I agreed that this was so, indeed, and then, partly because I saw that Bucky was itching to get back to his questions, but also because I wanted to see if Charlie's latest maneuver could really succeed with his own contemporaries, I said, "He seems in great spirits. It's only natural: you don't get to be eighty-two every day in the week."

The two men looked at each other.

"Eighty-two," P. J. said ruminatively. "Ah well, it don't matter much. . . ."

But Bucky was not so tolerant. "Hold on there, P. J.!" he said indignantly. "*What* don't matter? Be careful of that, P. J. Don't say the truth don't matter. The whole of the civilized world is against you there. Man, woman, and child. And when a man that's well known to be eighty-one stands up bold as brass and shouts 'Have a look at me, I'm eighty-two!' where does the truth go there? That's the question before us, P. J. What happens to the truth in a case like that? I'll tell you what happens to it: *it goes out the window and into the ash can.* That's what happens to our friend the truth!"

"Now now," P. J. said calmly. "What's the good of all that? We all know what's what. We all know Charlie. . . ."

"I'm a man for the truth!" Bucky said loudly. His face had grown very red; clearly, he had forgotten all about me. "And what's the truth about the eighty-two? Who's the one man in this room today that's *exactly* eighty-two and no lies about it?

[56]

Who is that man? We all know that, P. J. We all know that man is myself. *I'm* eighty-two: that's who's eighty-two. And last year I was eighty-one. And when I was eighty-one I didn't hold turkey dinners for myself to tell the whole wide world I was eighty-two or ninety-two or a hundred and two. And why didn't I? I'll tell you why I didn't: *because the truth's the truth.* There's a matter of principle there, P. J. I have the finest minds of our time to stand with me on that one!"

It was an impassioned defense, not so much of the truth as of Bucky, but it suddenly occurred to me that such passion could hardly be welcomed by those closest to old Charlie. Uneasily I turned to see how Mary had taken this onslaught, but she was not there. Characteristically she had melted away without our noticing that she had gone, and now I saw that she was on the far side of the room, talking to Agnes. So the probability was that she had not heard — and also, that no one else had. The room by now was noisy, and there was no sign that Bucky's voice had cut through the din. Obviously, he did not care. He continued to complain loudly, refusing to be pacified by the mild murmurs of P. J. (who, although older than all of them, seemed relatively undisturbed by old Charlie's claims), and it was only the announcement of dinner that at last subdued him. His voice trailed away into a little groundswell of grumbles, and he stumped off to the dining room, accompanied by the tranquil figure of his old friend.

As I started off in the same direction John joined me.

"Everything all right?" he said, and once again I caught the look of quick appraisal. Apparently I passed inspection; he said, "You look chipper enough. All buoyed up by the festive occasion?"

"All buoyed up by P. J. and Bucky, I'd say. We've been renewing old acquaintance."

"I saw you. If you got in more than ten words you were doing well. Still, P. J. is a good old scout. I could do without Bucky easily enough. And his wife."

[57]

This surprised me. "Is there a Mrs. Bucky? Still alive?"

He nodded. "He leaves her at home. She's quite content. She sits there, hooking rugs." He said gloomily, "She's hooking one for me. She calls me up at the rectory to tell me how it's coming along. Progress reports. I have a choice of mottoes, apparently. And Bucky's taken to paying me little visits. He wants to talk to me. Do you know what he talks about? His grave. How's that for a subject for the early evening hours? He's concerned about it; he's terribly afraid someone will slip up and that it won't get perpetual care. He's made it quite clear that when he's gone he wants to be weeded, mowed, and trimmed, every hour on the hour. Isn't it wonderful, Hugh? Bucky Heffernan, in his eighties and almost at the end of the line, comes to Holy Mother Church with one last supplication: a grave like a putting green!"

He shrugged, and we separated as we entered the dining room. Before I reached the table I was stopped by Frank O'Donnell.

"I didn't have a chance to tell you I saw the Bishop one day last week," he said.

His voice was low and private, and I thought I knew more or less what was coming. As a physician Frank was not indiscreet, but he had been the Bishop's doctor for years, and occasionally he liked to pass on to the lesser clergy, in a tone of great confidence, some small piece of inside information about his patient's health. I think this gave him the feeling of being a valuable link, of being somehow mixed up in diocesan affairs; a surprising number of laymen enjoy this sort of thing. I said, "You do far better than I do, Frank. I haven't seen him for months."

"He came in for a checkup," he said. "Pure routine, actually. He's in fine shape. That kidney obstruction we were a little worried about has cleared up nicely."

I hadn't worried about it; I hadn't known about it. But I said, "That's good news, Frank."

"Not that I really thought it would amount to anything, but we had to be sure. You remember Monsignor Kilrain." He looked meaningfully at me.

"Yes. That is, I remember him, but I don't remember anything special about him. Should I?"

"Mmm," he said, suddenly becoming guarded, cloaked in his profession; it was clear that confidences were over. "The diagnosis there was perhaps a little . . . but that doesn't matter now." He put his head back slightly and looked me over carefully, up and down. This was no amateur's survey; this was the practiced eye. Then he nodded briskly; I had, apparently, passed another inspection.

"Congratulations," he said.

I murmured something, anything; this was all a little embarrassing.

He added firmly, "Good work!"

And for one awful moment I thought he was going to clap me on the shoulder and tell me he was proud of me. But Charlie was now impatient and was calling from his position at the head of the table; Frank left me with the benediction of another short, encouraging nod. And I went to my place, thinking that Frank was undoubtedly a good doctor, a good husband, and a good man, and also that I found him, on most occasions, to be just about unendurable. . . .

And now we were all at the table; John said grace; and then, finally, we sat down to Charlie's dinner.

5

M Y FATHER, in his discussions of Charlie, had often
spoken of the birthday dinners — for they had been
begun several years before his death — and he tended to dismiss them as inferior occasions. He had never attended them,
although he told me that he had been asked now and then,
but he said that he knew Charlie quite well enough to imagine
what any such dinner would be like.

"A mean little meal, I'd say. Corned beef, a dab of cabbage,
a boiled potato, and a small piece of lardy pie. And oilcloth
for a table cover. Not only because the man is stingy, mind you,
but because there's nothing like a ten-cent meal to remind people of things. It reminds all the relatives, don't you see, of the
sort of meals they used to eat in the old days. In the days
when they were poor, back before the great day when Charlie
sat up and looked around and decided that everybody else was
wrong, that two and two *did* make five, if only you worked it
the right way and had the good sense to keep out of jail. Do
you know about Danny Conroy? The bricklayer who got left a
million dollars by a crazy aunt in Limerick? He'd invite you to
his big new house, the one the lawyers got for him, and when
the butler let you in, out would trot Danny in an old pair of
pants with no seat in them. It was his way of reminding the
world how far up the line he'd come since the days he carried

the hod. And the birthday dinners are the very same class of thing: they're nothing but Charlie's pair of pants."

But my father, who was right on most points about Charlie, was entirely wrong on this. Assuming, that is, that the meal to which I sat down was at all typical of the birthday dinners. It was no mere dinner: it was a feast. It was a feast to which I made a fairly poor witness, as I drank none of the wines which were poured with a surprisingly lavish hand (and here, once again, I saw that my abstinence did not escape sharp eyes) and while I'm not indifferent to food, still, it doesn't matter as much as it did once. But even so, it was clear that this meal was something special, from the great, fat, chilled oysters down to the cathedral of a cake, an awful baroque masterpiece of frosting and flame. It was astonishing, because even allowing for Charlie's high opinion of the day, there were still the limitations of his kitchen to be considered. Gertrude, the Carmody cook, was, like Agnes, an old retainer of solid but simple gifts. Could she have soared to such heights? No. The answer came soon enough: for this occasion, Charlie had not relied upon his household staff. Now and then a muffled shout could be heard from the kitchen, and Agnes, as she stomped around the table, was red-faced and furious — unmistakable signs that outside authority had been secured and was in charge.

I found myself seated between Charlie's sister, Julia Burke, and young Anne O'Donnell. And in a sense this was an awkward arrangement, because we were really strangers to one another: I'd met Ted's wife only an hour ago, and I had never known Charlie's sister well. A year or so younger than her brother, she had married early and had left the city; for many years now she had been a widow, coming back home, I think, only for these reunions. She was a slight woman with a faded and rather mournful face; she looked nothing like her brother, and appeared to have none of his turbulent vitality. (Although this was undestandable, for she must have been about eighty. I had to keep reminding myself that Charlie and his friends

[61]

were probably not typical octogenarians.) As she began to eat she huddled over her plate, as if to guard it from her neighbors, and her eyes moved about in continual examination of her fellow guests. She said suddenly, "It's grand to come back and see the old friends once in a while."

There was a pause, and then I realized that she had been speaking to me, although at no time had she looked at me. I said, "You don't get back too often, Mrs. Burke?"

"No, no. Not since Martin died. You didn't know my Martin, Father?"

"No, I'm afraid not. . . ."

"A saint," she said firmly. She continued to eat and to look across the table at Helen, Bucky, John and others. "A livin' saint. Sick and on his back five days out of the seven from the time I married him, and never a complainin' word. One kidney, no gall bladder, a bad liver, and blood so thin you could hardly call it blood at all. The doctors'd come to the house in busloads just to have a look at him and poke him and lift him up and strap him down. They called him The Wonder Man. And never a complainin' word out of him. He'd just look at me with his weak little eyes and say, 'Julia, there's worse off than me.' And many's the time I felt like sayin' 'If there are, where are they?' " She shook her head and said, "A livin' saint. Your father would of known Martin. How long is your father dead now?"

"Nine years, Mrs. Burke."

"Martin's dead *ten*," she said, a strange, lively note entering her voice. It was almost a ring of triumph, as if she had just announced the winner of a particularly grisly competition. For the first time she looked directly at me; I think she was daring me to dispute the victory of The Wonder Man. I said nothing and, presumably satisfied, she went back to her plate, saying again, "Yes, yes, it's grand to get back and see the old friends now and again. And see Charlie on the birthday."

I saw her eyes stop moving now and rest on our host, who,

seated at the head of the table, seemed to have forgotten his guests for the moment: he was concentrating entirely on the food before him, eating in silence and with great speed. I wondered now how Julia, almost at the end of her life, viewed Charlie, for in a way she was closer to him than any of us. They had grown up together, brother and sister, in the same tenement house, and they stood now as the only survivors of that once large brood of children. And so what were her special thoughts on her brother as he sat, so obviously hale and hearty, in his old age? Response came suddenly, as if she had heard the unasked question; she sighed and said, "Poor Charlie. He's gettin' terrible frail."

Which seemed far enough from the truth to call for a mild dissent. I said, "You surprise me, Mrs. Burke. I'd say he looked very well."

But either she didn't hear me, or else — as old people sometimes do — she had already lost interest in her subject, or else she had not really been talking to me at all, but to herself as much as to anyone — in any case, she made no answer. She said, "This is a very nice soup. Nourishin'."

Then she sank into silence, although her lips continued to move slightly, as if she were whispering secrets to herself. And so, with Julia locked up tight in her own private world, I turned from the very old — at least for the moment — and went to the very young.

Or so Anne O'Donnell seemed to me now. This may have been largely a matter of contrast — the inevitable post-Julia reaction, for certainly this handsome, well-groomed mother of two was no gawky schoolgirl. Yet it was more than contrast; I saw this as soon as she began to talk. There was a freshness, a youthfulness to her speech, a kind of natural, running forthrightness which I found entirely agreeable. I found it also, at first, a bit surprising, if only because most people — including self-possessed young women — aren't so completely at their ease when talking to priests they've just met. Memories of old catechism classes undoubtedly linger long; as a consequence, there's usually a fair amount of preliminary tiptoeing around.

But not here. She talked about her children. I had complimented her on them: she had agreed with the compliment.

"They *are* good, aren't they?" she said cheerfully. "Although it's not much credit to me, I'm afraid; I don't spend nearly enough time with them. But we have a wonderful nurse, and they've picked up all their good manners from her."

I said, "I'm behind the times. I thought children's nurses had all disappeared, long ago."

"Well, they have, mostly. We were terribly lucky to get this one. And we have to pay her a *fortune* every week, but I think it's worth it. The children don't whine, they don't stare, they're not too noisy, and they do manage not to tear *too* many things apart. The result is that we love them quite a lot and bore everybody to death by talking about them all the time!"

I noticed that the children were not at the table with us. They were off having their own dinner with the remarkable nurse, and this seemed to me a prudent move. I had the suspicion that our company of ancients and the clergy might not be quite up to the mealtime behavior of two small children who just managed not to tear too many things apart. . . .

She talked about her wedding; I explained — too quickly? — that I had not been in the city at the time.

"Yes, I know," she said, disconcertingly. But then she went on, saying frankly, "You really did miss it, Father. Even though it was mine, I think it was a lovely wedding. And the reception was absolutely fabulous. Old Mr. Carmody drank carloads of champagne and kissed me and even cried a little. That's fairly unusual, don't you think?"

It was practically unprecedented; I said sincerely, "I wish I'd been there. Tell me, now, a little about Ted. What's he doing these days?"

"Well," she said, "the latest is that he may run for Congress.

In fact it's almost certain he will. Or had you already heard that?"

"No. I hadn't heard a word." About that, or about any of Ted's recent intentions or activities; I was no more up-to-date on him than on the rest of the Carmodys. In fact my strongest memories of Ted were far removed from the present: the most vivid picture I had was that of a small, isolated figure, standing on stage in a junior high school auditorium on a long-ago Armistice Day, declaiming in a brave and breaking voice, "We *have* kept faith, ye Flanders dead. . . ."

And now he was running for Congress — so much for my memories. I said, "Good for him; I'm glad. And you, Anne: how do you feel about it?"

"Am *I* glad, you mean? Yes," she said, "I think I am. The trouble is that I like the way we're living now, and I expect that if he gets elected there'll be all sorts of changes that I won't exactly be mad about. But then, it *is* exciting. And of course Ted can hardly wait. He pretends to be terribly blasé about it, but he's actually much more excited than I am." She said, in an oddly solemn, proud voice, "He's been quite politically active in the last couple of years, you know."

"No, I didn't know." And then I asked her which side of the political fence he was active on. It was an innocent question, but it seemed to startle her; she looked at me as if I had just spoken the inconceivable. After a moment she said — rather patiently, I thought, "Ted's A.D.A. So am I, in a way."

"Ah," I said, "I should have known." Should I have? Was it self-evident? Were there alternatives? The Young Republicans? The New Republicans? The New Young Republicans . . . ?

But she laughed suddenly. "I don't know how you'd know. But I always talk as though *everyone* should know. I can't believe that there's a living person who doesn't know A.D.A. is practically Ted's life's blood. And of course a good many more people *will* know when they endorse him for Congress."

[65]

I said curiously, "What does old Mr. Carmody think about this? Not the A.D.A.; I mean the running for Congress?"

"Oh," she said lightly, "I haven't heard. I'm not really sure that he knows."

And now it was my turn to be startled: *I* had just heard the inconceivable. On a family matter — or what old Charlie would surely regard as a family matter — he had not only not been consulted: apparently he had not even been informed. This to old Charlie, who had ruled his own children with such a rigorous hand, and to whom for so many years all decisions had been reluctantly, perhaps, but unfailingly referred. But now Anne had spoken casually, not as if they were deliberately keeping information from him, but rather as if his knowledge or lack of knowledge was . . . well, simply was not important. And this came as a shock to me: the old man with the iron hand over all his family did not even enter the lives of his grandchildren! The gulf between the old and the young was clearly wider than I had suspected: here was another reminder, if I needed it, of just how isolated I'd become. I looked at this young girl seated next to me, smiling at me, and I realized that I knew nothing about her at all. Only that she was Ted's wife, the mother of his children, and that she was not a local girl. As for the rest, nothing: not even who she was or where she had come from or who her parents had been — all the little points of basic information that everyone in Saint Raymond's seemed to know within five minutes of a new name's being mentioned. . . .

And I was to gain no knowledge now, for from his position on the other side, P. J. called over to me, "You're at Old Saint Paul's, is it, Father?"

Conversation was about to become more general; I said, "I am, Mr. Mulcahy."

"That's a great old place," he said approvingly. "Oh, a great old place entirely."

Bucky joined in. "Now now, P. J.," he said warningly. "Easy

on that, there. I don't know as we could say it's such a great old place *today*. Once upon a time it was a great old place, yes. All right. That we know. That we agree upon. But is it a great old place *today*? I put the question to Father, here. What about that, Father? Is it a place a man would want to be at all?"

"Well, of course, I'm there," I said. "That may make a difference. But I like it. It's not what it used to be, but I think you'd recognize everything easily enough." Almost as if it were a point of pride, I added, "The church and rectory haven't been touched for years."

Julia said unexpectedly, "Many's the time I was to Old Saint Paul's. When Father Con Dolan was pastor. There was a man you wouldn't forget. He had a neck like a turkey and died of the croup."

"Ah, but it's the people that's different," Bucky said. "The old crowd's gone and forever. We can't deny that. Scattered to the four winds." Obligingly, he named these. "North. South. East. And West. That's what changes things. When the people pack up and say goodbye. I don't get over that way much these days, but they tell me there's nobody there now but Chinamen and Egyptians. And yourself, Father," he added politely.

A younger voice was heard; Dan had decided to join the conversation. "Speaking of Egypt," he said hurriedly, "I once found myself in the company of ex-King Farouk. What had happened was that I'd gone to Paris on business and one of the men I was calling on — a banker named Dorville, who used to be with Rothschild — took me to this little *bistro* one night. There at the next table was this fat man with three or four pretty girls. And who was it but Farouk? It turned out that Dorville actually knew him fairly well, but for some reason we didn't get the chance to meet."

His wife laughed. "Hobnobbing with royalty, dear," she said.

"Right!" said Dan.

There was a pause.

[67]

"I never knew there was any Egyptians in Old Saint Paul's," P. J. said thoughtfully. "There was a feller from Egypt once lived over on Harvey Place. He looked like a Jew. D'ye remember him, Bucky?"

Bucky nodded vigorously. "I do. A fat little feller with slick hair."

"No," P. J. said. "Thin as a rail, with one eye. They called him Frank. 'Twasn't the name at all, of course, but you couldn't get close to the real one. So they called him Frank. He had a job in the rubber company. They kept him out in the back office. He was good at the addin' and subtractin'."

"And damn poor at payin' the rent," said Charlie, suddenly and grimly breaking his silence. His plate, I saw, was being refilled. "I remember that lad. He lived at 34, in a nice clean little room with a sink. And the bathtub only a few steps down the hall. But come the first of the month and you'd need a blowtorch to get the rent out of him. He'd hide in the room, don't ye see, and make believe he wasn't to home. And then I'd peep in through the keyhole and sure enough, there'd be the one eye, lookin' out at me. Oho!" he cried. "There was a bad lad! I'm a kind man and I hold no grudges, but there was a lad should of been locked up for fifty years! Or shipped out of the country like an Eyetalian gangster!"

And he went back to his plate.

"Egyptians are very good at arithmetic," said Bucky. "That's a well-known fact. They do it with beads. On a board. It's old as the hills."

"This is lovely meat," Julia said. "Very tender. You'd need no teeth at all. I wonder, Mary, could I get a piece that's a little more crispy? Somethin' a little better done?"

"Of course, Aunt Julia," said Mary anxiously. She signaled to Agnes; the exchange was made.

"Raw meat gives you cancer," said Julia.

"It was a queer thing," said P. J. meditatively, "what happened to him. He died. One night. And d'ye know how they

[68]

found him? *On his knees.* The man died sayin' his prayers!"

"Ah well now!" Bucky protested. "One moment with that, P. J. Hold on there. We've no evidence for that. No evidence whatsoever. All right: the man was on his knees. That we know. That I give you. But how do we know he was at his prayers? How do we know he wasn't down there looking for his collar button? And had a heart attack? How do we know that?"

"The face," P. J. said calmly. "You could tell by the face on him. He was too far gone for the doctors so they gave me a call. The boys and myself went along and fixed him up as nice as you please. He hadn't a dime to his name but they gave him a little funeral all the same and put him up in the Sacred Heart Cemetery. At the north corner. Up by the walnut trees and Dummy Dolan."

"The very best part," Bucky said resentfully.

"On account of the shade," agreed P. J. "Well, what I was to say was this: when I first went into the room and took a peek at him, what d'ye s'pose was on his face? A smile. A nice, peaceful smile. I tell you, Bucky, there was no mistake about that one: there was a happy little Egyptian when he died!"

"All the same," Bucky said, "I wouldn't want a church full of them of a Sunday morning. They're a tricky lot, P. J. If we know anything from what the whole of history has to tell us, we know that. *Egyptians are a tricky lot.* And very poor supporters of the Church as well. Oh, a bad bunch when the collection comes round. A church full of Egyptains means a basket full of buttons. That's a well-known fact the world over!"

All this from the springboard of Old Saint Paul's, which in fact — not that it mattered — had no Egyptians at all. The conversation continued for some moments in much the same way, and as I listened to it, with amusement and delight and nostalgia, it was so familiar to me that it almost seemed as if I'd never been away from it — and this in spite of the fact that I hadn't heard it for years now. But it was the same talk

[69]

with which I had grown up, the talk which belonged, really, to another era, and which now must have been close to disappearing, the talk of old men and old women for whom the simple business of talking had always been the one great recreation. And so the result was the long, winding, old-fashioned parade of extraordinary reminiscence and anecdote and parochial prejudice and crotchety improbable behavior: in the world of old Charlie, Bucky, and P. J. — and my father — the newer, smoother tolerances had not yet arrived. I wondered, now, as I listened, how the young would feel about all this. Ted and Anne, for instance: were they shocked? Or entertained? Or bored? The young sometimes have severe standards: could they really appreciate what it was that was going on here before them?

This much was certain: they could appreciate far more easily than they could participate, and this went for the rest of us as well. For there was no doubt that this dinner belonged to the old people; their talk may have been unhurried and wandering, but it was also proof against interruption. Only Dan had tried: fearless Dan, with his sporty story about Farouk. He had failed. The great slow silence had swallowed up this attempt at intrusive liveliness; then the conversation had proceeded along its former, and proper, course. And I had listened, drifting along with the tide of words, and as I did the feeling of familiarity grew and grew, the sense of being once more at home in a place I knew. . . .

Yet despite the easy flow, I was puzzled by one thing: old Charlie's silence. He had broken it only once, to recount, with vigor, the circumstances of his landlord-tenant duel with Frank the Egyptian. Otherwise, nothing. I knew that he had always been a dedicated eater, but then he was a dedicated talker as well — and under the highly favorable circumstances of his own birthday, could food alone have silenced him so completely? I thought it unlikely. But it was not until the dessert was brought in — the huge, ornate cake, with all its candles blazing — and the ritual of blowing and cutting and serving was completed, that the mystery dissolved, for it was then that Charlie rose slowly to his feet. Clearly, this was the moment for which he had been saving himself: the time for talk — talk that counted, *his* talk — had arrived.

"Well, well," he said, "here we are again at the table, on another birthday. All together, family and friends. Happy as clams, and," he added, "full of the finest food that money can buy!"

A useful reminder, but an odd touch from a host. I caught John's shooting, sardonic glance. Helen, I saw, sat calmly, without changing expression; Mary, at her father's side, quietly radiated obedience. Charlie's children were ready.

"How do I feel?" Charlie asked rhetorically. "How do I feel on this day of days? How do I feel now I'm eighty-two?"

There was just the slightest emphasis given these last words; Bucky shifted noisily in his chair and his face worked furiously, but he said nothing. Charlie continued.

"I'll tell you how I feel: I feel *grand!* I'm here to tell you I never felt better in all my life. I went up to the Clinic for a couple of days last week and the lads up there flipped me up on the table and ran me around the room like a squirrel. When it was all over I said to them, 'Well, doctors, when do I make out my will?' And they said to me, 'By God, Mr. Carmody, if everybody had your pump and your art'ries there might be no wills made at all! No man lives forever, Mr. Carmody,' they said, 'but you'll come damn close to it!' Oh, they're smart lads up there at the Clinic. I wouldn't go anywheres else!"

"Hold on there, Charlie!" said Bucky. "Here's the question before us: *Is the Clinic all that good?* Let's examine the facts, that's the thing to do. And the facts are that they're all boys up there. Smart boys, yes. That I give you. But boys all the same. Give me a doctor that's got the experience behind him. A doctor like Dan Doyle. That's my doctor and I'm a well man today. Dan Doyle knows all the tricks. A hero of World

War Two when he took out a Frenchman's appendix with a soup spoon! I leave it to Dr. Frank O'Donnell here to back me up on Dan Doyle!"

Frank smiled and shrugged his shoulders slightly. "Dan Doyle's an excellent surgeon, of course. I've known him for many years. He was a classmate of mine. . . ."

"Dan Doyle's an old man," said Charlie abruptly. "As doctors go, that is. Doctors go very fast. Up at the Clinic there's nothin' but young doctors fresh from their books with all the brand-new tools in their kits and all the latest dope in their heads. If a new bug comes along on Monday, on Tuesday they got the pill to kill it. I tell you, mostly young people today are a bunch of bums, but I'm a great man for the young doctors. The old ones don't keep up. You go to Dan Doyle with a pain in your belly and chances are he'll give you an aspirin and a cascaret and tell you to take a good long walk in the woods. Then the next thing you know he's sharpenin' up his soup spoon again. No no, the young ones are the best. Old doctors go over the hill in no time at all. I wouldn't trust a one of them who was past forty!"

I wondered how Frank, the exact contemporary of Dan Doyle, felt about this. But he seemed unperturbed. At any rate, he continued to smile; I suppose it was quite possible that over the years he had grown used to his father-in-law's conversational style.

"So the art'ries are all right then, Charlie?" said P. J.

"Free and clear," Charlie said. "The blood goes whishin' through them like a fire hose!"

"Art'ries is terrible hard to tell about," said Julia, "from one day to the next. They clog up very fast. Like drains. That's what happened to Martin."

"By God, everythin' happened to Martin!" Charlie said, with some exasperation. "If he wasn't et by lions it was only because he never went near the zoo!" And then, quickly, with an impatient flourish of the hand, he waved away Martin and even the far more congenial subject of the Clinic; from his manner, even from his stance, it became clear that he was now ready to speak on graver matters.

"So here I am, feelin' grand, and eighty-two," he said. "And I can't help but think as I stand here that all over the city and the country too they're chiselin' out tombstones for people younger than me. There's not a day goes by I don't pick up the paper and see where they're sayin' the Dead Mass for someone who was still in knee britches while I was already a married man with a family on the way. There's people in this very city who spent their whole lives plannin' on what they'd do with what they got once I was out of the way and six foot under, and now the queer thing is I look around me and they're all gone and their houses are up for sale at cut-rate prices, and here am I, eighty-two, and still goin' strong. I tell you," he said, "it's little things like that make a man feel good!"

He had settled into the groove, speaking easily and with great verve; it occurred to me to wonder if this was his invariable performance on these occasions. Had his captive audience — apart from myself, of course — heard substantially this same tune many times before? I had no way of knowing, and of all those around the table only P. J. furnished a possible clue. He was sitting as upright as before, but now his eyes were closed. Significant? Or just the normal reaction of a very old man who has heard too many speeches after too many dinners, and knows that he cannot conceivably hear anything new . . . ?

Charlie continued to talk about the blessings of old age.

"I tell you what cheers an old man like me up sometimes," he said, "and that is that there's still a few others around as old as me that ain't dead. Although now I come to think of it most of them might as well be. They're all in the hospital or the Old Folks Home or some asylum somewheres. I was out to Saint Vincent's the other day to see poor Frankie Ferguson. Frankie was always a big strong feller, a year younger than me, who'd walk around in a snowstorm without any overcoat, and wear the cotton B.V.D.s instead of good wool underwear, and laugh at me because I'd bundle myself up like a sensible man on the cold days. Oh, Frankie was the great one for pokin' fun at you when there was other people around. 'Here comes Charlie Carmody, all wrapped up in blankets and hot water bottles and rubber boots!' he'd yell. 'Hey there, Charlie, where's your Eskimo hat? I hear, Charlie, you got underdrawers made of fur! Keep warm, Charlie, so's you don't catch a cold!' Oh, many's the laugh he had at me in times gone by, and all the other loafers with him. But I'm a kind man who holds no grudges. I forgive them all. They're all dead now anyways except Frankie, and he's out in the ward at Saint Vincent's all curled up like a doughnut with arthritis and with a string hangin' out of his mouth. Poor Frankie. Yes, many's the good laugh he had at Charlie back in the old days. I don't think he laughs much now. Well well, that's the way it goes. We mustn't complain."

And so once again I was face to face with this special form of resignation, so peculiar to Charlie. It did not appear to impress Bucky. He had been toying irritably with his knife and fork for some moments, and now he said loudly, "Now now, Charlie! One two three on the facts, if you please. Fair's fair; we're all agreed on that. And what we know is this: that there's plenty of people alive and well today as old as you *and older.* In the very pink of condition. People like—"

"People like yourself," Charlie said, cutting in swiftly. "Like yourself and P. J., there. Oh, don't I know that, Bucky! And ain't I grateful for it! I tell you, I don't know what would become of old Charlie if anythin' terrible happened to his old pals Bucky and P. J. And there's not a night goes by I don't get down on my knees and say a prayer it don't. 'Oh God,' I say, 'please don't let nothin' happen to Bucky and P. J. Don't let that little twitch around Bucky's mouth amount to a row of beans—' "

"*What* twitch?" cried Bucky. "What twitch is that?"

"Shh shh shh," said P. J. composedly, still with his eyes closed. "You're interruptin' a man at his prayers."

"Oh yes yes," Charlie said, "busy as I am, I'm not the man to forget an old pal. Every night, Bucky, I'm on the knees. And s'posin', in spite of it all, somethin' terrible did happen to you? God help us, I hope it don't, but if it did, I'd be the first on hand to see you were made comfortable. I'm not a rich man today, taxes bein' the way they are, but I'd see you got a nice little room somewheres with plenty of sunshine and round the clock care. And every now and then I'd see you had little things sent in to you: a nice soft custard, a bit of fruit. . . ."

"Custard!" Bucky shouted. His whole face, even his eyes, now seemed to inflate oddly, as if he were holding his breath — which, all too clearly, he was very far from doing. "Not by a damn sight! I don't want your custard! I won't take your custard! You'll send no custard in to me! I say that now for one and all to hear: *Charlie Carmody will send no custard in to Bucky Heffernan!*"

"No thanks are due," Charlie said magnanimously. "I never forget an old pal, sick or well!"

"Cup custard," Julia said. "Martin was the one was fond of cup custard. There was days at a time he wouldn't eat nothin' else. He was that thin you could put your hand on his belly and feel his backbone, and I'd say to him, 'You got to eat, Martin, to keep up your stren'th. Wouldn't ye have some lovely chicken soup with all the fat skimmed off?' But he'd look up at me with his little smile and say, 'Only the cup custard, Julia. That's my fav'rite. I'll eat that till the day I die.' And he did," she said.

"Old pals," Charlie said. The bright blue candid gaze rested benignly on Bucky — so benignly, indeed, that it was only for an instant that I seemed to catch the quick glint of malicious satisfaction. I looked around the table and no one seemed un-

[75]

duly bothered by this spirited exchange between host and guest. But they were all veterans at these dinners — by now, even Anne — and presumably something more or less like this had been expected as a natural part of the program, a regular feature of Charlie's day. All the same, I wondered if they might not now feel a certain suspense, an uneasy speculation as to which of them might be the next recipient of Charlie's special birthday benediction?

"Old pals and the family," Charlie said. "I remember them all, day and night, in the prayers and out of them. And plenty of others as well. Busy as I am, I'm thinkin' of people every hour of the day. All kinds of people, big or small, it makes no difference to Charlie. Bankers and clerks and cops and sewer workers." There was just the slightest perceptible pause. "And priests," he said.

It was a neat hierarchy. Automatically I looked across the table at John and found that he was already regarding me with a significant eye. Which was hardly a surprise; no stroke of his father's, however casual, ever eluded this ready man. . . .

"And the little children, too," Charlie said. "I'm a great man for the little ones. A soft touch, as they say. Nothin' makes me feel better than to walk over to John's parish school of an afternoon and watch the boys and girls playin' their little games. And many's the time I've leaned over the fence and had little talks with them and told them who I was and what I was goin' to give them all some one of these fine days: lots of brand-new bats and balls and hockey sticks. Oh yes, I'm thinkin' of those lovely little children all the time. And what I wonder sometimes," he said, his voice suddenly becoming rather sentimental, "is do they ever think of old Charlie? The way he thinks of them? I wonder do those boys and girls ever stand up by their desks in school, say, and all together recite a little prayer out loud for Mister Carmody? Wouldn't that be lovely? But I don't think they do. I never heard that they do."

John said briskly, and not at all sentimentally, "Maybe

they're waiting until they see all those bats and balls and hockey sticks."

Did Charlie blink? I wasn't sure; in any case, he said instantly, "I hope that ain't true, John. I wouldn't want it on my mind, if I was a priest, that the little children in my parish school were bein' taught to hang around the school gate with their hands out, waitin' to get somethin' free from an old man. I don't think I could say my prayers at night if I knew the little boys and girls God put me in charge of were learnin' money grubbin' instead of their catechism!"

John said, with obvious irritation, "It's not at all a question of —"

"I blame no one!" Charlie said, putting up his hands. "There's no need to apologize to your dad!" Was this his most infuriating gambit? Very probably. He said, "It's all in the times. The whole world wants somethin' for nothin' these days, even the little kids. I never go by the school but I don't look in and see one of them throwin' a beanbag at somebody else, and I say to myself, 'Well, Charlie, in another year or so that'll be a rock. Or a bomb.' Oh yes, the kids of today are all a bunch of hoodlums. We pay our good money to send them to school where they're s'posed to be taught good manners and their ABC's, and what do we get? A city full of little maniacs in overalls, runnin' around all night stickin' up fillin' stations, lettin' the air out of tires, breakin' windows in my apartment buildin's, and stabbin' old ladies with jackknives. Oh, I tell you," said the soft touch for children, "I'd jail most of them the day they were born!"

P. J.'s eyes opened suddenly. "I see where Dolly McNamee was jumped at the other night whilst crossin' the park," he said. "By a dwarf."

"Dwarfs do a lot of harm," said Julia. "In their way."

"This one's been runnin' around for a good bit now," said P. J. "Jumpin' at people and scarin' them. In the dark. He hides in the bushes and then he jumps. They think it's a puppy

[77]

until he laughs. Oh, the cops have been after that feller for a long time now. The Laughin' Dwarf, the papers call him."

"There was a dwarf like that out in Kansas City one time," said Julia. "When Martin was in hospital out there. Nobody could catch him. He would go where they couldn't, ye see. He was that small. What they fin'lly did, they put a little policeman onto him. One his own size. He looked like a toy in his blue suit, but he was strong as a bull."

"They have very powerful arms, I'm told," P. J. said. "All their stren'th goes to their arms. Dwarfs have very weak little legs. But I'll tell you what I never knew about dwarfs, and that is what's the difference between them and midgets? That's a thing I'd like to know."

"Dwarfs are more delicate," said Julia. "The one out in Kansas City they found hidin' away in the stump of a tree. They took him off to the jailhouse and kept him nice and dry, but he died in a week. They don't last when they're cooped up."

Dwarfs don't keep. This was a subject, surely, on which Bucky could be expected to have opinions, but Bucky was saying nothing. Apparently his last exchange with old Charlie had left him with the sulks; he sat, now, staring down at the table, sunk in gloomy, stubborn silence.

"To get back to the main point," said Charlie, rather irascibly; the interruption had been a long one. "To get back to what makes sense and not a lot of nut talk. To get back to what I was sayin'. The newspaper fellers come up to me and say, 'Mr. Carmody, we'd like to hear how you got where you are, now you're eighty-two. Give us your best advice, Mr. Carmody.' And what d'ye think I tell them? No smokin' or drinkin'? Get to bed by sunset? Don't eat fat? No! I tell them: *Keep thinkin' of other people*. That's always been my rule and that's why I'm a happy man today. And I mean thinkin' about full-size people, not dwarfs or midgets or small cops. Regular people, the kind you meet on the street or in church or go waltzin' with or sell things to. That's the kind of people I been thinkin' of all my life, no matter how busy I was, and that's why I'm a happy man today at the age of eighty-two!" He paused and looked slowly up and down the table, and then, in an oddly tragic voice, said, "Despite the disappointments."

And was this declaration really greeted by the sound of a vast if smothered sigh? Or was it only that, from the glum contortion of John's face, I was sure there *had* to be such a sigh? No matter, for Charlie continued without breaking his stride.

"Oh yes, I had my disappointments, the same as anyone else," he said. "Only worse. And I have them still. I tell nobody about them, but I have them all the same. I see people goin' by me on the street, turnin' their heads around to look after me, and I know what they're sayin' to themselves, every last one of them. They're sayin', 'There goes Charlie Carmody passin' by, it must be wonderful to be him. With all his money, and bein' so popular, too!' And how many times have I felt like goin' up to them and sayin', 'True enough, but that ain't everythin'.' And it ain't," he said. "Not by a damn sight it ain't. Just because a man's got a little bit of cash in the bank and everybody likes him don't mean he's got no troubles. Oh no! Some of the troubles I got would of broke another man. And I don't just mean troubles like Roosevelt and his crazy gang with their big taxes, or the city tearin' down half my lovely tenements to build a playground for bums. No no, it's somethin' different but just as bad. Somethin' more personal. Somethin' so personal I keep it all to myself. That's the way I am. I tell my troubles to no man. Except," he said expansively, "to all of you here today. Family and friends, I don't mind them hearin'. What's a man good for if he can't trust the old pals? So I'll tell you what I never told anyone, and I think you'll be surprised a little. You've known old Charlie a long time now, and I know you think he's a hard old feller, and what he's goin' to tell you I know you wouldn't of guessed in a million years. It'll come as a hell of a shock, I guarantee you

[79]

that!" He leaned forward, the blue eyes looking out at us all; he smiled, a little sadly. "Well, here it is," he announced. "The thing is this: *I'm lonesome.*"

If this came as even the slightest shock to his listeners, they concealed the fact well. There was no stir, not a single sudden start; the room remained perfectly calm; glances were exchanged between Helen and John, between young Ted and Anne. It was quite clear that Charlie's quick venture into the pathetic had surprised no one, and that to all in this room — myself excepted — the words to come would be, at the very least, a twice-told tale. . . .

"Happy but lonesome," he said. "That's a funny way to be, ain't it? But that's the way it goes with old Charlie. Sometimes I get up in the mornin', feelin' like a million dollars, and I go downstairs nice and early, and no one else is up in the whole house, and I get my breakfast for myself, and I sit eatin' away by the kitchen window, feelin' the grand warm sunshine comin' into the room, and lookin' out into the back yard at all the birds singin' away for me, and I think to myself that it's great to be alive, and I'd love to live to be a hundred and ten. But then, right in the very same breath along with it, d'ye know what else I think? I think: *Poor old Charlie. Nobody cares!*"

And to this Mary reacted. Seated at her father's side, she looked up with a troubled expression on her wide, placid face; Charlie saw this, nodded slowly, and reached down to pat her on the arm.

"You're a grand girl, Mary," he said. "You're the same grand girl your dad brought you up to be. What I say has nothin' to do with you. Or not much, anyways. No, you're a grand girl and you do your best. In your way. As does Helen. In her way. As does everybody. Everybody's fine and dandy. Old Charlie never complains. But it ain't the same since your ma died. Somethin's been different with old Charlie since then. Oh my yes. Over thirty years ago, and there's not a day goes by I don't think of your dear ma and the way she'd look up with the soft brown eyes and whisper, 'God never made a finer man than you, Charlie Carmody!' Oh, I tell you," he said, "that's the kind of stuff a man likes to hear. He likes to know there's someone *understands* him."

"Rose was a lovely girl," said P. J. "I was always very fond of Rose."

Julia agreed, somewhat peculiarly. "A martyr if ever there was one," she said.

Which hardly seemed the sort of endorsement Charlie would welcome; I saw Bucky's eyes gleam with a sudden interest. But Charlie, possibly because he was concentrating on his disappointments, apparently did not hear; he said, "No, I get nothin' like that any more. Twenty years gone, and I miss her today just as much as ever. Nobody knows how much I miss her. Or how much I miss little Charlie. There was a lad for you," he said wistfully. "Little Charlie. There was a lad you could pin your hopes to. And then dyin' like he did, way before his time — oh, I tell you, I never got over that one. I used to look at him in the mornin' as he lay in his bed, sleepin' away, and I'd say to myself, 'Well, Charlie, here's the lad you can leave the business to. Here's the lad will appreciate it.' A man works the whole of his life like a slave, buildin' a grand big business up out of nothin' at all, just so's he can leave it to some one of his sons, and what happens? Nobody wants it. Nobody cares. John packs up and goes off to the seminary, and I s'pose there's nothin' to be said against that. We got to have priests. Some of my best friends are priests. But you can't leave a business like mine to a man that lives in a rectory. And then there's Dan."

Here Charlie closed his eyes, as if the mere remembrance of Dan's various destinies was too much for him. Dan himself seemed not in the least downcast. He was sitting straight up, his head cocked alertly, his lips pursed as if he were about to whistle. He was not the most sensitive of men to begin with, and I imagine that time must have toughened him still more against these pointed reminiscences of his father.

"But there was always Charlie," old Charlie continued. "Little Charlie. Charles Carmody Junior. There was the one I depended on. I'm a great man for lovin' all his children, none greater, but I s'pose Charlie was the pride and joy. There was the lad that loved the business. You just had to look at him to know that. A chip off the old block. There was somethin' about him made you say, 'There's the one will step into his dad's shoes. There's the businessman born!' And he was. Oh, the plans I had for little Charlie! I was goin' to take him into the office with me, fix him up a desk, make all the rounds with him, show him all the deadbeats to watch out for. Oh yes, I had it all set for him to step in and take over. And then what happened? He died. All of a sudden and in one night he died, and the whole kit and caboodle, all the grand plans, went right to smash. I had nothin' left. Nothin' at all."

His speech had become slower, and his voice was so rich with grief as he recalled the loss of the son who had been his only successor that for the first time I felt myself genuinely moved — and then suddenly, and with a shock, I remembered that Charlie Junior, the businessman born who was so dedicated to his father's affairs, had been, at the time of his death, exactly two years old. . . .

"All gone," said Charlie, "and that ain't the whole story. Not only the wife and little Charlie, but my best old pal as well. I don't have to tell you who that was. I'm a man that's got lots of good old pals like P. J. and Bucky here, but I mean no disrespect to them when I tell you what you all know: that the best old pal of all up and died on me ten years ago, way before he should of. Oh yes, all of you sittin' here today know who that was. And one of you sittin' here *specially* knows who that was!"

And he looked directly at me. For an instant nothing registered, then — a suspicion. An incredible suspicion. Could Charlie really mean . . . ?

He could. "Right you are, Father!" he cried. "Your very own dad. Dave Kennedy, that's the man I mean and that's the man I miss. My old pal, born on the same block and in the very same year. Oh yes, all my life I knew Dave Kennedy, and what have I got to say about him? Nothin' but nice things. He was just like me. There was people used to take us for twins. Playin' together, goin' to school together, growin' up together, side by side — oh, I tell you, you don't forget a man like that in a hurry. Many's the time we spent the whole night together, talkin' away down by the firehouse, him tellin' me things, and me tellin' him things. And I can see him just as plain as if it was yesterday, puttin' out his hand and touchin' me on the arm, and sayin' to me, 'I'll tell you what I want, Charlie old pal: I want my boy Hugh to grow up to be someone just like you!' Wasn't that a lovely thing to hear? I don't hear nothin' like that today. Just rememberin' it and seein' Father Hugh sittin' here with us all makes me feel good. There's nothin' could make me feel better unless it was Dave himself could come back and be here with us at the table, and say with his little smile, 'Here's to Charlie on the happy birthday: I hope he lives to be a thousand!' "

I tried to imagine this scene. I was not successful.

"But," said Charlie, with a sad smile, "he can't come back. None of them can. They're all gone. All but me. I'm alive and kickin' and happy. But lonesome too. Never forget that. Never forget that as happy as he is and with all he's got, it ain't all roses for Charlie. As the Monsignor used to say, we all got our crosses to bear. Only there's some of us got heavier crosses than others. But let's never mind about that now. I don't want to bother anybody. I tell my troubles to no man, as I said before. I mentioned it a little bit here today only because we're all family and friends, eatin' up good food and laughin' and enjoyin' ourselves, and I know that anythin' I got to say won't spoil the good time. And that's the way I want it. That's the kind of a man I am. And if, while all the smiles and jokes are goin' on, somebody looks up and catches old Charlie maybe not smilin' as hard as the rest, I want no one to feel bad. All I want is for them to say to themselves, 'It's only old Charlie, feelin' a little lonesome. He'll be better in the mornin' once he's had his good night's sleep and a bowl of oatmeal under his belt!' Oh yes, that's what I want them to say. And I know that that's what they will say."

Once more the sad little smile appeared and lingered briefly; then, abruptly, and in quite a different voice, he said, "Well, so much for birthday greetin's. Just a few little words to make you all feel at home, to make you glad you came. And now we've all et up, let's go back into the livin' room and have a grand old time!"

Although, with Charlie's final glum reflections to serve as a springboard, it struck me that this injunction was easier delivered than obeyed. Indeed, once we were back in the living room, it turned out that the one who had no intention of obeying it was Charlie himself, who now announced his own plans. He was going to bed.

"For my nap," he explained. "I take a nap every day of my life. You can't beat naps. They're the things keep a man strong and healthy. Oh yes, everybody ought to take naps!"

There was neither protest nor surprise at this announcement; apparently it had been expected. Charlie began to circle the room, shaking hands with his guests, once again thanking them for coming, and now bidding them goodbye. Clearly, the grand old time in the living room was destined to be a remarkably short-lived affair. And now, as he came up to me, for the first time I saw the signs of a change. For at last the day had begun to catch up with Charlie, and a few of the marks of fatigue were showing through. Some of the bounce had left his step; the bright blue eyes were now touched with a faint cloudiness; and all of a sudden it became easy to remember that Charlie Carmody was a very old man. . . .

In spite of which there was not the slightest change in his voice; this came through as strong as ever.

"A great day, Father!" he said. "And I don't mind tellin' you that your bein' here was what made it all the greater for old Charlie. I mean that, Father. Nothin' made me feel better than to look out of the front window and see you marchin' up the front steps again, just like you used to. A bit late," he said thoughtfully (mere fatigue could not conquer the essential Charlie), "but still here. And that's what counts with a man like me. I tell you, that made me feel grand." And then he added, "Even though we didn't have our little chat."

It was the first I had heard of any little chat. Would it have revealed why I had been asked here today? For this still remained as much of a mystery as ever; John had been quite wrong in guessing that old Charlie would show at least a part of his hand. I said, "It was a good day even without the chat, Mr. Carmody. We'll have it sometime later. Some day when you're not so busy."

"I'm never too busy for you, Father!" he cried magnanimously. "We'll have the chat all right. We'll have *lots* of chats." Then, cryptically, "With all we got to say to each other."

Another surprise. Did I have things to say to Charlie? No. Did he have things to say to me? Apparently. But what? In any case, he was not going to say them now. He shook my hand again and then hurried away towards the stairs; in a moment, still waving, he had disappeared.

And this marked the end of the birthday party. We stayed in the room for some minutes more while Mary made her large, slow, troubled way among us, explaining rather doubtfully that there was no need to go, that her father really expected us to stay. I think she convinced no one. It was obvious that when Charlie went the party went with him and now, one by one, the guests began to follow his example.

Dan was the first to go. With a smiling Flo on his arm, he walked around the room with a quick, pert step, almost like a vaudevillian's dance, hurriedly saying goodbye, and excusing his departure on the wildly improbable ground that "duty called."

To me he said jauntily, " 'Rivederci, Hugh. Auf wiedersehen."

Cosmopolitan Dan. I wonder that he didn't say goodbye to me in Egyptian. A few phrases from Farouk. . . .

Julia drifted off silently towards the second floor, the only one of the party to be a house guest as well. Bucky and P. J. left together, P. J. polite and gently abstracted, Bucky with a farewell jab at his host.

"There's those that need naps," he said to me, "and there's those that don't. I tell you this, Father: Bucky Heffernan don't. When does Bucky Heffernan sleep? At night! The proper time! No real healthy man jumps into bed every noon! The very best doctors agree with me there." Then he said, "I'll be over to see you one of these days, Father."

I said, "I'm always there, Mr. Heffernan."

"I've a matter to discuss," he said. "A very important matter. Dealing with my plans. My plans for the future. There's some people don't seem too interested in those plans. Some people with their short answers!" He looked across the room at John; the look was one of the darkest dissatisfaction. It occurred to me that the nightly talks on the subject of Bucky's grave might not have been going too well; it was more than likely that by now the thin surface of John's patience had begun to wear away.

"I mention no names," said Bucky, his voice suddenly much louder, "but there's some people certain and cocksure they've got other people all sewed up. What do I say to those people? I say this: Be careful. A man could change his mind!"

Was this intended as a ghoulish ultimatum: Bucky, threatening to take his final custom elsewhere? The elsewhere being, specifically, myself and Old Saint Paul's? But the threat was either ignored or unheard by John and Bucky said no more. He merely gave me a glance which seemed at once both triumphant and conspiratorial, and went off to rejoin P. J. at the door. As he did so, Ted and Anne came over to say goodbye.

"Come and see us, Father," she said. "Will you? Some evening for dinner?" Quite without irony she added, "Any evening you're not too busy."

I thought of the possibility of there being "too busy" evenings at Saint Paul's, but I thanked her and said evasively, "I'll try. It's a little difficult to arrange right now because I'm shorthanded; I have only the one curate. And while the parish is not demanding, it does cover a good bit of ground. . . ."

"All the same," Ted said, in his quiet, pleasant voice, "I wish you'd come, Father. I haven't seen you for years, and today almost doesn't count, does it? As far as any talk goes, I mean. And I'd like to have a talk." He smiled and said, "As a matter of fact, I'm out for some advice."

I said, "Is this the voice of the candidate?"

He looked at Anne, then back at me, and smiled again. "Possibly," he said. "Would you like to become an *éminence grise?*"

"I don't think they're much in demand these days, are they? Anyway, I'd be a particularly bad choice; my political counsel is nonexistent."

"Oh," he said, "I get all of that I need. And more. How much good it'll do I don't know. We'll see. Meanwhile, come on over, Father. You'd be doing me a favor. I mean it about the advice."

Just what kind of advice was not expressed; they left with the invitation open, Anne promising to call me soon, and now, in the diminished party, I was joined by Helen.

"The great thing is," she said, watching her daughter-in-law, who was managing the two children towards the door, "that she really is as lovely as she looks. Did you get a chance to talk to her at all, Hugh? I hoped you would."

[87]

"I did indeed. I liked her, very much. Who is she, Helen? Would I know any of her people?"

"No, I don't think so. She's from Chicago; Ted met her at a college dance, years ago. The family story is a little unusual. They used to be quite poor, and then one day her father invented a way to mix some sort of milk with something else in a tin can, and you pressed a button and out came floods of whipped cream. You know the kind I mean: it doesn't really taste good, but there's lots of it. Well, the result of that was that the family is now rich. Quite a bit richer than we are, I suspect."

I wondered how this went down with Charlie. Self-made himself, pleased by his achievement, did he welcome an alliance with another of the same who, apparently, had achieved even more? Helen answered the question without my asking it.

"Daddy patronizes him. First, because he made his money some thirty years after Daddy did, and you know how we old established families feel about the *nouveaux riches*. And second, he's part French-Canadian. There's some County Mayo there, but there's also a large chunk of Montreal, P. Q. That makes Daddy feel better. Which I don't mind at all; I find the father rather hard going myself. But the daughter's a different story."

"No chip off the old block here?"

"Far from it," she said. "And thank heaven for that. Anne's absolutely first class. Ted couldn't have done better; to tell you the truth I was staggered that he managed to get her. You're smiling: what's wrong?"

"Not a thing. I was just wondering if Ted knew he had this vote of confidence."

"Was it a lack of confidence, Hugh? I imagine it was at that. I don't know," she said reflectively, "I keep hearing of these mothers who feel sure that their sons will come home with the perfect choice, but I never felt that way. Not for a minute. And you know me, Hugh: I've never played Ted down. He's a fine boy, and he has his father's good looks, and a great deal of quiet charm, and he's really extremely intelligent. And I must say that all through school he managed to pick out girls who were nice enough. But somehow I always had this terrible feeling that when it came right down to the wire, when it came to picking a *wife*, he'd go to some impossible extreme. You know, that he'd come in to me either tugging some little thing who owned the biggest collection of rosaries in college, or someone with taffy hair and a wide mouth who liked to dance on table tops. Instead, he came in with Anne. I tell you, Hugh, it was the greatest moment of my life!"

I looked at her standing there, a handsome woman in her middle years, happily married, with life turning out well for those who mattered most to her, and I thought now that of all the Carmodys it was probably Helen who had come the closest to satisfaction and contentment. I said, "You're a lucky girl, Helen."

Her reply was odd.

"Am I, Hugh?" she said quietly. "Yes, I suppose I am. At least that's what people almost always tell me." And in her voice I thought I caught a queer touch of sadness, but I may have imagined this, and in any case it was gone in a moment, and with all her old interest and warmth she said, "All this talking, Hugh, and all I really want to say is how good it was to have you back today. Will you come back often? Really often?" With a little smile she said, "Now that the ice is out of Sebago?"

It was an echo from childhood. There had been, in our neighborhood, an egg man named Mr. Collingwood: a gaunt and leather-faced old Yankee, with bits of straw and chicken feathers clinging to his invariable old gray suit; he went from house to house, delivering his eggs and pronouncing upon the weather in a powerful and lugubrious nasal voice. And one day, at the end of one winter, we had all trooped into the Carmody kitchen just as Mr. Collingwood, standing in the center of the room, shedding his usual feathers, was saying with a solemn joy, "The ice is out of Sebago, Mam, the ice is out of Sebago!" This had become a phrase with us and somehow a sign of spring, as reliable a harbinger as any robin or bluebird, although it was not until years later that any of us found out that there really was a Sebago: a lake in Maine with presumably significant thaws. . . .

I said, "Good old Sebago. I haven't even thought of the name for years."

"Well," she said, "I have. Often. I go poking around through most of the things that happened then. We had great fun, didn't we, Hugh?"

I nodded, and she said, "But then I imagine most children do. It's just that the older you get the more likely you are to think that you had it all."

"I suppose you are." And then I said, "You're how old, Helen? Fifty-four?"

She smiled slightly. "Not old enough for this line of talk, you mean? Yes, you're right, of course. But somehow all of a sudden I've become one of the world's easy marks for nostalgia. I think the sight of a seesaw might make me weep. Maybe that's what being a grandmother does for you; you keep on thinking about the day before yesterday. Although," she said, more matter-of-factly, "I don't know what all this has to do with your spending a little time with us from now on." She spoke as if this were something that had been settled, long ago. "And listen, Hugh: one more thing. Are you going to drop in on Ted and Anne?"

"They asked me to, just now. . . ."

"Yes, I know," she said, almost impatiently, as though she had known of this invitation even before it had been offered. Which she probably had. "But the point is this: are you going to do it?"

"It was more or less left up in the air." Out of habit I went on. "It's a question of timing, of coordinating the schedules of Ted's house and Old Saint Paul's. . . ."

"You're not really too fond of direct answers these days, are you?" she said. "Come on, Hugh. Don't duck me. Give in, just a little. And do me a favor by going to see Ted and Anne. I'd like you to. I'd really like you to very much!"

And there was an urgency underlying these words which surprised me, because Helen was not a particularly urgent woman, and because a casual invitation from an attractive young couple — who surely could have been in no desperate want of company — hardly seemed to require such insistent support. And then it occurred to me that it was all being done for my sake. For my own good, as they say. One more string to draw the hermit from his lair, a line of communication open to the world of youth. Which was all well enough, and probably even necessary in a way, but still. . . .

Still, for this reason or some other, it was clearly important to Helen. She stood waiting for an answer, and so I said that I'd be glad to go. I intended to push this matter a little further, but now our conversation, as conversation so often had done that afternoon, came abruptly to an end, for John approached us, plainly eager for departure.

"We ought to be going," he said to me, looking quickly about him, as if suspecting that the nap was really only a ruse, and that at any moment Charlie might come sneaking down the stairs, ready to spring on those who had delayed too long. "If we're going we should get started."

We might have been going to Spitzbergen. But I said goodbye to Helen; I said goodbye to Mary; and, out on the front walk, I said goodbye to Frank O'Donnell. He was coming in from his car.

"I've just been out to get my camera," he said.

Now that everyone had gone. He held it out to me; it was a handsome and obviously expensive piece of imported machinery. I admired it and he said, "A present. From a German industrialist named Kessler: his firm makes them, among other things. They flew him over for surgery last month. Bile duct. They have perfectly good surgeons over there, of course, but someone had badly muffed this one. It was a mess, but he's all right now. Or," he said carefully, "as right as he'll ever be. They never quite . . . mmm." He put out his hand and said, "Well, Hugh."

Was he going to congratulate me again? But all he said, simply, naturally, and surprisingly, was, "It was very good to see you again."

And I said, "Thanks, Frank. Thanks very much."

I was halfway down the walk when he called to me.

"Hugh?"

I turned, and with a little flourish of his hand he said, "My best to His Excellency."

He was back in stride. I opened my mouth to tell him, for the second time that afternoon, that I almost never saw the Bishop these days, but — I didn't. Why spoil a ritual? I said, "All right, Frank."

He waved once more, and I turned back and went to the car to which John had hurried immediately upon sighting his brother-in-law. He looked at me, shrugged, but said nothing; then he pressed the accelerator and we pulled swiftly away from the Carmody house and the scene of old Charlie's party.

6

ALL THROUGH dinner John had said very little, and now, on the ride back to the rectory, I was sure that the dam would break, and down would come the fierce waterfall of words. But here I was mistaken, for what the afternoon seemed to have done, more than anything else, was to depress him, and when he spoke he did so wearily and with an air of moody reflection.

"I'm tired," he said. "Bone-tired. Exhausted. Drained dry. I feel as if a thousand suction pumps had been working over me. How about you? Aren't you tired?"

"No more than usual. . . ."

"Well, I don't know what that usual is. But I'll tell you what's usual with me. I'm almost never tired. Why that is I don't know, but it's so. I get up to say the early Mass and I go to bed late at night. In between I can take care of a funeral, speak at a Communion breakfast, baptize babies, visit the school, hear confessions, talk to the Ladies' Sodality, conduct novena devotions, and meet with one or another of those endless committees we seem to have at Saint Raymond's. If it's a really unlucky day I may even find myself at a Brotherhood Dinner. Listening to the speeches. Try that sometime, just for fun. The point is that I can do all this and still feel fine. Or at least all right. But give me one short gala hour at my father's house and I have barely enough strength left to make the front door!"

He drove on. I think I must have been a poor audience for him, for I was looking rather than listening — looking, not at John, but out at the streets and houses and trees and grass and old stone walls that seemed to float by through the drowsy stillness of the summer afternoon. This was the old part of Saint Raymond's parish, the part where Charlie lived, the part which, after all the years, remained so absurdly unchanged. Suddenly I had the feeling that if I closed my eyes and then opened them, very quickly, I would see, walking along the streets or sitting on the front porches of the large wooden houses, people I knew well but had not seen for a long time. And so I did this — foolishly, like a little schoolboy playing his games. But the streets, late on this Sunday afternoon, remained deserted, and in any case I think that people no longer sit on front porches, rocking away through the twilight; apart from one little girl in a buttercup frock, gravely tossing a red rubber ball at the sky, I saw no one. . . .

We came down the long and slowly sloping hill, and around the corner there was Saint Raymond's itself: neat, rose-brick, surrounded by its green geometry of lawn. And as I saw it now, I felt a quick pang — which was natural enough, I suppose. I glanced quickly at John, but he was looking straight ahead at the road, and I knew that he was thinking neither of me nor of Saint Raymond's; his thoughts were still in old Charlie's dining room. . . .

We turned into one of the side streets, and there, on the far corner, I saw another vivid landmark: a small variety store, which had been in this location since . . . when? Since before I was born, certainly. It had been established here mysteriously, in violation of all zoning laws; it had become a neighborhood essential, an emergency supply depot, dealing in such items as milk, bread, household staples, ice cream and penny candy: its owner had always been Mr. Avedesian, a tall, silent, bald

Armenian with great brown eyes and massive hairy hands. These hands were a legend to the children of the neighborhood: it was said that Mr. Avedesian had trained them to such a point of terrible deftness that each scoop of ice cream he served had a great pocket of air in the center; wary youngsters, wanting a cone, always preferred to wait for Mrs. Avedesian, who, it was whispered, had not been able to master the trick despite frequent and horrible beatings given her by her thrifty husband. Mr. Avedesian had one son, Dikran, a boy of my age who was a notable exotic in our simple racial group, and who brought strange lunches to school. I had not seen him for decades, and now, as we passed the store, I saw a stout, middle-aged man gazing out the window. Was this Dikran . . . ?

The store marked the end of the older section, and we came now to a newer, smarter section for newer, smarter families. We were still within the limits of Saint Raymond's, but when I was a boy, fields had been here: fields, and a dumping ground. Now fields and dump were gone. It had become a residential area for the well-to-do. And, not uncommonly, for the well-to-do children of those who had done well in the older section: it was here, for example, that Helen and Frank O'Donnell lived, in one of the more impressive of the comfortable, conservative, semi-stately brick homes. Each generation found its own environment: old Charlie in the sprawling and faintly dilapidated mansion on the hill, Helen and Frank here in the undoubted setting of the successful professional man, Ted and Anne — where and how? A ranch house? In a good suburb? For it suddenly occurred to me that despite the invitation I had no idea where they lived. I was about to ask John when abruptly he came out of his thoughts and said, "It's the talk that does it, of course."

I said, "That does what?"

"Tires you," he said. He had not yet left the dining room. "And not just my father's. Everybody's. Around that table, I mean. They all have that special, dreadful kind of talk that doesn't exist anywhere but here. It's not conversation. It's not anything. Just a suffocating cloud of words that keeps on growing and growing and coming and coming. Like a fog." He looked at me and said, "It didn't bother you, did it?"

"No. Of course I hadn't heard much of it for a long time. Not until today. And then I haven't your high standards for conversation. I thought it was all rather wonderful."

"What was so wonderful about it?" he said; irritation was now gaining on fatigue. "It's exactly the same talk I've heard since I was a child. There's nothing picturesque or romantic about it. And it's nonsense about 'high standards'; I simply like talk to have some point. And this had none. It never does. In the first place because no one is talking *to* anyone. They're just *talking*. And secondly, because in all rational talk, no matter how much you digress, you usually come back to the main road once in a while. But in my father's house no one comes back to the main road for the simple reason that there *is* no main road. Everybody there deals exclusively in detours." He fell silent again, and then after a moment he said broodingly, "They fool you, of course. As well as you know them, they fool you. And they fool you by beginning what they have to say with something that sounds simple and sensible. Nothing wildly interesting or startling. Just sensible. Something about the way the income taxes are collected, say, or about the state roads being in bad repair. All right. This is the start. And then just as you think that maybe this time there just might be a possibility of some sort of logical progression you suddenly find yourself trapped in the middle of some lunatic story about a man named Danny McGee who always slept in a maple tree or Little Philsy Kerrigan who once saved up a trunkful of doughnuts. And there you are. God knows how you got there, but there you are and there you stay. Once they get started it's an escape-proof vault and let's see you get out. I know; I've been trying all my life."

No comment seemed necessary or, indeed, desired; at any

[96]

rate, I offered none. There was more silence, and after a while he said in a milder tone, "Anyway, now you know about the famous birthday parties."

"Yes. If today's was a fair sample, that is."

"Oh, very fair. Exactly like all the others. Word for word, you might say. Except for the fact that your father was brought in for considerable mention. That was new. Usually my mother and little Charlie have that part of the speech reserved for them alone. By the way, was it your impression that your father and my father were such great chums?"

I said again, "They were boys together, of course. . . ."

"Yes," he said. "That's the same answer you gave my father, isn't it? All right. Now another question: Do you know yet why you were asked? I won't go so far as to accuse my father of forthrightness, but did he give you any clues by indirection?"

"Not a blessed one. You were all wrong on that."

"I know, I know," he said quickly. "But that's nothing unusual. No one can ever really do more than make a wild stab at what's on my father's mind. Not even Helen. And certainly not me. For a long time the great parlor game in our house used to be What-Will-Daddy-Do-Next. Well, I was never any good at it, and what's more I stopped playing years ago."

But by now we had arrived back at Old Saint Paul's, and as we pulled up in front of the rectory John said thoughtfully, "I wouldn't mind betting, though, that it all had something to do with this place."

And I said incredulously, *"Saint Paul's?"*

"Why not?" he said. "Come to think of it, it's the only answer. It makes perfect sense. You don't see it?"

"Not even remotely."

"You're handicapped," he said. "You're the pastor; you see Saint Paul's as a church. My father is not a pastor. He's a businessman and you can bet everything you've got that he does *not* see it as a church. He sees it purely as a piece of real estate which sooner or later the Bishop — even this Bishop — will

[97]

have to tear down. Well, that will leave what? Land. My father likes land. He owns a great deal of it over here and he'd like to own more. I know you're not interested in such things, but you might like to know that there's a good chance that in years to come all property over here will become rather valuable. Now, the only question for my father is when this land will become available and how best to get it. And of course here are you, right on the scene, and even better than that you're reputedly on good terms with the Bishop. I tell you, this is just the kind of situation to which my father responds from the depths of his being. Like another man listening to Mozart. It's irresistible!"

He spoke forcefully and with a certain excitement; despite all claims to dissociation, it was perfectly clear that an old family parlor game was now being played right up to the hilt. What-Will-Daddy-Do-Next died hard. But what he said made sense and his argument was plausible; the one trouble was that it left me unconvinced. Somehow I felt that whatever Charlie had wanted, it was something quite different from news about the demolition of a parish church — particularly when the demolition as yet existed only in his son's expectations. And, moreover, if he had wanted such information, he had certainly made no attempt to get it; in any case, there was the simple truth that I had none to give. So I said, "Maybe. But I think you're wrong on this one, too."

He shrugged. "I may be blinded by filial affection, you think?" he said, drily. "Well, we'll see. Or rather, you will. You can depend on that." The subject was finished; he looked around him at the rectory, the church, the dreary surroundings; without expression he said, "Home again."

"Home again," I said. "Come on in."

"No, I can't. I have to get back. Something rare is going on in my place right at this moment. Do you know what it is?"

I did not; he said triumphantly, "Nothing. Pure, blessed nothing. For a wonder. Apparently through some oversight

[98]

nothing, absolutely nothing, has been scheduled for the next couple of hours. Not a parish dance in sight, no Bucky and his friends, no visits from the Young People's Committee for a Better Liturgical Art, no conferences with distressed couples. And two curates on hand to take care of emergencies. And so I'm going back and I'm going to read. R-e-a-d. Which I can assure you in Saint Raymond's is an exotic pleasure. And then if my luck holds out, later on I may even be able to slip into the church and say a prayer. Privately. All by myself. Without anyone creeping up behind me to whisper in my ear the battle cry of the old Saint Raymond's hand. Do you know that one, Hugh? It goes like this: 'Excuse me, Father, I know I shouldn't be interrupting you like this, *but*. . . .' Roughly translated, this means that they've been hanging around all week, playing peek-a-boo among the pillars, just waiting for the chance to interrupt you, and now that they've got it God Himself couldn't pull them off! Well," he said, bringing himself up abruptly, "so much for gentle thoughts from a kindly old pastor. At the end of a farcical day. I have to be going." He turned the ignition key; standing on the walk I reached back into the car and he took my hand. "Goodbye, Hugh," he said. "We'll see each other soon. I'll give you a ring. Or you give me one."

"Goodbye, John. And thanks for everything: the transportation, the talk. . . ."

And I wanted to add that I thanked him, too, for the concern which he tried so hard to conceal, but this would have left him wretched with embarrassment. Still, in this final moment it emerged again; with a great casualness he said, "On the whole, this wasn't too bad a day for you, was it? Everything went all right? It seemed to."

"Oh, much more than just all right. It went surprisingly well. Your father's birthday turned out to be a very good day. For me, as you say. You're a more severe judge."

"There's a difference," he said. "You're watching the circus. I'm in it. Well. As Dan would say: *'Rivederci!'*" And, with the

[99]

stab of a smile, and a jerky nod of his head, he drove off swiftly down the empty street.

After a moment, I went into the rectory, not directly, but through the church, pausing for a quick kneel and a nod and a word. Unlike John, I had no fear of interruption; the importunate parishioner is hardly a problem in Old Saint Paul's. . . .

In the rectory, Father Danowski was waiting for me. He was standing in the front hall, dressed for the street; he was on his way to his usual Sunday night supper with his family. His appearance, always neat and unbelievably boyish, was especially so on these occasions, as if he took extreme care to scrub up well in order to pass muster before that extraordinary man, his father. It was possibly to atone for this appearance that his manner at such moments became even more elaborate than usual.

"Ah, Father!" he said. Graciously. "Well well. Did you have an enjoyable outing?"

An enjoyable outing. Over the river and through the woods, to Grandfather's house we go. I said, "Yes, yes. Most enjoyable."

"How glad I am to hear that," he said. "And what a sight it must have been to see: old Mr. Carmody surrounded by his well-wishers on his birthday. That remarkable old gentleman! How I would like to see him again, if only in memory of old times, when I was just a child. Still, I doubt whether he would remember me after all these years."

Every once in a while Father Danowski is impossible to resist, and so, a little unkindly, I said, "I don't know about that at all. Curiously enough, only this afternoon he said, 'How I wish I could see young Stanley Danowski again. If only to give him ten thousand dollars for his church.'"

Amazement. Suspicion. Then, more slowly, comprehension and a knowing smile. "Ah ha ha, Father," he said. "You almost caught me that time with your little jest!" And then, all unconsciously, he paid me back; he said, "How good it is to see you so merry!"

Merry . . . !

We talked for a bit about parish affairs, the few things that needed to be done; as I had expected, nothing had happened in my absence. Then, as Father Danowski was leaving, he stopped at the door and said, "Tonight at supper I must remember to tell my father about this birthday party, Father. You know, I believe, that he and old Mr. Carmody used to meet frequently in the old days. On the matter of rent. Mr. Carmody was always a most adamant man, but my father, although without formal education, is a brilliant debater. How often I heard them crossing their swords, exchanging their little pleasantries. Poor as we were, my father always gave as good as he was given. I can imagine how interested he will be to hear this latest news concerning his redoubtable old foe!"

John and old Charlie, my curate and his father: it was a day for the expression of filial feeling. Of somewhat different kinds. . . .

Father Danowski left; the rectory was silent. Old Mrs. Addione, who cooked and cleaned for us, had gone off long ago; she went to her own home each day after the noon meal, leaving behind the ingredients for our light supper at night. And Roy, whose hours were at best unpredictable, almost never appeared on Sunday, save during the Christmas and Easter seasons, when — much to Father Danowski's annoyance — he abandoned his policy of grumbling evasion and became lively and conspicuous, ostentatiously sweeping and polishing, genuflecting often, crossing himself piously, and otherwise suggesting that here was a laborer worthy of far more than his hire. Which, God knows, he may well have been; we paid the poor fellow little enough. . . .

And so, alone in the rectory, I went up to my bedroom. It was by now late in the afternoon, coming on towards evening, but the summer sun was still high, and it would be a good three hours until darkness. Not that I was especially longing for that to come, although strangers to Old Saint Paul's often remark — usually with at least a little of the air of the phrasemaker — that there, darkness undoubtedly benefits the view. Which is true enough, I suppose, but by now I've grown so used to the parish, both by dark and by day, that it doesn't seem to make too much difference. And in any case I spend little time evaluating the view. . . .

Although now I was doing just that. The large low window at the foot of my bed was open to the late afternoon; standing by it, almost leaning out of it, I could see that the first shadows had already slipped over the edge of the sidewalk and into the gutters of the street. They were the shadows of buildings. Once along these walks, there had been trees — maples, I think — but changes had been made and trees grow poorly in concrete; therefore — buildings. On both sides of the street these buildings were uniformly four stories high and were of a pale yellowish brick which could never have been particularly attractive; they had soiled easily and had not been cleaned. All had once been private homes; now they were rooming houses, and many had small shops on the first floor: a Chinese laundry, a secondhand clothing store, a cobbler's, a dingy grocery. None of these seemed to do too well. Directly across from the church was a religious goods store. Until recently it had been a delicatessen; then, one day, six months ago, its freshly washed window had revealed an assortment of luminous crucifixes and sugary Madonnas. It must have seemed a good idea to someone; these stores pop up like mushrooms in the neighborhood of churches; some are wildly successful. Not, however, around Saint Paul's. Here the consumers had proved peculiarly resistant; the venture had been a failure from the start. Now it was about to close its doors. Only two weeks ago the proprietor had paid me his first visit: he was a pudgy, middle-aged man with harassed eyes. When he came into the rectory he was

[102]

smoking the stump of a cigar which he snuffed out and put carefully away in his pocket.

"What do they want?" he asked, throwing his arms wide; it was a flourish of bewilderment and despair. "What do they want, Father? I got all kinds of stock. The best, the latest. I got a one-piece cross. Big. Strong. Like steel. You could *chin* yourself on that cross, Father. They don't want it. I got a special kind of rosary, they make it up in Canada, it's so tough you could jump around on it, it wouldn't break! And you drop it in the water, what happens? It floats! They don't want it. And I'll tell you what else I got, Father. I got a Mary that *cries*. Real tears!"

I said, "Like a mama doll."

"Right!" he said. "But religious! Nice! They don't want it. *Anything* I got, they don't want it. So — back to the wholesaler." Then, looking across at me, he said quickly, "Unless maybe you could help me out a little, Father. You know: maybe drop into the store, be seen a little. . . ."

I said, "I don't think that would be so good. And anyway, I don't really think it would help very much, do you?"

"No," he said hopelessly. "I guess you're right. They call it a religious country, but they don't know. I could tell them." Suddenly he said, "You're not busy, Father? I'm not taking up your time?"

"No."

"*I'm* not busy," he said sadly. "All I got is time!" And then he pulled his cigar out of his pocket and began to tell me all about himself. He talked for a long time; he was a fatalistic, oddly likable man who had not had much luck in either his home life or his business affairs. He had no plans for the future, but then he had had no plans when, unexpectedly, one morning, he had found himself in the religious goods business. With a somewhat surprising optimism he announced that something would turn up; it always had. . . .

These were our immediate neighbors, then: the glum, mottled rooming houses and small shops which bordered this part of the street. The street itself was a long one, and while certainly neither grand nor spacious, it was broader than most in this section — in the long-ago residential past, it had been the principal avenue. It was still paved with the old cobble-stones, and was seldom entirely clean. Usually — any day, to-day — it was covered with its thin litter of newspapers, fruit peelings, candy bar wrappers, a few odd bottles, and dis-carded fragments of clothing: a single sneaker, a shirt-tail. The lightest breeze passing over its surface raised its private dust storm. Early each morning the city trucks came around to clean and to sprinkle, and sometimes, curiously, through this early morning dampness there came the unmistakable smell of horses, although there hadn't been a horse over here for more than a decade. It was just one of the old smells which often cling to a neighborhood through time, which the years seem to bake into the stones, and which every now and then mysteriously gain fresh strength and come breathing back into life. No doubt just to serve as a reminder. . . .

But this was the "good" neighborhood, the respectable part of the street; two blocks away, the bars, the cafés, the cheap wine shops began. Old Saint Paul's is thus protected by a small buffer zone — created, I'm afraid, by a city ordinance rather than any deep religious feeling. The local Skid Row is well within the limits of the parish, however, and not so long ago, before Father Danowski came, when I was here alone, I used to walk about a good bit at night, more often than not coming back to the church by way of the Row. Sometimes I still do this, although not so often now. But whenever I do, at some point or other during the walk I think of a single scene I once saw in a moving picture, many years ago. It was a scene in which a priest was walking alone at night, through a district which I'm sure was intended to be very much like this one. It was sordid enough, suitably down at the heels, yet in the film it had an odd liveliness: one had the impression of neon and noise and motion. There was a peculiar wailing music in the background, and from the darkness came an occasional scream of violence. Through the shadows one could see the tottering and seedy drunks, the faded streetwalker, the few sharp-eyed hoodlums. And then the priest appeared: an erect man with a steady stride. He was quite handsome. He was also obviously a familiar and impressive neighborhood figure. Although his coat collar was turned up he was recognized at once; the recognition produced a chain reaction of edifying behavior. The drunks managed to straighten themselves and tug respectfully at their hats; the streetwalker, suddenly ashamed, turned away, pointedly fingering the medal at her throat; the hoodlums vanished in their evil Cadillac; the cop on the beat relaxed for the first time, twirled his night stick happily, and hummed a few bars of "The Minstrel Boy." The "padre" was passing by, and the district was the more wholesome for his presence. As for the "padre" himself, he continued to walk forward as strongly as ever, something about him managing to suggest, however, that he was in a dream — a muscular dream. His smile was compassionate but powerful: one had the feeling that here was a mystic from some ecclesiastical gymnasium, a combination of Tarzan and Saint John of the Cross. A saint, but *all man*. . . .

Well, what bothered me about this — and what made it so memorable — was not the priest, but the setting. This ludicrous Disney-parson, provoking these electric responses: all right. Or rather, *not* all right, but at least expected. Any priest in any movie is almost by definition a parody. Which in a way is understandable enough. I don't think many people know very much about priests — I'm not talking now about anything so complicated as the psychology of the religious, or the motives for vocation; I mean just the ordinary simple matter of how priests live from day to day, how they fill in their idle hours — and those who do know aren't necessarily in Hollywood. Not that this would matter much if Hollywood hadn't discovered

[105]

that the priest can be a useful addition to a good many films. The result has been that extraordinary succession of clerical stereotypes, ranging from the old Galway-born pastor (cranky but lovable, with the wisdom which seems to spring from arthritis) to the more modern native product: the quaint, pipe-smoking sportsman who, but for the unfortunate fact of his ordination, might well have become a fine second baseman. . . .

So then, as I say, the priest was no surprise. But the setting and the people, the whole scene itself — this was something else again. For here the material was surely familiar: the slum is no secret, and the phenomenon of Skid Row is unfortunately everywhere. It should have been no great trick to present this with some authenticity. Yet everything came out wrong, all wrong, so wrong that it hurt. The pathetic slum street proved to be a kind of cheaper Barbary Coast, a shoddy but still vital enclave. And of course the truth is that a place like this is not vital: it has, in fact, no life at all. There is no whirling motion; there is no clarinet in the background; the air is not filled with screams in the night. There is no noise. When I walk along this street at night I hear my own footsteps; the people I see are silent and motionless and wrapped in their own despair. They don't respond to me; they don't even see me; they don't see anything. And when, in this terrifying quiet, now and then the siren sounds, it is usually the ambulance, not the riot car, and it means that among these sad men who are so slowly dying, one has gone a little faster than the rest.

Actually, crime, sensation, violence are comparatively rare in a place like this; here, life — or the end of life — tends to become a matter of the slow leak rather than the explosion. Which is not exactly an improvement; of the two, I prefer the explosion. For what is really dreadful, what I find genuinely frightening, is this spreading, endless despair, hanging low like a blanket, never lifting, the fatal slow smog of the spirit.

[106]

And I've often thought that among all the afflicting sights of the world, none can be much more so than this one short walk along three city blocks, where night after night it's possible to see — indeed, it's impossible *not* to see — these faces from which hope and joy and dignity and light have been draining so steadily and for so long that now there is nothing left but this assortment of indifferent, damaged masks. They belong to human beings who, after a lifetime of struggling to become one thing or another, have succeeded only in becoming the rough sketches of their species, recognizable but empty, the bruised and wretched bodies and souls of the saddest people on earth: the people who no longer care. This is an awful situation about which you know you can do little, but about which you have to do something — because of course you are implicated. As a human being. And, more, as a human being who happens to be a priest. And when, moreover, that priest happens to be someone like myself, someone who but for the favor of God's good grace might not now be discussing this problem with such an easy objectivity, why then, the responsibility, the implication, is rather heavily underlined. Yet how to exercise that responsibility in this situation is one of the great questions. At least it is for me. I've said, I think, that this is not the kind of parish in which a great rapport obtains between the shepherd and his flock. We are all more or less strangers to one another. And most of all, I'm afraid, I'm a stranger in this smallest and dreariest part of my parish where — all moving pictures to the contrary — I can assure you that the priest is not this legendary, revered, and welcome figure, capable of healing with a glance. Or in any case this priest is not. I've thought, often enough, that someone else, someone with an easier manner, someone of a more zealous temperament, or — of course — simply someone holier, a more dedicated and a better priest, could do far more towards breaking down the wall. I'm sure this is true, and yet even he might not have an easy time of it. For — to put it mildly — they

[107]

do not reach out eagerly. This is understandable enough, too: at a certain stage of misery, the miserable want mainly to be let alone. And yet there's no hostility, no resentment; if I'm noticed at all I'm sure it's in precisely the same way that the mailman is noticed: as someone who is occasionally on hand, who is set apart by reason of his uniform, and who has no real significance for them; over here, they are not deluged with letters from home. . . .

This sometimes changes at the end. There are those moments of extremity when, even here, people do suddenly and desperately send for the priest. At this point I respond to the summons, usually arriving in some filthy little cold-water room, where even the cold water is a myth, and where a dying man is surrounded by all those who are closest to him: the landlady, who has seen it all before; the policeman, who is on duty; the young intern from the city hospital, who is beginning his career. These leave the room for a little while, and it is then that I hear the hurried, often incoherent, often barely audible final confession of this lonely, gasping man who, in a matter of hours, minutes, even seconds, will certainly die.

In these moments one hears extraordinary things. Not the sins: these people are not monsters, ingenious in depravity; they offend God in much the same unheroic and uninventive ways that the rest of us do. But there are the other things: strange irrelevancies which would seem to have nothing to do with the solemn fact that death is on the doorstep and pushing hard. I suppose people die in as many different ways as they live, and that in this incomprehensible interval when life is ending and death is slowly moving in, anything is possible. No one can begin to guess what queer churnings go on in the expiring mind and memory; no one should be surprised that the wildest incongruities sometimes result. And yet I am surprised. Not always, not even usually — for usually, nothing surprising happens. I hear a man's confession, I give him Holy

Communion, I anoint him for the last time; there is a silence, an exhaustion, I suppose, and then a soul goes to God — one hopes in peace. But sometimes in this moment instead of silence there is a kind of bubbling turbulence, and I find myself listening to words that seem to come driving out of this dying man. He *has* to tell me this story. And what is the story? It can be the oddest and most unimportant fragment from the man's past, fetched up to the surface for some unfathomable reason to completely engulf the final, fading attention. I can remember that at such a moment a man told me, in tones of the greatest urgency, of a Laurel and Hardy movie he had once seen: fat Oliver once again discomfited by thin Stan. Another man, in obvious pain, suddenly broke off in the middle of a groan to tell me that once, years ago in Hong Kong, he had had a dozen suits made for him. They had been cheap, but all had been short in the arm. And an old woman whom I had thought dead suddenly popped her eyes open and said loudly, "Listen to me, Father: *listen to me!*" Then with great logic and lucidity, and for perhaps two minutes, she told me of the occasion on which she had shaken Al Smith's hand in 1928. She finished this story in a strong voice, looked at me with clear, bright eyes, and died. . . .

And one can't help but wonder at a time like this whether they know what's really going on, whether they know that within a very few minutes they may die. I don't know; I think they do, in a way. But there's a clue, perhaps, in the loneliness of these people. Some of them who have drifted into a place like this, after having lived God knows where and how, have been locked up so tight within themselves and their unhappy lives for so long that for years they haven't talked — I mean, *really* talked — to another soul. Now, suddenly, there is this moment and the sense that time is closing in on them; they see the priest, and perhaps memories of other and happier days may come back, and they may want, more than anything else, just to talk to tell someone of something, anything, that once happened in a better time, before the bitter, recent, isolated years. . . .

As I say, it may be something like that. Or it may simply be that among people who have lived — as many of these people have — close to death for a long time, who have faced it obliquely every day, there is developed an instinct for postponement, like that of a child who every night delays the hour of his bedtime by standing in the center of the living room and saying desperately to his parents, "Wait, wait, wait, I want to *tell* you something!" What's coming is coming, yes, but meanwhile, if you can just keep talking, it might not come so fast. . . .

In any case, this is what happens from time to time, as the people over here die. And something else happens as well. Another reaction, of a quite different and more positive kind: one which takes place often, and one which, although given emphasis in a place such as this, is by no means restricted to the deathbed in the slum; sadly and ironically, it happens frequently and everywhere. It's happened to me most often in this way: as I'm bending down over a bed to watch the tumbling, muttered recitation of sins, to hear what may be the last words on earth of some poor soul who, for most of the years of his life, has been hungry, dirty, battered, harassed, pursued, and lacerated by every sort of pain and humiliation, he may now, upon suddenly realizing that all this will soon be over, shoot bolt upright on his mattress and with frightened staring eyes and panicky lips say incredulously, "I'm not going to *die*, Father? I'm not really going to *die*?"

And by this question he establishes his one last tie with most of the rest of us. Because the truth seems to be that no matter how bad life has been for us, we do not leave it willingly. And this is not simply out of any uncertainty of what's to come, or a fear of punishment, or a dread of the void. I believe with all my heart in the mercy and providence of God, and I believe in a future unimaginably brighter and better than anything I have known here — and yet of course the whole difficulty is that I *have* known and have loved "here." Very much. So that when the time comes for me to go, I know that I will go with full confidence in God — but I also know that I will go with sadness. And I think for no reason other than that . . . well, I have been alive. An old priest who was dying, one of the saintliest men I have ever known, one of those who had greatest reason to expect God's favor, many years ago surprised me by telling me, with a little smile, that now that he was going, he wanted desperately to stay.

"A single memory can do it," he said.

And I suppose he was right. The memory of an instant — of a smile, of leaf-smoke on a sharp fall day, of a golden streak across a rain-washed morning, of a small boy seated alone on the seashore, solemnly building his medieval moated castles — just this one, single, final flash of memory can be enough to make us want to stay forever. . . .

Which is just another curious part of the human predicament. And which is also a fairly elegiac strain to be inspired by a long glance down a slum street. And which is hardly why I came up here to my room in the first place. For what I had intended to do was to go over the whole afternoon in my mind — this afternoon about which I had had such misgivings, but which had developed into a warm, funny, richly satisfying day of a kind I hadn't known for years. In old Charlie's dining room, I had felt at home. And I came up to think about this, and about the Carmodys themselves: about Helen and John in particular, and the various small ways in which they, like all of us, had changed, and the ways in which they had remained just the same. This, as I say, was what I had intended to do; what I had done instead was to forget them all in an instant. Charlie's party had served as little more than an excellent springboard into the familiar world of my own affairs.

So then, back to the Carmodys — except that this was not to be. For the telephone rang at this moment; it was for me. Not for me personally; for "the priest." I'm always half surprised when the ringing phone really turns out to be for the rectory. A great many of the calls received here are misdirected; most of them are for a cigar store, run, apparently, by one Andy. (Same number; slightly different exchange.) Can so many people really want cigars? No. Andy has a sideline. He is a bookie — a fact revealed by some of the more explicit calls. I've been meaning to have our number changed for some time now; Father Danowski counsels this vigorously. He has had the bad luck on several occasions to be called by some of Andy's less satisfied clients. Each such experience leaves him outraged; each brings him posthaste to me.

"*Again*, Father! Yes, again! I tell you, Father, in my opinion this may be quite deliberate. Even over here, and in this day and age, the Church is not without its enemies!"

A revival of The Terror, its spearhead the off-the-track bettor . . . ?

Still, the last such call had brought a small change in the wind; Father Danowski had rushed in to announce a triumph.

"I brought him up with a word, Father! I cut right in upon him. I said to him," he said, his voice swelling with heavy irony, "I said, 'I am afraid I must inform you, my good sir, that you do not happen to be speaking to "Deadbeat." And that you do not happen to be speaking to "Welsher." You happen to be speaking, my good sir, to the *Reverend Stanley C. Danowski of Saint Paul's Church*. That is whom you happen to be speaking to!' I think I can promise you, Father," he said complacently, "that the person who made that call today will not do so again in a hurry."

I think that Father Danowski is really my only reason for not having this phone number changed.

But today the call was not for Andy. It was a sick call, and I went, not to the Skid Row district, but some blocks in the opposite direction. It was here that most of the small group of recently arrived Puerto Ricans had settled; over the phone, a frantic young voice, which urgency and accent had left almost incomprehensible, had informed me that Mrs. Sanchez was dying.

Mrs. Sanchez was not dying. Mrs. Sanchez was very far from dying.When I went in to her she was lying on her bed, a huge rosary in her hands. The room was small and dark; on a table by her bedside was a large and vivid picture of the Virgin, before which a blue votive lamp burned. Mrs. Sanchez was praying rapidly and audibly; the look she gave me was one of extreme annoyance. She was small and brown and very old; she looked rather like an unkind monkey. I might have seen her once or twice in church; I could not be sure. At any rate, we were strangers to each other, and Mrs. Sanchez, her moment of fright over, was not disposed to be cordial.

I had been prepared for this by the doctor, who was leaving as I had arrived. He had spoken of his patient without great sympathy.

"Epilepsy," he said shortly. "I've seen her before. And I'll see her again. She has medicine but she won't take it. Right now she's as cranky as a bear, but she's perfectly all right. There was no reason to drag you over here, Father, I told them all that, but they were running around here like squirrels, scared blue. I don't think they even heard me. So she's all yours."

Clearly, there was no need for the last rites here. But I could at least hear her confession; somewhat grudgingly she agreed that this might perhaps be done. I talked haltingly to the old lady; she had no English, and my Spanish is primitive, barely sufficient to cover the minimum needs of these occasions. However, Mrs. Sanchez's confession was not a complicated one. It developed that she was conscious of almost no sins at all, and that these few were venial; as she spoke of her blameless life I found myself distracted. Something in her tone reminded me, more than anything else, of old Archbishop Gartland, a severe and autocratic man, who was once asked by a bold reporter what he considered his besetting fault to be. If, that is, the Archbishop considered himself to have a besetting fault. The Archbishop did.

"I am rather too lenient with people," he said.

The Archbishop and Mrs. Sanchez: there was a distinct link here. When I left her, before the door had closed behind me I could hear her voice, already raised once more in sighing, sputtering prayer. She was resuming the devotions into which the intruder had so rudely broken.

Outside, I was in the one remaining room of the apartment. It was clean enough, but unbelievably crowded. Two small windows were open, but the room was airless, and although the day outside was cool and pleasant, here it was stifling, as if the last outpost of the heat wave of a week ago had battled its way in and had stubbornly refused to depart. There was a faint and probably permanent smell of gas — the small stove in one corner was old and looked dangerous. Cluttering the room were improvised partitions of blankets and beaverboard; a pile of mattresses; cardboard boxes from the supermarket; the stove; a sink; a crisscross of clothesline. Wedged in among these was the family of Mrs. Sanchez. It was huge. Or at least so it seemed in these close quarters: a regiment, an all-Sanchez regiment, of every age, of every size. And while by this time conditions over here are hardly new to me, nevertheless I told myself once more that so many people could not possibly live in so small a space. Yet I knew that they could, somehow, and that they did. They came towards me, smiling, obviously grateful, embarrassingly grateful, for I had done little enough. As, certainly, the old matriarch would have readily agreed. But they had laid out a small table of refreshments: coffee, pieces of cake, a bottle of wine. An elderly man — Mr. Sanchez? — held out his hand, in it was a dollar

[114]

bill. And the problem was how to refuse all this without wounding feelings, without hurting sensitive, decent people who have quite enough to put up with without encountering even unintentional rebuffs. And so, rather clumsily, I explained that I couldn't take anything, that it was impossible for me to stay, that I had the Blessed Sacrament with me, that I had to go now. They seemed to understand, and then I was reminded that of course the younger ones, at least, knew English, for a pretty dark girl said to me, "Thank you, Father. Mama will be all right now?"

I said, "Mama will be fine." Which was true enough: Mama would probably outlive us all.

Then we stood staring and smiling at each other, no one saying anything. There are these moments over here when suddenly I pull up to a dead stop — when, in other words, I haven't the faintest notion of what comes next. At such times I feel that my parishioners and myself are separated by a gap miles wide and unmeasurably deep, and yet I also feel, curiously enough, that so simple a thing as just one word, if it were the right word, could throw a bridge across the gap. But now, as always, the right word did not occur, and so, rather awkwardly, I said goodbye to the smiling Sanchezes and the small, steaming apartment, and drove back to the rectory.

It was almost dark now. I sang Benediction in the church, as I do every Sunday night. A few people came — not more than half a dozen. Mr. Yee was among them. Then, back in the rectory, I sat in the kitchen and ate my supper. It was a smaller supper than usual, for I was not hungry; Charlie's midday feast had taken care of that. As I ate, I turned on the small radio which Mrs. Addione keeps on the kitchen table. It is her great companion. As she peels, cooks, and cleans, she listens to all those serial dramas of domestic distress; every day this simple, healthy, long-married old woman is washed with fresh waves from the fascinating, storm-tossed sea of divorce, disease, and mental imbalance. Often, in my room or in the rectory office, I can hear the sounds of the broadcast sobs, and I know that all is well.

Now, on the radio, a man was talking: the talk was inspirational. Almost evangelical. A minister? A rabbi? A priest? No. Somewhat surprisingly, a vice president of a great air line. He was talking about brotherhood. Some years ago, it appeared, his air line had flown him to Africa, a land largely inhabited by . . . whom? Black men. Or so he had always believed. But while there, one day, quite by chance, he had observed one of these black men standing before a blackboard.

"My friends," he said, "I saw at once that against this background of *pure* black, the so-called black man was not really black at all! He was merely *a darker shade of white*. . . ."

Similar revelations had followed. His air line had taken him everywhere: with each trip a prejudice had peeled away. In India he had seen a so-called brown man, wearing a pure brown blanket; in Japan he had seen a so-called yellow man, eating a piece of pure yellow fruit; in our own Far West he had seen a so-called red man silhouetted against a pure red sunset. The contrasts had been startling, the lessons unforgettable. . . .

". . . yesterday our fathers, who had not the advantage of our modern transportation miracles, thought of people whose skins were a little different from our own as 'colored people.' Today we know better. Today we know that there is 'no such animal.' Today, in our great air age, as our giant aircraft set us down in the remote corners of the world in the twinkling of an eye, the modern traveler steps out into a strange land, looks at the faces of the inhabitants who have gathered there to greet him, and he says to himself, 'Why, here is something I never realized until now: *we are all white men together*. . . .'"

The strangest things come out of Mrs. Addione's radio. . . .

Usually, after supper, I go to my room and read until bedtime. I suppose I read now more than I ever did. Nothing particularly new or adventurous, but all the old, well-worn trails: Saint Augustine, Gibbon, *War and Peace*, Newman. Familiar enough territory for a priest who likes to read and who spends a good bit of his time alone. Tonight I picked up *The Grammar of Assent*, as I often do — Newman in particular is an old hero of mine, who gets no less so with the years. I read him over and over again, always with pleasure, always with benefit, and yet tonight I put the book down only a few minutes after I had picked it up. Because I wasn't really reading at all; old Charlie and his world kept crowding in, and the strong, lucid, flowing prose faded before the recollections of the day: Charlie whirling around his living room in that queer, astonishing kewpie-doll dance of welcome; Helen coming smiling across the room; John, lean and impatient, one eye on his watch, the other on the exit; Bucky's belligerent little face working out its wrathful patterns; P.J. seated at the table with his look of ancient, chalky calm; Ted and Anne, so new, so young, so attractive, so different from us all; poor anxious Mary; Agnes with her tray of sherry; Julia with her memories of saintly, undernourished Martin; and Saint Raymond's itself, its soft bricks trapping the sunshine of the afternoon. . . .

I kept coming back to them all, but mostly, I'm afraid, I kept coming back to myself — just as I had earlier in the evening. And this isn't usual with me. That is, I don't habitually sit here night after night, systematically reviewing the past and thinking about what is as contrasted to what might have been. The truth is that I almost never think about it any more. But today had been different; today the past had been all around me, I'd been swimming in it, and so I suppose it was inevitable that now, for the first time in months, I began to go back, once again, over all those years which were quite long enough in fact but which seemed even longer than time itself, those years

[117]

which I can look back on with no pride but only the deepest shame, those years which nevertheless turned and shaped and fixed my life as no other years have done. . . .

It's hard to tell when anything really begins, impossible to pinpoint a particular instant and say that before this everything was light, and after it, dark. Personal histories have no such neat boundaries. But in my own case, I can surely say that those first years at Saint Raymond's were all light and no darkness at all. For I came here on my first assignment as a young priest; here, to my own boyhood parish. It was an assignment in which I rejoiced, for I had none of John's glum feelings about "coming home." And so both of us were satisfied: he because he was to be kept at the seminary to teach, I because I was coming to Saint Raymond's. To me, it was the best possible beginning, the luckiest of breaks: I was delighted to be here, working among the people I knew and liked so well. Even in the rectory, where so many young priests come up against their first stumbling block in the presence of capricious authority, life was close to ideal, for the old Monsignor, although crotchety and even maddening at times, was nevertheless a good pastor, showing a surprising understanding of, and kindness towards, his younger curates.

So then, I was happy in the way that young priests so often are. This is, I think, a special kind of happiness, one perhaps peculiar to the priest, and, moreover, to the priest when he is just beginning, when he's in the very morning of his new life. Which is not to say that happiness must fade as the priest grows old: it can change its quality, it can deepen, ripen, become richer. But *this* kind of happiness will fade, because it belongs to the young: a mixture of innocence and awe, of freshness and wonder, of reverence and excitement, of joy and of a disbelief, almost, that, for example, it is really *you* who, in this church and on this altar and before these people, are now at last to have the great privilege of consecrating the Body and Blood of our Blessed Lord. Here the miracle and mystery of

[118]

God's grace strikes home so overwhelmingly, with such fresh-ness and clarity, that it stuns your heart and fills your whole being and nothing else matters at all. And these moments, once known, no matter how long ago, can never be really for-gotten. Never, never, never. . . .

Although of course it's not quite this unmixed; one's day is not filled with moments like this. You're not unaware that the Roman collar has given you new significance in another sense; I think it's a rare young priest who could remain entirely un-affected by the deference which is now suddenly paid him. Particularly when, in his new role, in his new vestments, so to speak, he comes back to familiar surroundings and finds that an old woman who a few short years ago would have cracked him over the head with a thimble now flatteringly solicits his judgment. On what subject? On any subject. Probably in no other walk of life is a young man so often and so humbly ap-proached by his elders and asked for his advice. Which, by the way, is almost always received gratefully and forgotten promptly. Although the young priest, at this stage of the game, mercifully does not know this. . . .

It was a time when I was busy and worked hard. In a parish like Saint Raymond's, a parish usually described as "up-and-coming," there can be a truly staggering list of parochial ac-tivities. In no time at all I was deep among them. In addition to the regular duties of any priest anywhere, I was organizing baseball teams for the altar boys and choir boys, dances for the young people, father-and-son outings, bridge parties, picnics for the Holy Name Society, lectures, concerts. I regularly gave talks in the parish hall; I liked to talk. My Sunday sermons in those days, while far from rivaling the Monsignor's stupendous pro-ductions, were fairly elaborate and, I'm afraid, rather long. I can remember my father coming, Sunday after Sunday, to whatever Mass I said, sitting there and listening to what his son — the priest — had to say. He always sat in the same place, and I always saw him from the pulpit; I was happy he was there. He was a man of intelligence, taste, and ironic appreciations; he was also mildly anticlerical. And I wonder now what he must have thought of a good many of those sermons, spoken so zealously, and with such assurance. But he said nothing; I think he was proud of me. . . .

I was active; I was talked about; I think it was generally agreed in the parish that I would "go far." I think I may have been in some accord with the general agreement. But it made no great difference, for fifteen years passed by in this way so busily, so happily, and so quickly that at the end of the time it literally seemed as though it had been only a matter of weeks since the Bishop, before the main altar of the Cathedral, had placed his hands upon my head, and I was made a priest forever. I suppose that in this time I must have changed in a hundred ways: we all do, fifteen years *are* fifteen years, after all, no matter how short they may seem, and a man of forty is not a boy of twenty-five. But I felt unchanged; I was working as hard as ever; my enthusiasm was still strong; and when I looked about me I was supported by the comforting signs of some accomplishment: a new parish hall, an improved choir, a disciplined corps of altar boys, more weekly communicants among the men, a greater number of boys bound for the seminary. Not all my doing by any means, but I had had a hand in much of it, and if I wasn't satisfied, still, on the whole, I think I was fairly well pleased.

Then, suddenly, I left Saint Raymond's. Not of my own volition; I was transferred. I was, in fact, promoted. I was given what every curate looks forward to; I was given a parish of my own. . . .

This was Saint Stephen's. It was not an enormous change; as such changes go, this was a slight one. For Saint Stephen's, located not far away from where I'd been, was a somewhat smaller, somewhat poorer Saint Raymond's. That is, it was another of the old Irish parishes which had not come along quite so fast or so far as Saint Raymond's, and although it was far from being in distress and, indeed, enjoyed its own measure of modest prosperity, still, there was a chip on the parish shoulder whenever Saint Raymond's was mentioned, an instant racial readiness to suspect patronage from this slightly more elegant neighbor. It was good Saint Stephen's practice to speak of the parishioners of Saint Raymond's as being "high mucky-mucks" — a derisive reference to the latters' supposed wealth and burning social aspirations.

Yet I liked Saint Stephen's. It was not the flourishing parish that I'd grown used to, the work was hard and required more than a little tact — for after all, priest or no, I *had* come from Saint Raymond's — but after a cautious beginning on both sides I got along well enough, I understood the people and their problems, and there were no great difficulties or heartaches. Moreover, I enjoyed being the pastor, the boss, and I suppose that at the back of my mind there was always the feeling that this was somehow temporary, a stage on the road, and that one day, if all went well, I would be back in Saint Raymond's, this time as the pastor. A simple enough ambition, surely. Too simple? A little too parochial, too snug? Not entirely consonant with "Going therefore, teach ye all nations"? Yet there it was, something to be considered. I considered it often. . . .

It was five years after I came to Saint Stephen's that my father fell ill. This was sudden. He was a man who was never sick; then, one day, he was. After some argument, he was persuaded to see a doctor. There was an examination; there were tests; there were more tests. And when the tests were completed, the results were given, not to my father, but to me. My father had a gastrointestinal cancer; he had had it for some time. It was not curable; it was not controllable. It was as simple as that. The doctor who told me this was a kind man who spoke gently, but what gentleness of speech can cushion such a verdict?

"I'd say six months," he said, concluding. "Maybe a little

less, maybe a little more. I wish I could tell you something quite different, Father, but I can't. It goes without saying that we'll do all we can for him."

I said bitterly, "Which doesn't sound like much, does it?"

A disagreeable and an unfair thing to say to a perfectly good man who was doing his best, and whose only crime had been a failure to produce a miracle. But I think he understood; at any rate, all he said was, "No. No, it doesn't Father. And I'm afraid it isn't. Nevertheless. . . ."

And we continued to talk — or rather, he did. I'm sure he was sensible, even consoling. I don't know. I didn't hear a word. Or if I did I don't remember it. For what was there to hear? He had given me his message in the first few minutes; after that, what more could be said? That could make any difference, I mean? But I do remember that as I was leaving his office I said, just as if the possibility had not occurred to me until that last moment, "The pain: will there be much?"

The kind voice said, "It's probably something we shouldn't even speculate on now. He may very well have none."

"But on the other hand . . . ?"

He hesitated for just an instant, then looked directly at me. "But on the other hand," he agreed, nodding. "Yes. It's a possibility, Father. We can't tell in advance. You see," he said patiently, "it's just one of the things we don't know about. We'll have to wait and see."

And so we waited, and my father began to die.

When you are every day with someone you love and whose death you know is very near, you find that the emphasis is always shifting: what is important now becomes not so important a week from now; two weeks from now it may not count at all. In the beginning, when my father was still fairly active, when he looked precisely as he had looked for years, when there was not a mark of his illness upon him, when his only complaint was a rare, puzzled confession of having felt "a bit queer" a day or so ago, I worked furiously to collect and nourish all those thin, pathetic, isolated shoots of hope which always sprout up, however wanly, at a time like this. And it seemed absolutely vital that I keep downing the old placebos: doctors make mistakes, no man who looked and moved and talked the way my father did could really be so close to death. Yet all the while I was terrified that he would somehow discover how close he was. Fortunately, he seemed to have no suspicion. The doctor had spoken to him in the most general terms of a temporary stomach upset, and my father, who had had so little personal experience of sickness, had accepted the vague diagnosis without question. He trusted the doctor.

"A nice lad," he said to me. "I knew his father well. A good smart man who kept a drugstore and had two wives. The first was this lad's mother: a fine little blue-eyed girl who was great for the dancing. She died young, and then what do you think? He married another, the very image of the first! God knows where he got her from; I always thought he might have advertised in the papers. You know, with a snapshot of the first wife, and saying underneath, 'If you're a Catholic girl that looks like this, then I'm your man.' I remember there were a few little jokes about it at the time. But the joke was on us. She turned out to be a grand girl, just as grand as the first. And so he had two good wives. That's very rare."

He came to Saint Stephen's regularly now: to Mass on Sundays, dropping in on me at odd times during the week. And I began to call on him more often, taking care not to be too attentive. Even so, this was remarked upon late one afternoon as we were in his kitchen, and he was standing in front of the stove, making tea for us. He drank numberless cups of strong tea, the color of Burgundy, every day of his life. Now he said conversationally, "I see more of you now that you're pastor over there than when you were one of the hired help next door. How is that, I wonder? I was always told that pastors were very busy people, with great responsibilities. Although now I come to think of it, the ones that told me that were mostly pastors themselves."

So then, it probably wasn't suspicion, but just another stroke in the old game he loved to play. Relieved, but still cautious, I said, "I'll tell you a secret about the successful pastor: he discovers very quickly how to delegate these responsibilities. That's what I do. I leave everything in the hands of those two extremely capable curates I have. The hired help, as you so reverently call them. This leaves me plenty of time to come calling on the more rebellious laity. The curates really run the parish; I'm needed only for certain decisions."

"Such as will we have the fine big sirloin steak with the fresh asparagus tonight? Or will it be the rib roast with the strawberries for dessert? Oh," he said, "I know those big decisions you lads have to make, all right. It's a great wonder any of you live to be fifty. What with the terrible wear and tear on your nerves. To say not a word of your digestion. Will you have a cup of tea? It'll help to ease your difficult life."

So spoke the ferocious anticleric. It was familiar talk and good to hear, but as I looked at him, and listened to his voice, and took the cup of tea from the old, slender, strong hands, it almost broke my heart. . . .

This was the calm period, relatively easy on my father, which rather quickly came to an end. He grew weaker; he came to Saint Stephen's less frequently; his appetite was poor; and he spent a longer part of each day lying down.

"I've no more strength than a chicken," he said. "I don't dare to blink my eyes for fear it will tire me out. Denny Callahan was in here yesterday afternoon and said that he felt the same way a while back, but a good big meal fixed him up fine. It might fix me up too if I could only eat it, but the funny thing is, I've no appetite at all. It's a very queer business indeed."

Then, slowly, the pain began. As the weeks went by, it became clear that there was no reason for even the most carefully hedged optimism, for the pain did not lessen. It was not constant, but the bouts came more often and with increasing severity; my father was now in bed most of the day, much of the time under sedation. He complained very little, but I think it was now that he realized how seriously ill he was, for, quite suddenly, he stopped talking about it. Whenever the doctor or I tried to support him with the usual bedside reassurances, he smiled, agreed, and very soon changed the subject. And one afternoon as he was lying there, awake but with his eyes closed, and I was talking to him in a way that was intended to be encouraging, his eyes opened, and he gave me a slow and weary wink.

"You wouldn't kid an old man, would you, Hughie?" he said. It was the saddest question I had ever heard.

But for the most part his spirits were good, surprisingly good, and in pain-free intervals he would talk at length of days gone by. He was a man who had always taken great pride in keeping up to the minute, in reading all the papers, in knowing what went on in the world around him, but now the present no longer seemed to interest him, and he talked only of the past. He talked especially of my mother, and this was unusual with him. My mother had died in an influenza epidemic when I was very small. I had only the faintest recollections of her, and here my father had been of little help: on the subject of my mother he had been curiously reticent. I wondered about this often, of course, although I never questioned him. I think, now, that the truth was simply this: that her death had been without question the great catastrophe of his life, striking him so harshly and with such finality that he never really got over it, and could not bring himself to talk about her as she had been, not even after all the years, not even to me. And while he spoke of my mother often and fondly to me, he always did so incompletely, in a strangely peripheral way, so that I grew up with a picture of her which was really little more than an outline. Was this unfair, an injustice to me? It must seem so, and I suppose in a way it was. And yet we all have within ourselves those private spaces which are uniquely our own, and which we cannot share. This was my father's: the heart of his grief which he chose not to expose. It was only now, in these last months before his death, that the outline was filled in, that, without preliminary or explanation, my father suddenly began to talk of my mother as he had never talked before, in words and phrases lit with a bursting, lyrical warmth and love which had been stored up and held within him all this time, and which was now released because, I think, he knew his own time was so short, and because he did not for a moment doubt that very soon now he would be joined to her again. . . .

So there was a feeling of joy here, and there was joy too when he talked of his boyhood days in this city which by now had changed so greatly, and when he talked of the good old times which must also have been fairly hard old times, but from which a kind memory had removed the sting. And, of course, when he talked over and over again of the old friends and the old enemies, the varied, picturesque *dramatis personae* who had always been the great stock company of his anecdotes, led always by the chief protagonist, old Charlie. It was in these days that my father balanced the books on Charlie for the last time, and I remember his final verdict well. It was delivered towards evening of a day late in spring. My father was sitting up in bed, backed by numerous pillows. He had had a fairly good day, he had talked somewhat more than usual, and Charlie had evidently been on his mind — at least, the talk today had been about no one else. My father sat now, poking without interest at the small tray of bland and negligible food before him, and looking with preoccupied eyes out the window at the still and darkening evening. Two fire trucks went screaming by; my father said absently, "I wonder where that one would be?" I went to the window and looked, but I could see nothing; when I told him this he merely nodded and went on thinking whatever it was that he was thinking. The moments went by slowly, as they do in a sickroom; then, suddenly, out of the silence, and as if to himself, my father spoke aloud his last opinion on this man he had known and studied with such fascination all his life.

"Charlie Carmody," he said thoughtfully. "As fine a man as ever robbed the helpless."

The last view is not always an indulgent one. Although my father continued to talk and to reminisce in the days ahead, he did not mention Charlie again.

As he grew sicker the anecdotes grew fewer, and were more frequently punctuated with pain. My father required greater care now, and this was not always easy to provide, because he remained at home, refusing to go to the hospital. The doctor had tactfully suggested such a switch for, as he put it, "a few days' checkup." But on this point only my father had been stubborn. This was his home; this was where he would stay. And so he stayed, under conditions which were not ideal, but which were the only ones possible. This continued for some weeks, then came sharply to a halt. The illness now entered a new and terminal stage; the hospital, which so far had been little more than a suggested alternative, now became a necessity. And so my father left his home at last. He did not protest; he could not. For by this time the disease in its wild progression had reached his brain, and now my poor father no longer knew where he was, nor — mercifully — did he care.

It was an agonizing time — although when I say this I'm speaking selfishly, because what I really mean is that it was an agonizing time for me. What it was for my father no one could tell. It may even have been a time of some relief: the long periods of mental wandering, of mumbling oblivion, of not remembering at any one moment what the last moment had been like, must at least have interrupted the continuity of his pain. I don't know; I hope so. But I could reach him only rarely now, and everything, even the hospital room itself, seemed to contribute to this sense of separation. Sickness had changed my father's appearance — he had lost a great deal of weight, his face was small and hollowed — and here in the gleaming, impersonal, almost polar bleakness of this strange setting, he seemed further altered, reduced, lost. There were times when, sitting by the side of his bed, I would shift my position and look away for a bit, thinking of something else, and when I turned back to him again it would be as though something had blinked behind my eyes, destroying recognition, and on the white trim bed I would seem to see a total stranger, a small and shrunken figure in a vast, shapeless nightgown of hospital flannel, staring at me with great, glazing, senseless eyes, and talking on and on in an endless sad parade of urgent, crazy words. And I would have to *remind* myself that this was my father, and then I would close my eyes and tighten the agony one turn more by trying desperately to recall him *exactly* as he had been, down to the very last detail. . . .

And so my father died. All through his illness I had said my Mass for him each morning; every day and every night I had prayed that he might be allowed either the miracle of recovery or the blessing of a happy death. These prayers were not answered. My father did not recover, and he died witless and in pain. And why this should have been I have no idea at all. He was a very good man who had lived a very good life — yet he died a very cruel death. This is the hardest sort of thing to accept; for some, it's impossible. Because here is the old, baffling problem which has always been with us and will be until the end of time: the problem of reconciling pain and suffering with an omnipotent and merciful God. There are all sorts of answers suggested to this problem, most of which are as old as the problem itself; some are foolish, others are as reasonable as the mind of man could possibly devise. But here it seems to me we deal with something reason cannot reach, and with that part of man which reason does not touch, for when someone stands fixed and helpless before another's suffering — espe-

[128]

cially in those cases when those who suffer are plainly innocent of any guilt — then the cool light of reason may not be of much help. A syllogism does not support a mother who has seen her baby burned. And here, I think, faith comes in. I myself believe that there is no such thing as purposeless pain or suffering, although I must confess that for much of it I can see no purpose at all. But the point is that if one accepts God, one accepts Him totally, accepts what He does and what He permits. One accepts it, but one does not necessarily understand it. Surely it's a question of vision, for as we are, we can see, but only to the corner; we cannot begin to see the whole design. . . .

But this is not a theological treatise, or a piece of apologetic. What I'm saying is really a preliminary to an explanation — or rather, not an explanation at all, but an account — of my own behavior after my father died. For I saw him die, I sat through the two days of his wake, I said his Requiem Mass, and I buried him by my mother's side, and while there was ache and grief enough, there was certainly never the slightest thought of personal rebellion, of a turning away from God because of an unanswered prayer. No, what happened, happened much more slowly and subtly, and without my quite realizing, for a long time, that anything was happening at all. But shortly after my father's death my life began to change, and it was now that I began to do heavily and steadily what before I had done lightly, occasionally, and in a very different spirit, that I began to drink seriously, and to my own danger, and to the danger of my parish.

This is not a pretty story, and I have neither the intention nor the desire to go back over all the details — details which even in memory would be humiliating enough to any man, but which are infinitely more so when that man is a priest. For here there is a double betrayal: of the dignity of a man, of the sacredness of a vocation. In any case, it was in these weeks following my father's death that I began to spend most of my time by myself. This was a great departure for me; as I've said, I had always been a gregarious and an active priest. For example, ever since I'd become the pastor of Saint Stephen's, I'd kept up my old ties with Saint Raymond's; there was considerable visiting back and forth. This now stopped. Not all at once, but it stopped. And it stopped because . . . well, because *I* stopped, and when one way of a two-way exchange stops or dries up, the other invariably does, too. So, loyally, they continued to come over now and then, and the visits were always pleasant enough, no one was ever not cordial to the other, but the mutual encouragement, the nourishment that keeps friendship and affection going was lacking, and by-and-by all visits ceased. It was in this way that over a period of time I came to lose all touch with even the Carmodys.

Within the parish the situation was different; the results were the same. Here I was bound by duty as well as friendship, yet without deliberately planning it, without ever waking in the morning and announcing to myself that this day I would remain a little apart, I began to withdraw from my parishioners. There were of course the parish functions — at first I went to them as usual, but now I found myself slipping away at the earliest possible moment, and as the weeks and months passed by, I found myself not going at all. It wasn't that I had turned against the people; it wasn't even that I had now anything so positive as dislike for these gatherings which had once been such a part of my parish life. It was simply that somehow they had stopped mattering, and now it seemed the easiest and indeed the most natural thing in the world to sidestep each one as it came along.

In the rectory I built up further insulation. People came, on any of the multiple errands that can bring the people to their priest, and for a while I continued to see them. Somewhat more briefly than before, however; I managed to discourage the cherished habit of the casual, gossipy, infinitely expanding "chat." Eventually, gradually, I stopped seeing them altogether;

for the first time in my life as a priest I now regularly sent down word that I was "out," and passed the problem on to the younger and more willing hands of my curates.

And as for my curates — these two young men who lived with me, who were in my charge, and for whom I was supposed to serve as some sort of example — I'm afraid it was towards them that I behaved worst of all. Not by harshness or severity, but by apathy, neglect. From me they deserved care and respect; they received not even attention. They came to me now with parish problems which I settled perfunctorily and in haste; they no longer talked to me of themselves for the good reason, I suppose, that I no longer asked them about themselves; our rectory small talk grew smaller and smaller, then disappeared entirely; at meals, in the rectory living room, in the sacristy of the church — in short, in all the places where we normally met — my eagerness simply to *get away*, to return to the solitude of my own room, was all too unconcealed. Before their young and puzzled eyes the old, easy harmony of our life together vanished; a chasm cracked open and was never again bridged by either pastor or curates. All this was my fault, and the fault was not a small one. Because there is a sense in which a priest is dependent upon no one quite so much as another priest, for he has no wife, no child, and — in the ordinary meaning of the word — no home. His home is the rectory; his family, his fellow priests. And so while it's true that I was never deliberately unkind or cruel to my curates; it's also true that I was guilty of a graver offense. For what I did was to destroy the spirit of their priestly home. . . .

In this way I came to be alone. I spent most of my time in my bedroom: a pleasant enough room, although this couldn't have mattered less; I wasn't there to bask. Just what I was there for remained an unanswered question. It somehow seemed terribly important that I should be there and that I should be there alone, so that I might do . . . what? Whatever it was that I had to do. An odd restlessness had come over me; I began many things, and finished nothing. I would come into the room, close the door, sit at the table or in the armchair, and begin to read, or to say my office for the day, or to prepare a sermon for the next Sunday. But whatever I began, in no more than a few moments, I would drop the pen and put the book aside, and I would be thinking of my father. And thinking, strangely enough, not of anything big or important that he'd said or done, but of the small things, the little fringe touches: the way his lips formed into a slow, soundless whistle as he went through the careful ritual of filling his pipe; the slight limp in his walk on a damp day (he had broken a bone in his foot as a young man); his habit of courteously saying, "Ah yes, that's a very good point indeed!" — which was his inevitable preliminary to total disagreement. I have an accurate memory, which is not always a blessing, and as these recollections purred soothingly along, they were so fresh and strong in their exactness of detail that I sank into them easily as if they were the only realities that counted, as if they could and would happen over and over again, at any time: now, tonight, tomorrow morning. Then, suddenly, would come the sharp, clearing sweep across the inner eyes, and I would come to, and remember that this was only a memory, an echo of something which was gone and which could never be again. And this would always take me to still one more memory, this one of the memory of my father as I had last seen him: wasted, senseless, unrecognizable. And then. . . .

And then I would rise, walk up and down the room — sheer motion, the great therapy of the restless man, pour myself a small drink — which seemed to help, go back to my chair, and begin again the farce of preparing to get down to work. And in a while the whole procedure would be repeated, and then, later, it would be repeated again. The only change was one of emphasis; as time went by, the small drink got no smaller. Slowly it became more important, and over the months the occasional help came to be the steady necessity. At all hours; at night so that I might sleep; the first thing in the morning, to deaden the passage into the long, dull empty ache of the day. . . .

Which is the classic story, of course. It's been told over and over again, especially in recent years; the reformed drunkard is a ready raconteur. It's the familiar story of the trap: does it become much different merely because the narrator is a priest? Probably not — except, of course, that one may wonder why the priest, if caught, stays caught, for surely there must be aids, sources of strength available to him which should be tapped at once. And this is what I tried to do — not at once, but at last. For, strange as it may seem — especially since, in the confessional, I had heard these case histories outlined a hundred times or more — I didn't for the longest time realize just what it was that was happening to me. And then one morning I woke with a clarity rare to me in those blurred days, and suddenly I seemed to see my whole predicament before me, etched in the sharpest, most unsparing detail, complete with every certain consequence. I saw this with a sense of shock, and I remember that, heavy-headed, heavy-eyed, I pushed myself up in bed; I scourged myself — with words; I shook my head clear and reminded myself that this had become a habit, and that habit could be broken with a strong will; I got to my feet; I made a firm resolve.

This firm resolve lasted for twenty-four hours. It was succeeded, after a while, by another firm resolve, which lasted not quite so long. This was in turn succeeded by another . . . then another . . . and another. . . .

And then, finally, I did what I should have done from the start. Shame, pride, may have held me back; I don't know. But now I remembered that I was God's priest; I went for God's help. I went desperately, because by this time I was badly frightened — but the discovery I now made frightened me even more. For I found that, just when I needed to most, I could no longer pray. I could kneel, I knew the words, I could say

[133]

the words — and they meant nothing. At night, in the silent room, I could hear myself whispering phrases which I had known from the days when I first knew any words at all, which once had been charged with richness and fervor and love, but which now were empty formulae, dry wisps blown up from the desert of memory. I was praying — and it was nothing more than a child with jackstones in his hand, singsonging his way through the gibberish of games.

And yet — how to explain this? — I never stopped believing: in God, in His goodness, in His justice. I did believe, but prayer is always a kind of talking to God — and now I could not talk at all. I went through the motions, straining to drive into the lifeless words some breath of hope, of devotion. But you can't do this if it isn't there, and now prayer was little more than a succession of distractions, and I seemed to be speaking a language which I had always spoken but whose words no longer had reference to anything I knew, and sometimes it seemed as though a part of me had left me and now stood on the sidelines, observing, a detached and melancholy witness, mourning the vain performance, and whispering back to me, "It's no good, it won't work, you just can't do it any more. . . ."

Then one night, or very early one morning — it must have been three o'clock or so — I awoke in the darkness and, surprisingly, I was neither drowsy nor fuddled. I was wide awake; I had come from dead sleep into an almost preternatural alertness: I was trembling. This passed, but I could not go back to sleep. I tried what had come to be my unfailing remedy; it failed. And so I lay there, forced to think, and finding myself in one of those brief cool spaces of lucidity which now, to tell the truth, I did not particularly welcome. And what I thought about was of course myself: as I was now, nearing fifty, the respected pastor of his parish who was in fact a solitary drinker in his room, dazed most of the time, indifferent to his people, irresponsible in his duties, a spiritually arid priest for whom the wellsprings had dried up, for whom life had been reduced to a problem of concealment and routine. And then the inevitable contrast: the young priest of not too many years ago, zealous, devoted, with fresh and unimpeded hopes, whose parish was his life, whose days were active and busy and full of joy. How had the one become the other? The distance between them was the distance between the poles, yet it had been eclipsed, and in no time at all. How? Why?

Lying there on my bed in the black and silent morning, in this moment of queer lucidity, I found an answer. It was an answer which began back in those early active years, back with the new parish hall, the improved church grounds, the spick-and-span school band, the bridge evenings for the women, the weekly gatherings of men, the outings, the school plays — all those things of which I'd always been so proud, and to which I'd given so much time. And, suddenly, there was the clue before me: the "so much time." So much time that there had been no time for anything else, and I saw now, in a flash of long postponed revelation, and with a sense of shock and dismay, how little by little the unimportant had become important for me, how those things which belonged properly on the edges of my life had in fact become the center. The young priest, without realizing it, had become little more than a recreation director: a cheerleader in a Roman collar.

And it had been so easy, so innocent. There are, after all, certain social duties which a priest has towards his parishioners, and if that priest is as I was — energetic and gregarious, with an aptitude for such occasions — these duties and occasions have a way of multiplying. There's a great attraction to this: he's doing what he likes to do, and he can tell himself that it's all for the honor and glory of God. He believes this, quite sincerely, and he finds ample support for such belief: on all sides he's assured that he is doing the much-needed job of "waking up the parish." Which is not a hard thing for a young priest to hear; he may even see himself as stampeding souls to their salvation. What he may not see is that he stands in some danger of losing himself in the strangely engrossing business of simply "being busy"; gradually he may find that he is rather uncomfortable whenever he is not "being busy." And, gradually too, he may find fewer and fewer moments in which he can absent himself from activity, in which he can be alone, can be silent, can be still — in which he can reflect and pray. And since these are precisely the moments which are necessary for all of us, in which spiritually we grow, in which, so to speak, we maintain and enrich our *connection* with God, then the loss of such moments is grave and perilous. Particularly so for a priest — particularly for a priest who suddenly finds that he can talk more easily to a parish committee than he can to God. Something within him will have atrophied from disuse; something precious, something vital. It will have gone almost without his knowing it, but one day, in a great crisis, say, he will reach for it — and it will not be there. And then . . . then he may find that the distance between the poles is not so great a distance after all. . . .

This was the answer which came to me on that morning. It was not a consoling answer; is it ever consoling to learn that you've been most mistaken in something of which you've been most proud? It brought me closer to desolation than I had ever been before. From that moment on, I grew more desperate and my predicament became more extreme. I did not drink less.

Yet how curious it was that, although this went on for a long time, very few in the parish really knew about it. While I was rarely available to them, I was at least visible: I always managed to say my Mass on Sundays, and while they surely must have sensed the change in me, I've found that towards a priest most people are apt to be either innocent or charitable. Probably a little of both; at any rate, they don't readily suspect the worst. I think they thought I was ill; from time to time I heard reports of their concern. The curates, of course, were another matter. They knew. They could not help knowing. They lived in the same house with me, and in any case priests always know about another priest who drinks. It must have been an intolerable time for them; I must have continually scandalized them. But they said nothing; I'm sure the poor fellows had no idea of what to say or do — nothing in their seminary training had prepared them for the drunken pastor.

Meanwhile, I grew less discreet. I left my room at night now, and wandered about the rectory. Occasionally I was conscious of the guarded creaking of a bedroom door: my progress was being observed. I did not care. Then, one morning, I was found in a stupor on the hall floor, just outside my room; I was helped to bed. I was now becoming more public, and it was only a question of time until what had to happen finally did happen. I was summoned before the Bishop.

At this time the Bishop of our diocese was not the man who had appointed me pastor of Saint Stephen's. This Bishop was new. He had arrived fairly recently to take charge of the diocese; none of the priests knew much about him. He had come here from the West: a large, square-faced, uncommunicative man, as bishops go neither young nor old — roughly the same age as myself. He had come to us preceded by none of the usual tendrils of advance clerical intelligence — for once, the reliable diocesan grapevine appeared to have broken down — and he continued to remain a mystery to most of us. He was certainly a mystery and a stranger to me as, on that morning, I stood before him, in disgrace.

He said only, "Sit down, Father."

His voice was low, and suddenly it occurred to me that I had never heard him speak before except on public occasions. Now, here in the privacy of the room, his voice seemed curiously uninflected, without expression of any kind. I sat facing him across the old Bishop's desk — a great mahogany lake; the wide gray eyes were heavy and as expressionless as the voice. So far, there had been no touch of anger or reproach. Or — less

[137]

comforting — of sympathy. The low voice said, "How long has this been going on?"

The tone was impersonal: it was like a company physician making a routine inquiry into the history of abdominal pain. I said, "A long time, I'm afraid, Your Excellency."

"Which means . . . what? Weeks? Months? Years?"

I hesitated, and he added, in exactly the same voice, "Since your father died?"

And this was a different kind of question, one which surprised me; clearly, the Bishop was better posted than I had imagined. I nodded, and then, because it seemed important not to use my father's death as any kind of prop, or as the basis of a plea for pity, I said, "Although I don't think it's as simple as that. The cause-and-effect, I mean."

He looked at me, but in an oddly reflective and neutral way, so that I somehow felt that he might really have been studying himself as much as me. He said nothing, and in the silence, I wondered if it was now my move, if he expected me to continue with an explanation, with some attempt at justification. But apparently not. He got to his feet and walked slowly over to the windows, and stood there, looking out at the long broad slope of lawn which stretched away down towards the avenue. It was the middle of a summer morning, and the windows were open: from somewhere outside came the sound of a lawn-mower, and there was the smell of freshly cut grass. And the Bishop stood there, looking out, motionless and silent, for what seemed to me a very long time, and then at last, without turning to me, but still looking out the window, he said an astonishing thing. He said, quietly, calmly, simply, "I don't want you to do it again."

And that was all — then there was silence. I said nothing; I was stunned by mildness. All I could do was sit there and stare at him; instead of the thunderbolt, he had delivered a tap on the wrist. Why? He turned now, and once more the wide gray eyes took me in with that curious, reflective stare; he said slowly, "What did you expect me to do, Father? Crucify you?"

I said, truthfully enough, "I don't know, Bishop. I don't think I had the slightest idea." And then, because he had been so fair, so decent, and because surely something more than this inarticulate bafflement was called for, I said, "I'd like to thank you. It's very generous. . . ."

But he did not acknowledge this. Instead, he returned to his desk and sat down; he said, "There was some feeling that you should be removed from your parish. Not so much because of what you had done as because of what you might do in the future. The course of prudence. That doesn't surprise you?"

I shook my head, and he said, "Prudence is all right. Still, it can become the easy way out. And then there are other factors. You have a good record in the diocese. And to take a man's parish from him is bound to be a humiliating affair. I don't want to humiliate you, Father." He was speaking evenly and steadily, in a voice which remained as subdued and unemphatic as before: a soft and private voice in which he seemed to be listening thoughtfully to his own deliberations. Suddenly he said, "You were ordained . . . when?"

I told him, and he nodded. "Yes. I thought so. My year. If I had come from this diocese originally we would have been classmates in the seminary. That's not important. But it is another factor. You're not some young curate who comes in here to be reprimanded and sent back to his pastor. You're a man of my own age. You've been a priest as long as I have. What am I to say to you, Father?" He looked at me, and with the look came another of those long and absolutely still pauses; after a while he said, "That a priest has grave responsibilities? That you haven't lived up to yours? That what you've done is wrong, seriously wrong? You know all that. Almost everything I could say to you now you know as well as I do. To give you a talking-to, a lecture, would simply be empty punishment. Rubbing it in. I'm not much interested in that. What I am interested in is seeing that all this stops. As soon as possible. Right

[139]

now. That's all I say to you, Father: I want you to stop." And very simply and directly, he said, "Will you? Can you?"

Again, easier said than done — especially since the doing was up to me. But I said, "I think so. I give you my word I'll do my best. . . ."

It seemed inadequate, thin: like a Scout's brave pledge at a troop meeting. But he made no comment; he said only, "This problem of yours: I haven't asked you to tell me about it in any detail. Not because I'm not interested. But because I thought you might find it difficult." He said objectively, "I'm not the easiest man to talk to. Also, there are others who know far more about this sort of thing than I do. Experts. They might be of some help. You might want to talk to them."

I mentioned my confessor; he said, "Yes, obviously. But you might also try it on another level. Establishing certain physical safeguards. A different approach. Do you know Father Luke Leary?"

"No. . . ."

"Alchoholics Anonymous," he said bluntly. There was another of the pauses; he said, "Does that shock you, Father?"

"No." Although this was not quite true; it did, a little. I said tentatively, perhaps defensively, "It's just that I'm not quite sure I fit the category."

"No. I don't say you do. But I think it does no harm to talk to someone who understands drinking. A doctor. Or Father Leary. He's a sensible man. Not brilliant, but sensible, practical. I have the feeling that he knows what he's talking about. He drank heavily himself at one time. A bad situation. But he got out of it and since then he's been helping a few of the priests here in the diocese. You see, you're not unique, Father." The low voice seemed to grow more remote; he said, "These things happen. Why, I don't know. Loneliness, I suspect, as much as anything else. They forget what they . . . Well," he said, coming back to me, "think about it. Your confessor, prayer, yes, of course. But I wouldn't ignore the other.

[140]

The two go together, I'd say. At least they do in my experience." He stood; the interview was over. "Goodbye, Father. I'll give you my blessing."

I knelt for the blessing, and kissed his ring. When I rose, I said goodbye, and thanked him once more for his kindness.

He said thoughtfully, "I don't know that it's kindness. It's more a matter of balance. I can't let anything happen to any of my parishes. But on the other hand I can't afford to lose a good priest. I think the second is as important as the first." With no change of voice he said, "Good luck, Father. Do well. Keep busy."

I had almost reached the door when he said, "Father?"

"Yes, Bishop?"

"But not too busy," he said. "Too many things go on. Save a little of yourself, Father. For what really counts."

It was a shrewd and unexpected stroke. Once again I was reminded that this strange man, so short a time in our diocese, had informed himself surprisingly well. And now I left him and returned to Saint Stephen's: relieved, even happy in a way, somewhat apprehensive, a little uncertain of what was to come, but above all full of high resolve. The second chance had been given, and given with the greatest generosity; from now on, I would make the most of it. . . .

So much for good intentions.

Two months. Two months in which I had not the slightest trouble with my parishioners (there had never been public scandal; news of what had happened had been kept within the rectory). Two months in which my curates were nervously eager to demonstrate to me that nothing, really, had happened at all. Two months in which I talked to my confessor (a stern and careful old man who sat in his chair, his long old body bent forward, his head supported by a veined, translucent hand, his eyes closed; from time to time he would sigh deeply and murmur "Yes yes," with a kind of discouraged impatience which suggested that he had heard this same dreary tale many times before and knew far in advance of the telling exactly what the next detail would be). Two months in which I did not, despite the Bishop's urging, call on Father Luke Leary (for I had no wish to approach the peculiar apostolate of the confessed alcoholic — mainly, I suppose, because of the obvious implication). Two months in which I prayed and tried to recover some sense of dedication; two months in which I stopped all drinking; two months in which, slowly, optimism grew, and I began to feel a confidence that at last a corner had been turned. In short, two solid months of progress and of hope: the prelude to the quick collapse.

Because it was quick. Quick — and mortifying: I capitulated in an instant. There was, one night, after a good day, a sudden onslaught of depression — why, I don't know. I found myself for the first time in weeks smothered by this unaccountable sadness; it seemed to me that everything I'd done for the past two months was purposeless, foolish: the steady strides forward were in fact the steps of an ant up the side of a mountain. It was a mood of despair I couldn't shake. The more I looked at myself and what I was doing, the more it seemed to me that everything I'd prized most belonged to the past, that my father, my own hopes, my life as a priest, my friends, were all gone or damaged forever, and that my future consisted of an endless succession of days in which I would slog along the treadmill, whistling to support the delusion that I was coming ahead by leaps and bounds, while in reality I was moving nowhere: a gray, pathetic, neutral figure, kidding himself until the end of his time. . . .

Bleak moods assail everyone; most of us have our defenses. That night I had none, and as it grew worse there came a moment when suddenly, automatically, without any sense of arriving at a decision, I walked quickly out of my room, and out of the rectory, and down the dark night streets to the familiar door of a neighborhood package store. And so it was that, within the matter of an hour, the hope, the optimism, the confidence, the accomplishments of the past two months were gone, and I was back where I started.

Or rather, much farther back than that: before, I had always had at least a measure of discretion; now, I seemed to have none. My audience was no longer limited to two appalled and extremely unhappy young curates: I had broadened my field. Now, restless and foggy, I not only left my room at night but I left the rectory as well, and often very late at night — or very early in the morning, long before dawn — I walked and walked — alone, aimless, slightly unsteady — through the streets of the parish. The darkness was some protection, but not much; of course I was seen and of course I was recognized. The rectory secret was now a secret no longer. The whispers began and spread and grew louder: the pastor became the public scandal. I did not even spare myself the authentic comic touch: very early one morning, on the front porch, as I was fumbling for the key, I was discovered by whom? The milkman! The traditional encounter: the pure farce. I did not laugh. . . .

Nor did the Bishop. This time the summons came quickly; within a few weeks I was back in his office. He was as expressionless, as impassive as ever, but he had come to a decision; he said at once, "It was a mistake. And not only on your part, Father. But now we have to do what some would say we should have done immediately. Perhaps they're right. Although I don't know. . . ." He looked at me and said quietly, "I'm appointing Father Molloy administrator of your parish."

And so I had lost Saint Stephen's. But of course by now this was inevitable, so much so that even when I heard it announced in so many words, I felt no new pain. I said, "He's a good priest. They'll like him." There was a pause — an awkward one. Then I said, "I'm sorry, Bishop. Genuinely, sincerely. . . ."

And what I meant was a sorrow, not at having lost my parish, but at having failed it. I'm sure he knew this; his head moved

[143]

forward in a slow and rather absent nod, as if acknowledging the words. But he said thoughtfully, "I think most people who do something they know is wrong are sorry afterward. And genuinely so. The sinner who rejoices in his sin: that must be fairly rare. Everybody's sorry. I'm not trying to cut you off, Father. Or to minimize the value of your sorrow. But I am suggesting that sorrow by itself doesn't really help much. It's too easily neutralized. It doesn't last long. Something else is needed if anything is to be done." The low voice said unexpectedly, "Do you know The Cenacle, Father?"

Or not so unexpected, because this, too, was inevitable. I knew The Cenacle — or more accurately, I knew about it. Located in the desert country of Arizona, it once had been the home of a national figure wealthy enough to be called eccentric; twenty years ago it had been purchased by the Church and had become . . . what? A retreat? A rest home? A hospital? A recuperative center? At one time or another over the years I had heard it called all these things, but whatever the euphemism, The Cenacle was in fact a way station — and, in some cases, a final home — for the errant priest. To be sent to The Cenacle was . . . well, it was not exactly a boost to one's self-esteem. Was the Bishop at this moment thinking of my self-esteem? I thought it unlikely. I looked at him, and once again I saw the slight nod.

"Yes," he said. "There are alternatives. But I think this is best. All things considered." And then this strange disciplinarian asked, "Does it appeal to you at all?"

And what could I say? That I was overjoyed to join the company of broken clerics like myself? I hesitated, then said, "Not very much, I'm afraid, Your Excellency. Although I wouldn't have thought that was a particular consideration at this point. . . ."

He did not respond to this; he said only, "You may feel differently after you've been there awhile. It's not a penal colony. It's a place where you can be put on a decent program. And work with intelligent people. People who understand what it is you're up against. People who can help you. That's what's essential. Independent effort is all very well, but if you're really in trouble, I think it's seldom good enough. We depend upon each other, Father. All of us. We're meant to. In a way, that's what it's all about."

There was another of those extraordinary pauses, in which he seemed to be communicating with himself. Then he said, "But you know all this. I think most people know it. And I think that a man who does know it and would let his pride, for example, stand in the way of such help would have to be a very short-sighted man. Almost a foolish man."

There had been not the slightest shift in tone before this last remark to suggest the special pointedness — yet there was no mistaking that it was there. It was the closest the Bishop had come to the direct rebuke. He stood now; another of our interviews had ended, this one far less happily than the last. He gave me his blessing again; he wished me good luck again; and as I left his office he said again, "Father?"

I turned; he said simply, "Goodbye. And remember, it's not forever. We'll have you back with us again."

It was on this vague note of promise that I left the diocese and went to The Cenacle. . . .

I was not there forever; I was there for four years: a long time. Yet it was a good time. Not always a happy one — particularly in the first few months — but in the end a deeply rewarding one: far more so than I could ever have expected. Because, for one thing, it worked; it did the trick. Here in what was really, I suppose, a desert reformatory — a queer sprawl of adobe building, stripped of the lunatic splendors of its former owner — among a fellowship I had joined with reluctance, with resentment (for it's quite possible to resent what you admit to be just), and with a sense of shame, I did what I could not have done alone: I came to terms with myself; I came to terms with God.

It's pointless to go into any step-by-step account of what happened — although I remember it all, every bit of it. It's easy enough to say, I think, that from the beginning I was given every help by a few compassionate and knowledgeable men. One was a layman, a doctor who had been out there for some years; one was a priest who, although still fairly young, had in fact started The Cenacle, nearly two decades before; three or four more were priests who had no connection with the staff, but who were there because they had been sent there: like me, they had come to be cured. And so, professionals, or merely those who had been through the mill themselves, these men were there to help. The odd thing is that I don't think any of them were what would ordinarily be considered wise men. I look back on our conversations, and I remember little that was at all remarkable: certainly no one was conspicuous for his piety or learning. Yet they had what I needed: they had their experience, they had a clear, hard, practical view of my problem and position, and with an odd combination of bluntness and delicacy, they managed to point out to me just where I stood and what I was. Moreover, they made themselves available to me at any hour, and for what was I think the first time in my adult life I came to have no hesitation in calling on someone to help me, if only to talk to me, when I was at my lowest, when sometimes it seemed as if I might quite literally go mad. Because the moments of despair still came, but now I was no longer allowed the reliable obliteration. And so there was nothing else to do but face them. They were endless, and they were awful. Even with every kindness and encouragement from those around me, it was a bitter and a desolate business. . . .

And yet this bitterness and desolation did not last. Gradually I began to improve, to respond, to notice and even to take an interest in this new world in which I found myself. It was a world completely new to me; everything about it was different, even the setting. Especially the setting. I woke each morning to the bright heat of the desert day, to the pale high sky without a cloud. The house was cool, protected by its thick adobe walls. I could look from my window across the enormous sweep of silent space and watch the play of the morning light on great and distant mountains; at night the sun went down at once, and from a window in the west I could see the dramatic, shifting rush of amethyst and gold flood the sky before the instant, final drop of darkness. It was all strange and completely fascinating to me. I had grown up in the East and had never left it; I had grown accustomed to the smaller scale, the close horizons, the crowds and the places where crowds live, and the sudden spiteful turns of weather. Out here there was none of that: only a vast, unbroken grandeur, the majestic monotony of the hot and brilliant days. I never got used to it; I never got tired of it. I would sit for hours by the window, motionless, thinking, watching, listening to the immense, sunbaked stillness. I suppose it was all a part of the therapy that was going on every day; in any case, it worked wonders for me.

At this time there were perhaps twenty priests at The Cenacle. In addition to the staff, that is, but including the three or four priests I've already mentioned as being especially helpful. During my stay — which, as I've said, was a long one: I could have left earlier, and in fact the Bishop once suggested it, but this time I wanted to be sure — this number varied: sometimes there were more, sometimes less. They came from dioceses all over the country. Like me, most of them were middle-aged, and had come here for the first time and for the one reason; again like me, they had arrived filled with shame and the desire to keep to themselves. But there was in this house an atmosphere — an atmosphere of help, really — which broke down exclusiveness, and this, plus our common bond of all having failed in the same way, sooner or later brought each one into contact with the rest. I came to know them all and to hear their stories — just as they came to hear mine. We talked freely, even insistently: after all, our Topic was there. As in any institution

[147]

where all the inmates suffer from the same malady, we compared our notes and our cases: the causes, symptoms, expectations of recovery. And I found to my surprise that there was a great similarity to all these stories; in every one, I saw something of my own. As the Bishop had said, I was hardly unique. The telltale thread wound its way through all: the slow neglect of the nourishment of the spirit, the failure to realize that unless this is daily deepened and enriched, then, when the fervor and the drive of the young priest fade — as they must — there will be no replacement by a living, ever-growing love, and then, when the aging priest going through the years meets the inevitable disappointments, crises, or sometimes just the sudden burden of his loneliness, he may meet them with an emptiness where fullness should be, and the result of that will not be a happy one. Because if a priest has not this continuing current of love, he has nothing. He can turn to no one; his marriage is to God, and if he fails in that, his strength is gone, his very purpose is gone. And so, what then? The Cenacle? The Cenacle — if, that is, he's fortunate. If not, there are other roads and uglier destinations, and the priest, like any other man, is not immune to these. . . .

But the priests who were with me were firm and unanimous in one intention: to return to their dioceses, to pick up their lives as parish priests, never to need The Cenacle again. Most of them succeeded in this; they did not come back. Yet there were the sad exceptions, and I can remember with great affection and sorrow one priest who, even during my stay, left and returned four times. He was a small, pale man with a fragile and strangely gay face; he must have been more than fifty, but there was about him such a persistently youthful air that he might have been in his thirties. Each time he came back he was a washed-out, shaking ruin, but he had an astonishing ability to recover, and in no time at all he would be out walking around the grounds with his springy, chipper step, whistling, joking, looking like a mischievous boy. I talked with him often;

never once did he admit to being an alcoholic. He never in fact so much as mentioned drink — and this, in The Cenacle, was an extraordinary reticence. Instead he spoke in the vaguest terms of a mysterious respiratory ailment which attacked him recurrently and left him drained and helpless. It was, he explained, a matter of climate.

"I tell you, Hugh, this place works miracles for me!" he said enthusiastically. "It's the steady heat that does it. The bacilli or the viruses or whatever they call those organisms these days simply perish: it's genocide the moment they hit the Arizona state line. Here is where I flourish, yet there I am, nailed to New England. They say that it's the tropics that destroy health, but have you ever stopped to consider who the 'they' are who say this? They all come from Bangor or Providence. Not one of them ever mentions the simple medical fact that the month of March in the Massachusetts bronchial belt is infinitely more debilitating than malaria time in Panama. It's no accident that all the country's best hospitals are in Boston, you know: they want to be close to the source of supply." We walked along, and he whistled cheerfully; every now and then we paused while he traced in the dust with a stick a quick, deft caricature of some diocesan acquaintance. "John Riordan," he said. "The clumsiest priest in America. For some reason he got interested in Boy Scout work and they appointed him spiritual director. His bishop had to remove him after two months. He'd go to the meetings and insist on being one of the boys. You know: splitting firewood, hacking away with hammers and axes and knives. After every meeting he'd come back to the rectory covered with blood. It was wonderful first-aid practice for the Scouts, but this pastor saw that unless something were done in a hurry this priest who'd formerly been all thumbs would very soon be no thumbs at all. So the bishop removed him. No," he said, returning to an earlier theme, "I'd like nothing better than to get out. Of New England, that is. Wouldn't you, Hugh? Don't you ever get fed up with it back there? Wouldn't

[149]

you like a transfer? Wouldn't you like to wake up one morning and find yourself the only priest in some impossibly hot, impossibly arid land?"

"An American Desert Father? Or someone like Charles Foucauld? No, I don't think so. Not very much. Not at all, really."

"Wouldn't you? *I* would. Oh, wouldn't I!" We continued to walk, and after a while he said gaily, "I might found a new order: The Congregation of the Little Fugitives of the North Atlantic Seaboard. Do you think that Rome would look with favor on it? You could join, Hugh. We'd all ride camels and every year we'd have a grand celebration on the day the first flake of snow falls in the Berkshires. We'd burn a rubber boot. Or a ski. I'm convinced I'd never know another sick day."

He was wonderful company on these walks: imaginative, witty, lighthearted. He was also extremely plausible, and once, early in my stay, when I first met him, I discussed his case with the priest who was the Director of The Cenacle.

"But isn't it possible that there's something in what he says? I don't mean that he isn't an alcoholic, but in back of all the excuses, couldn't it be true that the climate might have a little to do with it? I know people up there who sniffle and whoop and cough six months of the year; I'd imagine that if he's at all susceptible in that direction it wouldn't help his main problem. Probably some sort of transfer. . . ."

"Transfer," the Director said. "To where? He's been practically everywhere you can be transferred to. He's told you about the terrible attrition of the New England winters? Naturally. Did he also tell you that he hasn't spent a winter in New England for the past ten years? Nominally he's attached to a parish there; at least I think he still is. But he's the greatest traveler I know. They're unbelievably indulgent with him in that diocese. I suppose it's because he's so likable. And he is. He's one of the most agreeable, likable men I've ever met. But he's also most unfortunately a drunk. In New England, in California, in Alabama, in South Bend, Indiana, and in a monastery in

[150]

the Kentucky hills. No, climate has nothing to do with it. Our friend doesn't discriminate. Hot or cold, wet or dry, he finds his drink. And takes it."

"Then what can be done about him? Nothing?"

"Well, I can only tell you what we can do about him here, and *that's* nothing, all right. We can straighten him out for a few weeks or a couple of months, but that's about it. You see, he just won't play ball. You can't treat a man who refuses to be treated. He won't tell me the truth and with the others he's even worse — especially doctors, psychiatrists. He's very charming with them and tells them these fanciful stories. They're trained men, of course, and naturally they don't believe a word he says: they know right away what they've got on their hands. But he pays no attention to what they tell him. I once told him point-blank that of course he was an alcoholic and that it was high time he stopped his nonsense and faced up to it. You would have thought I'd told him he was twelve feet tall. He professed to be astonished; he cautioned me, in the friendliest possible way, against being ruled by an obsession. He explained that it was a common fault of the specialist to interpret everyone in the light of his specialty. And he said that while he did occasionally take a drink to kill the pain — just what pain he didn't say: that's usually left rather indefinite — that was a far cry from being an alcoholic. Alcoholism, he said to me, was a *disease*. So there you are. He won't admit to a thing, and this stops us before we can even get started."

"Yet he knows what this place is specifically for. And he must know what he's doing and what he is. Do you think it's possible that he could not know? I mean, that he could have talked himself into believing that he's not really a drinker?"

"No, he knows, all right. He may not admit anything, but he knows. He's a very intelligent man."

"And he continues to come back, time after time? Have you ever made any difficulties about taking him back?"

"Oh no," he said. "I can't do anything for him, but I'll always take him in. If I could think of anything better to do with him I would, but I can't. So I'll take him. It's a treadmill, but where else can the poor fellow go? Everybody likes him, but no matter where they ship him it's the same old story. A short, delighted honeymoon, then — bang! No one's going to put up with that; no one can afford to. So his bishop and I have a little arrangement, and whenever he goes off the rails they bring him back from wherever he happens to be — and it's not always easy to find him, by the way — and out he comes for another stay. That's all right with me. As I say, he's a most likable man. And by now a fairly helpless one, in spite of the way he looks and walks around here. I think he may be happier here than he is anywhere else; I wouldn't be surprised if he's come to think of it as his home."

A week or so later, the priest we had been discussing and I were taking one of our usual walks. As always, it was clear and hot, and as we walked, little bright-eyed lizards skittered away in the dust before us, coming to a stop yards away, and freezing into immobility. He said, "I'll miss seeing those lizards. They look like half the people I know."

I wasn't paying the strictest attention; I said drowsily, "There's no need to miss them. They'll be here every day."

"Yes, but I won't," he said. "The time has come, Hugh. D day. I'm leaving on Friday."

This woke me completely. "So soon?"

"It is soon, isn't it? I take no credit: it's all due to long walks in magnificent sunshine. I don't cough any more and apparently my chest has cleared completely. Of course a return to God's country may fix that, but probably not this time: I hear they're having the best summer they've had in ages. Two consecutive days without rain: all that sort of thing."

I said carefully, "Still, it's unpredictable at best. I should think you'd be better off if you didn't rush back. Why not stay out here a bit longer and give yourself a chance to build up some resistance?"

"Do you know, that's just what the Director said? I thought it was extremely nice of him, especially since I must be all kinds of a nuisance around here. Considering, that is," he explained, "that I have no right here in the first place. This establishment has its own special purpose: it's not at all geared to my kind of trivial complaint. But they've been wonderful with me all the same."

"Then why not stay a while longer. . . ."

"No," he said. "No, I have to get back. I have so many things to do. For one thing, I'm anxious to get working on an idea I have for a diocesan pageant. We have one every year, and of course it's always pure lunacy. You know the sort of thing: your friendly neighborhood dentist suddenly popping out from behind the curtain and announcing that he's Saint John of the Cross. Isn't that terrifying? Of course the Episcopalians go even more hog-wild; they've taken to staging little Biblical dramas in modern dress. There's one rather fancy divine in California who presents the Twelve Apostles in berets and Bermuda shorts. We haven't gone in for that yet; at least I don't think we have. But what I want to do is something quite traditional. You know Claudel's *Le Soulier Satin?* Well. . . ."

And, in the highest of spirits, he went on to tell me about his plan, which was, in a way, brilliant, and which, I knew, would reach the same stage of completion as all his other plans. The diocesan pageant could much more safely rely on the friendly neighborhood dentist.

When he left we said goodbye warmly, promising to keep in touch with one another. The railroad station was some twenty miles away; he was to be driven there in The Cenacle's old ranch wagon, and he sat in the front seat beside the driver looking small and sunburned and happy. At the last minute

[153]

he stuck his head out the window, said goodbye to me again, and then took a slow and last look around the flat, still desert landscape.

"Do you know what I'm doing, Hugh?" he said dramatically. "I'm saying a special goodbye to The Cenacle. It's not like saying goodbye to you, because for one thing in the years to come you and I will probably run into each other a hundred times. But somehow, with The Cenacle, I feel it's *final*; I don't expect I'll ever see it again. In a sense that's a little sad, isn't it? Because it's a very pleasant place, and everyone out here was so good to me. But I have to go home, and when I get there I gather I'm to be given all sorts of new responsibilities, the kind that will keep my nose to the grindstone until even the grindstone is worn out. So I really don't imagine I'll be getting out this way again. Ergo. . . ."

And he waved a great flourishing wave, which included all the premises; then he drove off, still waving, at me and at The Cenacle.

He was back in six months. By the time I left The Cenacle — which was a couple of years later — he had been back three times more. And always — after the first few days, during which he kept to himself — he seemed gay and undismayed, although at times a little older, a little more worn. And never once did he speak of his drinking. Now, today, where he is, or how he is, I don't know. I've written to him several times; the letters were not returned, so I suppose he got them. But I've never received an answer: not even a card. I pray for him regularly, as I'm sure many others — whom he met as casually as he met me, and whom he never saw again — do: he's not a man who's difficult to pray for. I hope he's all right, and that wherever he is or wherever he goes someone will be found to take a little care of him now and then, to occasionally do for this poor, engaging, bright-faced wanderer what another man, not necessarily any better, but maybe just a little more prudent, or even a little more selfish, would by instinct do for himself. . . .

I left The Cenacle. I left it at last, thanks to the help, the kindness, the example of those I've already mentioned, and thanks above all to the grace of God. When I left I had been there — as I've said — four years, which was far longer than I had expected, and was I suppose much longer than was strictly necessary. But I was cautious, I wanted no mistakes this time, and the Bishop, understanding this, allowed me to set my own pace. And so I stayed on, gradually becoming almost a part of the place, occasionally helping out with some of the new arrivals — trying to do for them at least a little of what others had done for me — and then too, helping out with the regular, routine physical chores of the place. The staff was small: there was plenty for everyone to do. Then, as time went by, I was quite often sent out from The Cenacle into the surrounding districts to lend a hand wherever a priest might be needed. In that big country there was a shortage of priests, and The Cenacle had become a convenient supply depot: a kind of clerical replacement pool. I would drive off in the jeep to spend a few days assisting at a parish church in one of the towns, or at an army base, or at one of the little Indian missions (Bucky, apart from his romantic notion of the priest on horseback, had not been far wrong in his suspicions). It was work of a kind I'd never known before, and along with everything else, it helped. Often, driving back to The Cenacle at night, I found that I could think about things I hadn't really thought about for years. And there were moments when, bumping along on a bucket seat over a freeway of baked mud, passing through the strange quiet and the clear shining darkness of the desert night, I would suddenly become aware of a stillness which was something quite apart from the stillness of the night. It was an interior stillness, a stillness inside me, a stillness in which there was the absence of all distraction and unrest, a stillness in which, quietly and without effort, I seemed to come together, to be focused and attentive, to be really *present*, so to speak, a stillness from which it seemed natural, even inevitable, to reach out, to pray, to adore. . . .

And this is what I mean by saying that slowly, but at last, I came to terms with myself and with God. In the end, this is what The Cenacle meant to me. I left it with gratitude and regret; in a way I didn't want to leave at all. But I did leave. I had been there long enough; it was time to go back to the diocese where I belonged.

I went first to the Bishop. Four years had not changed him; he was as undemonstrative as ever. Yet I knew that he was pleased to see me, and after a brief welcome he said, "We have the problem of where to put you. I could keep you here in the chancery for a while, but I thought you might like to get back to a parish."

"Yes, I would. If there's one available, that is."

"We're limited in choice at the moment," he said. "There aren't many vacancies. A few, in different parts of the diocese. None is as agreeable as your old parish." Then he said, "There is one vacancy in your own city. How do you feel about that? It's a question of whether, immediately, you want to go back."

To the scene of the crime? It was a question indeed: I'd thought about it often. For The Cenacle was one thing; the old home town was quite another. And even though it wasn't Saint Raymond's or Saint Stephen's, still, whatever parish it was, it was in the same city, people moved about and talked: encounters, awkward encounters, were inevitable. But just as inevitable was the fact that one day, sooner or later, I would go back: I knew that; postponement wasn't much of a solution. Besides which, it was, after all, an offer, and I was in no position to go about rejecting parishes. And so I said, "I think it might be well to go back right away, Your Excellency."

What did I expect him to do? Clap me on the shoulder, say firmly, "That's the brave priest?" No. Hardly. Which was fortunate, because all he did say was, "All right. In that case . . . do you know Old Saint Paul's?"

I knew Old Saint Paul's. I think every priest in the diocese knew Old Saint Paul's — or at least knew about it. Just how many of them knew or even suspected that it still survived as a functioning parish was another matter. For the majority, I imagine, it was merely a part of ancient diocesan history; now, abruptly, it had become a part of my history. I tried to feel enthusiasm. I remembered when I had last seen this church. It was on a day about seven or eight years ago, when I had been driving back across the city to Saint Stephen's. Normally the route I traveled took me nowhere near Saint Paul's, but on this day there was a detour, and as the traffic slowly edged its way around through the slum district, I had every chance to take in the tattered neighborhood and the church itself. And just as I was passing the church, a priest — an elderly priest — came out of the rectory next door. I knew most of the priests in the city, but for some reason I didn't know this one. He was a tired-looking man with a dusty soutane; as he walked up the church steps he paused and with one foot nudged an empty bottle and a tin can off the steps and out into the gutter. Then, slowly, he walked into the church. I remember feeling a sympathy for him, and wondering who he was, and what he had done to warrant this albatross around his neck.

And now the albatross was mine. . . .

"Down at the heels," the Bishop said candidly. "It's no prize. But there it is, and it needs a pastor. You've been inside the church? The rectory?"

I said, "Yes, but many years ago." Did I say this hopefully? For, after all, there was the possibility that improvements had been made. . . .

The Bishop doomed the possibility. "Then you know what to expect," he said. Now, once again, as on my first visit to this office, he rose from his desk and walked over to the window, where he stood in silence, looking out. Today the window

[157]

was closed; there was no sound of the lawn-mower and no smell of cut grass. It was a day in the middle of March, and there was snow on the ground; a few minutes before freezing rain had begun to drive down. A gray day, suitable for gray tidings. . . .

The low, private voice said suddenly, "It's an odd place. Grubby. Unexciting. Out of date. They've been after me to tear it down. On the ground that it's a dead loss. They're right, of course. But I have a feeling for Saint Paul's. It's a church that has meant a lot in its time. It stands for something in the diocese. And it's still needed. People know it; it's familiar in a way that a new church could never be. I can't afford to restore it, but at least I can keep it together." He looked over at me and said, "It's not an additional punishment, Father. I agree it must seem so, but I don't mean it as such. It won't be like anything you've had before, but I think you may find it has its own compensations. We'll see. If it doesn't work out I'll arrange something else. But give it a try."

And so at least I had a promise of reprieve. I left the Bishop's office and came directly to Saint Paul's. There had been no dramatic changes: that much was clear at once. The whole place seemed exactly as I had remembered it. I went into the rectory and established myself in the pastor's bedroom; the priest who had been here on temporary assignment greeted me and shook my hand. He shook both hands. Fervently. I think no man could have been happier to see another; I think his bags must have been packed for days. He would not stay the night but left immediately, repeatedly assuring me that Old Saint Paul's was now "all mine." I'm sure he thought I was about to bolt, leaving him once more in full and unhappy possession. . . .

Alone, I began to walk around the rectory in a slow examination of the premises. It was not a cheering tour. There was dust and dirt and ample evidence of mice; light bulbs had burned out and had not been replaced; from old rooms on the top floor came the smell of damp and mildew. After a while I went downstairs and crossed over into the church. It was too dark by now to see what it was really like, but I had a fair idea. I knelt in the sanctuary for a few moments, then I went back to the rectory and into the kitchen. I was suddenly hungry; I looked for something to eat. Provisions, however, were slim: the priest who had left so abruptly seemed to have lived here as if he were camping out in a haunted house. But there were various items scattered around, and from them I put together my first meal as pastor of Old Saint Paul's: a can of Vienna sausage, a glass of nonfat milk, and an apple. Scenes of clerical gluttony: I thought of my father's notes on the theme. And then, because it had been a long and not a particularly exhilarating day, I went back up to my bedroom and there, in the quiet of the rectory — or what passed for quiet in an old building full of mysterious creaks and snaps and sighs and the whispering scurry of small paws behind the walls — I finished my office for the day and went to bed.

The next morning — for no reason at all I remember that it was a Tuesday — I said my first Mass in the old and virtually empty church; there was not even the usual complement of the curious, eager to inspect the new pastor. Here in Old Saint Paul's, they couldn't have cared less. I saw two or three old ladies and, seated halfway back in the church, a Chinese: it was my first glimpse of Mr. Yee. After Mass, I returned to the sacristy to find a thin, dark man with evasive eyes waiting for me. This was Roy, the janitor; he was making what I was later to discover was one of his infrequent appearances. He introduced himself to me; he apologized profusely for not having been on hand to meet me when I had arrived.

"Only," he said, "when you got here, Father, you know where Roy was?"

I did not know.

"*In jail*," he said. "With cops around him."

It was all I needed. The parish, the rectory, the church, and

[159]

now a janitor who had arrived fresh from jail. And, moreover, one who spoke of himself in the third person. He continued, even more alarmingly.

"Roy said to them, 'It ain't right to keep me here. You got no right to coop a man up unless you got charges.' They said, 'Oh, we got charges all right. You know we got the charges. We got all kinds of charges. You're one smart cookie, Roy, but we got you at last. You pushed it too much this time, Roy. Smart as you are, you can't never get away with no *kidnapping!*' What you think of that, Father?" he said. "A man that works in church every day and they finger him for a kidnapper! Roy was burned up, Father! Because why? Because here he is, he should be over at the church to do his work and say hello to his new priest, and where is he? In jail on a frame!'"

At some point in this narrative belief had suddenly collapsed under the burden of absurdity; I found myself looking at Roy, who had begun to breathe heavily, slap his sides, and stamp on the floor in order to emphasize this account of jailhouse injustice, and all at once I knew that at the moment when he should have been here to meet me he had in all probability been asleep in his bed. There had been no kidnapping charge, no jail, no cops. Roy was, quite simply, embroidering, although with a somewhat wilder hand than most. I congratulated him on having gained his freedom so quickly; he replied darkly that Roy knew the ropes.

"He knows the ropes," he said, "and he knows his rights. Roy don't need no mouthpiece, Father. Not Roy. Not when the right is on his side. He put them cops right in their place. He said to them, 'Look here, you better let Roy go and be quick about it. You better not keep no man from the Catholic church where he works his fingers to the bone each day. You better not keep him from his new priest or that new priest might get mad and come on over here and blow his stack at you!' That's what Roy told them, Father. So they had to let him go. Only," he said regretfully, "too late for him to be here on time."

"Now that you are here," I said, and began to talk to him about the many things that needed to be done about the church. He seemed delighted.

"Roy's been *waiting* to begin," he said. "Just tell Roy where to start, Father."

I told him; he nodded enthusiastically. "That's a good place," he said. "Just let Roy at that place!" But then, suddenly, he left me, saying that he would return early that afternoon. I did not see him for a week. . . .

In this way I began my new pastorate. It was more or less the way I had expected; life in Old Saint Paul's held few surprises. But it did hold one — and that one was the great surprise of my own contentment here. For in spite of all the obvious drawbacks, in spite of every sad expectation having been met, I was not unhappy in Saint Paul's — not even in those first hours of glum exploration. It's not easy to explain, even to my own satisfaction, but for some reason I seemed to feel that in a peculiar way I fitted the parish, that there was some sort of rough equation between Saint Paul's and myself. I'd never been in a parish remotely like it before, yet I didn't feel at all strange or in the least out of place here. There was a quality which drew me to it, made me oddly comfortable — although this was probably nothing more at first than the sheer *calm* of the place. It had the quiet, the absence of turmoil atmosphere that seldom visited backwaters often have. It was so peaceful, so undemanding a parish that to have moved here from The Cenacle seemed actually a very slight transition. I had my parish duties to perform, of course, but as I've said earlier, these were neither many nor arduous. And because my polyglot parishioners kept pretty much to themselves, I found myself with a great deal of time on my hands; with no curate, I found myself alone for long intervals. But this loneliness no longer bothered me. I read more than I had in years, I thought about what I'd learned in The Cenacle, I began to take the long nightly walks through the district, and I worked regularly around the church and rectory, painting and making a few minor repairs, trying to pick the place up a bit. I was helped in this by the acquisition of Mrs. Addione; the hiring of this silent, efficient woman, just a week after my arrival, was a major move. I even came to some sort of rather equivocal relationship with Roy: I raised his salary. Not much, but all I could afford; no matter how little he did, the poor fellow deserved more than he'd been getting. Now, in gratitude, Roy came irregularly but more frequently, each time with a different excuse, or — failing that — some fanciful tale from his imaginary past. He told stories of having been a chef on a transatlantic liner, a professional dancer, the fire chief of a small town in Connecticut, a rum-runner during Prohibition, a newspaperman, a jockey, a Communist. I found these glamorous fictions ingenious and entertaining, but poor Father Danowski, when he came, found them unendurable. He was baffled by Roy; I think he was even a little afraid of him. Sturdy, even powerful, himself, Father Danowski had the strong man's fear of the suspected lunatic, and Roy's sudden plunging movements and occasionally rolling eye made him uneasy. I remember in particular one encounter between them; it took place shortly after Father Danowski had arrived in the parish. Roy had been painting the back of the rectory; Father Danowski had come out and had been cornered. From my room I could overhear a chilling account of Roy's career as a middleweight boxer. The career had been a short one, for it appeared that Roy, once maddened by blood, was uncontrollable. The knee, the thumb, the elbow, the savage kick were all vital parts of his fighting technique; after nearly destroying an opponent twice his size in a memorable bout in San Diego, he had been barred from the ring for life. It was a preposterous story, but

Roy was a vivid raconteur and told it with great conviction. Father Danowski was clearly impressed.

"Well well," he said nervously. "Well well, Roy. That is quite a horrible tale. I trust that is all in the dead past now." Then, apparently feeling that a certain facetiousness might now be useful, he added, "I trust Father Kennedy and I may feel safe from your assaults? Although to be sure you undoubtedly would not commit the sacrilege of striking a priest."

Roy had not been reassuring.

"When the mood is on him," he said, "Roy would strike *anything!*"

"He is a wild person," Father Danowski said, reporting this conversation to me some moments later. "A wild and a violent person, Father. Mark my words, we had better have a care or we will all be murdered in our beds!"

But Roy stayed on, and nothing happened. And indeed, in another and larger sense nothing happened: the phrase might almost have been the motto of the parish. For situated as we were, in the middle of the slum, we had few points of contact with the life of the large and active city; the slum served as an untidy but efficient moat. When I came to the parish all sorts of changes and developments were occurring in the city. The winds of political reform were blowing, there was talk of urban renewal, one transportation crisis was succeeded by another, civic bankruptcy was said to be upon us — yet none of this seemed to penetrate the passive, dusty enclave of Old Saint Paul's. I was in the city in which I had spent most of my life and in whose affairs I had taken a small but always interested part; I might have been a thousand miles away. I soon saw that I need have no fear of old acquaintances running up against me bearing fragments of the past in their hands. Now, I met almost no one I had known in the old days. Sometimes an occasional visitor came to the rectory: someone who'd been one of my parishioners in either Saint Raymond's or Saint Stephen's. We talked pleasantly enough, although not for too long; then they went away and did not return. I wondered at first what was behind these visits. Curiosity? Kindness? A little of both, probably. But in any case such visits were few. No one came casually to this part of the city; no one "dropped in." One had to make a special, deliberate point of visiting Old Saint Paul's, and I think that many of those I had known so well hesitated now to make this point, feeling — quite rightly — that under the circumstances the first move was surely mine. I realized this; I knew that for many of them it was their sensitivity to my feelings, their fear of my embarrassment quite as much as their own, which kept them away; I knew that if any hands were to be extended, it was up to me to reach out first. But this I did not do. For several reasons, I suppose: prudence, a sense of shame, a feeling that to evoke even those few parts of the past which meant the most to me — a handful of people, three or four places — might in the end bring the whole thing sweeping in on me: the old principle of inviting the camel's nose under the tent. And so I did nothing. I told myself that there was plenty of time, that one day, some day, perhaps I might make the move. But meanwhile, secure in Old Saint Paul's, I did what seemed best or at least safest: I simply stayed away.

Until, that is, today. . . .

And now it was the end of today, and this — not so briefly — is what I thought about as I sat by the window in my room, looking up the length of the now dark street, listening to the quiet night, drifting back through so many years in this long, slow flow of memory which had begun with an old man's birthday party on a summer afternoon. How strange it was that when at last I did go back, it should have been through the unlikely auspices of old Charlie; I wondered what my father would have said to that. And how strange it was, too, that all the fears and anticipations had been for nothing, and that in Charlie's house what I had felt mostly was enjoyment and a full, warm satisfaction that I hadn't felt since — well, since a very long time ago. So long ago that I'd almost forgotten. And it was only now, I think, as I sat here with so much of the past and present summoned up and laid before me side by side, giving me a kind of comparison test — a before-and-after picture of myself — that I realized how much I had really changed. For everything that had happened, beginning with my father's death and ending with The Cenacle, had left me, not a sad man, certainly, but a silent and a solitary one. In the old days, whenever I was with my parishioners, I always felt a sense of apartness, to be sure — that apartness which any priest must feel in the company of laymen: the mere fact of his collar alone is an effective badge of separation — but at the same time I always felt at home. I don't think I was ever quite so much at home as in those large parish gatherings where throngs of people were squashed into a hall, and I mixed easily and eagerly with them, sharing their high spirits and their stories: I think, at the time, I even had a mild reputation as a neighborhood raconteur. In other words, the popular priest. Today, of course, I don't mix, there are no parish gatherings over here, and time has brought a new taciturnity to the neighborhood raconteur: I'm fully aware that my conversation consists largely of the small, necessary key words and phrases of acknowledgment, plus an assortment of short and noncommittal sentences which really don't do much to keep talk going. In many ways I've become a modified and muffled man — which, when you consider the unmuffled version, is not necessarily a turn for the worse. And the curious — and fortunate — thing is that it takes no effort to keep the muffler on. That is, every day is not a heroic struggle against the pull of the past; by and large, I have no desire at all to do the things I used to do, to live the way I used to live. I suppose this happens to everyone to a greater or lesser degree: as we grow older or endure experience certain parts of us are awakened, certain other parts, which were alert, responsive, gradually become dull or die out entirely. Which is

[165]

all right with me: in this case I do not mourn the dead. Yet all the same, every now and then, a flicker of nostalgia shoots up through: probably a special kind of homesickness reserved for the aging man instead of the boy at boarding school. I'd felt it this afternoon, with old Charlie and Bucky and P. J. and Helen and John: the dead tissues twitched a bit. All of which is natural enough, probably even inevitable. And does no harm, I think: a one-time visit to old Charlie can hardly upset the balance of my days. . . .

It was late now; I'd been in the chair by the window for hours. I got up and began to get ready for the night. Father Danowski came in, returning from his family evening. He has the habit — which I wouldn't discourage for the world — of coming in to see me every night before he goes to bed, like some big, clumsily formal, obedient puppy. Tonight he was full of the impact of the name of old Charlie upon his father.

"Memories, Father," he said. "It served to bring them back in a flood. How well my father recalled his many dealings with that shrewd old person! What tussles they had over the years! At one point Mr. Carmody sought to intimidate my father by threatening to raise the rent. But he did not know my father. My father said to him, 'Have a care, Mr. Carmody. You are not talking to just anybody. You are talking to Casimir Danowski who is quite aware of your many obligations in this matter. And unless you see to it that the kitchen windows are freshly puttied and the bathroom drain is unplugged *immediately*, do you know what will happen to you? You will be subjected to severe penalties *in a court of law!*' Oh yes, Father," said Father Danowski admiringly, "my father was almost an attorney in matters of this kind. It is no wonder old Mr. Carmody came to have such a deep respect for him." He nodded his head wisely, in thorough comprehension of all such merited respect; he rose on his toes and sank back on his heels; he looked around my room in his final nightly survey. "Well well," he

[166]

said, "the end of yet another day. It has been a good day for you, Father?"

"Yes," I said. "Yes, a very good day."

"A little change," he said sagely. "Something that is advisable for us all now and then. How glad I am for you, Father!"

That extraordinary expression of ponderous benignity once more clumped down on the young round features: I thought he might have been about to bless me, to tell me to go my way in peace. Still, whatever the manner, there wasn't the slightest doubt that he meant what he said, that he really *was* glad for me — which, after all, is all that matters. Or so I remind myself — rather often — in my conversations with my curate. He said good night, and then, just before he left the room, he said, "Oh, by the bye, Father: you remember that earlier today I mentioned the possibility of Mr. Carmody's one day expressing his interest in Old Saint Paul's? From a financial point of view? I wonder if you recall my speaking of that?"

"I do indeed. Vividly." So then, hope had not died entirely with the appearance of Charlie's ordained son. . . .

"I spoke of it again this evening," he said. "To my father."

"Ah. And what was his reaction?"

"He laughed," Father Danowski said regretfully. "Loudly. Almost to scorn, you might say. My father is a man of eloquence, Father, in the tradition of the old country, but I have seldom heard him express himself with such feeling! He said to me, 'Stanley, you are living in a fool's paradise. I will tell you what that old man will give you. He will give you not a thing. Count on yourself, Stanley. Do not count on other people. If you count on Mr. Carmody you are counting on a man who will see you ground to dust in your grave and your church crumbled to little pebbles before he will give you so much as a dime!' Am I correct," he said, "am I correct, Father, in assuming that this opinion somewhat coincides with your own?"

"Somewhat," I said. "Although I think your father's being just a little extreme. . . ."

Which was a fairly lukewarm defense of the little old man who had been my host that afternoon. Father Danowski said proudly, "Yes, that is his way. His *style*, so to speak. But substantially, Father? In *essence* . . . ?"

"In essence." And it was with at least a twinge of guilt that I said, "Well, yes. In essence, I think you could say that your father's not too far wrong."

He nodded, but said nothing. After a moment he said good night once more and left the room with slow steps. He was not easily discouraged, but I think now he saw all too clearly that Charlie had been nothing more than a false dawn, that the brighter, brisker, spick-and-span Saint Paul's remained as far away as ever.

I went downstairs and over into the church; I usually do this before going to bed. The church now was absolutely still. I prayed, and after a while I went back to my room. I was tired, and I knew that tonight, after this long day, I would go to sleep very quickly.

But not immediately; the day was not quite over. Almost as soon as I got into bed the telephone rang, and once again, with something of the surprise I had felt on that morning only a few days ago, I heard the voice of Charlie Carmody.

"Father? You're not asleep yet?"

"No, no, Mr. Carmody." I added quickly — and, I hoped, meaningfully, "Not yet."

"Ain't that grand!" he said approvingly. "Oh, I tell you, Father, it does an old man good to hear your voice: nice and loud and clear as a bell. That's the way a priest should sound, night or day! On the job! If there's anythin' I hate is to call up a rectory on the telephone and hear some sleepy little voice sneakin' out at me from under the pillows! Oh, there's a dreadful lot of lazy priests around the diocese today, Father! Grown men, supposed to be out on the altar, and where are they? Up in their beds, makin' little tents for themselves under the covers and comin' out only for meals! I know them all, Father. They're a bad bunch!"

I had a sudden and rather frightening vision of old Charlie, clad in his nightgown and posted by the telephone, late at night and very early in the morning grimly dialing all the rectories in the diocese, checking up on clerical sleep. I said, "You're a hard man on us, Mr. Carmody."

"Not on *you*, Father," he said magnanimously. "Oh no, not on you. I make an exception of you. You're just like your poor pa: up at all hours and ready for anythin'!"

As a description of either my father or myself this was staggeringly inaccurate; I said quickly, "Anyway, I'm glad you called. It gives me another chance to thank you for today."

"Not at all, Father!" he cried. "Not at all: the boot is on the other foot. I'm the one to thank *you*. That's what I called you up for now. I had it in mind all the time to thank you for comin' all the ways across the city just to see an old man on his birthday. But then d'ye know what happened? I couldn't remember! What d'ye think of that, Father? I couldn't remember if I did or not!"

Was this credible? Could old Charlie really have been so disturbed at the thought of not having thanked me — or anyone else, for that matter? I said, "You did, Mr. Carmody. Although there was certainly no need. . . ."

"I couldn't remember," he said again, and this time he spoke sadly, and the old voice sounded weaker than before. I recognized another of Charlie's quick changes into pathos. "But I don't remember anythin' these days. Not a blessed thing. That's because I'm an old man, Father. Oh, I know what people say. They look out and say, 'Take a look at old Charlie: ain't he a livin' miracle? At his age with a mind like a steel trap and a memory that forgets nothin'!" But they're all wrong, Father. Lately I forget nearly everythin'. They don't know that, and I'll tell you this: I'm glad they don't know. I

[169]

wouldn't want to trouble them. I get down on my knees at night and pray to God they'll never know. 'Oh God,' I say, 'don't let these nice people know that Charlie Carmody's an old old man that's fallin' apart more every day. Don't let them know there's mornin's he wakes up without rememberin' who he is or where he is or is he rich or poor. Don't let them know, dear God, because I'm the kind of man that bothers no one!' That's what I pray," he said, "but I s'pose no matter what, they'll all get to know sooner or later anyways. I s'pose I'll get worse as time goes by. I s'pose one day I'll do somethin' crazy, like forgettin' where my own house is, or walkin' out on the street with no trousers on. They'll all know then, Father. I can't stop them from knowin' then. And what will they do about it once they do know? I hope they won't poke fun. I hope they won't laugh at each other and say, 'Look at old Charlie, he's lost his marbles!' Oh, I hope they won't say nothin' like that. And I don't think they will. People are nice and kind, as a rule. I always loved people, Father. That's the kind of man I am. And so I s'pose when they see me like that they'll just shake their heads and say, 'Poor old Charlie. He can't remember nothin' now. He's slippin' away into nothin' at all. And what a grand man he used to be!' I s'pose that's what people will say about old Charlie, Father!"

It was a woeful recitation, a far cry indeed from the jubilant account of old age that he had delivered earlier in the day. By now it was almost out of sheer instinct that I said, "I'd imagine the loss of memory would be an enormous inconvenience to anyone, Mr. Carmody, but especially to someone like yourself. Your tenants must be constantly coming up to you, asking questions about the rent, finding out how much they owe. And I can understand what a predicament this places you in. You can't tell them because you really can't remember. And so I suppose they slip away, often without paying anything at all. I can see how that would happen."

This personal vision was greeted with a moment of silence.

[170]

"You can see that, can you, Father?" Charlie said at last, and once again I heard the grim, dusty little chuckle. "By God, then, your eyes are better than mine. I tell you they are. Because I don't see nothin' like that at all. Oh, they give it a try now and again. They come up to me, shufflin' with sad little steps, smilin' the little whimperin' smile, and sayin' ain't it a grand day, Mr. Carmody, and didn't the wife pay you somethin' on account the twelfth of last month, the day you didn't have your book with you? Oho," he cried, "they're sly! I'll give them that, Father. People are sly. Sly and bold. Bold as brass. I know them all. They're always out to take advantage of a man that's got a soft heart. But I see right through them. They look different to me than to you, Father, I can tell you that. You see them in church of a Sunday, with their hands folded nice in front of them, marchin' up to the altar rail, and you say to yourself, 'Here come the saints.' But I look at them and I say to myself, 'There go the burglars!' Every damn one of them, Father! I know them all. I spent my whole life learnin' about people, and most of them would cut your heart out with a post-office pen for the sake of a ten-cent piece! And if they know a man's got a kind heart and likes to do nice things for people, they come runnin' full speed to him with nothin' in their pockets and gravy on their chins, cryin' help, help! 'Oh, do somethin', Mr. Carmody!' they yell. 'Help us out or else little Nora will have to give up the ice-skatin' lessons, and the man from the store will be up with the van to take away the grand piano that turns into the television set when you punch a button! Oh, save us, Mr. Carmody! Do somethin' for us!' And I do," he said. "I'll tell you what I do for them, Father. I hand them a little bill and, nice and soft, I point out the day it's due, and then I tell them they'd damn well better pay up and in full, or else little Nora will be out on her backside on Clancy Boulevard with mud puddles next to her mattress. She can skate on them when they all freeze over. That's what I do for them, Father, and it's what I do because I know them all

[171]

like the back of my hand. Swindlers all!" Then, astonishingly, he added, "But live and let live!"

It was another of the irrelevant but supporting mottoes which apparently served Charlie so well. There was a pause now, and, because it was late at night—at least, late for me—and because I was tired, I said, tentatively, hopefully, "Was there something special, Mr. Carmody. . . ."

But I doubt that he even heard this, for just as I started to speak he broke in, saying heartily, "Well, good night, Father. That's what I called you up for. To thank you and to say good night. Pleasant dreams, Father. And say a prayer for Charlie."

And, oddly enough, this seemed to be all he had called for. The mystery of the day remained unraveled, and by now I was too tired to care. I said, "I will, Mr. Carmody. Good night. Sleep well."

"Oh, I sleep grand," he said. "Like a baby. A little child. It comes from doin' nothin' bad, and bein' a friend to all!"

And was I wrong, or was there once more, at this, the sound of the old dry chuckle? I don't know, because as he hung up I was already falling asleep; the memorable day was over at last.

II

II

7

AFTER CHARLIE'S party there was an interval of quiet in which I neither saw nor heard from any of the Carmodys. In a way, this was not surprising. For one thing, I made no effort to reach them. Not because I didn't want to, or because I wouldn't enjoy enormously seeing them again, but because I still felt, really, as I had from the first moment of Charlie's first call: that in this situation, here in Saint Paul's, with everything going so well, it was simply safer and wiser to leave the past alone. As for Helen and John and their promises to keep in touch with me from now on, I had no doubt that these promises were sincere and would be kept. But in good time; after all, they were not adolescents, frantic to communicate every hour on the hour with their friends. Like myself they were middle-aged; we had been apart a long time; we had grown into our own lives and fixed routine; there was a kind of logical inertia; there was no hurry. I knew that sooner or later, in one way or another, I would hear from them. It was a knowledge that did not bring me unmixed comfort. . . .

Still, while the silence of Helen and John did not surprise me, the silence of their father did. Clearly old Charlie had mysterious business of some sort with me which was yet to be finished, and he was not a man who let go easily. I had expected — and half feared — a sequence of rambling telephone talks, all occurring at times of maximum inconvenience. But I was wrong. The calls did not come at all hours; they did not come at all. Charlie became a part of the Carmody quiet, and in this quiet I went about my daily duties, occasionally looking back on the birthday, remembering even the insignificant details — the boy from the orphanage, greedily savoring in memory each taste and smell of the Christmas feast! — and wondering every now and then what would happen next, and when.

But I did this fairly seldom, largely because I suddenly found myself with no spare time. The pace had unexpectedly picked up in Old Saint Paul's; two events took place, one immediately following the other, which stirred us to unprecedented activity. The first of these was the visit of the Bishop to the parish.

This was a formal visit; it called for preparations. Unfortunately, most of these preparations depended upon Roy, but this always unpredictable figure astonished me with furious spasms of scrubbing and sweeping and painting, so that on the day before the Bishop arrived, both church and rectory were, if not spotless, at least at their most presentable.

Father Danowski said, "Well well, Roy. You see what can be done if only you give of your best efforts?"

This tribute was not well received.

The Bishop came on a Sunday morning, and sang a Solemn Mass at ten o'clock. There was a small, improvised choir; Father Danowski had relentlessly drilled the altar boys; and by the standards of Old Saint Paul's the resulting ceremony was elaborate, even magnificent. And yet there was one disappointment: although the visit of the Bishop had been announced well in advance, the people came in no great numbers. Attendance was adequate, but no more than that; the old, large, half-empty church was full evidence that the parishioners of Saint Paul's did not easily respond to the occasion.

Mrs. Addione, however, *had* responded; after Mass the Bishop came back to the rectory for what was really a handsome breakfast. He ate slowly and well, and over the breakfast table, while the calm, apart, impersonal manner remained the same, and there was no sudden thaw into chumminess, I found myself easier with him — partly, I suppose, because the setting was my own, partly because the circumstances of this meeting were considerably less forbidding. The Bishop talked freely, not at all about the events of that morning, but about diocesan matters in general. There were just the two of us; Father Danowski, who still had the final Mass of the morning to say, had been able to join us for only a moment. When he left he did so in his most formal manner, managing somehow to suggest the departure of some vast, bulky courtier from a *levée* in another century. But as he was in the middle of this exit, the Bishop did a curious thing. He smiled faintly and suddenly said something in a language I did not for the moment place. Father Danowski, startled completely out of his disguise, flushed, and stammered something to the Bishop in the same language. He left the room like a schoolboy, his steps awkward, but his round face shining with pride.

The Bishop said to me, "My mother was Polish. And my father was German. Born in Milwaukee, but still, that's German enough. Or it was in those days."

The Bishop had a German name, and I wondered now why I hadn't thought more about this before, for in this part of the world the bishop who was not drawn from solid Irish stock was something of a rarity. There was no good reason for this, other than the reason of tradition — that this was the way it had always been, ever since the old days when virtually all the priests and all the people were immigrants from the same land. This had all changed, of course, but traditions last long, and I thought it entirely probable that this present bishop was the first "non-Irish" one the diocese had ever known. I mentioned this to him; he nodded.

"Yes. It's a precedent. Not a terribly important one, but in a certain sense it is. There are obvious disadvantages. A small percentage of any old guard dies hard. Especially here." After a moment he added thoughtfully, "The danger of course is narrowness. A confusion of aims. . . ."

It was a cryptic start, but he did not go on; instead, he broke off and turned to a discussion of the affairs of Saint Paul's. It was hardly a searching discussion; for the most part he asked questions about parish maintenance, the cost of repairs, revenues acquired, funds needed. But the questions were perfunctory rather than penetrating; I even had the impression that he felt no particular interest in them, but asked them only because they were the routine questions which, at one point or another, had to be asked of every pastor. They went on for a few minutes, then abruptly he said, "You've been here . . . how long? A year? A little better than that, isn't it? How does it seem to you now?"

I told him about the parish, hinting, rather than stating explicitly, at what it had come to mean to me. And I added, "It's still a little strange, though. I think it would always be, no matter how long I was here. And it's not just the matter of racial mixtures or different languages. It's the queer isolation. In a way, it's like a foreign mission, yet here it is, right in the heart of the city, and completely cut off at the same time. You sometimes feel that you have no lines out to anywhere."

"Do you find this depressing? Discouraging?"

"No. I seldom think of it, to tell you the truth. Very little about the parish depresses me; as I've said, I get along here remarkably well. However, I could wish I knew the people a bit better. That's a situation which seems to remain fairly static."

But he made no comment at all on this; instead, he drank the last of his coffee. Then he said slowly, and as if to himself, "A year." No more followed; he sat looking down thoughtfully at the empty coffee cup, and it seemed to me as though the atmosphere was changed; I had the feeling, almost the certainty, that the Bishop was on the point of saying something of

[178]

the greatest importance to me. I suppose it was the soft phrase "A year" that did it: was he announcing the end of a period of probation? Was he in fact about to tell me that my stay at Old Saint Paul's was over? That I had done well enough, that now a bigger, better parish could be mine? Suddenly I felt certain that this was exactly what he was going to say, and with this I felt a quick panic: I had no wish, none at all, to leave Saint Paul's. But I must admit this: at the same moment there flashed into my head, wildly, another thought, and I almost said aloud: *Saint Stephen's!* Not Saint Raymond's, for John had that, but the next best thing: my old parish. It was astonishing, even impossible: it was the last thing I had wanted. But now it occurred to me instantly, leaping into my mind as an exciting possibility, crashing headlong into all panicky regrets about Old Saint Paul's. It lasted for only a second, then went as quickly as it had come, but it left me confused, shaky, even ashamed. It was a moment which had taken me completely away from the Bishop. I looked at him now and saw that his eyes had left the table and were considering me quietly, and I was suddenly completely sure that I could read in him the very words which would tell me of the change. . . .

I was wrong. For what the Bishop actually said was, "Spanish. Do you speak it at all, Father?"

Spanish. So much for prescience, my powers of intuition. It must have been a long moment before I finally said, "Some, Your Excellency. Not very much."

If there was a delay he didn't seem to notice it; he said only, "I would think it might be of some help over here."

But he didn't pursue this; he went back to talk of general matters, and shortly afterwards he left. In many ways the visit had been a successful one, but for me it had been reduced to one unsettling moment. Over the next few weeks the memory of this moment — of that crazy surge of delighted anticipation for something I'd convinced myself I no longer wanted — came to me often and disquietingly, reminding me that we

[179]

are seldom as fixed and sure as we believe ourselves to be. Sometimes just a puff of temptation, and the backbone cracks. . . .

However, the visit had no such melancholy effect on Father Danowski. He was ecstatic; he said to me, "What a remarkable person he is, Father! How fortunate we are in this diocese, to have a leader of such calibre to guide the reins of our destiny!"

Which certainly may have been true enough — although not necessarily because our leader knew how to say goodbye in Polish. . . .

And now the second of the two events occurred; this once concerned Father Danowski directly. Less than a week after the Bishop's visit he was taken to the hospital for an emergency appendectomy. He had come into my room very late one night, gasping for breath, and repeating, "I have a very bad pain, Father, I have a *very* bad pain!" I called for an ambulance; he was taken to the hospital and operated on immediately. He came through with flying colors, and when I went to see him on the following day he was slightly fuzzy from opiates but otherwise in good shape.

"Thanks," he said, grabbing my hand as soon as I came near his bed. "Thanks a lot, Father." Then, already beginning to recover his dignity even under the fading anesthesia, he said thickly but formally, "Your quick action, Father, saved my life."

"I made a telephone call. It doesn't take too much quick action to dial a number; that's about what it amounted to."

"Nevertheless," he said solemnly. "*Nevertheless.*"

And then he went off to sleep.

It was in this week that I met, for the first time, that almost legendary figure, Father Danowski's father. I met him one afternoon in his son's room; to my surprise, he turned out to be a very small man — was Father Danowski, I wondered, a physical sport in his family? Or had he derived both size and strength from his mother? — with a face full of creases and a heavy gray brush of a moustache. I guessed him to be slightly older than myself and, far from being the firebrand of his son's stories, he seemed a mild and even a submissive man — although this may have been the effect of his surroundings; hospitals seem to overpower and diminish people. On that afternoon he said very little, but Father Danowski took in every word with an obvious pride and later, when his father had left, he said comfortably to me, "Well, Father, do you see what I mean now?"

"Yes. Yes indeed."

"How pleased I am," he said, "that he took to you so quickly. That is most unusual with him."

Another surprise. "You felt he took to me?"

"Oh yes. It was quite unmistakable, Father. One could gauge it from his very silence alone. Perhaps you observed his occasional periods of silence?"

"Yes, I observed those. . . ."

"Out of respect to you," he said, nodding. "That is what they were, Father. My father is a talker of great skill, and with those he does not take a liking to, I have often seen him overwhelm them with his words. But with you he displayed another side."

"A becoming reserve," I suggested.

"*Exactly*. And now, Father, what of the news of Old Saint Paul's? I trust your additional labors are not proving too burdensome for you?"

My additional labors were not proving too burdensome for me, but with Father Danowski missing and no one to take his place, there was no doubt that they existed. Which is why — as I've said earlier — I had less spare time than usual for thinking about the Carmodys and their concerns. And when I did think about them, it was always with the feeling that one day, any day now, I would be hearing from them. In this I was right — although not quite in the way I had expected. For when I did hear, it was in the form of a visit rather than a telephone call, and my visitor was not Helen or John or even old Charlie: it was Dan.

He came to the rectory early one evening, a few days before Father Danowski was to be released from the hospital. I went to the door and there he was, alone, looking sharply pressed and vaguely sporty, something about him suggesting, as always, that he had just left the barber's chair five minutes before. He said, "Hello, Hugh. Surprise surprise."

It was indeed; he was a puzzling guest. Still, he was also a welcome enough one; he came in and after the first words of greeting I said, "I had no idea you were still with us, Dan. Somehow I thought that right after your father's party you were moving on to other fields."

"Other and *greener* fields," he said, correcting me. "Quite a bit greener, actually. Of course they'd have to be. There's not much for me in this city. There never was, come to think of it. I suppose it was a question of temperament and ambition as much as anything else. But I don't have to tell you that, do I? You spotted it years ago. I can't tell you, Hugh, how often I've looked back on what you said to me then and wished I'd had the plain common sense to follow it up. But you know how it is: a crazy kid won't listen. He knows all the answers; you can't tell him anything. It's a funny thing, Hugh, but I was talking about it to Flo only the other night. 'I don't have many regrets, Flo,' I said. 'I'm a happy man, doing well, and with a good wife. And yet I don't mind telling you that every now and then I think about what Father Hugh Kennedy said to me when we were still really only boys, and I wish I'd followed his advice. It would have saved me plenty of grief in the past!' "

And what was all this in aid of? What advice? Had I ever said anything significant to Dan about his life? No. Had I ever said anything at all to Dan about his life? No. I said carefully, "You remember my own words better than I do, I think. . . ."

He laughed and shook his head ruefully. "I have more reason to," he said. "With everything that happened. No, Hugh,

I remember it as if it were yesterday morning. I met you one day outside Casey's candy store; I think you'd just come back from your first year in the seminary. We talked for a while about nothing in particular — small talk, you know — and then all of a sudden, I remember, you put your hand on my shoulder and said, 'Dan, take my advice. Get out. Get out while the getting's good. Get out before we break your heart. This city's not for you, Dan. We're a city with a past, but we have no future. Whatever you try, we'll beat you down. We'll never give you the scope someone like you needs. We'll never even understand you.'" The blue eyes of his father now gazed at me — but in the son, they wavered just slightly. "How right you were, Hugh!" he said feelingly. "Oh, how right you were. If I live to be a thousand I'll never forget what you said to me that day. Don't tell me you don't remember!"

It was incredible; the conversation before Casey's candy store was as rooted in fact as those nonexistent football games we used to play. I said, "Not quite in those words. . . ."

"The land where time stands still, Hugh," he said. "That's what this town is. Conservative, old-fashioned, suspicious. You bring new business methods, new investment possibilities here, and they're on you like hawks. They hate new ideas, Hugh. They want that good old five per cent. At least a dozen times I tried to show them how they could double, even triple their original investments. I tried to put them on to a few good things I had. And what happened, Hugh? They misunderstood. They got the whole thing wrong. Once or twice they even got a little nasty about it. You may have heard something about that at the time."

At the time — or rather, at the times — it seemed to me that I had heard very little else; old Charlie was among those who had "got nasty." But this was hardly the moment for candor; I said that I had heard nothing of the kind.

"There was never anything to it, of course. But it did something to me, Hugh. I can't deny that. I got angry. I swore I'd

[183]

leave this town. And I did, right then and there. Ten years after you advised me to, but I finally left. It was the best move of my life. Ever since then I've been all over the world, I've met interesting people, I married Flo. I've been successful, Hugh. Highly successful. Successful in a way I couldn't have dreamed of being if I'd stayed here. And do you know what the key to that success has been, Hugh?"

I had no idea. From the general tenor of his approach to me, it wouldn't have surprised me greatly if he'd said, "Prayer." But when I shook my head, he said, "I've kept flexible. Flexibility's the answer, Hugh. Don't tie yourself down to a single narrow activity. Keep your eyes open; move around. That's what I've done. The result is that when I see a good thing I can jump aboard, right from the beginning. That's how I happened to get in with this new mutual fund group."

A faint memory of our last conversation rose to the surface; I said, "I thought you were in wool?"

"That too," he said instantly. "That too, Hugh. I usually manage to keep two or three balls in the air at the same time. Although to tell you the truth — and this is confidential: I wouldn't want it to get around — I'm thinking seriously about dropping the wool end of it. It's not what it used to be, Hugh. The new synthetics have hit it hard. No," he said, "I give most of my time these days to our mutual fund company. It's a fascinating business, Hugh. Highly competitive at the present time, of course, but our outfit is a little bit different from the others. Quite a bit different, as a matter of fact." And although we were alone in the rectory, his voice now dropped into a tone of confidence so low that it was barely audible. "I don't mind telling you who's in this with me, Hugh. Although I wouldn't want it to go any further." Dramatically he paused, then said, "Will Altgeld!"

"Will Altgeld?"

"You don't know Will Altgeld?"

Astonishment. Incredulity. I said, "No. Should I?"

"Well, no," he said, somewhat disconcertingly. "Not really. Because you're not primarily interested in the Who's Who of high finance, are you, Hugh? No. I didn't think so. You never were. I can remember back when we were kids together you were never much for thinking about money; you used to say, 'Oh, I'll leave that to Dan; that's his department. He has the head for figures!' But anyway," he said, "even if you *were* interested, you wouldn't necessarily know much about Will. He's one of the magic names, but he prefers to remain pretty much of a mystery. He's an enigma, Hugh. One of the most successful financiers of our time, but an enigma. There are sides to Will that nobody knows. He has a private chapel in his home, Hugh."

An enigma, but a pious enigma; I said, "Ah. . . ."

"As well as I know him," Dan said, "he never ceases to amaze me, Hugh! Here's the man who in two months, singlehanded, brought off the Farley-Poore collapse. Here's the man who really engineered the Otis Incorporated–Keisler Grain merger, no matter what you may have heard to the contrary. And at the very moment that merger was going through, at the very moment when some of the biggest men in the Middle West were breaking their necks to get in touch with him, where do you think he was, Hugh?"

"In the chapel?"

"Right!" he said. "That's a good guess, Hugh. That's just where he was. He was in the chapel. I don't know about you, Hugh, but a thing like that makes me stop and think. About myself. About other people I've been associated with, socially and professionally. Top men in their fields, Hugh. And what it all comes down to is this: I've never met a finer man than Will Altgeld! Or one that I was prouder to know!"

I decided it was time to pull the conversation back into some touch with reality; I said, "And so now you're with him in this mutual fund arrangement?"

He nodded enthusiastically. "We've really got something,

Hugh. Something entirely new. As Will said to me about a month ago, 'Dan, we don't promise our investors the moon. With the program we've worked out we can only promise them two things. One: *bigger* returns. Two: *quicker* returns. And do you know, Dan, somehow I have the feeling they won't object too strenuously to that?' " He laughed and made a motion with his arm; for a moment I thought he was going to nudge me in the ribs. But then he grew suddenly sober, and said gravely, "Actually, Hugh, that's why I'm still in town. I wouldn't be too eager to have this get around, but I've persuaded Will to let me tell a few old friends about our program. So that they can get in on it right from the beginning."

And it may have been that age had slowed me, or it may have been merely that what was happening was so ludicrous, so impossible, that I couldn't have anticipated it, but in any case it was not until Dan had spoken these last words, so earnestly, with such an attempt at conviction, that I realized what it was that he had really come to see me for. I said, "Dan —"

But he had started now; he was not to be stopped. "Naturally I thought of you, Hugh," he said hurriedly. "I don't know, I think it's probably always bothered me that I've never been able to do anything to repay you for the advice you gave me so many years ago. Oh, I know it didn't mean anything to you, but it meant all the world to me. I don't forget things like that, Hugh. I mentioned it to Flo only the other night, and what she said nearly knocked me over. She said, 'If you feel that way, Dan, don't you think it would be nice if you did something for him now?' And as I say, Hugh, it nearly knocked me over. Because it's so *simple*: the first thing I should have thought of the moment I saw you!"

I said again, "Dan —"

But it was no use; nothing short of a cannon shot could have stopped him now. The salesman's pitch had begun. It was something I was fairly familiar with; any priest who lives in a rectory for any length of time acquires great experience with salesmen. They come constantly and in great numbers: the wifeless cleric is a juicy target, an easy mark. They come selling shoe polish, life insurance, Cadillacs — anything. Depending pretty much on the apparent prosperity of the parish. Old Saint Paul's is largely ignored; the expert knows poor grazing grounds on sight. But in earlier years I must have met hundreds of them, and I suppose I even became a kind of connoisseur of their various approaches; now, as I sat looking at Dan, hunched forward in his chair, talking too eagerly and too quickly, smiling too confidentially, a natty but vastly imperfect mirror of his father in action, I suddenly found myself wondering if he had ever been able to sell anything to anyone. And of course he had; his narrow escapes from the wrath of purchasers were evidence of that. But it seemed to me now as step by step the "program" unfolded, and a sunlit pyramid of facts, figures, and tax-free benefits piled up before my eyes, that everything about him must have been a signal to the buyer to beware: the urgent glowing words, the laugh, the manner, each gesture, all suggested the carnival performer in his checked suit, manipulating the walnut shells over the concealed pea. And I wondered, as I listened, uncomprehending, to what he was saying, if there was any truth in it at all? For instance, was there really a program? Was there even really a Will Altgeld . . . ?

He continued to talk, growing more animated and euphoric by the minute, until finally — and loudly — I said, "Dan!" It must have been a shout, for now he did stop, abruptly, a look of bewilderment on his face. "What?" he said. "Did you say something, Hugh?"

I nodded. "I want you to do something, Dan, before you say anything more. I want you to look around. Around this room, that is. Take a good look."

Obviously still puzzled, but willing to go along with a customer's whims, he turned obediently, taking in the small drab office, so poorly furnished, so completely without a hint of prosperity. In short, a promoter's nightmare. But he turned back to me, smiling doubtfully, and said, "I don't get it, Hugh."

"You didn't look hard enough, then. I should have thought it was crystal-clear. Dan, we're a poor parish. I'm sure your investment scheme is all you say it is, but it couldn't matter less. We haven't any money to invest. The plain fact is that we haven't any money at all."

His face cleared instantly. "Oh," he said. "I see what you mean. You think I came over here to get you to invest parish funds?"

Had I wronged him, then? I said, "I'm afraid that's what I did think. . . ."

He laughed. "Come on, Hugh," he said. "Everybody knows that Old Saint Paul's hasn't had a quarter in twenty years. Why would I be doing that? No," he said, settling back into earnestness, "no, what I'm here for is to give *you* the chance, Hugh. Not the parish; you. What I'm talking about is a sure-fire investment for *you personally!*"

For me. Personally. Poor Dan. I said, "Look, Dan. First of all, thanks a lot. Its good of you to think of me. But you couldn't be barking up a worse tree. I haven't any more money than the parish. I'm just not an investment possibility at all."

This time the laugh was not free of anxiety. "You're joking, Hugh," he said. "I mean, of course I know you're not a rich man and that this isn't what you might call a boom period for you, but still, over all the years. . . ."

"The nest egg? It doesn't exist, Dan. At one time I did have a little money that my father left to me. Not much; a small insurance policy. But it went. Quite quickly and foolishly." I added drily, "You may have heard."

"I know, I know," he muttered hurriedly. "We're all proud of you, Hugh. Enormously proud. A great comeback. A fine example. But . . . look," he said desperately, "I may have mis-led you. As a matter of fact, I'm sure I did. You see, what's

[188]

needed isn't a *lot* of money. You don't have to be a million-aire. In fact you don't even have to have much at all; I'm actually almost embarrassed to tell you how little you need. We're letting a few of our friends in for practically nothing; just enough to get them started. . . ."

His voice trailed away as he saw that I still shook my head, and then, for no special reason other than that he looked so suddenly defeated, I went on to assure him that if I'd had any money, his proposition would have been close to irresistible. He did not seem cheered. Still, it was impossible for him to stay downcast for long; a long line of similar disappointments in the past must have fortified a natural resilience. After a moment he said, "Well, that's that. Although it's a shame, Hugh. It really is. I could have put you in the way of a first-class thing. A once-in-a-lifetime proposition. But that's the way it goes." He said suddenly, "I don't suppose, by the way, you know of any other priests around who might be interested?"

Had this become his specialty? Was he "working" priests these days? I said, "No, I don't think so. . . ."

He continued as if I hadn't said a word. "They'd have to be close friends of yours, of course. I could only take them in on that basis. As a personal favor to you."

"I can't think of a single soul, Dan." As a precaution against any further relaxation of standards, I added, "Close or other-wise."

"I see." There was silence. "Well," he said, "that's the way it goes." And I remembered that on at least two occasions I had heard old Charlie breathe approximately this phrase: was it a family formula of resignation? Except that Charlie remark-ably combined it with his victories; Dan, more traditional, used it in defeat. There was a difference.

But now he got to his feet; his mission, while unsuccessful, was over. "Well, Hugh," he said, "I'm sorry it didn't work out. It would have been a great thing. But it's grand to have seen you again, anyway. And your place." Once more he glanced hastily around the room in which we sat. "And your place," he repeated. "Very nice. Very nice indeed. Fine. I have to go along now and tidy up a few odds and ends before I leave town. I expect to be pulling out early tomorrow morning. I'd like to stay around a bit longer, but business before pleasure. Will seems to need me out there; apparently everything's moving along in a hurry. Bigger and better than we had anticipated, in fact."

Presumably "out there" was headquarters: the lair of Will Altgeld; I did not ask. I walked with him to the door, and then, just before he left, I couldn't resist asking, "You haven't suggested to your father that he come in on this with you?"

"No," he said quickly. "No, I haven't done that, Hugh. Dad's a fine businessman, of course, and he'd see the potential in a minute, but he's a little too conservative, a little too *inflexible*, if you know what I mean, for this type of operation. I think he might very well get the wrong idea. So I don't plan to mention it to him. As a matter of fact, Hugh, I'd just as soon you didn't say anything when you see him."

"I won't. Not a word." Then, half facetiously, I said, "Your program is safe with me."

"Yes, well, I wasn't thinking about the program. Exclusively, that is. What I really meant was that I'd appreciate it if you wouldn't mention my being here at *all*. You see, Hugh, I don't believe he knows I'm in town at the moment. We had a little talk the other day, and I think that somehow he got the impression that I was going off to the West Coast. Immediately. So that if he found out that I was still here he might be a little surprised, don't you see? Not that it matters of course, but he might misunderstand."

I had a sudden hunch: old Charlie had very probably supplied funds for the California trip. In the past he had often — if reluctantly — come through with what could be described only as get-away money for his son — had Dan now pretended the need for this once more? But it was hardly my business. I promised I would say nothing, and he left with a jaunty enough wave and a cheery farewell; he had quick powers of recovery. He drove off to his greener fields in a new, lime-colored convertible, and just as he was pulling around the corner I noted a final and rather characteristic touch: the car had dealer's plates. Was this another instance of Dan's boasted flexibility? Or was there merely somewhere in the city an unsuspecting dealer, hopeful of a quick sale? Either alternative was highly probable. . . .

Two days later Father Danowski returned from the hospital: paler, thinner, but otherwise unchanged. And on this day, in the early afternoon, I had another surprise visitor: old Charlie. He had forsaken the telephone to appear in person; like his son Dan forty-eight hours before, he stood waiting for me on my doorstep. And when I saw him standing there, memory worked one of its queer tricks, and all I could think of was something my father had said many years before.

"There are two men in this city that come to your house and they're always smiling," he had said. "One is Father Phil Riley from the missions, and the other is Charlie Carmody. I like Phil Riley the best. The smile means nothing at all, but at least a man knows what's behind it. He's come to tap you for a dollar and ten cents to help put up a clay statue of some little Italian that went out to the jungle two hundred years ago and put trousers on the black lads and stole bananas from the baboons and now they've decided he's a saint. But with Charlie it's not so easy. The smile is on his face, all right, but the minute you open the door he's into his dance, don't you see, running up and down the piazza, saying ain't it a lovely day today, and do you think the tomatoes will get ripe early this year, and do the little children still play hopscotch down by the barn? I swear there's times God Almighty Himself could hardly tell what he has up his sleeve!"

But this afternoon the smiling Charlie was a miracle of forthrightness. After the briefest of greetings he said briskly,

[191]

"Well, Father, they tell me you had a caller the other day!"

So the circumspect Dan had not been successful; however he knew, old Charlie undoubtedly did know. Still, I had made a promise; I could at least go through the useless motions. I said, "Caller?"

"Dan," he said. "My boy Dan. That's the caller I mean, Father. Oh, I tell you, Father, you're a lucky man! Havin' Dan come to see you is like havin' old King Rothschild himself drop in for a cup of tea! You'll be a rich man in no time now, Father! Is it a new way to make gasoline out of pump water he's got these days? Or I wonder is it a jelly bean mine? Whatever it is, put your money in Dan's hands, Father, and your fortune's made!" He said sharply, "You gave him nothin', I hope?"

But this was an old war, and none of my affair; besides, I suspected Dan might be having trouble enough without any help from me. I said "Actually, he just came by to say hello."

"Hello," Charlie repeated grimly. "Oh, I know these hellos, Father. I heard these hellos almost all my life." More moderately, he said, "But so long as you gave him nothin' I s'pose no harm is done. Where is he off to now, did he say?"

Solicitude? Parental concern for a fifty-year-old fledgling? I thought not; it was just Charlie, checking up thoroughly. I said carefully, "I think he mentioned something about the West Coast."

"The West Coast," he said. "Or China. Or the South Pole. It don't matter much. They all got telegraph offices. I'll be hearin' soon enough. Oh, I tell you, Father, there's a cross for a man to bear! Along with everything else. I don't wonder people walk around the city today and say, 'There goes poor Charlie Carmody. It's a miracle he ain't all bent over with all he has to put up with, what with Roosevelt and the big taxes and Dan!'"

In all this we had not moved away from the front door, and now I suggested to old Charlie that we go inside to the small

[192]

office — where, presumably, we would continue to discuss Dan. But he shook his head and said, "No no, I didn't come to stay, Father. I was just over this way lookin' at a buildin' or two I still got in spite of everythin' and I stopped by here on my way to the hospital. Would you go over there with me, I wonder, Father? Just for a bit? To say a few words to Bucky?"

This was a surprise: both the invitation and the news. I said, "Is Mr. Heffernan in the hospital? I'm sorry; I hadn't heard. What happened: anything serious?"

"No no no," said Charlie, almost contemptuously. "Nothin' like that, Father, nothin' like that at all. Bucky's a great man for hospitals. There's some of us goes through aches and pains every day that'd kill most men, but we do what we got to do and say not a word about it. Not a single word, Father: that's the way some of us do. But if Bucky wakes up with so much as a sneeze in the mornin' he's halfway to the private room and the nurse and the thermometer in the mouth like a cigar. And the wife lets him go; I think she's tickled pink. She leads a hell of a dull life, Father, sittin' there every night, hookin' rugs and lookin' at Bucky. Well well," he said expansively, "that's the way life goes. We mustn't complain."

Once again the old refrain. But he had provided an out for me, for while I was used to hospitals, and went to them often as a priest, I wasn't especially eager to make a trip to one just to see a malingering Bucky. And so I said, "I'm relieved to hear that nothing's really wrong, Mr. Carmody. And I think that in that case I won't go along; it might be more of an intrusion than anything else. . . ."

But Charlie was having none of this. "Not so fast, Father!" he said instantly. "Not so fast, there. We got to be fair. We got to be fair to Bucky!" Had I been unfair, then? But Charlie continued, swiftly back-pedaling. "I don't say for *sure* he's got nothin' wrong with him. I couldn't say that at all. I don't know what he's got. Oh, he's always been a great one for goin' to the hospital for what you might say was the fun of it, but that don't mean he ain't got somethin' *now*. By God, Father, a man could die of a hangnail when he's as old as Bucky. If someone came up to me on the street and said, 'Excuse me, Mr. Carmody, I know what a busy man you are, but I wonder could you tell me what Bucky Heffernan is like these days?', d'ye know what I'd have to say to them, Father? I'd have to say that Bucky was like an old wool sweater that looks fine and that you think could last forever, and then all of a sudden one day one little thread comes loose and before you can say 'Jack Robinson' the whole damn thing is nothin' but a puddle of yarn on the livin' room floor! And nobody knows that any better than Bucky himself, Father. I tell you, I wouldn't be s'prised if that ain't what he's thinkin' about right now, lyin' there on his back in his little room. A man at his time of life, Father, if he ain't really dyin', is doin' the next thing to it: he's *thinkin'* about it. That's why it'd be a lovely thing to go over there today and say a few nice words to him. Just to cheer the man up."

I had my doubts about the cheering effect of Charlie in the sickroom: would he hearten the moribund Bucky by telling him about the puddle of yarn? The extraordinary thing was that as he talked his voice was hearty and detached, as if, in discussing the thoughts of the old and the possibly dying, he was able to exempt himself completely from any connection with such a fraternity. He kept on talking, and in the end — which means, I suppose, in a very few minutes — I agreed to go with him, although I was by no means convinced that the trip was necessary or even desirable; invitations from old Charlie had a way of inspiring uneasy reservations. . . .

I went upstairs to change, and before I came down again I looked into Father Danowski's room to tell him I was leaving. He was not there; I had not heard him walking about, but obviously the convalescent was stirring. At the head of the stairs I looked down and saw that he was in the front hall — and that he had already joined Charlie.

"Here you are, Father!" Charlie cried, sighting me. "Oh, I

tell you, Father, ain't this one for the books! Would ye believe this one? I knew this lad when he was a little feller no higher than a hydrant! And now look at him: a giant of a man and a priest to boot! Ain't that grand? Oh, don't that make me feel good! The very same lad you got for a curate today once upon a time lived in one of my nice houses over in the East End! There's a coincidence for you, Father! What d'ye think of that one?"

"I had begun to walk around slowly upstairs," Father Danowski said sedately to me, "for the purpose of exercising my legs, Father. The physicians impressed upon me the importance of doing this. Suddenly I looked down the stairwell and whom should I see before my eyes but Mr. Carmody! I recognized him instantly, of course, from former times, and came down to make myself known to him. As I was just a small boy in those days, little did I dream that he would remember me!"

"Not remember you!" cried Charlie. "Oh, that's a good one, Father. Old Charlie not remember little Kazmeer!"

"No no," Father Danowski said gravely. "Casimir is the name of my father, Mr. Carmody. *My* name is Stanley."

"Right you are!" said Charlie exuberantly. "Little Stanley! Oh my! Those were the great days. I can remember it all like it was yesterday. In I'd walk to the East End tenements to collect the rents, and there'd be little Stanley and his little Polish pals lookin' at me with big eyes and sayin' to themselves, 'Here comes Mr. Carmody with the penny candy and the gumdrops!'"

This last had the savor of the myth, but Father Danowski did not comment upon it. Instead he said, "My father is the one who has always recalled those days with a special affection, Mr. Carmody. How often, through the years, he has spoken of your visits!"

"Kazmeer," said Charlie. "There was a fine man for you: always on time with the rent. God never made a finer man. I tell you, the world'd be a better place today if we only had

[195]

more Kazmeers. And how long ago was it he died, Father?"

"No no no, Mr. Carmody. You have been misinformed, I see. My father did not die at all. On the contrary, I assure you, he is quite alive. Alive and in the very best of health."

"Ain't that grand!" Charlie said. "Alive! Oh, that's the way to be, all right. And now you're over here with the son of my best old pal. Over here with Father Hugh! Oh, ain't life funny? We never know! I tell you, Father, you're a lucky man. You couldn't find a better boss in the whole diocese than Father Hugh, here. Or a holier one!"

Father Danowski inclined his large head in solemn politeness; I said quickly, "Will you be the boss yourself here for an hour or so, Father? I'm off to the hospital with Mr. Carmody to see a friend."

"To see Bucky on the bed of pain," Charlie said. "Yes, we got to be goin'." Addressing himself once more to Father Danowski, he said, "Well, Father, you're in a grand old place here. It might not look like much now, but once upon a time it was the best there was. They came no finer than Saint Paul's. The showplace of the diocese, you might say. The pride and joy." And then, with that special gift which must have been literally invaluable to him in his business affairs, that gift of somehow darting instantly at the vulnerable spot, he said musingly, "I s'pose it could be so again."

It was irresistible bait; Father Danowski leaped. "Do you feel that, Mr. Carmody?" he said eagerly. "How happy I am to hear you say so! If Father will permit me, it is what I myself have strongly felt —"

"Oh, yes, yes," Charlie said, and now a soft and decidedly dreamlike expression settled on the old face, "I got a great feelin' for Old Saint Paul's. When I look at it today, all run downhill the way it is, I tell you there's times I feel like cryin'. I dunno, maybe I'm too soft-hearted for my own good. I s'pose I am. But nothin' in the whole wide world would make me feel better, Father, than to see the old place neat as a pin, bright and shinin' once more like it used to, the whole shebang all done over in great style, with the organ boomin' away, and the crowds of people knockin' each other over tryin' to get inside of a Sunday! Oh my, wouldn't that be a grand sight! Wouldn't that make me feel good!"

Father Danowski said fervently, "It is truly extraordinary, Mr. Carmody, how close your feelings in this matter are to my —"

"And what would it take?" asked Charlie rhetorically. "What would it take to make this a grand old place again? Would it take a miracle? It would not! A few buckets of paint, a scrubbin' brush, a little cement, and a couple of carpenters and there'd be your miracle for you! Oh yes, all it would take," he said softly, *"is just a little bit of money!"*

There was a hush; the old, bright blue eyes were fixed upon their object in the gaze which was open, innocent, inviting, *kind;* Father Danowski stood there, open-mouthed, hypnotized. All unsuspecting, he had started out to exercise his legs; he had blundered into the realization of his dreams! But it was becoming a cruel performance; I said, "Cash isn't necessary, Mr. Carmody; we'll take your check."

The blue eyes shifted quickly to me, and I saw that the guilelessness had been replaced by a look of quite another kind — one of shrewd, hard amusement. And was it my imagination again, or did one old eyelid drop in a tiny, flashing wink? In any case he said, "Oh my my. You're your pa's son, Father, and no mistake about it. A chip off the old block. I tell you, just hearin' your voice speakin' up like that so clear and saucy does me good." And while he was saying this he had turned to Father Danowski; before he had finished he was already shaking his hand and beginning his retreat. "Well, goodbye, Father," he said crisply. "Maybe we'll meet again some day."

Opportunity was fading, fast; Father Danowski leaned forward as if hoping to catch up with it before it disappeared entirely. He said hurriedly, "Perhaps we could continue to discuss this matter at some other —"

But Charlie was already at the door. "Goodbye!" he cried. "It was grand to see you. And give my regards to your dear pa Kazmeer. Tell him I remember him and I'm tickled to death he's still alive! It's great to be alive! Come along now, Father. Poor Bucky's waitin' for us, and you can't say 'Hold on there!' to a dyin' man. Come along or we'll miss the visitin' hours!"

So, with a nod to Father Danowski, I left the rectory with Charlie. And on our way out to his waiting car, it seemed to me that on every step of this short march down the steps and across the sidewalk we were accompanied by my curate's eyes, following along behind us: large, round, baffled, disappointed, but somehow still lit with a reawakened hope, and unwilling to let go. . . .

Charlie did not employ a chauffeur; he drove himself. His car was large, old, and unfashionable; he drove it slowly and with excessive care. As we rode along, traffic piled up behind us on the narrow streets; horns blew impatiently; on those few occasions when a car behind did succeed in pulling out and passing us, I saw angry faces and furious eyes; sometimes there were shouts. To all this Charlie paid no attention at all; I doubt if he was even aware of it. He seemed in an especially benign mood, perhaps placed there by his fortunate encounter with Father Danowski; he drove along serenely and talked of the blessings of the automotive age.

"You can get from here to there in a minute and a half now," he said. "If I could of done that when I was a lad just startin' out, Father, I'd be a rich man today. But I didn't learn to drive a car until I was near fifty; all my boys and Helen too could drive before I did. I took trolley cars and walked. All over the city. I didn't mind. I'm a great walker, Father. I always was. I walked every inch of the city in my time, keepin' my eyes open, collectin' the rents. I bet I got more miles on me now than any man alive. Your pa was a great walker, too. D'ye remember that, I wonder?"

I nodded. As a young boy I had often gone on long walks — very long walks — with my father. They were never walks with any particular destination — or at least I never took them to be so. We just walked and walked, anywhere, and then at some point my father would decide we had walked far enough, and we would turn around and come home. But as I remember it, unlike Charlie we did not walk all over the city; in that day, the city, although large enough, was of course considerably smaller than it is today, and easier to get out of — a mile or so from our house, and we were in the country. Not wild country, certainly, but pleasant rural country, with hayfields and farms and barns and cattle and small, unforbidding woods — it was here that I remember walking with my father.

Charlie must have been reflecting along almost exactly the same line, for he said now, "Your pa was a queer man when it came to the walks. Many's the time I'd see him startin' off by himself, and I'd say to him, 'For the love of God, Dave, if it's a walk you want, why don't you stop all this foolishness and come along with me and I'll show you what a real walk is. A sensible walk. We'll go down the Boulevard to Sheridan Avenue to have a look in the stores and see who's buyin' what, then over to Division Street down past the depot and see is the rubber company layin' anybody off, then out to the East End while I make a few little calls, and back up through Little Italy to watch the Eyetalians havin' one of their nut parades and maybe see if a place or two is up for sale, and then home by way of the car barn. That's the kind of a walk that makes sense!' But he wouldn't come along," Charlie said, "not ever. Instead he'd start off on the railroad ties out to Limpy Coyle's meadow, and from there he'd go miles and miles to who knows where. I swear to God where he went there was no place to go. And nothin' to see. I remember one night I was just gettin' home to my supper about dark, and I looked down the street and who did I see walkin' along, slow and easy, like they'd just gave him the Bank of England for his birthday, but your pa. And I ran down from the house to him and I said, 'I s'pose you're just back from the walk?' And he said, 'I am.' And I said, 'All right. Now tell me this: you been gone the whole of the afternoon.' 'No, Charlie,' he said, 'I been gone the whole of the *day*.' 'All right then,' I said, 'so much the worse: you been gone the whole of the day. And what I want to know is this: in all the whole day, what did you see? Did you see anythin' at all? Anythin' worth seein', I mean?' And what d'ye think he said? He said, 'I'll tell you what I saw, Charlie. I saw a couple of cows, a brook, a hawk, a haystack, and a sunset. That's what I saw, Charlie!' And by God, Father," Charlie said, "I give you my word he meant it! The whole day, and that's what he saw! Oh, he was a queer man on the walks."

And of all the times that Charlie had mentioned my father to me, it was only now that what he said moved me at all, or indeed even made sense to me — I suppose because it was only now that what he said rang true. For once Charlie had neglected to supply my father with that absurd dialogue meant to suggest infrangible old palship; instead, he had dredged up a recollection so genuine that I could hear my father's voice. Moreover, in the telling of this story Charlie's own voice and manner seemed to have changed; it was as if, quite without realizing it, he had succumbed to his own memories. That is, as if he had been so caught up in his reflections that he had temporarily forgotten whatever role it was that he was playing for my benefit and had been, quite simply, himself. For the first time I had the impression that he had said what he would have said whether anyone had been with him or not, and it occurred to me that this surely must have been among the rarest of events: old Charlie saying exactly what he thought. . . .

But it did not last; he said suddenly, "Old Saint Paul's: it's a ramshackle old place you got there today, Father. I hear there's those that think the Bishop will tear it down and sell it for scrap."

It was clearly a question; Charlie waited for an answer. Had we come to the point at last? Had John been right? Was his father now about to present himself as the logical receiver of dismantled churches and — of course — their attendant properties? Was this really why I had been so suddenly cultivated as a chum? It seemed so, certainly, and — pompously enough, I'm afraid — I said, "I keep hearing that, but I don't know anything about it. It's my own guess that the Bishop has no intention of tearing down or selling."

But he surprised me by quickly agreeing with me. "I hope not," he said. "I dunno why he would. There's no place in the diocese means more to us all than Old Saint Paul's. Tearin' it down would be like tearin' down half the city. No no, I hope he don't do anythin' crazy like that!"

And strangely enough, I believed him. I think Charlie was not often ruled by the softer sentiments, but he had spoken these words with something very close to fervor, and I could only conclude that although the razing of Saint Paul's might ultimately put money in his pocket, he preferred — for whatever private and mysterious reasons — to see it upright and intact. A small inconsistency — as my father used to say, "Like the time Queen Victoria gave five pounds to the Famine Fund"— but there it was, and since it was, I was as far away as ever from the secret of what he was really up to with me. I decided now to pursue the theme of Saint Paul's a bit; I said, "It's not impossible that it could be renovated to some extent. I think that Father Danowski even had the feeling that you were about to take on the project yourself."

"Little Kazmeer!" he said enthusiastically. "Oh my, they come no better than Kazmeer. A grand lad." He added thoughtfully, "But he's like all the Poles, Father: *they got no sense of humor.* No no, they can't tell when you're havin' a little joke with them!"

[201]

Sentiment stopped, apparently, this side of madness; Charlie had been saved by his sense of humor. Poor Father Danowski.

We reached the hospital. As we rode up in the elevator Charlie said, "I s'pose P. J. will be here. He don't do much these days, so he comes in and spends his time with Bucky. Mostly he goes to sleep. And then there's the other feller. Bucky couldn't get a private room this time; they were all full up. So he's in with another feller. A feller that says nothin'; I dunno is he a dummy or not. By God, if he ain't Bucky'll drive him dumb with his line of gab!"

He chuckled happily at the thought; we got out of the elevator and walked down the corridor to the room of the ailing Bucky. When we entered he was sitting up in bed, his chin in his hands, his elbows supported by his knees, his attention fixed on a television set located some ten feet away. My immediate thought was that the sick man looked remarkably well. As predicted, P. J. was in the room; as also predicted, his eyes were closed. The silent roommate I could not see, yet I knew he was there, for in the second bed was a curled and invisible figure, sheet and blankets pulled up tightly over his head. Was he so ill as to want only this dark, small isolation? Or was this rather a protest against the television set, which seemed to be turned up to its full volume? As we came in, Charlie had to shout to make himself heard.

"Here we are, Bucky!" he cried. "Here we are! Myself and somebody else you didn't expect to see in a month of Sundays! Hello, P. J. Look who I brought along with me today, Bucky! Look who I brought all the way over here to have a word with you! Here's Father Hugh Kennedy himself! Ain't that grand? Speak up, Bucky! Say hello to Father, here!"

It was a boisterous entrance to a sickroom. P. J. opened his eyes, murmured quietly, and smiled slightly. Bucky, however, looked up, frowning, and said shortly, "Hello, Father. For the love of God, Charlie, quiet down! Be fair! Be considerate to all!" Was he concerned about his roommate? His fellow patients? Apparently not; he said, "I'm watching my program."

Charlie said nothing, but raised his eyebrows at me in an expression of great magnanimity, suggesting that he would endure much to humor a sick friend. We sat down and watched the final moments of Bucky's television program. It was lugubrious entertainment. A stout, plain-faced, middle-aged woman was standing on a stage, a false tiara perched ludicrously on her head; she was weeping. By her side a small man was jumping up and down, winking and laughing; he was like a demented puppet. From time to time he addressed the weeping woman facetiously as "Your Majesty." Suddenly he began to push gifts at her. Piles of gifts: flowers, fruit, furs, candy, articles of clothing, a portable radio, a food freezer.

"She's the winner," Bucky said superfluously.

There were greater rewards which would come when the program was over: a tour of night clubs; dinner with a film star; a ride in a helicopter. Each new item of largesse was proclaimed by the small man in an exultant, bullying voice; he continued to wink, jump, and laugh. The woman, for her part, continued to cry, and I wondered why. Hysteria? Sheer joy? Did the puppet and his presents stand for dreams come true . . . ?

The program ended; Bucky sighed and said, "That's a grand program. One of the very best I watch. Turn it off, Charlie. There's nothing on now but the cowboys."

P. J. opened his eyes again and said unexpectedly, "I like the cowboys. The daughter has a television and I watch the cowboys all the time. It's very easy to tell the good fellers from the bad. The good fellers wear white hats and eat apples."

Charlie, snapping the set off, said with some irritation, "That's the damnedest thing I ever saw, that program there. What in the name of God was all that nonsense, Bucky?"

"No nonsense at all!" Bucky said sharply. "There's no nonsense to a program where people do grand things for other people, free and for nothing. Don't say nonsense to that one,

[203]

Charlie! The whole wide world is against you there! I leave it to Father if that's not so!"

The arbiter. I said, "I saw so little of the program I don't think I'm quite sure what it was all about. . . ."

"Do good to your neighbor!" he said. "*That's* what it's about, Father. The women come up to the man there with their hard luck stories every day and he helps them out."

"I see by the paper Rose Gormley died the other night," P. J. said. "There was a woman had hard luck. D'ye remember Rose? She married Funny Phil Hanrahan that sold the soda? A very homely man. I don't s'pose I ever saw a homelier man than Funny Phil. But a beautiful singer. He had a lovely voice. That's the only reason Rose married him. She was very musical. And then what happened? She went deaf! A year after they were married, she was deaf as a post! That's hard luck."

"One moment there, P. J.!" Bucky said. "Don't make too much of Rose. She was a hard luck woman, yes. We're agreed on that. I knew her well. But she wasn't in it with these women on the television. These women have all got husbands that left them or they're sick and they'll never get better or somebody swindled them out of their last nickel or their house got smashed to bits in a hurricane. And the man on the program helps them out! The one that wins he gives grand things to!"

It was the pictorial version of Mrs. Addione's radio; I said, "And the winner: how is she chosen? Is she the one who's had the hardest luck of all?"

"That's it!" he said approvingly. "You're getting it now, Father! The hardest luck of all is the thing!" He went on with the enthusiasm of the true fan. "Sometimes it's very close. Sometimes you can't tell at all. Oh, I'd hate to be the judge on some of them! But today it was easy. Today you could tell from the start. The woman that won is a widow that's got bad sugar diabetes and her daughter got hit by a bus."

Charlie snorted. "So they give the woman a box of candy and a ride in an airplane. By God, that'll make everythin' fine! Maybe she'll have more good luck and fall out of the plane. Then she can come back on the program again and win more crazy stuff!"

"That's it, Charlie!" Bucky said angrily. "That's the way! Be like you always were and always will be! Laugh at things you don't understand! Like giving away things for free! Be careful, Charlie! Don't laugh at charity! The wisest men we've got don't dare to laugh at charity! Let alone the man who used to charge his very own kids dimes to ride downtown with him in his automobile!"

It seemed a time for intervention; I was about to break in with at least an intended pacifying word when Charlie made another of his sudden switches and said soothingly, "Now now, Buck, don't get all riled up. I meant no harm. Old Charlie don't visit his pals in hospital to pick fights with them. Watch the television as much as you like. I don't give a damn if they hand out diamond stickpins to every bum in the park with a bellyache. If it helps an old pal in hospital get well, I say good luck to them, Bucky! I take my hat off to them!"

Bucky looked at him with some suspicion; after a moment he said grudgingly, "All right then, Charlie. There's no offense taken where none was meant. Forgive and forget! We can't do better than that."

Charlie moved to another plane. "You're feelin' good today, Bucky?" he inquired solicitously.

It was the first time the sick man's health had been mentioned. Bucky nodded and said, "I am. Dr. Dan Doyle was in the first thing this morning. He said I can go home tomorrow. Or any time I feel like."

"Ain't that grand!" Charlie said admiringly. "Well well well. As quick as that! And at your age, too! I tell you, Bucky, there's not many people could do that. You'll live way past us all!"

With no pause, and in the same tone of high compliment, he said, "There's no trouble, I s'pose, in keepin' the hands and feet warm? They don't take cold at the tips of a sudden?"

"No no. Nothing like that," Bucky said. He seemed now faintly condescending. "You're way off on that one, Charlie. What I had was nothing like that. At no time."

I said politely, "What *was* wrong, Mr. Heffernan?"

He smiled. "Ah," he said. "What was wrong? That's the question, Father!"

"I met Johnnie Corrigan yesterday," P. J. said thoughtfully. "In front of the paper store. He looked very bad. I think he might of had a stroke or somethin'. When he talks he makes faces."

"He had no stroke!" Bucky said indignantly. "Talk sense, P. J.! I keep hearing that Johnnie Corrigan's had strokes! He's had none! Not a single one! I know! I talk to all the doctors! He makes faces because he always made faces! Even when he was a little kid! Did anyone say he was sick then? No! But now he makes faces and pretends he's had strokes!"

"They're different faces now," P. J. said. "Oh, very different!"

Bucky was not persuaded. "Everybody knows what's wrong with Johnnie Corrigan," he said. "And that's the same as it's always been: nothing! Not a blessed thing, P. J." He turned to me and said, "But they didn't know what was wrong with me, Father. They didn't know that. They tried to find out but they couldn't. I'm a great puzzle to the doctors, Father."

"But you're all well now," said Charlie. During the preceding exchange he had been patiently silent; now he said, "That's the thing that counts, Bucky. That's the thing I like to hear. All well! And goin' home tomorrow! I tell you, that makes me feel good. Was it just Dan Doyle said you could go, Bucky? He didn't bring in some big doctor to see was he right?"

"They come no bigger than Dan Doyle," Bucky said flatly.

"A good man," Charlie agreed. "Old, but good. Oh, I tell you, it must be grand to be all well again. The head is nice

[206]

and comf'table, I hope? No cracks when you switch it from side to side? No stabbin' pains in the back of the neck, there? Right over the collar button?"

Bucky looked at him; he said shortly, "Why would there be pains where I never had a pain in my life?"

Charlie's head bobbed up and down; the answer seemed to delight him. "Ain't that grand!" he said. "And no little sweats? You don't feel clammy at all?"

"No!" Bucky said, his voice suddenly very loud. "No I don't have little sweats! No I don't feel clammy! No I don't go blind two hours each day! No I don't swell up at night! I'm sorry to have to tell you that, Charlie, but I don't! Now what else is there? What else would you like to know? Aside from the fact that I feel only one way and that's A-Number-One! *That's* the way I feel!"

We were nearing another danger point, obviously, and again I went to cut in, but again this was unnecessary, for Charlie abruptly stopped his little game. So abruptly that I somehow had the feeling that his heart hadn't really been in it, that the needling of Bucky had been enjoyable but more or less automatic — just another of the little bonuses — but that his main purpose in coming here today was something quite different. He said now, "Easy, easy, Bucky. Is that a way to act when an old pal asks a few questions to find out are you as good as new? And when Father here comes all the way across the city just to see are you livin' or dyin'?"

From my point of view this was something less than the ideal approach, but it seemed to work. Although not completely: when Bucky replied it was obvious that a few feathers remained ruffled. He looked at neither Charlie nor myself but straight ahead, giving the impression that he was addressing the now inactive television set.

"Father knows I thank him," he said. "He's not the kind of a man that has to be told every little thing. He knows I feel all the better for his fine visit today. And he knows that, not just

[207]

because he's a priest, but because he's a decent sensible man that knows how to behave himself in a hospital! Not like some people that come in here and run around and yell and treat a man's sickroom like it was a zoo! Not like some people that could give a man a bad relapse! I mention no names, but they better be careful, those people! The doctors have been told! The whole hospital knows about them! They better mind their manners and be more like Father, here! There's the kind of a man does you some good when he comes to see you!"

The visitor whose very presence heals: since I'd been in the room, had I said ten words? No. Still, I had my uses: the wall off which all shots could ricochet.

Charlie gave no sign of having been hit. "Right you are, Bucky!" he said heartily. "Oh, right you are on that one! A few minutes with Father Hugh is like a month in the country! He's just like his pa for that. No one knows that better than me. Didn't I realize it today when I went over to Saint Paul's to pick him up, right when he was havin' one of the very busiest days of the year!"

This was quite untrue, but it was only the beginning. For now, as Charlie continued to talk, invention took over altogether; he reached new heights of fantasy.

"Oh yes," he said, "I went over in my car to pick up Father Hugh. I like to give him a little ride, a little fresh air, on a nice day like this. He's all cooped up in the parish there, and he don't like to leave because he's so busy. But he comes out every now and again for an old pal. I remember when I had the birthday, he said to me, 'I don't go many places these days, Mr. Carmody, because I got so much to do, but I'll come to your party if it's the last thing I do. I know that's the place my pa would want me to be on a day like this. Right by the side of his old pal Charlie!' I tell you, I damn near cried when he said that to me! Wasn't that a grand thing for a man to hear? But I hear lots of nice things from Father. Oh yes, I tell you we have the great talks about his dear pa and the good old

[208]

days. And when I went over there today and said to him, 'I'll tell you what's let's do, Father, let's forget about our little ride today and go over to see Bucky instead. What d'ye say to that?', well, I tell you, he had the coat and the collar on before I finished gettin' the words out of my mouth. 'Let's go, Mr. Carmody!' he said. 'Let's be on our way! Anythin' you say is all right with me, just like it would of been with my pa! Besides,' he said, with his grand little smile, 'I'd like nothin' better than to go over there and cheer Bucky Heffernan up!' So over we came, Bucky, the two of us. And oh, ain't we glad we did! Ain't we glad to see you up and around and lookin' so well! And to hear you're goin' home first thing tomorrow! Oh my, won't that tickle your lovely wife! I'll have to bring Father over to say hello to her one day soon! Oh, yes yes!"

Unexpectedly, Charlie had broadened the base of his spurious anecdotes: they now starred me, as well as my father. A wildly unrecognizable picture was emerging: a picture of me in my shabby rectory, drudging away like a dedicated mole, pausing only to glance anxiously at my watch — surely it must be time for my father's old pal to arrive to take me for my weekly ride! Charlie talked on; the picture grew in definition. The pal of the father had become the pal and patron of the son, and although Charlie did not say so explicitly, one somehow had the feeling that all this was in response to a deathbed request. I was, then, an inherited responsibility. But I was more than that; Charlie did not sell me short; our association was no mere one-way street; I too had something to give. Examining the dialogue assigned to me in this improvised reminiscence, I saw that I was insipid, yes, but I had my qualities: I was obliging, attentive, cheerful, consoling. In my grand little smile there lurked a quiet strength. . . .

It was maddening. Comic, too, I have no doubt, but at this moment mainly maddening — if only because I felt so helpless. Obviously I should do something — but what? Should I protest? If so, to whom? Bucky? P. J.? The roommate under the blankets? And against what? Charlie was committing no crime; at most he was intimating rather strongly that we were far closer friends than actually we were. Which was annoying, but hardly actionable. And against which — especially under the circumstances — the protest would have the rich ring of the fatuous: "Excuse me, gentlemen, but as a priest I am compelled by duty to inform you that the claims of this eighty-one-year-old man to that most highly prized of commodities — my friendship — are in fact quite without foundation!" No matter what the words, this was what was bound to come through; I was sure of it. And so I could do nothing. Nothing but sit and wait for the farce to finish. Did Charlie know this? Did he count upon it? I was certain that he did. The certainty made me feel no better.

And of course — once again — there was the question of motive. Why on earth was he going through all this? What possible end could these absurd stories serve? Because the fact that they weren't true was no doubt reprehensible, but it was not, after all, so astonishing. Charlie notoriously rode truth with a relaxed rein, and while fictional autobiography may not have been a family habit, it was a habit shared by at least one other member of the Carmodys: earlier in the week I had been a conspicuous figure in Dan's faked recollections. But that had been different; there was no mystery to that. Less gifted than his father, Dan could keep nothing up his sleeve; his purposes were crystal-clear and always the same: he wanted money. That was simple. But what did old Charlie want? That was not simple at all. . . .

I watched him now, bubbling along, and as I did, and saw the clear old face shining with enthusiasm, the bright blue eye occasionally turning to meet mine in a candid, fond, paternal gaze, without wavering an inch, without even the faintest touch of shame, I found that in spite of everything my annoyance began to disappear, and I began to feel not only a wry and slightly uncomfortable amusement, but also — I'm afraid

— a kind of awful, guilty admiration for the sheer unblemished gall of this incredible old man and his whole preposterous performance.

What P. J. and Bucky felt it was impossible to say. P. J. had closed his eyes again, and Bucky, who at first had been, if not fervently attentive, at least passive, now began to give every sign of a growing impatience.

"All right, all right!" he said at last. "All right, Charlie! One moment there! Hold on! There's other people besides yourself that knew Dave Kennedy. For the love of God, the man wasn't a stranger you met all by yourself on top of a mountain in Zanzibar! The man lived here every blessed day of his life! Right here in the city! There's plenty of people that knew him and liked him! Just as much as you. And there's plenty of people that know and like the son. Just as much as you!"

Charlie gave him a soft, almost a pitying, smile. "It ain't the same thing," he said mistily. "No, it ain't the same thing at all. I'd explain that one to you, Bucky, but you wouldn't understand. No no no. Not in a million years you wouldn't. But I don't blame you for that. It don't matter now anyways. All that matters now," he said, his voice suddenly springing out of the soft mists and ringing with bounce, "is that you're all well and goin' home tomorrow! *That's* what matters. *That's* what makes me feel good. Oh yes! Hooray for Bucky! My old pal is good as new again!"

And for a moment I thought he was going to circle the sickroom in one of his bounding, enthusiastic dances, but instead he remained by the bed and contented himself with pumping Bucky's hand vigorously. This terminal heartiness, if it did nothing else, at least forestalled further battle; a moment before Bucky's face had begun to darken again at the suggestion of mysteries he could not comprehend. Now, however, he seemed mollified, and when, a few seconds later, he thanked Charlie for coming in to see him, he did so in an almost effusive manner.

"You make a man mad at times," he said, "but you've got your good points, Charlie. I'm one man that says that!"

To me he said, "I thank you for coming here today, Father. I'll be over to see you one evening at your place as soon as they let me." He added significantly, "I've a matter to discuss with you. A matter I mentioned to you before. A matter one certain priest in the diocese won't be too happy about when he hears what I plan to do. One certain priest we all know well. I mention no names."

John and the grave; it was a talk to look forward to. I said goodbye to him and went over to say goodbye to P. J., but the old man rose from his chair and said in a thoughtful voice that since he had been here all afternoon, he now supposed that it was time for him to go home, too. And so the visit ended; we all said goodbye to Bucky once more, and then we left the room.

Or rather P. J. and Charlie left the room; as I was leaving, something curious and totally unexpected occurred. I was walking slightly behind the two old men, and as I came to the door, and as they were already in the corridor outside, I heard someone in the room behind me say, quite loudly, "Father!" The voice was not Bucky's. I looked back and saw that the roommate, whom by now I had completely forgotten, had emerged from under his blanket and was sitting up in bed. He was a man in his late fifties, I should guess: thin, mostly bald but with patches of dusty gray hair that had been mussed by the blankets, and with a great pale dome of a forehead that bulbed out prominently over the bony, rather pointed face below it — so much so that one's first impression was apt to be of the skull rather than of the man. Around his neck he wore scapulars and a medal on a silver chain; on his pajamas was pinned a small badge of the Sacred Heart. The pajamas themselves, I noted, were not hospital issue; they were blue pajamas on the right breast pocket of which had been stitched, in red thread, the single word *George*. I couldn't remember ever having seen

[212]

him before, but he nodded at me and smiled in an oddly expectant way — was recognition called for? Hurriedly, he beckoned me over to his bed.

"Hello, Father," he said. "How come you're over here, hey?"

So I was known, at least — but who was he? I said carefully, "Hello. How are you these days?"

But it was not enough. He looked at me anxiously, and said, "You don't know me? From the parish?"

So he was from Old Saint Paul's, which wasn't too much of a help: one more among the many, rather than the few, whom I still did not know, not even by sight. And of course the intelligent thing, the only thing, to have done was simply to admit this, but he seemed to want so badly to be known, and there was, after all, that clue on the pajama pocket: the irresistible temptation to the smooth deduction. I said, "Yes, of course. How are you, George?"

It was a mistake, clearly; he looked baffled and said, "George?"

In that case, whose pajamas? It didn't matter; he said urgently, "I'm *Albert*. You know me, Father. You know me good. Albert Savastano? The fruit stand? Up by the swill trucks?"

It was pinpoint identification: up by the swill trucks. Still, it did the trick: I knew who he was now. About a mile from the church, at the northern end of the parish, there was a side street where a row of empty sanitation department trucks usually stood parked; apparently they were now — at least to judge from Albert — a neighborhood point of reference, like a monument, or a cathedral. At the corner of that street there was a small fruit stand: a pushcart, really. It was filled with fruit which looked good and was good; often, in walking by, I had stopped to buy an apple or a pear. I must have passed the time of day fifty or sixty times with the vendor who stood under the umbrella in back of this cart, yet it never would have occurred to me to connect him with the man in bed before me now. True, I had at least some excuse: at his trade he wore, always, a great, broad-brimmed felt hat which concealed his mighty dome; without it he was to me unrecognizable. And then of course there was the old difficulty of coming upon the familiar object in unexpected surroundings. But excuse or not, the simple truth was I didn't recognize him because I'd never paid any attention to him; I'd never even bothered to find out his name. And so all I could do was to hope to ride over embarrassment, and to say, "I'm sorry, Albert. I didn't expect to see you here. What have they got you in for?"

"Stones," he said succinctly. "Look, Father: how you like that for a stone?"

He pointed to the white table at his bedside. On the table was a glass jar, and in the jar was a round, grayish, granular object about the size of a golf ball. Someone — a nurse? — had fixed a large gummed label to the jar and on it had drawn a crude picture of the stone. In the tradition of perky, postoperative humor, the stone was smiling; underneath it had been printed simply: *Albert*. It was more reliable, at least, than the pajamas. . . .

There was a pause; he was waiting. I said — warmly, I hoped, "That's some stone."

"You bet," he said proudly. "How you like to have a stone like that, Father? No good, hey? Like a rock. The biggest stone they had all year. The doc told me." He reached over and took the glass jar from the table; he held it up before him, inspecting it fondly. "You know what I do with this stone, Father? I keep it. The doc, he say, 'Go ahead, Albert. It's yours.' So I bring it home and put it somewheres." He laughed and said, a little abashed, "And why? What do I do with a stone?"

I said without thinking, "You could put your name on it."

And as soon as I said this I was sorry, because I didn't want to make fun of him, or hurt him. But it was all right; he merely nodded and said seriously, "Or paint it, maybe. Different colors." He put the jar back and said, still looking at it, "That's a real big stone, all right."

I said, "But you're feeling better now, Albert?"

"Oh, sure, sure," he said. "Real good. In two days, three days, I go home. Hey, Father, you been up by the stand lately? You're surprised I ain't there? You miss the good pears, hey?"

I'd been up in that district only three days before; I hadn't missed the good pears; I hadn't missed Albert. I hadn't even noticed they were gone. I said lamely, "You'd better hurry up and come back."

"Sure," he said. "You bet. Don't worry, Father. Real soon. You come up the first day, I give you a pear free! The kind you like: Comice. Good, big, juicy! On the house, Father!"

I thanked him, and promised I'd be there. I stood there, and there was another of those awkward pauses as we looked at each other in silence: with the fruit stand and the gall stones, we had exhausted our topics of common interest. From the corner of my eye I was suddenly aware of Bucky. He was leaning forward in his bed; without turning, I could just manage to glimpse the expression on his face. He was attending this scene with an incredulous and rather hostile curiosity: I was *his* visitor; here was encroachment! And this made me think in turn of P. J. and Charlie; I said, "Can I do anything for you here before I leave, Albert?"

"No," he said. "No thanks, Father. It's nice here. Real nice."

And then, not that it made any sense, because he was getting out himself in a day or so, but because, I suppose, I still felt a little guilty, I said, "Do you want me to deliver any messages for you? Tell anyone I've seen you?"

He shook his head. "No," he said. "I got nobody."

He said it cheerfully enough, and certainly didn't appear distressed; all the same, it was a sad and lonely thing to hear. Had I been his only visitor, then? Even if an unintentional one? Very probably; almost certainly. So I had performed a kindness as well as a pastoral duty. By accident. . . .

[215]

I left him now, and as I went out of the room I was careful to say goodbye to Bucky again — but in pantomime only this time: a smile and a wave. It seemed the more prudent thing to do. Out in the corridor I saw P. J. and Charlie; they had apparently been waiting impatiently at the nurses' desk, down by the elevators.

"Here he comes!" cried Charlie, in his voice not meant for hospitals. "Here he comes, P. J. By God, Father, we were just goin' to send the police out lookin' for you. We thought you might of got lost! Or that Bucky maybe threw a fit in there!"

I explained about the roommate; Charlie professed to be greatly impressed.

"Think of that!" he said, as we rode down in the elevators. "The first time the man's said a word since he's been in there! Ain't that wonderful, Father? Don't that show the powers of the clergy?"

And he looked at me with an innocent eye; I said nothing.

"From Old Saint Paul's," P. J. said musingly. "Savastano, is it? I s'pose there's more Eyetalians in the city today than anybody else."

"There was one time," Charlie said, "I had nothin' but Eyetalians in my tenements. They're a bad gang, the Eyetalians. Great big families, singin' and stampin' around all day and night, wearin' the buildin's out. The kids tear hell out of the plaster with their fingers!"

P. J. nodded. "Eyetalians have very strong fingers," he said. "That's why they make such good cobblers. Savastano," he said again, slowly. "I don't think I know him. There was a man named Sebastiano once lived over there. He used to play the cornet and dance in hotels. He called himself Don Peedro or some such name as that. So they'd give him the jobs. He was a nice young lad."

Charlie shook his head impatiently. "I don't know the man," he said, dismissing the subject. "I never heard of him."

"He died," P. J. said. "Very young. He was dancin' around

[216]

one night in cheap stockin's and got a blister on his heel. After a while poison got into his blood and he died. The boys and myself buried him."

"It's a hell of a note," Charlie said, "when a grown man can make a livin' runnin' around the city doin' crazy dance steps and callin' himself fake names!"

"Well," said P. J., "he's dead now."

Just deserts? We had reached the ground floor; as we walked out of the hospital to the car, Charlie said, "I'll ride you home, P. J. I'll drop off Father here on the way."

But I had decided against riding; it was a good day, and a long walk back to the rectory, and I felt like walking. I told this to Charlie; it met with his approval.

"Just like his pa!" he said. "And just like me! A great walker. Not like the rest of these young bums today. No no! All right then, Father. Have your walk and I wish I could join you. It was grand to see you anyways, and we'll be gettin' together soon." In an even louder voice he added — obviously for P. J.'s benefit, "As usual. As usual. Goodbye now, Father. And don't forget the prayers for Charlie. He needs them all!"

And so we all repeated again the formulas of farewell, and Charlie and P. J., in the huge old car — like themselves, I suppose, the survival of a more spacious age — rolled down the drive in slow monopoly, and I began my walk through the late summer afternoon, a walk away from old Charlie and his persisting mysteries, back to the plain predictability of home, of Father Danowski and of Old Saint Paul's. . . .

8

FALL CAME: always a lovely season in this part of the world. Old Saint Paul's was hardly the ideal observation post from which to glimpse its glories — the first frost brings no riot of color to the neighboring delicatessen — but the weather was clear and perfect, the days seemed to ring with the sharp autumn light, and all the smells of the season were in the air. In this section of the city we were virtually treeless, but all the same, every day, towards late afternoon, invisible smoke from burning leaves drifted in from somewhere. It was the time of year I'd always liked the best, and I suppose I still did, but now my ground had shifted slightly: as the pastor of Old Saint Paul's, I thought of the fall in terms of the coming winter — and I thought of the coming winter in terms of tons of coal. The rectory, with so much of it shut off, was easy — or at least relatively so — to keep warm; the church was something else again. It was only during the winter months that I became really aware of the sheer *size* of the place: the huge, drafty nave would have been a challenge to any heating system and was an outright defeat to ours. The old furnace was enormous, cumbersome, inadequate and voracious; coal disappeared like snow in May; fuel costs mounted at a staggering rate and easily became our most considerable parish expense. Despite this the church remained uncomfortable, and from mid-October until late in the spring pockets of damp, frigid air, seemingly sucked from the stones and impossible to dissipate, lurked in corners, the slightest opening of a door sending them swirling around the interior. Veteran parishioners knew the location of every steampipe; this did them some good, but not much. And, at the altar, saying Mass, I think I was never quite free of the anticipation that at any moment now the next bone-chilling assault would begin, as the frontal edge of some new cold-air mass knifed its way unpredictably towards my ankles, my neck, the small of my back. . . .

Which is something less than martyrdom, but which makes its impression all the same; at the beginning of the new winter I find I have no difficulty at all in remembering the old. Yet now it was still early in the fall, the days were pleasant rather than cold, and in those moments when I thought of thermostats and coal trucks and heating bills, I was content to think of them as being still some weeks away.

Not everyone was so dilatory. Roy, whose working tempo was ideally suited to the hot and drowsy days of summer, distrusted and feared the sharper months to come; by the end of September he had begun to plump for the heated church.

"Because why?" he asked rhetorically. "Because the doc said to Roy, he said, 'Roy, a man like you, he's a tiger, but his blood don't run in cold weather. That's what you got to watch out for, Roy. That cold weather. That blood just lays around, froze. You better be careful of that froze blood, Roy.' That's why," he said, "Roy dropped that great big box in church this morning when you was saying Mass. Whang on the floor from his cold hands! You hear the crash, Father?"

I had heard the crash all right, but when Roy was puttering around the back of the church, crashes were no novelty. I said unfeelingly, "I doubt that it would be the cold this early in the season. It might be some sort of circulatory condition that a minor operation could clear up nicely. I'll tell you what: why don't we run you over to Saint Vincent's Hospital sometime today? They could probably fix you up in no time at all."

So that stopped all complaints for that morning. But three days later he was back again: same thing, different tack.

"You know what Roy saw on his way down to church this morning, Father?" he said, meeting me in the front hall of the rectory. "On a puddle? Ice!"

"On the first of October?"

He was prepared for disbelief; he threw up his hands dramatically. "October one," he said, in an awed voice, "and *ice*. Boy! Don't that make you flip your lid, Father? Ice! Right there on the sidewalk. Roy put his feet down on it and *crunched* it." With his heel, on the front hall rug, he demonstrated the crunching of the ice. "And then," he said, "Roy said to himself, 'Roy, you better get on in there as fast as you can and tell Father about that ice. Else he ain't going to know why it was so cold in church this morning!'"

"Cold?" said Father Danowski, coming in, and overhearing this. "Why, Roy, it is sixty-nine degrees on the thermometer just outside the kitchen window. That is balmy, Roy."

Father Danowski had just finished his breakfast: he looked well fed, contented, warm. Roy scowled fiercely and stared down at the floor.

"And yet," said Father Danowski, "it is curious how little we know about cold. How little we understand of the manner in which it affects different individuals. Some of us feel the cold greatly. Some of us do not. As for myself, ever since those days when I was a small boy I have seldom worn an overcoat. Today I do not even own one. In the depths of winter I will wear a topcoat, yes, but that is all. That is no credit to me; it is simply that I am not affected by the cold. I was reading a most instructive article on this very topic in the *National Geographic* magazine only the other evening. Perhaps I have spoken of it to you, Father?"

"No. . . ."

[220]

"It was absorbing," he said. "It appears that there is a tribe of primitive Indians at the tip of South America who are positively immune to the wintry blasts of that forbidding region. They are clad in savage nothingness, yet on the coldest nights they sleep out of doors and on the bare ground, their bodies exposed to the driving snow and the wildest winds! How remarkable that is! Reflect on that, Roy: how much it teaches us of what the human being is capable!"

"Roy ain't no Indian," Roy said sullenly.

"There was no implication that you were, Roy," Father Danowski said, with that dreadful benignity again. "No no, that was not my point at all. We know that you are not an Indian, Roy. We know full well what you are. Here in the parish of Old Saint Paul's, you are the good right arm of Father and myself. That is what you are!"

Roy responded to this tribute by scowling more fiercely than before and rolling his eyes in his most threatening manner. Then he left us and went down into the church yard, muttering and shaking his head; as he passed the bottom step he kicked it, hard. Father Danowski watched all this with the greatest satisfaction. He had recently decided that he understood Roy, and had taken to viewing him in a more indulgent light.

"Look at him, Father," he said complacently. "See how embarrassed he is: it is unmistakable. And why? Because a few kind words were unexpectedly addressed to him. How wrong I was, Father, in once suspecting him. He is like a child: a great and awkward schoolboy!"

The schoolboy disappeared around the corner of the church; we did not see him again for nearly a week. He returned to the rectory rumpled, red-eyed, and still shaking; he had an explanation. He had been stricken by a sudden and paralyzing disorder.

"From his hips down to the ground," he said, "Roy could not move a muscle!"

[221]

Father Danowski returned to suspicion. "If you ask me," he said severely, "Roy has been *drinking*."

The fine weather continued; in spite of this, so did Roy's complaints against the cold church; I was not moved. Meanwhile, parish life went on, and the Carmodys began to become a part of it. Or, more exactly, not of the parish life, but of mine. Old Charlie came at least once every ten days or so, sometimes alone, sometimes with Bucky or P.J. He would talk at great length, always of my father and the old days; then, abruptly, he would rise from his chair in the little reception room and he would leave, the mystery of his visits still unsolved. And John came: he had telephoned once or twice, and then, one Sunday morning, and at his suggestion rather than mine, he came over to Saint Paul's to say Mass. I mention that it was his suggestion, not because I wasn't pleased to have him, but because the timing was so odd: both by custom and diocesan regulation each pastor is strongly encouraged to remain in his own parish on a Sunday morning. John knew this, of course; he referred to it when he telephoned to arrange for his coming.

"My flock can get along without their beloved pastor for a day," he said briskly. "It will do them a world of good. Not to speak of what it will do for me. As a matter of fact it all works out rather nicely: there's an extra hand staying in the house for the next week or so. A touring English cleric. A convert. Naturally. He's too good to be true, Hugh. He really *is* languid, loose-jointed, and impenetrable of speech. The absolute archetype. And with a wonderful chumminess about the Church; he speaks of the Apostles as if they'd just borrowed money from him. So I'll let him take over for me this Sunday. My only regret is that I won't be there to see my father's face as my replacement starts talking about 'Queer, dear old Saint John.' Still, we can't have everything. So I'll be over. Besides, it's important I come on a Sunday; I want to see your place at its peak."

[222]

And so he came, to say the eight-thirty Mass on Sunday. The church was perhaps a quarter full; this — whether he knew it or not — was the peak of which he spoke. A change indeed from jammed Saint Raymond's. I watched him from the sanctuary as he said his clear and beautifully articulated Mass: not a word slurred, not a movement slighted. I think that, in a way, I would rather have watched John Carmody say Mass than any other priest I knew. He was entirely at his ease in Latin — he had been from his earliest days in the seminary — and he had a swift, delicate dexterity which is rare and which is not at all the mere facility which can come with time and practice. And which can be dangerous: a certain glibness on the altar is more than just a bare possibility. For when we do anything, however important, over and over again, when by repetition we reach the point where we could do this thing without thinking, the danger is that we *will* do it without thinking. The result is that sometimes we will pray to God, say, in the same automatic way that we will tie our shoelaces. I mentioned prayer because it's so peculiarly liable to this sort of thing. We know our prayers so well and have said them so often that before we know it we've said them again — and again without a shred of thought or meaning. I suspect it's very hard for most of us to pray — to pray well, that is. The mechanical act of falling upon one's knees and saying The Lord's Prayer every day is one thing and a simple thing, but to say even the first half-dozen words of that prayer with the attention they deserve is quite another and not at all so simple. I think every prayer well said is a shot through a barricade — and the barricade surrounds the altar as well as anywhere else. The priest saying Mass knows exactly what he is doing, he knows that the words he repeats day after day are the gravest words he will ever speak, that they are in fact the very core of his belief and of his being, yet in spite of this there comes that moment when, with a sudden shock, he realizes that his mind has been wandering — for exactly how long he does not know

[223]

— and that the words of the Divine Sacrifice have been little more than a buzzing background blur. Which is a strong signal to keep his guard up in the future. But because the dangers of routine are what they are, and — more important — because we are what we are, this is easier said than done, and so, sometimes and unhappily, there are priests who unintentionally but carelessly begin to elide, to speed up, even to skip, until in their hands the Mass becomes a lightning travesty of itself, and startled parishioners find that they are out of church almost as soon as they came in.

Of this John was never guilty. Judged by the standards of the stop-watch, his Mass was undoubtedly what could be called a "fast" Mass, yet what counts is not minutes and seconds, but one's attitude, and his was one of reverence and attention. I think it was here on the altar that he was really at his best as a priest, for it was here that one could see a side of him that was nowhere else revealed, and it was here too that one had not the slightest awareness of the brusqueness or impatience that otherwise trembled almost visibly beneath the surface of his skin.

His sermon that Sunday was on actual grace. It was a crisp and intelligent sermon; it would have gone over extremely well in a seminary classroom. Here, in the decidedly nonacademic atmosphere of Old Saint Paul's, I had my doubts. So did John. Back in the rectory after Mass, he said, "Hardly a turnaway crowd, would you say?"

"No. But then there's this consolation, if you need one: it's as turnaway as we get."

"I was devoured by a pair of Chinese eyes," he said. "I spotted the owner right at the beginning of the sermon; he stayed with me to the bitter end. Very flattering. Is he one of the regulars?"

"Oh yes. That's the invaluable Mr. Yee." Should I tell him of Mr. Yee's unfortunate limitation? I thought not; under the circumstances, surely, this detail was better omitted.

But I needn't have bothered even to think about it, for he said immediately, "Mr. Yee speaks no English, I imagine? And understands none?"

I said, "I'm afraid that's about it."

But all he said was, "Lucky man." He finished his coffee and said, "Thanks for the hospitality. Now, where's my coat, and I'll be on my way."

"So soon?" He had said nothing of his plans for the day, but somehow I'd expected a longer visit. I said, "Don't rush off. Stay a while; savor our local scene. Saint Raymond's can wait for an hour or so."

"Or forever, if it were up to me," he said. "But I'm not going back to Saint Raymond's. Not right away, that is. I thought that as long as I was taking the day off I'd drive out to Deerford. I haven't been back there since I was transferred. By your omnipotent friend, His Excellency."

I passed this over and wondered: a sentimental journey? A pilgrimage back to happy days? It sounded unlike him, and indeed it would have been; he explained by saying, "Actually, I've got to go out there sooner or later. I left some things — books, etc. — that I need, and then I ought to look in on this doctor."

"Doctor?" This seemed even more unlike him; I said, "Is this something new?"

He shrugged. "Neither old nor new. I'm not ill, if that's what you mean. I had a little stomach trouble a couple of years ago and this doctor came in to the rectory to see me. He made me promise to check with him every once in a while. And so I do. From the health point of view it's absurd: I never felt better and the entire physical examination takes about a minute and a half. But I promised and he's a decent enough fellow; I think he simply wants someone to talk to. Deerford's not Paris, you know. If you're hard up for conversation you talk to the squirrels. And if you're really desperate, you try the natives. So it's not everybody's cup of tea. But," he said, with

[225]

a grim wistfulness, "it suited me. Right down to the ground."

I said, persisting, "You're all right, then?"

A queer reversal of roles: now *I* was asking the questions about health. But I got no immediate answer; all wrapped up in his thoughts of Deerford he seemed not to hear me until, with a little start, his head snapped up and he said, "What?"

I repeated the question. He looked puzzled, as if I had just asked a question rooted in lunacy: had he grown any feathers lately, had he walked upon the waters? He said, "Of course I'm all right. Why? Do I look all wrong?"

He did not. He looked fine, first rate — so much so that it suddenly did seem an impertinence even to inquire. I told him so and he nodded. "Well, there you are. I'm good for another fifty years at least. The only trouble is that every last one of them is apparently to be spent in Saint Raymond's. A prospect of pure enchantment." He got up and said, "It's a good three-hour drive; I'd better be getting along."

I went out with him to his car. I thanked him again for coming and saying Mass; I half promised I'd do the same at Saint Raymond's one day soon. Half promised; that's all. And before he drove away the last thing he said was, "I hear my father's been favoring you with his little courtesy calls. In fact I hear that he practically comes in with the morning milk."

"Nothing as often as that. He does appear from time to time."

"I'll bet he does. What's he up to? Have you found out yet?"

"No, I haven't. I'm not even close. If he's really up to anything, that is. I'm beginning to think that he isn't."

"Famous last words," he said. "Stop talking like one of your altar boys. I still say that what he wants is a few thousand square feet of metropolitan land, at present inconveniently occupied by one church and one rectory. Wait and see. The day of the bulldozer is close at hand. Or so my father profoundly hopes."

He spoke with conviction; he was sure that he was right; I

was just as sure that he was wrong. I felt that whatever Charlie wanted, it had nothing to do with Saint Paul's. And there were even those times — few and far between, to be sure — when I almost felt that it had nothing to do with me. The point is that Charlie's mystery, the great conundrum which had puzzled me for so long, had now begun to lose its edge. I still thought about it, of course, but it was no longer a matter of daily speculation, and Charlie himself I received, not without suspicion — I had been far too well brought up for that — but with a first quick leap of wary wonder which then was apt to fade entirely until he came the next time. I suppose the truth was simply this; I found that in a way I looked forward to him with a sense of pleasurable expectation. For my days were trouble-free and agreeable enough, heaven knows, but even with Father Danowski and Roy on hand to provide minor variations, the pattern was admittedly something of a monochrome; Charlie brought me a touch of color that I may have missed more than I had known. In any case, I came to welcome the sudden, frequent, and always unannounced appearances on the rectory doorstep, and it was never hard for me to watch and listen as this little, incredibly lively old man bounded about the rectory reception room, bubbling out his exuberant monologues, each one a virtuoso's grab bag of gossip, extravagant self-praise, spurious compliments to me, crocodile tears, unlikely reports of kindly deeds performed, and — above all — eloquent recollections of the vital, parochial, picturesque and vanished world in which he and my father had been young. . . .

". . . they made Little Georgie Casey's boy head of the rent control last week and before he had the chance to warm the seat with his pants he was up callin' me names in the papers! Did you read about that, Father? Did you read about Charlie Carmody the rent-gouger? Oh my, ain't that a terrible thing to be called? By the son of Little Georgie, that I knew all my life like a brother? And then the papers get on to me and say, 'Ain't it awful, Mr. Carmody, when a young feller like that calls a fine man like you names? Have you got a statement for us, Mr. Carmody?' And what do I tell them, Father? I tell them the truth. I say, 'I got no statement but forgive and forget. That's the way Charlie Carmody is and that's the way he'll always be. He holds no grudges. I got nothin' against any man, specially when he's Little Georgie Casey's boy that was brought up with practically no father at all, what with Little Georgie bein' away for so long for stealin' the penny stamps out of the post office. . . .'

". . . you got the place lookin' grand, Father. I tell you, you're makin' a palace out of a dump. Good hard work: ain't that better than money? Oh yes, everybody the whole city over is talkin' about it. They're sayin', 'Have you seen Old Saint Paul's lately? Father Hugh Kennedy is makin' it look like Saint Peter's in Rome. . . .'

". . . dreadful lot of bum kids roamin' the city today. I'd put them all out peddlin' papers. That's a great thing for a boy, Father: scootin' around on a winter night, deliverin' papers from house to house, with his nose runnin' and his fingers frostbit and his cheeks all red with the cold! That teaches them to be on the go. You show me a lad peddles papers and I'll show you a lad can grow up to be President of the United States. I used to peddle papers, Father! What d'ye think of that? And today, when I'm walkin' along the street all by myself, and I see a lad with an armful of them to sell, lots of times I might stop and buy one and give the little feller a dime and tell him to keep the change. . . .

". . . the time they were after your pa to go into politics. They wanted him to run for the Council against Silly Jack McCoy. There was a man I never liked, Father. I'm a man that likes most everybody, but I never liked Silly Jack. A big tall clown of a feller with a face like an ash tray that was always goin' around laughin' at nothin' and whackin' people on the back. He was in the Council twenty years and gave

[228]

out free beer at all the picnics and wore a fireman's hat in the parades and kissed all the old ladies' hands and sang 'O Sacred Heart, O Love Divine' in the Cathedral on Sundays and sold me a secondhand car that the motor fell out of in two weeks. Oh, I tell you, Father, there was a man they should have jailed the day he was born! Well, in the end he went crazy, the way a man like that would, and got all soft in the head and started doin' mixed-up things like handin' out cigars to little babies and cherry lollipops to grown-up men. That was when they decided to get rid of him and asked your pa to run. But he wouldn't. Not even when his best old pal asked him to, he wouldn't. I said to him a hundred times, I said, 'For the love of God, Dave, get on out there and run and save the city from that dirty cheat. He was always a dirty cheat and now he's a crazy dirty cheat!' But he wouldn't. He said that if he had to sit in the City Council for as much as two weeks he'd be crazier than Silly Jack. Besides, he said he liked the man. Your pa was a queer damn man with some of the people he liked. . . ."

So Charlie talked on, visit after visit. And not only Charlie, for by now I had another caller: this was Bucky. He had come with Charlie once or twice, but on those occasions he had for some reason been a subdued and subordinate figure; now he came by himself, perhaps half a dozen times in all. Unlike Charlie, he did not come unannounced; each visit was preceded by a telephone call. Each call was guarded, faintly conspiratorial: the tone of the first set the pattern for the rest.

"You'll be at home tomorrow night, Father?"

"Yes, I expect so, Mr. Heffernan. I'm here most nights." Then, as a prudent addition, I said, "I'm afraid I go to bed rather early."

"I'll stop by. For a minute or two. If I may. I don't like to intrude. I'm not like some people I could name. Some people not a million miles from here, Father. Some people that barge right into another man's house like it was their own."

No comment; I said instead, "There's no intrusion, Mr. Heffernan. None at all."

"I have this *certain matter* to discuss with you, Father. A very confidential matter. I'll say no more about it on the telephone. *I think you know what I mean.*"

"I understand, Mr. Heffernan. Come along, by all means."

So he was still at war with John; from now on he would discuss the question of his remains with me. A signal honor . . . ?

On these visits, he came always at night, usually arriving just as I had finished dinner. The signal for this arrival was the sound of the Warren Avenue bus, making its way with difficulty around the sharp corner; two minutes later the doorbell would ring. (Bucky had no car; during the next few weeks I was to learn that he was a patron of, and an authority on, the city's bus lines. He rode everywhere: an old man, still active, with time on his hands, he had apparently taken to buses as other old men take to their beds. It was not unusual for him to spend a good part of the day simply riding around in these buses, going nowhere in particular, but transferring from one to the other with the ease and finesse of the accomplished traveler, and finally, at the end of the day, winding up near home and Mrs. Bucky and his supper.) Here in the rectory — again, quite unlike Charlie — he wasted no time on preliminaries; there was no conducted tour of the church for Bucky; he made none of the customary regretful comments on the transient glories of Old Saint Paul's. He was a man with business on his mind, and he got down to it at once.

It was fairly astonishing business — even though I'd been warned about it, and even though I'd imagined I knew what it would be like. For very old people sometimes talk about death with a peculiar familiarity, dwelling on it almost with relish, and those younger than themselves often find this unsettling, even ghoulish. I suppose it is, and yet one's ideas of what is or is not ghoulish undoubtedly change as, gradually, the obituary page comes to replace the front page as the main attraction in one's morning paper. In any case, it's a common approach among the old, and I was prepared to meet it in Bucky.

But Bucky surprised me. He was concerned neither with death itself nor his preparation for it; he was concerned only with the little niceties to follow.

"It's all here, Father," he said, producing a thick, sealed, and rather soiled envelope from his coat pocket. "All written down. In black and white. In the Will. Be prepared. Leave nothing to chance. The greatest generals in all history are with me on that one." He did not open the envelope; instead, he replaced it in his pocket. "I'll tell you all about it," he said.

He began with his coffin. He had already selected this. Nearly a year ago he had gone shopping with P.J., who had supplied invaluable professional advice. The coffin had been bought, paid for, delivered. It was now in Bucky's basement. Waiting.

"Very handsome," he said. "Dignified. All walnut and the very finest steel. The kind of a coffin a man can be proud of. Yet only half of what you might expect to pay. On account of the shopping around. And P.J.'s discount."

He had chosen his undertaker.

"Arthur Dacey and Son will do the job. When the time arrives. There was a little argument at first on account of my already having the coffin but that's all fixed up now. They have their instructions, Father. Down to the very last detail. They know just what to do. I told them, 'I'll have no silly smile on my face! Remember that!' Friendly but solemn, Father: that's the way to go. I'll wear the navy blue suit, the dark blue tie with the little white dots, a white carnation on the lapel, and the black kangaroo leather shoes with the plain toes. I'll have my wedding ring and my Knights of Columbus pin. I'll have my rosary beads in my hands. And that's all!"

He explained why he had taken this upon his own shoulders.

"The wife is a fine woman," he said, "but you couldn't trust a woman with a thing like this!"

He had drawn up his specifications for the funeral: a High Mass from Old Saint Paul's at eight o'clock in the morning; myself to sing it; a quartet in the choir loft; eight bearers, chosen by name: Charlie and P.J. led the list. There were also substitute bearers, in the event that any or all of the originals should predecease him.

He went on. There was to be a two-grave lot in Saint Paul's cemetery, the exact location of which was yet to be determined (I had the feeling that he was currently spending hours wandering through the cemetery, his sharp old eye on the watch for prime sites). His tombstone — like the coffin, already purchased and delivered — was an enormous rectangle of white polished marble. He produced a small card and showed me, in printed letters, the epitaph which he had composed and which would be incised upon the stone:

HERE LIES

A MAN BELOVED

BY ALL

CORNELIUS J. HEFFERNAN

And underneath:

AND HIS LOVING WIFE

MARGARET B.

A strange final equation, surely: short shrift for poor Margaret B.!

He talked with special zeal of the care of his grave. It should be perpetual; he had read only recently of a new grass admirably adapted to this purpose: green the year round, it required little mowing. He had already written to inquire if this grass were suitable for these latitudes.

There was more, but at last he finished. He breathed out hard, then sat back in his chair, clearly waiting for his due. I could at least be truthful; I said, "You've thought of everything, Mr. Heffernan."

"I left out nothing," he said with satisfaction. "Did you notice that, Father?"

"Yes. Yes indeed."

"All tied up in a bundle," he said. "No loose ends. Neatness counts! That's what they used to tell us in school and that's what I've always believed. I've lived neat and I'll die neat. No man can argue with that. But what's the good of it all, Father, unless you can trust people? To carry out the plans. Just as I made them. Right to the dot. That's the question the whole wide world asks, Father: Who can you trust? The big books all ask that one. And I ask it too. Who can I trust, Father? Some priest who's so busy trying to get out of the room the moment he sees you coming in he can't hear a word you say? Some smart-aleck priest who always knows just what you're going to say ten minutes before you say it? No no, Father. I'll trust no priest like that. No matter how well I know his pa. I say it now for one and all to hear: *If a priest has got no time for Bucky Heffernan, Bucky Heffernan has got no time for that priest!* Alive or dead. Not after all the trouble I took to make everything come out nice. And that's why I'm here tonight, Father. Right here. In Old Saint Paul's rectory. I'm here to get a priest I can trust!" And then he actually said the words; he said, "Will you bury me, Father?"

It was both a compliment and a request — of a somewhat special kind, to be sure. And how to respond? What in the world could you say to this? Because the whole thing was so close to farce, so divorced from the meaning of death, so wildly, comically out of proportion that for a moment I was almost tempted to answer in kind, to suggest little graveside ingenuities of my own. But then I looked at Bucky and saw his eyes staring at me with passionate earnestness, and I suddenly realized that, despite all the ludicrous trappings, here was an old man who really *was* going to die soon simply because he was that old, who wanted terribly to have everything "come out nice," and to whom it was a matter of the most enormous importance that Bucky Heffernan, once he had ceased to be Bucky Heffernan, be borne in glory to the ground and treated grandly every day. A queer piece of terminal vanity, and hardly the ideal obsession before the fact of death, yet there it was, obviously — all too obviously — the spark or the vision that kept him going, the object which entirely filled his skies. And so, in a situation like that, do you try to shoot the object — however preposterous — out of an old man's skies, or do you try to come to some sort of terms with it? Or rather, with the man himself? I said carefully, "Look, Mr. Heffernan: I'm sure you know what the Church has to say about something like this —"

But these were unfortunate words, probably — inevitably, come to think of it — suggesting censure, or outright prohibition. Or so he apparently thought, for instantly he raised his hand to stop me. "One moment, Father!" he said triumphantly. "I have you there! The right is on my side! One hundred per cent! I can go where I want to be buried from! I've looked it up in the books! Popes and bishops back me up on that one!"

A new side of Bucky: the canonical side. I said, "Yes, I know you can. You can be buried from whatever parish you like. It's your privilege, Mr. Heffernan. And if you really want to be buried from Saint Paul's, whenever the time comes, of course you can be. And if you really want me to say your Mass, of course I will —"

"That's it!" he cried. "I thank you, Father! Those are the words I came to hear! Those few words! From a priest I trust!"

And he shot to his feet; he had all the appearance of one who was about to leave at once. I said quickly, "I even have a few words more." And the question was, of course: Where to begin? With a short catechetical talk on death? Hardly. A try at an apologia for John and Saint Raymond's? I said, "You know, I would think you might want to give another thought to your own parish, Mr. Heffernan —"

"Aha!" he said scornfully. "That's all they'll get. From now on. They'll get Bucky Heffernan's thoughts, yes. *But they won't get Bucky.*"

I'd never before met anyone who had such a fond apprecia-tion of his own dead body; he spoke of it as if it were a casket of rare gems. I said, "Yes, but listen, Mr. Heffernan. In the first place, if I were in your shoes, and looked as well as you do now, I wouldn't be thinking of my burial as being imminent. But when it did come, I think I might want it to come from a place where everyone knew me, from my home. And after all, Saint Raymond's is your home, isn't it? You've lived there all your life; all your friends are there. I should think a man with your sense of the fitness of things would prefer to be there." Was this effective artfulness? I looked at Bucky. No. I went on to the nub of the matter. "And as far as your plans — these arrangements you've so carefully made — are concerned, surely no one could handle them better than Father Carmody. He may seem a bit brisk or preoccupied at times, but I know he has a high regard for you. And he's an extremely efficient man. You could be sure that your instruc-tions would be followed to the letter."

Pacifying words. Which failed to pacify.

"He's had his chance!" Bucky cried. "And passed it up! Too busy! Too busy to spend a few short evenings with Bucky! And now Bucky's too busy for him! Opportunity knocks but once! We all know that! The boot's on the other foot now! And one day he'll know it! One day," he said, excitement and delight running across his face, "that certain priest will get what's coming to him! One day when the people start coming back and asking why they have to go clear across the city to look at Bucky's lovely grave! One day when the Bishop calls him up on the carpet and wants to know why a man with a

[235]

grave like that wasn't buried in his own home parish! And then," he chortled, "*then* that certain priest will have to eat crow! Ho ho! *Then* he'll have to speak up! For one and all to hear! He'll have to say, 'Your Excellency, I'll tell you why he's not buried at home. In his own parish. Where every man belongs. He's not buried there because of me! It's all my fault! I was too much of a smart aleck for my own good! Too high and mighty! I see it all now! He came to see me! Of his own free will! To discuss the matter man to man. And what did I do? I thought I had him all sewed up. I was too cocksure. I gave him no time. So off he went to Old Saint Paul's and never came back! That's what I did, Your Excellency! *I drove Mr. Heffernan away.* I confess it all. The whole works!' "

I did it with my little hatchet. . . .

And the curious thing was that I had begun all this in the hope of restoring a little sanity, some small sense of proportion, to the evening. So much for good intentions. We had arrived at a vision which, however incredible it seemed to me, clearly left Bucky in near-ecstasy. As he contemplated each savory detail of John's glorious abasement, he chuckled and his shoulders shook; his eyes bulged; his face was red and smiling; he was breathing happily and hard. And once again there was this peculiar *swelling* of his whole being — I had noticed the phenomenon before, at Charlie's birthday dinner, although then the cause had been a different emotion. It did not matter: he seemed to inflate equally with rage or joy. He seemed also, now, to have no disposition to leave; apparently in the last few minutes he had changed his mind; he sank comfortably into a chair and seemed ready for a fine, full, macabre evening. . . .

Still, it didn't turn out quite that way; he stayed, but not too much longer. He continued to talk; we did not — or could not — change the subject; every once in a while I made my bid for a slight shift of emphasis. Not on anything central or theological — this, with luck, could come later — but on cer-

[236]

tain small practical points which, to put it mildly, stood in some need of revision. There was the matter of the epitaph, for instance; subtly, I plumped for greater justice for Margaret B. On this and other points Bucky paused to listen with an appearance of solemn attention, the way old men sometimes do when they're catching their breath; I do not think that he was deeply moved. By the time he left, a great deal had been covered and as far as I could see, absolutely nothing had been changed. In short, an ideal evening for Bucky. He shook my hand warmly at the door and professed to be enormously satisfied; he hinted strongly that this was by no means the last of such visits. I believed him. . . .

Yet the next morning I telephoned to John; I had had second thoughts on the subject of Bucky. Maybe it was that my long stay in such a placid pool as Old Saint Paul's had dulled my reactions; maybe it was that my infrequent and irregular contact with old men like Bucky had somehow softened me, brought me to a kind of rosy romanticism — in any case, it wasn't until I woke the next morning that certain suspicions began to suggest themselves, suspicions which, in years gone by, would have arisen the instant Bucky had opened his mouth. And so I called John, partly because I thought he ought to know what was going on, but mostly because I was sure that by now he already did.

In this I was entirely right.

"He's been here," he said. "Bright and early this morning. Dripping with triumph. I couldn't get rid of him. You've got a great supporter there, Hugh. He kept following me around and telling me that at last he could die in peace. He's all promise and no performance, unfortunately."

"I don't suppose you're interested in winning back my great supporter? Somehow I have the feeling that it could be done."

"Yes," he said drily. "Somehow I have that feeling too."

"Bucky has made his approach?"

"Oh yes. I was given to understand that while you had the

[237]

inside track at the moment, all might not be lost if I played my cards right. Of course the truth is that much as I want to, I haven't a hope of losing him. No matter how I play my cards. That coffin in the basement will wind up here, come hell or high water, and all the talk is just that: talk. In the good old Saint Raymond's tradition of meaningless eloquence. He's here, and here he'll stay until the end of time. Or at least until the end of his time. You couldn't blast him out of Saint Raymond's."

Which was perfectly true, and which I should have known by instinct from the beginning. In a way I felt relieved: it was where he belonged, obviously. Yet at the same time, remembering my own careful attempts at persuasion last night, I also felt a little foolish. I said to John now, "So it's all Bucky's little game, then?"

"Entirely. Pure pingpong. Back and forth. As fast as the buses will carry him. It must hardly have seemed worth his while when he had just me to annoy, but now that he's got you too, everything's fine and dandy. That's the great principle of life over here: the more people you bother, the better you feel. A little lesson I absorbed at my father's knee. No, your only defense now is to hide, Hugh. Or better still, pray for a bus strike. That would do it."

There was no bus strike; I could not hide; Bucky continued to call. He talked; I talked; we played his little game together. A certain monotony crept in, inevitably, for our single subject was not without its limitations, and Bucky as a narrator believed in repetition. Still, I was neither annoyed nor bored. Like Charlie, Bucky brought a peculiar zest, a flavor, to the day, and if much of his talk meant nothing at all — speculations about that cataclysmic shift which would never occur — still, there was a kind of fascination in listening to a man who could with such enthusiasm and in such detail outline the blueprint for his posthumous disposition, and who could see in his own grave nothing short of a civic monument. But beyond all this there was something else, something which did not belong in never-never land — not a dream or an antic fantasy, but a fact which belonged to the here and now. This was the plain fact of death itself, the sober side of the picture, which I sometimes forgot even existed as I listened to Bucky, but which — I'm convinced — he never forgot, not even for an instant. Because every once in a while, as he talked, underneath all the complicated and grandiose plans, I caught a note of uncertainty and fear, and after a time I was sure that this was what he was really talking about, and not at all the burial or the dramatic transfer of his bones. I may have been all wrong in this, reading too much into a tone or a look in the eye, but I don't think so, and in any case the least I could do was to listen. And perhaps now and then to offer a suggestion, a word of reassurance, some small help: you never know. . . .

But I was not Bucky's only audience in the rectory; there was also Father Danowski. He had never actually met or talked to Bucky — on all his visits, Bucky made a great point of his need for privacy: "Strictly between ourselves, Father! There's certain people would love to know my plans!" — but even in these moments of high confidence Bucky was apt to talk at the top of his voice, and Father Danowski, located a floor away, could often hear bits and pieces of what went on. He spoke of this to me, apologizing elaborately for having overheard anything: it was by no means, he assured me, by *no* means to be construed as eavesdropping. Which was true enough, certainly: one might as well have spoken of eavesdropping on a peal of thunder. As he went on to tell me just what he had heard, I discovered that he had at first been bewildered, then horrified by Bucky's zealous approach to his own interment. Suddenly, however, the mists had cleared, and in a flash he had understood everything. Bucky was joking. It was all in fun.

"What a merry old gentleman he must be! With that famous Irish sense of humor," he said indulgently, "which I have so often observed in *you*, Father!"

There are times when life with Father Danowski seems nothing but a series of invisible winces. . . .

So then, one by one the Carmodys had begun to turn up at the rectory; Helen was the last to do so. She came one afternoon about three o'clock, and when I went to the door, there she was, and without any preliminary at all she said, "Hugh. Tell me the truth: how many times have you been out this fall? Just to be out walking around, I mean? Taking a look at the leaves?"

It was as good a way as any to say hello, I suppose; I said, "I haven't looked at a leaf in years. Come on in."

"No," she said. "You come out. I have the two children in the car: Anne left them with me while she went off to do a little politicking for Ted. And I'm just riding around, looking: it's *so* beautiful, Hugh. And I'd like you to look with me. You don't need to tell me how busy you are, because I know very well *just* how busy you are. And you know that I do. So come along. Just as you are. You don't even need a light coat. It's a perfectly gorgeous day!"

She was right: about me (I was no busier than usual, Father Danowski could easily deal with anything that might come up on a midweek afternoon); about the day (it was soft and warm and drowsy, the unexpected return of summer for a one-night stand). And so I went out to the car with her. As we came down the walk I could hear shouts and laughter, but then we were sighted, and by the time we reached the car silence had dropped down, and from the back seat two solemn little faces regarded me as unwinkingly and as noncommittally as they had on Charlie's birthday. The back seat was covered with a litter of crayons and papers; not without pride Helen said, "I think you should show Father what you've been drawing."

[240]

Father was shown. They pushed forward a single sheet of paper. Reluctantly. I took it. Reluctantly. Although my reluctance was perhaps better concealed: the obligation of the adult. I think these situations offer no difficulty at all to those who are regularly with children, and yet if you're not — most priests are not, and certainly this priest is not — the older you get the more likely you are to find each such presentation a matter of some embarrassment. It's probably vanity as much as anything else: I think most of us, however removed from children, cherish the belief that we're rather good at getting along with them — that we can "talk" to them. Which belief is, unhappily, put to the test every now and then, for children sing, children dance, children draw — and children have proud parents. Or grandparents. There's a technique for dealing with this; I don't know it. What do you say about a child's drawing, for instance? To the child, that is? Without looking foolish? For of all artists, children are the most openly contemptuous of misinterpretation — and yet the gay blob that one supposes to be a cow is always a cat. Or a chicken. The drawing before me now was orange and green and purple and indecipherable; I felt Helen watching me with amused eyes; I played it safe; I said with a bouncy heartiness, "Ah well, this is first rate. This is . . . fine!"

Aesthetic appreciation. The two children said nothing but looked at each other again. Not that I blamed them. Helen was silent, too, and her expression had not changed. I said apologetically, "That comes pretty close to being the best I can do. I'm not quite in my element."

She laughed suddenly and reached out and took my hand. "Hugh, Hugh," she said. "I'm sorry. I won't do it again. That's the one exhibition of the day." To the children she said, "It's a beautiful house: the most beautiful I've ever seen. Now you do some more while we go for a ride. Huge houses: with lions and tigers all around."

The little boy said soberly, "And bears?"

"*And* bears," she said. "Loads of bears. The more bears the better. And then we'll show them all to your daddy and mummy when we get home." To me she said, "Now they'll be good as gold and quiet as mice. And as a matter of fact so will I."

We drove off, leaving the busy part of the city rather quickly — for curiously enough, despite all the building programs of the past few years and the nests of suburbs which had exploded into being, it was still possible to get into attractive country in a relatively few minutes, and in a few minutes more to reach the surrounding hills. After a while we turned off the main highway onto a narrower road, and then in a mile or so onto one still narrower. This was unmistakably a country road, one which wore its black topping badly. I knew it well: it had been the terminal trail of boyhood expeditions. Here and there along this road were the broken stone walls of the old farms; oaks and maples lined both sides, and slowly we passed by these multicolored blazing battalions of Indian summer. The road climbed steeply and ended illogically: all of a sudden it ceased to be, and you found yourself in a tiny clearing, completely surrounded by trees except for one small gap at the front. This gap was actually the brink of a high, sharp cliff, and if you stood back from it, and on a slight elevation, you could look down through the widening aperture on almost the entire sweep of the city as it swelled its way towards the south. It was, in its way, a spectacular site, the kind which in another locale would unfailingly have been called "Lovers' Leap"; here, more prosaically, it was known simply as "The Top," and as a tourist attraction it was a failure.

Yet I had always liked it. Helen brought the car into the clearing a little way, then stopped, and for a moment we just sat there, silent, looking around. It was very quiet — so quiet that automatically I turned to look at the back seat: I saw the twins had dropped their crayons and were now propped up against each other in the still, seraphic sleep of children. The car windows were down; there was not the slightest motion in the air; the light still held on the flaming trees; the car, ourselves, everything was ringed in color. Helen said softly, "How beautiful this is. Like living inside a rainbow."

I said, "It hasn't changed much, has it? The grass is a little longer. And the trees are a little bigger. Otherwise it's just about the same."

She said, "Treasure trove and pirate's gold. Ten paces from the great oak tree." Because almost half a century ago, the three of us — Helen, John, myself — had come to this spot one afternoon to dig for buried treasure. We had a map — a pirate's map; we dreamed of gold. Or at least two of us did, for I knew what the others did not: I knew that the map was a hoax, that it had in fact been drawn by me. One day I had found, in the attic of our house, a handful of old coins. They were quite worthless, as it turned out, but even so they held possibilities: I took them out to the clearing and buried them in an old, decrepit cookie can. Home again, I drew the map: I drew it on a piece of splotchy, time-discolored paper torn from an unread book someone had given my father long ago — I can even remember its name: *Traits and Stories of the Irish Peasantry*: a clue perhaps, to its remaining unread. Under the map I supplied careful directions, all done in approved Jolly Roger style, copied from *The Boy's Own Book of Buccaneers* — which explains Helen and the ". . . ten paces from the great oak tree." The next day I presented the map to Helen and John as my great discovery; I persuaded them — not much of a trick: they were all too willing to be persuaded — that the locale referred to could only be our secret clearing; swiftly we set off to find the buried treasure. We climbed, we paced, we dug, we *found* — and then, although I'd fully intended to keep my secret for weeks, months, *years*, I proudly broke the spell at once by confessing everything. Great disappointment, wild pummeling, threats of dire revenge — in a word, it was a good day, a fine day, the kind of day, I suppose, that inevitably seems even better and finer when viewed from nearly fifty years away. . . .

I said "I don't think I've been back here since. Once or twice after that, maybe, when we were still children, but apart from that, never."

"Oh, I have," she said. "Lots. I told you, I think, that I seem to spend most of my time looking for old footprints to step in. How about you, Hugh? How do you feel about old footprints?"

"It depends pretty much on the footprints. I'm all in favor of some of them. Others I'd just as soon skip."

A note of self-commiseration? But all she said was, "Yes. Well, we all have those stretches it doesn't do to make tracks over again. No, I try to be fairly selective in my old footprints. It doesn't always work, but I usually manage to give myself A for effort. But then I guess everybody manages to do that, don't they?"

It wasn't a question that needed an answer. It wasn't a question at all, really, but a kind of passive, sleepy drift of words; she had shifted her position in the seat so that her head was now supported by the frame of the open car window; relaxed, with her eyes lightly closed, she seemed to soak up the color and sunlight of the splendid afternoon. After a moment she said, still sleepily, "I'm as bad as the twins. How's your parish these days, Hugh? As good as ever?"

A for effort. I said, "Good for me, yes. How good it would be for anyone else I don't know. I think a more active pastor — someone like John, for instance — would probably go mad there."

"He doesn't do a bad job of going mad where he is," she said, "although for slightly different reasons." She sat up, smoothing her hair; her eyes were now open and alert. "I asked him the other day what he wanted me to give him for Christmas. He said he thought a machine gun would be useful. Under the circumstances. He gets more gregarious with each

[244]

passing year, don't you think? I don't know, perhaps a parish like Saint Paul's might have been just the thing for him; at least he wouldn't know everyone there."

"That's true enough," I added. "Although there are other factors." For I had, suddenly, a picture of John, situated in Old Saint Paul's: he was seated at his desk, busily writing; there was a knock at the door, a knock which, peculiarly, managed to be both deferential and important at the same time; the door opened and Father Danowski came bustling in, primed for informing conversation: *Pardon me, Father, but I wonder if by any chance you are aware that Roy has been behaving of late in a most singular manner. . . ?*

She said thoughtfully, "I'll tell you what I used to wonder about. What I wonder about still, for that matter. And that is why the Bishop ever decided to put John in Saint Raymond's. Offhand I'd say that was a fair example of a mistake in high places. Wouldn't you?"

It was a question I'd put to myself more than once, and I hesitated; she must have suspected evasion — not without some reason, remembering past performance — because she looked up quickly and said with a faint smile, "Come on, Hugh. Remember me? Honest Injun now: didn't His Excellency pull a boner?"

"I don't know." Her mouth moved slightly, which was enough: incredulity requires no massive pantomime. "No, Honest Injun or whatever else you want, I don't. For one thing, I don't know what he had in mind — or if he had anything special in mind at all. Don't forget that it was a perfectly good routine transfer. Saint Raymond's needed a pastor, and out in Deerford there was an experienced pastor who was due for advancement. And who, by the way, had the advantage of knowing Saint Raymond's from A to Z. So that if you look at it that way it was hard to beat as a logical move. And I think that's probably the way to look at it; after all, I doubt that the Bishop would have known anything about John's pet dislikes. Besides, if you take a look at the results, I'm not so sure that it was a mistake. Not from the parish's point of view, certainly; John must run it as well as anyone could."

She sighed. "You're a nice man, Hugh, and I adore you, *but*. But but but. You *do* beat around the bush — or at least you do lately — and that's what you're doing now. I'm not talking about the parish, and you know I'm not. I'm talking about John. What about him, Hugh? Was it a mistake for him?"

And here we were again, after so many years, back on another bit of familiar ground, although perhaps not covering it now in quite the same way as before. For I don't think that either of us believed any longer that the problem of John would be eased by the passing of time, that he would mellow and soften with age; having ourselves reached at least the outposts of age, we viewed its miracles with a harder eye. I said, "You used to ask easy questions. It could be a mistake, yes. And it could work out well, and it could work out badly. That's one of those answers you're so fond of, isn't it? But I don't know what else to say; it's too soon to make even a decent guess. I'd say so far, so good. He seems about the same to me; at least I haven't noticed any changes."

"Haven't you? I think I have. He's sharper, more withdrawn. . . ."

"Well, he's also older. It doesn't get easier for anyone, you know. Especially if you're someone like John."

"Maybe he should have been something else. Although I can't think what. And he *is* a good priest: I know that. . . ."

I agreed. "Even a remarkable one, in a way. But he's a solitary, Helen, and that's where the trouble comes in. That's fine if you're in a cell in a monastery, but when you're in a parish — any parish — the plain fact is that you have to deal with people. It's not much of a contemplative life. You're a sitting target for people, and you can't complain about it because that's what half the job is. It's that half that bothers John. So that if you mean is he happy, I don't think he'd be particularly happy in any parish. I'm not so sure that's the point, anyway. Although I agree that he might be happier somewhere else than where he is now."

"Now that's an odd one," she said slowly. "I mean, what you just said about being happier somewhere else. Because John more or less said the same thing about you."

And this took me by surprise. I said "Did he, now? And how did he arrive at that, did he say?"

"No. We were talking one day — about you, among others — and he just mentioned it in passing." She said, "Was he right, Hugh?"

I shook my head; I said firmly, "No."

She said gently, "Sure? John's very shrewd, you know."

"I know. But I'm still sure. Your shrewd brother is all wrong on this one."

She seemed to accept this; at least she didn't go on with it, and I was just as well pleased. Instead she said, "Mistake or no mistake, my shrewd brother is now rather articulate on the subject of the Bishop. I don't know how shrewd that is. But then I don't know the Bishop. What's he like, Hugh?"

"He's a strange man. I don't know him terribly well; it's John who's spread the myth that we're great companions. Actually, I wouldn't guess that many people knew him well; he's pretty enigmatic. Frank could probably tell you more about him than I can; he's his doctor, after all."

"Yes," she said doubtfully, "although that doesn't help a great deal. I find out next to nothing from Frank. And it isn't at all a case of doctors not telling, because Frank is really rather . . . well, *voluble* about some of his patients. It was a great shock to me at first. I'd always thought that the doctor was a bit like the confessor, but not at all. At least Frank isn't. He's full of odd, half-discreet tidbits about who's sick and what they've got and what their chances are. But with all that he really doesn't *tell* you anything: he's not much good at giving you *impressions* of people. Do you know what I mean,

[247]

Hugh? I don't mean that he's insensitive — although I suppose it must sound as though that's exactly what I *do* mean — but he really isn't much interested in them. Beyond, of course, what's wrong with them that he can fix."

"No probing of psyches?"

"No. Although I'm just as happy about that. Only sometimes . . . well," she said abruptly, "that's why I don't know about the Bishop from Frank. Do you like him, Hugh? You do, don't you?"

"The Bishop? Yes, very much. Of course I have every reason to, and that usually helps."

"These reasons," she said. "You wouldn't care to talk about them, I suppose?" And she said this so casually, so matter-of-factly, that it was a moment before I realized that with these few words she had not only changed the subject, she had pitched the conversation on another level entirely. I looked at her, and I didn't say a word, not because I didn't want to say anything, but because I had had no practice in talking about the things she wanted to hear, and I didn't know where to begin. She said simply, "It's been a long time. Five years, hasn't it? And I don't know where you were or what you did or whether you were sick or well or happy or sad. I know the beginning, and why you went away, of course, but beyond that I haven't heard a word. Except a short report from John every now and then, and I never knew, really, just how close he was to whatever was going on. So give me credit, Hugh: I've behaved myself pretty well up to now. I haven't asked you questions, and I won't ask you now if you don't want me to. Only I had an idea that you might want to talk a little about it sometimes. And if you would I'd like very much to listen. I would, Hugh. I really would."

And so sitting here in the car, a part of what must have seemed an absurd composite — the city pastor perched in a woodland clearing, clerical black bathed in gay autumn, two little children sleeping quietly and all but forgotten behind —

I did talk to her. I talked only about myself and what had happened to me: it was autobiography pure and simple, talk of a kind that one doesn't make — or want to make — more than once in a very great while, and sometimes doesn't make at all. For while it's true enough that we are often our own best topics, I think that apart from the usual sidewalk and sitting-room recitations of small boasts and complaints we almost never really talk about ourselves. In a *central* way, that is: in any way that means anything. And if we do, most of us have only a very few friends to whom we will so talk; some of us have no one; I had Helen and John. Perhaps, because of the situation, because we were what we were — not only old friends, but both priests, both ordained together — I should more suitably have gone first to John, but there was no deny-ing that Helen was easier. She lacked her brother's fierce auto-matic resistance to the spoken confidence, and although I knew that he would have overcome this for me, nevertheless Helen reached out where he did not and, probably, could not — and so I talked to her. For the first time since I had left the city I told the whole story to someone — the whole story, that is, in essence and in capsule. I left out certain details, but while these were important to me, they would have been to no one else: they were those moments, those parts of life, which are so purely personal and private that you can no more share them than you can share your heart or brain: in all of us there is that small and unsurrenderable core which . . . well, which in the end determines everything. But other than this, I told Helen pretty much all that had happened, right from the piling catastrophes that led to my first interview with the Bishop, down through the years at The Cenacle, and then once more back to the city, and to Old Saint Paul's and Father Danowski.

She listened. Intently, I think; certainly without interrup-tion. And yet what her reactions were to any given point in the story I couldn't say, for the simple reason that I didn't notice them. The truth is that, in talking, I somehow lost sight of her. Not deliberately, of course; there was nothing intentional about it; I didn't studiously avert my eyes at any point in the hope of sparing either of us embarrassment in an unheroic tale. No, I began by talking directly to her: directly and flatly and exclusively, telling her just what had happened, without any dramatic touches, and then gradually my attention must have lost its focus, because all at once I found myself listening as well as talking. Listening to myself, I mean. I'd become my own audience — a phenomenon not unknown among narrators. But it was curious: it was as though this story, this painfully familiar story, which I'd gone over in my mind so many times that it all flowed into place with the easy order of the alphabet, had now gained a sparkling freshness, a whole new life, simply by being spoken aloud, and the result was that I seemed to be hearing it for the first time. It was an odd and compelling experience, so compelling that I don't think I knew what was really happening until at last I came to the end and, with nothing more to say, looked over at Helen as if she might have been some sort of agreeable afterthought, and it was only then that I suddenly came to and remembered that the afterthought was in fact only the point of the whole narration . . . !

I don't know whether she noticed this or not — or whether she thought it was important. She said nothing immediately, but then this was natural enough: I suppose any confession or explanation of this kind creates its own afterglow of required silence. Finally she said quietly, "Well. That's quite a story, isn't it?"

"Yes, I guess so. I don't exactly go around telling it at parish suppers."

"In fact," she said slowly, "you've a little bit flummoxed me. All of a sudden I don't know what to say. It's quite a change, I know, but I really don't."

"You don't have to say anything, Helen. That wasn't included in the price of admission."

"Yes, but I'll let you in on a secret, Hugh: I had something all ready to say. I think I had it prepared even before you opened your mouth. I knew exactly what I was going to say the moment you were finished."

I said wryly, "Poor Hugh?"

She nodded. "More or less, I'm afraid. Do I say that a lot? I suppose I do. But I won't say it again. And I never meant it to sound patronizing or silly, but I guess something like that always does, doesn't it? No matter how you mean it."

I said, "You're unfair to yourself. I don't think you've ever said a patronizing word to me in your life, much less a silly one."

"Haven't I? Well, that's good. I'd like to believe it. Anyway, I'm not going to say one now. I think all I want to say is that it's a wonderful story, Hugh. At least it is to me: wonderful, and terribly moving. And awful, too, of course. Awful for you, that is: I had no idea the roof fell in so completely. I just wish. . . . You couldn't have come to us? That wouldn't have been any good? Or did you even think of it?"

"I didn't, to tell you the truth. I didn't think of going to anyone. Just the opposite, in fact. What I wanted to do, more than anything else, was to keep to myself. And I also had the feeling, I remember, that all my troubles would be over if I could only get away — from the people I knew, from the city, from everything. You get to the point where the simple switch in geography seems to be the answer. Well, I couldn't quite manage that in the parish, but I could arrange to be more and more alone. Which I did. With fairly well-known results." And then, because it was something I'd wondered about over and over again through the years, and because, even though it made no difference now, I still felt responsible and guilty and — somewhat less noble, this — just plain curious, I said, "How did they take it, Helen? I know there was talk, of course; there had to be — and a lot of it. But what kind of talk? Were they shocked? Hurt? Angry? Scandalized? A little of each? I never knew. Obviously it's not the kind of thing people come up and talk to me about. And I've never asked anyone. Until now."

"There was talk," she admitted. Unwillingly: I think that at this stage of the game the subject was probably far more painful for her than for me. "You know, about what you might expect. Most of it wasn't very reliable: rumors, gossip, someone knew someone else who knew an altar boy who knew the truth. Still, in a general way people seemed to know what had happened — you really weren't very secretive, Hugh — and I suppose that what they mainly felt was . . . well . . . rather let down. . . ."

Which was kind enough, surely — and also not quite true. For this gentle disappointment, this simple, sorrowful feeling of being "let down" might possibly have been the main reaction of a community of saints, but the people of Saint Raymond's and Saint Stephen's were . . . well, quite simply, they were human beings. And it wasn't at all hard to imagine the medley of whispers, pitying little nods, sardonic winks, outraged perorations, snickers, and small jokes that came up inevitably when groups got together — just as it was no harder to picture, on another age level, the schoolboy, safely out of sight of monitoring eyes, suddenly beginning to zigzag unsteadily along the sidewalk, mimicking for his admiring friends the evening gait of his former pastor. All this and much more took place: I was sure of it. And it took place, not because the people were cruel or vindictive or vicious, but because the capacity for just this kind of thing is so much a part of all of us — and the great mistake, I think, the mistake that surely leads to more misery, is for the victim to succumb to the normal temptation and take the part for the whole. For there is a balance here: the great majority of those who winked and nudged and raved and joked would, in the very next moment, have willingly given me whatever lift they could, and the same schoolboy who staggered with such derisive exactness would in an instant have given up his free morning to serve my Mass and drive me halfway across the state and back. We all share in a shattering duality — and by this I don't mean that soggy, superficial split that one so often sees: the kind of thing, for example, where the gangster sobs uncontrollably at an old Shirley Temple movie. I mean the fundamental schism that Newman referred to when he spoke of man being forever involved in the consequences of some "terrible, aboriginal calamity"; every day in every man there is this warfare of the parts. And while all this results in meanness and bitterness and savagery enough, God knows, and while only a fool can look around him and smile serenely in unwatered optimism, nevertheless the wonder of it all is to me the frequency with which kindness, the essential *goodness* of man does break through, and as one who has received his full measure of that goodness, I can say that for me, at least, it is in the long succession of these small, redemptive instants, just as much as in the magnificence of heroes, that the meaning and the glory of man is revealed. . . .

All this, from a phrase which had been thrown out in kindness by Helen! And which had been an answer to a question which should never have been asked in the first place. For, as I say, I knew the people, and I knew — by instinct, if by nothing else — what the real answer had to be. So then, why on earth badger Helen into uncomfortable evasion, merely out of some ludicrous, little-boy desire to feel a soothing hand on the brow and be reassured that the spanking had not really been so bad after all? We were all too old for that sort of thing; I felt ashamed. It was high time for a quick change of theme, and so I said, "If that was all they felt, they were very good indeed. But in any case it all belongs to history now. And sometimes I think ancient history; that's what being in Old

Saint Paul's does for you. After you've been there a while you somehow have the feeling that everything that happened to you before you came there must have happened a minimum of a thousand years ago."

"Well, that's probably good. At least it gives you the illusion of having lived a very long life." But she said this absently; she wasn't to be diverted from my trials so easily; she said, "I keep thinking of those last months at Saint Stephen's and you there, day after day, not seeing anyone, not talking to anyone . . . oh Hugh, it must have been absolutely miserable for you!"

Although it had hardly been unshared misery; I couldn't help thinking suddenly of my two curates in those days: those dutiful, embarrassed young priests, receiving such a wild baptism into the clerical life. *They* had been miserable enough, all right — and, irrelevantly, it occurred to me that I hadn't seen either of them since the day I left Saint Stephen's. Which was understandable: all things considered the connection was not one they could have been anxious to preserve. But all this left us still close to the same old subject; I said, "It wasn't much of a picnic. For anyone. But there's a little temptation to exaggerate it. After all, it wasn't something unique, you know."

She shrugged slightly. "I suppose not. Although that doesn't matter much, does it? I shouldn't think it did. I mean, if you cut your hand off, it hurts; it doesn't hurt any less simply because a thousand other people may have cut their hands off before you."

"No, but if you remember all those other hands you may be prevented from hiring a hall and giving a short talk on 'How I Cut My Hand Off.' I think it helps you to keep a sense of proportion. Otherwise you begin to fondle your own personal catastrophes, and that seems dangerous to me. I'm not at all out to demolish my own importance as the suffering object, but the plain fact is that a good many people have gone through the same thing. Or what amounts to the same thing.

There's always the question of degree involved, of course, but I think most adults have had crises, awful intervals, where there just didn't seem to be any way out. Haven't you? At one time or another?"

"Yes," she said slowly. "Yes, I have." And then for a few minutes she didn't say anything. We sat there, the light already beginning to slip away a little in the short autumn day, and when she did speak it was apparent that our direction had been changed at last. "I was talking about old footprints a few minutes ago," she said. "There are a few I never care to step in again. Although no matter how old they are they have a way of showing up every now and then, I guess just to prove that nothing you do fades out completely. I was remembering just now the year I came home from college. You weren't around then, Hugh."

"No." Although I remembered very well the year she had got out of school. I'd been away in the seminary, and so had John; because of that, neither of us had gone to her graduation. I said, "I didn't realize that anything crucial had happened then."

"I don't know that it was crucial, exactly. It certainly wasn't anything terribly dramatic: nobody died or lost his faith or fell in love or disappeared. It was nothing like that: in a sense it's really not much of a story at all. Except that at the time it was quite enough for me. I thought that every window in the world had closed up tight and wouldn't ever open again. That sounds fairly drastic, doesn't it?"

"Yes. Yes it does. It also sounds a little bit as though you were twenty-one."

"Well, yes. That was the point. Or part of the point: the *whole* point was that I was twenty-one and at home. You see, I hadn't really been home to speak of since Mummy died and I went off to school. For short stays yes, during vacations, but those were more like intermissions than anything else; there was always school to go back to. And I liked going back.

I really did. I'm hitting that point a little hard, Hugh, because you were always fairly snobbish about Saint Claire's, weren't you?"

Was I? And then, for the first time in heaven knows how many years, fragments of long-ago, scornful declamations came back to me; I said, "Yes, I guess I was. I'm sorry. Still, I had a little justice working for me on that one, didn't I? Academically, your alma mater wasn't exactly rigorous, was it? Not too many deaths from overwork?"

She said loyally, "It wasn't supposed to be the Sorbonne. It was supposed to be a very expensive and rather elegant school for Catholic young ladies whose fathers were rich enough to send them there. And what happened was that it was better than that. Much better. There were actually one or two people there with real brains, Hugh, there really were. It may have been pure accident, and they may have been found out and dismissed by now: all right. But they were there *then*. And that's all you can really ask for, isn't it? One or two? So it wasn't just a playground. Although," she said, less defensively, "we did have great fun. Quite a few of the girls lived within week-ending distance, and I used to go home with them. I must say they lived the full life out there; they had us beaten by a thousand miles. They had the loveliest parties, Hugh! And then even at the school we did surprisingly well. You know how these schools usually are: all the girls together under the unwinking surveillance of the Mother Superior and her band? But we managed to have the most wonderful dances — have you ever waltzed through nun-filled rooms, Hugh?"

"Never."

"Well, the thing is, neither have I. At least not at Saint Claire's. That was what was so wonderful; the nuns were quite different and extremely sensible. Whenever we had a dance — and we had quite a lot of them — there wasn't a wimple in sight; they simply melted away. And believe it or not, Hugh,

[256]

there was no Babylon; we just had a marvelous time. Oh yes, Hugh, I liked it. I liked it fine!"

And she seemed to nod to herself, as if reminding herself how grand it all had been. Had it, I wondered? I suspected some inflation: she had a strong romantic streak, and one or two of the points — those generously disappearing nuns, for example — had the rosy quality of legend. On the other hand, it may all have been perfectly true, for Saint Claire's was easily the luxury school of its kind: Charlie, so niggardly in so many ways, had always been astonishingly open-handed with his children's education, announcing loudly that they were to be given all the advantages he had been denied. My father had offered an explanation of this which had been perceptive if slightly uncharitable.

"Charlie's a man who lives in hopes," he had said to me. "And here he hopes, you see, that one great day when it's all over he can call his boys and girls into his living room and look at them with sad eyes and say, 'Well, it's no more than I expected all the while. I gave you my hard-earned money and my heart's blood too, and what's happened? With all that I gave you, not a one of you has done as well as me that started with nothin' at all!' Oh, yes, a moment like that is something to live for. It'll pay Charlie back a thousand times for every dime he's spent. That's all he really asks for: not the big rewards at all, but just the little satisfactions that come to a loving family man every now and then along the line!"

Be that as it may, Saint Claire's had surely been a matter of more roses than thorns; it was not here that bitter memories were rooted. I said, "These windows that closed up so tight: they came later on?"

"Yes. One day a vacation was over and all of a sudden there was no more school to go back to. I think I'd almost forgotten that schools eventually gave out diplomas — that that was really the idea behind the whole thing. Anyway, I had mine now, so there was no more reason to go back there. Or anywhere else, for that matter; you might say that suddenly there seemed to be an acute shortage of alternatives. So I just stayed on at home. It isn't what I would have done if I'd had a perfectly free hand, but I really didn't expect it to be too bad. I certainly didn't look forward to it with loathing. Although I thought I'd probably be a bit lonely."

"And you were?"

"I was," she said. "You see, you were off at the seminary, and so was John. And Dan was at school — at several schools, in fact." The cloudy look which touched all Carmody faces whenever this magic name came up now appeared — although in softened form — on hers. "Poor Dan," she said. "He was at it even then. I don't remember at *what*, precisely. I think in those days it was usually some sort of football pool that was fixed so no one could win. The school authorities were never very sympathetic and as a result he had to move about a bit. Anyway, he wasn't at home and that was bad luck, because no matter what he did he was always great fun around the house. I wouldn't call him the most dependable brother in the world, but he was always likable and gay, and at that point in history I would have settled for a little gaiety."

I said, "But you knew hundreds of people around here: old schoolgirl chums, that kind of thing. Some of them must have been available."

"Well, yes, except that I hadn't seen them very much for about four years. And the wrong four years at that: if I'd been older or younger it might have been different. But if you leave home at seventeen and stay away until you're twenty-one, then you come back to a place you've never been. Particularly if you're a girl. All sorts of people are married, new little cliques have formed, and your very best friend in junior high school, the one you used to show your poems to, is now reading all the novels of Faith Baldwin. Do you know what I mean, Hugh? I'm not exactly a Kafka girl, and I've read Proust, Volume One, and that's all, but still . . . anyway," she said,

[258]

"that's not so important. What *is* important is that by this time you're completely out of touch with every last bit of local gossip. And that really ruins the show!"

I said, "Does it, though? You think so much hangs on that?"

"I think just about *everything* hangs on that. Oh," she said, "I know we're all together in the brotherhood of man, and I really have read about that Western Heritage we share in common, but dear Hugh, these things *really* aren't what matters when you're on the telephone at ten o'clock in the morning with your second cup of coffee in your hand. *Then* what matters — what keeps the whole thing going — is whether Larry Reilly gave Kay McCormack the same ring he once gave Bessie Devlin, or whether Chet Dolan's going to get the City Hospital vacancy even though Mary talks too much, or whether Jack and Honey Keough had a fight over Jack's inviting Cissie Donahue to dinner at their house the night of the Yacht Club dance. And my trouble, Hugh, was that I just wasn't interested: I couldn't have cared less! I was interested in gossip, all right, but the people I wanted to gossip with and about were all a thousand miles away. Or at least most of them were. And that didn't do me much good here. And so the long and short of it is that while I went out now and then, I found myself at home more often than I'd expected. With Mary. And Daddy."

She stopped; I waited. I continued to wait, but to my surprise she said nothing more, and finally I said, gently, "And?"

But then a curious thing happened, for she looked directly at me and when she did I saw that something different had come into her eyes. It was no sudden, flashing signal, and I don't think it was even anything measurable or definable: it was just one of those small, faint changes of light or intensity which could have escaped notice but which, on the other hand, was quite enough to tell me that, for some reason, she had abruptly changed her mind. Whatever she had intended to say, she was not going to say it now.

[259]

"And," she repeated slowly. "And . . . nothing, really. I think I must be pretty much of a flop as a storyteller, Hugh. All start and no finish. Not that it matters so much in this case because the story I was going to tell . . . well, it just isn't worth telling."

I said, "A sudden decision?"

"Yes, I guess so. But a sensible one, I think. Do you remember the winter when we used to go down to the old Criterion on Saturday afternoons to see all those vaudeville acts? And do you remember what you used to say? That a bad act always followed a good one? Well, I'm not going to follow your story with mine. I'll confess something to you, Hugh: I happen to want — very much — not to seem silly to you, and the unfortunate thing is that the more I think over what I was going to say, the sillier and more trivial it seems. I'm afraid it's really nothing more than the story of a fairly spoiled girl who, at one point in her life, felt fairly sorry for herself — and I really can't blow that up into much of a tragedy, can I? Besides, it all happened a hundred years or so ago, and couldn't matter less today. Dear Hugh, I wouldn't waste a single minute of your time by even trying to tell it to you!"

I said, "Let's say my time isn't quite that valuable. And let's say I'd rather like to hear it."

Which was more or less what she had said to me a few minutes before, but with far better results: I had in fact talked my head off. But she merely said, "No, it's nothing, Hugh. Honestly. It would be childish, and I'm a grandmother: I can't afford it. Have a little pity: I feel foolish enough already. It wouldn't help to start in telling you now how I felt when I got a spanking in the fourth grade, or about the time I got my unrequited crush on the Manual Training teacher. And this is just as pointless, just as irrelevant. Really it is!"

Was she a truthful woman? Yes. Did I believe her now? No. For all this just didn't begin to square with what she had said — or, much more important, the way she had said it — earlier. But there it was, and since I knew that, in an entirely pleasant way — no pursed lips, no jutting jaw — she could be quite as stubborn as she needed to be, I thought it unlikely that we would move much farther in this direction. As if to reinforce this thought the two children, who had slept so obligingly for so long, now awoke, and this, together with the coming darkness, was the certain signal that our afternoon was near its end. We took one more look around, but now the light was dim and graying, and all the gay reflected colors of the day had gone — there was nothing more to see. So, slowly, we pulled out of the clearing and began our drive back to town.

We said little as we rode. I think Helen was probably somewhat embarrassed, in the way one is when both too much and not enough has been said. And for my part, I think I was . . . what? The abused confidant? The one who had given far more than he had got? I'm afraid there was at least a little of this, and yet, if so, it was unreasonable. Because the perfect equation of confidence, that tit-for-tat balance of trade which we find in the schoolyard — "I'll tell you my secret if you'll tell me yours!" — is almost impossible, for a thousand reasons, in the complicated, everyday universe of adult men and women — such a confidence, indeed, is seldom all our own to give. So then, to sit there feeling that, in some peculiar way, I had been short-changed was both unrealistic and childish, yet all the same I did sit there, radiating, I suspect, the silence of the injured party. . . .

But if we were silent, the ride was not: the children took up the slack. They had been quiet; they had been "good"; now it was time to atone. They began one of those mysterious children's games which become the more incomprehensible as you yourself become the more removed from childhood — this one took the form of a loud, energetic, singsong sequence of verse and antiphon:

"*I've* got a penny. . . ."

"I've got a penny. . . ."

"David's got a penny. . . ."

"Susan's got a penny. . . ."

"Donald's got a penny. . . ."

"Nancy's got a penny. . . ."

They had many friends; all had pennies. The game continued for some moments until suddenly Helen called a halt, and I wondered if they had crossed the permissible threshold of harassment? Or if the chant had only now broken in upon her thoughts? At any rate she half turned to the back seat and said firmly, "All right, now. No more names and no more pennies. And no more shouting of any kind."

The little boy said, "We were singing."

"Well, it was lovely singing. But let's not sing any more right now. You can sing on Saturday when we go to the zoo; that's the place where everyone sings. But if you sing any more in the car I'm afraid there might not be any trip to the zoo. That wouldn't be so good, would it?"

There was a pause while this threat was considered. Then the little boy said, "Are we going home now?"

"Yes. We'll be there in just a few minutes."

The little boy said, "Is he coming with us?"

There was no possibly ambiguity about the question; still, the little boy took no chances: one small forefinger pointed significantly at my neck. Helen looked over towards me and I recognized amusement, a kind of mock helplessness — so that at least the slight stiffness, the embarrassment, was over. She said, "That's what's known as the proper reverence for the cloth. They're little pagans." To the children she said, "Yes, I hope very much that Father's coming with us." And to me: "Will you come, Hugh? I know I didn't give you much of a story, but at least I can give you a very good dinner. We have a marvelous cook these days. What do you say?"

"I say that I'm tempted. Sorely. But I've been away from the rectory all day. . . ."

"Ah," she said, "there's really not much logic to that, is

there? One evening out hardly means you're a gadabout, Hugh. And that curate of yours will love a few extra hours of responsibility, you know he will. So come along. I just have to swing by the hospital and pick up Frank and then we'll go directly to the house. Ted and Anne are coming over for the children; I know they'd love to see you. And Jim and Polly Darcy are coming in for dinner, and you always liked them a lot, didn't you? I think we'd have a wonderful evening!"

It was all true enough; I didn't doubt it for a minute. I hadn't seen Jim Darcy for years; I liked him enormously. He was an intelligent, humorous man, a corporation lawyer with curious interest in a thousand things, from Seneca to practical politics. He had once run for mayor; he had been elected; he had done well in office but then, after a single term, he had chosen not to run again — although it was generally agreed that he could have been re-elected with ease. He was a civilized and stimulating companion, an odd stick, in a way, and a great raconteur with a formidable knowledge of the small and personal details of the city's past and present. I can remember his coming to our house, when we were boys growing up together, and talking more to my father than to me, pumping him for reminiscence. My father obliged. Willingly. He was fond of talking, particularly on this subject and to this audience, for Darcy was one of those rare boys to whom grown men will somehow talk rather freely, almost as if to an equal. Everyone had predicted, at one stage or another, that he would leave the city and "go far," but he had in fact stayed in the city and, indeed, in the same house in Saint Raymond's parish — for no other reason, I think, than that he liked both the place and the people. He must have known exactly when it was that I went away, as well as the reason for my going — it was the kind of thing he would hear about, almost as soon as it had happened — and yet I knew that I could meet him tonight at Helen's with no uneasiness, and without the slightest fear of awkward reference of any kind. So then, the

[263]

prospect was a good one: an agreeable evening, a pleasant throwback to old times.

So pleasant, so agreeable, that I knew I would not go. Was it absurd to think of this innocent, congenial gathering as a potential danger — as some sort of thin edge of the wedge? Possibly — but then, I was not exactly wedge-proof; I knew my own vulnerability. And so, for this reason, far more than any urgent need to hurry back to a scarcely overburdened Father Danowski, I refused the invitation — and in the end, after some further protestation, the refusal was accepted. But the reference to Darcy had reminded me of something else — something Helen had touched upon briefly at the beginning of the afternoon — and as we drove into the hospital yard I asked her about her son's political plans.

"They seem to be coming along," she said. "He's about ready to announce, I think. He's very keen on it now; so is Anne. So is Frank, for that matter. I'm not so sure that I am. Maybe that's because I'm not in the least politically minded or 'oriented' or 'aware' — whatever it is that we're all supposed to be these days. But I just don't know the first thing about it; we've never been at all a political family. Though that's a little odd in itself when you come to think of it, isn't it? I mean, so many around us were, and you'd have thought that Daddy, of all people, would have been in his element, charging around, pulling strings, swapping votes. But he never did. No, Ted's the pioneer — and I'm finding it a little hard to get used to."

I remembered what had struck me as most peculiar when I'd first heard of these plans; I said, "Has he told your father yet?"

"No. But I have." She sighed as she turned the car into a parking place outside the hospital entrance. "Someone had to, Hugh. It should have been Ted, of course, and I kept telling him so; he agreed to do it and I know he meant to. But he *does* procrastinate a bit, and I think that what really happened was that with all the running around he's doing these days he simply forgot." She smiled wryly and said, "It doesn't

[264]

sound possible, does it? I mean, that you'd actually *forget* to tell Daddy a thing like that?"

"No, not very. What is it: a case of the new generation not fearing the old gods?"

"Yes, I guess so. Something like that. Not that he doesn't love him and respect him, but . . . anyway," she said, "as I say, someone had to tell him, before he learned it from a stranger or read about it in the papers. Do you know, I even had the wild thought I might ask you to do it?"

And this startled me; I said, "Why me, for heaven's sake?"

"Oh, I don't know. Because you have the strength of ten. Because your heart is pure." She laughed and put her hand on my arm; she said, "No, the real reason was that you're so obviously *persona grata* these days. He still talks about you all the time: about you and your father. It occurred to me that you might be just the one to break the ice. But then I had a few second thoughts."

"I'm grateful for that."

"Are you? I think you would have done fine. Better than I did, at any rate; I'm afraid I was fairly clumsy. Of course it really wasn't very easy: what I had to do was explain why he was hearing it from me instead of Ted. You see, I don't think it ever dawned on him that he doesn't enter Ted's life the same way he did mine. Or John's. That he hasn't the same *relevance.* Do you know what I mean, Hugh?"

I did indeed; it was just this I had wondered about when I had seen old Charlie and his grandson together at the birthday dinner. I said, "Ted's a long, long way from the immigrants."

"And it's happened so *fast:* that's the thing. Look at Ted and some of his friends: the way they dress, the way they talk, the way they behave — and all a couple of generations away from the farm in Galway. Don't get me wrong, Hugh: they're good children, I'm proud of them, they've done beautifully, and I suppose what's happened was inevitable. All the same, it

[265]

can be a little hard on the ones who've been moved away from — once they come to realize it."

"And you think your father does realize it?"

"Yes, now. Oh, I invented what I thought was a plausible enough story, but I don't think he was taken in. He didn't shout or make any noise; he didn't even get that pathos in his voice that he does whenever he talks about little Charlie, or how lonesome he is. He just stood there and looked . . . well, odd. And *old*, I suppose. It's funny, but I never think of him as being old, but right then . . . anyway, a couple of days later I did get Ted and marched him in and the two of them had a long talk. And then he was more like his old self, but I could see that everything wasn't quite right. And do you know what I suddenly thought, Hugh? When the two of them were talking together, with Ted doing politely just what he was supposed to do, and Daddy bouncing around the room, giving lots of advice that wasn't really wanted and that I think he knew wasn't really wanted? I thought that maybe there ought to be a law to prevent very old people from even *seeing* all the wonderful young. Much less talking to them. It might be kinder in the end!"

She had been there, certainly, an eyewitness, and she was a sharp observer, and yet I wondered if she might not have been at least a little wrong. Not to deny the problem of the old versus the young, which is real enough, God knows, and often tragic enough, too, but to save me I couldn't quite picture Charlie as its immediate victim. He was a tough old man whose ego was in fact a fortress, and in all our meetings — those meetings which by now had become so frequent — I had seen no crumbling of the barricades. He remained as positive, as peppery, as exasperating as ever — I would have said a far cry from a broken old man who deserved the compassion of the middle-aged because he had been given the indifference of the young. And I would have guessed that if Charlie had sensed such indifference, his sorrow — if any — would have

[266]

been for the young rather than for himself. It was the kind of failure of appreciation which might well have seemed to him moving because it was so incomprehensible; it was entirely possible that he would have even pitied the guilty before removing them from his will. . . .

But Helen was obviously troubled and she was no fool. So there may have been something there after all — or, again, it may have been something else. I think that as she grew older — and, of course, as Charlie did too — she was perhaps increasingly disturbed as she looked back over what must have been, at best, an extremely uneven father-daughter association. For Helen had never had Mary's simple, plodding devotion; she was an intelligent, imaginative woman who must have felt for this baffling and difficult parent a great and shifting range of emotions, some of which — Helen being Helen — were fond and loving, others of which — Charlie being Charlie — were not. She must have had little enough to reproach herself with, but I suspect that she did, nevertheless — although admittedly this was all guesswork on my part, for she seldom talked about her father revealingly. This conversation now was by no means typical, and I was sure that the one she had begun earlier, back in the clearing, and then had stopped so abruptly, would have been even less so. . . .

But all such speculation came to an end with a renewal of commotion in the back seat, with the little twins — who once again had been forgotten by me — scrambling over each other to the car window and waving and calling out, "Grandpa! Here's Grandpa!"

Frank had appeared on the hospital porch. He came down the steps and over to the car; when he saw me he seemed both surprised and pleased. "Hugh!" he said, taking my hand. "Well well! It's fine to see you!" And then, as he had on our first meeting at the birthday dinner, he ran me up and down with that professionally keen look, the infallible scout's eye searching the placid plain for the bubbling discord under-

[267]

neath. And again, as on that first meeting, his head moved in an abrupt, satisfied, terminal snap; once more I had come through. The rewards of a continued sobriety: was I again to be congratulated? But I did him an injustice, for all he said was, "I'm glad you've come. We were talking about you last night; I said we'd never be able to pull you out of that rectory."

Helen said, "We haven't pulled too well; now he wants to go right back. Persuade him to come to dinner, Frank; he won't pay any attention to me."

He put his hand on my shoulder. Heavily. "Attention!" he said, in a queer, ominous, somehow theatrical voice. "Come to dinner! Doctor's orders!"

And he frowned darkly. For an instant I was puzzled, then I understood. He was playing the stage-medico. It was the end of the day; it was comedy time. He was having fun with Father. It was a side of Frank I had not seen before, and I found it embarrassing. Not only for him — and probably for Helen; tactfully, I did not look at her — but for me as well, because now, according to the rules of the game, it was my move, and I had grown out of the habit. What was required, clearly, was the Rotarian response: a snappy, facetious salute, an "Anything-you-say-Doc!" We were to be clowns in tandem. And I was paralyzed; I could no more do this now than I could have flown unaided through the air. But mercifully it developed that nothing of the sort was needed, for Frank did not expect response; he merely winked at me and turned away, reaching down into the back seat and grabbing the twins and lifting them up, one under each arm. "All right," he said. "Now what have you got for me. Show me!"

They showed him. The little boy and the little girl threw their arms around his neck and hugged him with a fierce delight: he was obviously a great favorite. There was no reason he shouldn't have been, yet all the same I was surprised — another injustice to Frank? — and much more surprised by

[268]

what happened next. For, planking them down again, he took charge and for the next few minutes, while Helen and I sat as silent spectators, he joked with them, made faces for them, and mystified them with a disappearing coin, his long, scoured surgeon's fingers skillfully manipulating the metal in and out of sight. And here, no matter what he did, he was not embarrassing at all; the children were noisy and enchanted; it was a performance I couldn't have duplicated in a thousand years, and one which I wouldn't even have known how to begin. I reminded myself that my situation was unlikely to demand such talents — was there room for the clerical conjurer of Old Saint Paul's? So then, was there any reason for envy? No. Was I envious? Yes. . . .

Helen said, neither with bursting pride, nor with any suggestion of apology, of trying to chalk one up for her husband after his earlier heavy foolery, but quietly, matter-of-factly, "He's very good with children. And with sick children he's absolutely marvelous."

But now playtime was over. Frank finished his performance with a vaudevillian's flourish, was rewarded with two great wet kisses from the children, and then, as Helen pushed over on the front seat next to me, slid in behind the wheel. "Now, where to?" he said. "Can we take it as settled, Hugh: you're coming home with us?"

But I still said no; for a few moments he continued to urge me. It was in a way absurd: he insisting as if I were some sort of lion, procured with difficulty, the particular catch of this particular season; I refusing as if virtue itself resided in a plate of Mrs. Addione's leftovers in Saint Paul's kitchen. Eventually it was agreed that I would be driven back to the rectory and that we would meet for dinner another day. We left the hospital grounds; as we rode along I noted with some surprise that Frank drove quickly rather than well. The deft surgeon's hands were not so adroit with a car as with the disappearing coin: Helen was easily the better driver of the two. We talked pleasantly, inconsequentially, and then, about the halfway point, Frank said, with an air of one remembering a detail, but an important detail, "Joe Sawyer caught me as I was going in to operate this morning. He wants to know if we'll go down to the convention with Lil and himself."

She said thoughtfully, "I'm not too mad about that. Do we have to?"

"No, there's nothing definite. I said I'd check . . . although it might not be a bad idea. Because of Marjorie."

"Yes, well, that's the only reason. And even that. . . . Frank, let's face it: Marjorie is really a *very* big girl now. She's not three years old and she doesn't suck her thumb. She's a married woman with a child! So that even if we do go. . . ."

"I know. Well, we'll see. You'd rather go down with Victor and Liz?"

"Much, *much* rather. . . ."

They talked some more; once again I saw that I had arrived at the border of the unknown land: the private preserve of husband and wife. Over the years I must have come to this precise spot literally a hundred times — I suppose most unmarried people have, but I think there may be a difference with priests, who by vocation are not only unmarried, but will always be so — and yet each time it never fails to jolt me a little, I imagine it's the sheer swiftness of the passage, for one thing: it always happens in an instant. One moment you may be talking to an old friend, someone you've known as long as you've known anyone, someone you may even have known so well you would have sworn there was very little left to know, and then suddenly that someone will turn and speak to someone else in an entirely different way: a way so special, so direct and intimate that you wonder why words were used at all — it's as if the two had met head on and fused somewhere in mid-air before a syllable was spoken. And this is the point at which you realize that the old friend you knew so well has in fact dimensions you will never know — just as you realize that this way of speaking, this kind of encounter which is so personal, so completely *shared*, is also something you will never know. Which is really no great revelation, you may have realized all this often enough before, but, as I say, each fresh recognition brings its own jolt home. Unless you are careful — and sometimes even then — it is a sentimental moment. . . .

It doesn't last, of course. You "count your blessings"; balance is restored — a restoration which is sometimes sharply aided by the turn of the tone within the forbidden preserve. And in any case such private conversations are usually self-limiting; you are suddenly remembered; there is a bridge of quick apology; the talk becomes general once more. As it did now and I, doing my part, asked Frank about his son.

"He has a good chance," he said. "Of course I'm not a politician, but everyone seems to feel he has a good chance. He's announcing his candidacy next week, which I'm told is a little early, but then he's not worried so much about the election. The hard part will be getting the nomination. He'll be running against Arthur Sullivan for that."

I knew Arthur Sullivan: an old party wheelhorse who had represented his district — and Ted's — in Congress for many years now. He was a large, hearty near-illiterate, a professional friend, of whom my father once said, "I take my hat off to Arthur. He's discovered how a man with no brains can become a great statesman. You do it by keeping your rosary beads in your pants pocket so they'll fall out on the sidewalk when you reach for your handkerchief — you'd be surprised the number of colds Arthur has in election time — and by wearing plenty of holy medals pinned on to your blue serge suit. In a hard campaign you can hear Arthur jingle for miles. 'This is my Saint Christopher, that was blessed by the Pope,' he'll say. 'And be careful of that one, Mrs. McCaffrey — that's my Saint Francis that was give me by His Eminence!' And what's the end of it all? Today he's in Washington telling the navy how many submarines they can have for the next two years. And that's not bad for a man who was thirty-five before he found out a submarine was something that went under water!"

Arthur Sullivan was among the last of his species, already an anachronism — but not necessarily in his own district. I suspected that there he was still powerful, and that he would be a very hard man to beat. I said, "Ted's got his courage."

He laughed. "Oh, he's got plenty of *that*, all right!" And was there, here, at least the hint that I knew where *that* came from?

Helen said, "I'm all for courage, but I'm all for prudence, too. And I'm certainly not crazy about my boy running for any office against anyone like Arthur Sullivan. I think that underneath all that bumbling and laughter and going to Mass on weekdays he's really one of the most ruthless men I know; I think he'll say anything or do anything to win. And I think it's quite possible Ted may be hurt by it!"

And Frank said, simply and quietly, "He's not a boy, Helen. He's a grown man. And what can you do?" It was unexpected and, to me, oddly touching: this pleased, comfortable man revealing, just for a moment, that he might not be so pleased, and that he shared his wife's concern. But then, as if to atone for weakness, he laughed again and said to me, "Helen's a strong minority of one. I think we'll have to get her father to give her a little talking-to. And by the way, Hugh, there's the one who's really excited by all this; you might think he was running for Congress himself. He's pleased as Punch. And proud — proud in a way that's quite unusual for him. It's a *quiet* pride; he doesn't say much about it; but you can tell exactly what he feels simply by looking at him!"

Helen said, "We turn left here, Frank. At this corner."

We turned on to the avenue; Saint Paul's was now in sight. And I found myself wondering which was the real Frank: the one who had spoken with such simplicity and genuine feeling to his wife an instant before, or the imperceptive, clumsily jocose, slightly pompous man of such undoubted good will towards me who, with no more than a single word or the slightest set of his lips could send me into such reasonless irritation — and had been able to do so, moreover, since we were small boys in school together? So now again I reminded myself that there *was* this good side, that he was both kind and good to Helen, that it was absurd for a grown man to cherish and nourish these schoolboy dislikes. It was all true, and so with this in mind, and with a determination to be at least *fair*, I looked at him with new eyes — and felt an instant and almost overwhelming desire to pitch him out of the car. . . .

Pastoral thoughts at twilight!

As we neared the rectory he spoke again, this time offering a final comment on his son's campaign; it was the comment of the professional man rather than the father.

"Of course we mustn't forget that there is the factor of health involved here. Arthur Sullivan's not a young man. He's not an old one, either, as ages go today, but he's never taken especially good care of himself. I'd say he's led a fairly hard life. I'm not his doctor but naturally I'm in a position to hear things. And then of course his heart isn't all that it might. . . . mmm-mm." He stopped; his look said that he could say no more. For the first time it occurred to me that Frank's peculiar brand of professional discretion might be rather adaptable to the requirements of a political campaign. "The main thing," he said, "is to remember that *we never know*. No, we never know!"

It was grave, terminal, faintly ecclesiastic: it might have been the last line of a thousand sermons. Fittingly, we had pulled up before Saint Paul's. I got out and said goodbye to Frank; also to the children, who gave me their customary stare of steady evaluation. Friend or foe? I was still being weighed, obviously. To Helen I said, "Thanks for everything: the day out, the tour. You're a good guide."

"A guide to the past?" she said. "I enjoyed it. We'll do it

[273]

again sometime if you can stand it. And, Hugh, I hate to be a pest about this, but do come to see us. I know you won't make a definite date — I ought to know by now — so I won't press you. But any night — any time — you feel like it, just come. I'd say that was a fairly open invitation, wouldn't you?"

It was, and Frank seconded it. Strongly. And then they left, with my promising — as usual — to visit them soon. . . .

I went into the rectory; Father Danowski was seated at the table, nearly finished with his meal. When he saw me he jumped to his feet.

"Ah, Father!" he said. "I began because I did not know the precise time of your return. I hope you do not mind?"

"No no. Far from it."

"Mrs. Addione has been good to us today. Bountiful, one might almost say. She has left us chicken soup and cold roast lamb. Both are delicious. Be seated, Father, and I will get you some." And before I could stop him he was off to the kitchen. He returned in a few moments with a tureen full of soup and a large plate covered with thick slices of lamb. It was a supper for an army. Or for Father Danowski. Yet he was so willing, so goodhearted, so pleased to set this mountain of nourishment before me that all I could do was thank him and try to look properly hungry.

"And it is every bit as good as it looks," he promised. "I can testify to that!" He went back to his place, saying, "And your afternoon, Father: I trust it was most pleasant?"

"Yes, it was. Mostly a long ride in the country. Very pretty, and the air was good. . . ."

"Fresh air!" he said. "How good it is for us all!" Then he was silent as he began to eat his dessert. It was a pink Jello. Strawberry? Cherry? Raspberry? With luck, I would never know. But Father Danowski now said appreciatively, "Cherry Jello: how refreshing it is on a tepid evening! Have you ever thought about Jello, Father?"

[274]

"No more than the next man, I imagine. And casually, I'd say, rather than profoundly. . . ."

But he gave me a glance which was quick and which might also have been suspicious: I've noticed that lately my curate seems to have become more alert to certain possibilities. A small testimony to my schooling? Or to my increasingly heavy hand? He said reprovingly, "I was referring, Father, to the *principle*."

"Of Jello?"

"Of its *invention*. Just consider, Father. Here is a man who one day long ago said to himself, 'Well, I wonder what would happen if to this flavored powder I should add a small quantity of boiling water?' And today, as a result of that one question, *that man is many times a millionaire*. It is the principle of simplicity, Father. All of our great inventions have been simplicity itself."

The wheel. The clothespin. Jello. Three or four swift spoonfuls and he was finished; he wiped his lips delicately and said, "Well, Father, it has been a tranquil day. There is not much to report to you on the doings during your absence. Once again our good friend Roy did not put in his appearance. And we are shortly to have another altar boy: little Paul Harju. He came around to see me this afternoon, sent by his mother. There is a lovely woman, Father. Mrs. Harju. She is a Finnish person. Almost a saint, one might say. Considering all that she has had to go through."

But I did not know what Mrs. Harju had had to go through; I wasn't even sure that I knew Mrs. Harju. I was reminded — not for the first time — that for all his mannerisms, for all his little preposterous touches, Father Danowski was doing his job. In his zeal he had managed to compile dossiers on an astonishing number of our parishioners — not an easy task in a district with such a floating population — and even though he had been here a relatively short time his knowledge of the parish was far more personal and detailed than my own. Which is not exactly a comforting reflection to a pastor. Ignorant, I said now, "Mrs. Harju has a difficult time?"

"Oh yes. Because of her marriage. To the well-known scapegrace." And his look was so meaningful that I couldn't bring myself to admit that the well-known scapegrace was known to me not at all. I said nothing; he said, "But the boy is a fine little chap, although somewhat in need of instruction. When he came into the sacristy today I noticed at once that his hat was still upon his head. It was a small hat," he explained "of the type which is known as the 'beanie.' You know the type to which I refer, Father?"

"Yes, yes. . . ."

"This one," he said, "had a propeller on it. I said to him, nicely but quite firmly, 'Now, Paul, one thing we do not do, we do not wear our hats in church. Ladies and girls do, yes, but men and boys do not. It is not respectful, Paul. It is also silly and out of place.' Then, Father, so that he might remember this, I decided to give him a small object lesson. I said to him, 'Now, Paul, I will *show* you just how silly and out of place it is.' And I showed him, Father. By taking his hat and placing it upon my head."

"You wore a beanie? With a propeller?"

He flushed. "As an *object lesson*, Father," he said, with dignity. "I wore it only for a moment. As an *example*."

It was an example I would have given much to see. He said hurriedly, "And then Mrs. Koury called. To arrange for the baptism of her new little daughter. Also I noticed, while I was in the church, that that man is back again."

"Which man is that?"

It turned out to be the old man I think I've mentioned before — the one I'd seen so often, always standing or kneeling or sitting in the gloom of the back of the church anonymous and unapproachable. He hadn't been around for some weeks now, and from time to time I'd wondered what had happened

[276]

to him. Had he been ill? Had he died? And if he had, did anyone know? Besides the few necessary authorities? Did he have any people? I thought it unlikely; most men like that are apt to be alone, and even when they aren't the people they have are so removed from them that the effect is just the same. And so, as I say, I'd wondered, and I'd even made an inquiry or two — from the cop on the beat, for example — but with no results. And now, apparently, he was back and I felt oddly pleased — oddly, that is, when you consider that I'd never so much as said a word to the man, and didn't even know his name.

Father Danowski was not so pleased; he did not like mysteries. He said, "He is a most peculiar person. When I saw that he was back with us today I went up to him and spoke to him. As a priest. I said that I had observed him on many similar occasions and asked if perhaps I might be of some assistance to him. And do you know what his response was? *He bared his teeth at me.* Like an animal of the wilds, Father!"

I said, "I think I wouldn't go up to him any more. I'd let him alone. He does no harm."

"Not as *yet,*" he said. It was clear that his reception had unsettled him; I'm sure he still believed that the priest was always a welcome figure. "But we do not know what may happen. A person like that who wanders into the church at all times and stays for literally many hours in the darkness by himself, avoiding even the clergy: who knows what a man like that may be up to? He could be quite crazy, Father. He could be a pyromaniac. That is a distinct possibility. They are becoming more numerous these days, I am told. And there is something about churches that seems to attract them. One single madman's match, and what would happen to Old Saint Paul's, Father? I will tell you what would happen: *we would become a fiery inferno!*"

I pushed back from the table; we both rose and said grace. As we walked out of the dining room I said, "I wouldn't worry about it if I were you. I think your madman is probably just an old man who spends a good part of his time drifting into churches."

"He impresses you as being a *pious* person?"

"I don't know about that. I don't think it's a question of piety, necessarily. It could be nothing more edifying than an old man who has the whole day to kill and not too many places where he can kill it. And at least in here he's out of the wind and he's comparatively warm and he's sure" — but then, remembering my curate, I changed this — "or reasonably sure of not being bothered: for a good many people that's not too easy these days. So that's something. Not much, but it's something. And then of course there is just the possibility that he may have come in to say a few prayers. He could do that, you know. Even if he is a little crazy. There are all sorts of reasons why people come into church. I think, though, the percentage of those who come in to set us on fire must be fairly small. Offhand I'd say the odds were against our going up in smoke."

He did not seem persuaded. We had reached the stairs; he started up towards his room. "Perhaps," he said. "Perhaps, Father." But then another thought struck home and he said, more brightly, "You do not think he could be a wealthy eccentric?"

"No."

"And yet one reads of them continually. Shabby old gentlemen who walk the streets with holes in their trousers, who nevertheless bequeath *entire libraries* to communities which have befriended them!"

Father Danowski has a romantic streak; from time to time it breaks through the sedate and formal front unexpectedly, like a crocus through the frozen February crusts. I knew that he was dreaming again of the bigger, brighter Saint Paul's to come. I said, "Nevertheless, I wouldn't bank on anything like

[278]

that in this case. I think that even Mr. Carmody would be a more likely bet."

Sudden guilt appeared on the round young face: he said apologetically, "I forgot to tell you, Father: Mr. Carmody telephoned while you were out. I meant of course to inform you of this the moment you returned, but our most interesting conversation quite drove it from my mind."

"That's all right. Did he say what he wanted?"

"No, there was no message. Except to say that it was not important and that he would call again. Although before he hung up he was kind enough to inquire as to my father's health. Also to exchange a few pleasantries with me. More and more, Father, I come to realize what an extraordinary individual he truly is!"

I agreed that he was extraordinary; Father Danowski said good night and went off up the stairs to his room. Although "went off" is not quite exact: he literally *skipped* off, his normal, solemn, episcopal step made joyous, I suppose, by the recollection of that "exchange of pleasantries." It wasn't hard to imagine what Charlie had said to him. The opportunity combined with the target: it was too easy, he could not have resisted. A few crafty hints of things to come — and now my curate went buoyant to his bed. And as I saw the stocky, boyish back go sailing around the corner of the upstairs hallway, and thought of the plans being made, and the dreams that would be dreamed of miracles of stone rising while crowds below cried *Jubilate Deo* — then I thought that perhaps it was high time I had a word with Charlie. A restraining word. For fun is fun, but my poor curate didn't deserve this; I would have to interfere in the interest of his sanity. To say nothing of my own. . . .

I left the rectory and went through the connecting passage into the church. It was empty, as it almost always is at night; the old man who had so gracelessly snarled away my curate's offer to disturb him must have gone home — or, at least, gone off — hours before; now there was no one here but me. As often as it occurs, this is a special moment for me, one which defies routine: I mean, this precise moment when I first come into the church at night. Because by night this church is quite different, and not merely in the sense of light and dark. In such a solid, dim building, that difference is not extreme; the night brings one more layer of opaqueness, the dark becomes a darker dark. But there also comes a change of atmosphere. Here the stillness of the night seems to have quite another quality from the stillness of the day: something far more positive than the mere absence of noise; there is a sense of solitude which is immense, boundless; one suddenly *feels* the consecrated space. It's a curious thing, but I can never enter the church at night in the same way I do during the day: as abruptly, as — I suppose — *unthinkingly*. Something, a feeling of awe, of being a little *overwhelmed*, pulls me up, and I hesitate at the open door. As I did tonight. And then, after a second or two, I go in and cross the transept into the sanctuary and there, at the bottom step of the altar, I begin my prayers.

And then. . . .

I begin, as I say, and I pray for . . . how long? A few minutes, perhaps, and suddenly the darkness is not so dark and the stillness is not so still. A board creaks, a pipe bangs, a streak of wind whishes through a vulnerable chink: competition to devotions. Successful competition. Tonight, for example, there was a change in the darkness overhead; my eye caught it instantly. A bluish, misty bar of light had entered through the broken window and now angled softly across the width of the church; it meant the moon had risen, and I found myself thinking that this was as it should be, that a brilliant night and a bright full moon were what a day like this deserved. And from this I went on to think about the day and my own complete enjoyment of it, and from *this* — well, from this I went on to shake myself clear of all such drifting, and to pull myself back to the altar and my prayers. But the alternation continued. One moment I would be in the middle of an aspiration, and the next in the middle of the clearing, surrounded by autumn instead of the dark, watching Helen's face as she suddenly decided she would tell me a story of a long time ago — and then just as suddenly decided she would not. Why? I wondered; I broke off wondering and came back to the present. Firmly. So firmly that possibly a full minute passed before I was back in the car, riding along the avenue, listening to an invitation to a good dinner and a good reunion with Jim and Polly Darcy, and then a little later I was still in the car, still in the front seat, but really ten thousand miles away as Frank and Helen slipped without knowing it into the language of their own cocoon, a special blend of semaphore and sound. . . .

Which is not new with me. When I was a young priest this happened to me regularly, but then I was quite confident that it would not continue: that with the years I would learn the secret of immediate composure, that the time would come when I would kneel at night, and with the very start of genuflection all distractions of the day would disappear — it was a matter of practice, devotion, discipline, control. This is true enough, I suppose — except that such a time has not yet come for me, and I know now that it never will. And isn't it absurd — to mention the least of the faults — when a man who's been a priest for more than thirty years still can't kneel down at the end of a day and simply say his prayers? Not heroically, but just attentively: at once, and from start to finish without the punctuation of a regiment of trivia? Because if crises, great events, problems impossible to solve were brought before me during the day and stayed on, refusing to be shut off, erupting through devotions, that would be one thing — at least it would be understandable. But here in Saint Paul's — as I've said so often — I have no such problems or events; the crisis is an unknown animal. The truth seems to be that my mind is a kind of happy hunting ground for the negligible: every night as I start to pray, even if the day has been as dull and unmemorable as one could possibly imagine, a hundred little items of no significance at all rise up from God knows where, and softly and painlessly begin to poke and prick away until suddenly, before I know it, all attention is leaking down a hundred little drains. Which, as I say, is absurd, which is humbling, and which nevertheless continues. . . .

And yet while it can — and does — still shame me, it no longer leaves me discouraged. For I discovered at The Cenacle that the one way I can pray is with patience. We all approach God differently, and I know that there are those who can do so devoutly, totally, immediately, who can, in a sense, fling themselves into prayer. I can't. I wish I could, but I can't. I've said before that prayer doesn't come easily to me — it probably doesn't to most of us — and the only thing I can do is to start to pray and to wait — to wait at night, for example, until the day runs down and dies. As it always does now; as it did tonight. But there's always the prologue of innumerable false starts — I suppose this is, for me, the preparation for prayer. Sometimes it takes a long time; sometimes not long at all. But however long or short, it's always there, until finally it goes, and then there comes a calm, a quiet, and, at last, prayer. . . .

Tonight I must have stayed in the church longer than usual, for when I got back in the rectory it was quite late. The house was quiet, and so I knew that Father Danowski had gone to bed. When he's up, odd smothered noises come continually from his room, as if he were moving furniture, or dropping heavy weights on the floor. I know he's a great believer in exercises, he does them solemnly, morning and night, but no one can exercise *all* the time, and probably the explanation for most of the noise is simply that noise goes where he goes, as he moves bulkily through a world of suddenly breakable objects. But now he was in bed, which meant that he was asleep — to go to bed and to go to sleep are, for my fortunate young curate, entirely coexistent deeds. He once told me of an uncle of his who was the family insomniac; he spoke of him with a certain puzzled wonder, as if he had been a dwarf. . . .

But tonight I was tired enough myself; I suppose it was the ride and all the fresh country air that now left me so sleepy. I went up to my room and I was in my pajamas, just about to turn in, when the telephone rang — and it was only then that I remembered Charlie. His timing was bad; I was not yet asleep.

"Hello, Father! You're still up, I hope?"

"Oh yes. I never sleep, Mr. Carmody."

"Aha!" he cried. "Oh my, that's what I like to hear, Father! A grand little joke before goin' to bed! Just like your poor pa. They tell us the Irish have got half of the fun and the wit of the world, and by God, Father, when I listen to someone like you, I b'lieve them!"

It was severe punishment for my feeble little stroke; I said quickly, "Father Danowski told me you'd called, Mr. Carmody; I'm sorry I was out."

"No need to be sorry, Father!" he said magnanimously. "No, no, no need to be sorry at all. I had nothin' to say that I couldn't say to you later as well. Such as now. And besides, I had a nice little chat with the curate. There's a good simple lad, Father."

It was not an endorsement that would have pleased my curate: he thought of himself in a rather different light. I thought, now, of beginning my new campaign in his defense, but it was late at night — at least, late for me, and far too late to start playing games with old Charlie. So I said only, "He is a good lad. And just about invaluable to me over here."

He agreed. Instantly. "Oh, don't I know that, Father!" he said. "I'm with you on that one all the way. I tell you, there ought to be more priests around the city today like little Kazmeer. The good strong back, that's what's needed. It's only the smart ones that make the trouble. Give me a good, hard-

[283]

workin' Pole any day to some of these lads with their questions and their big ideas. You'll get none of that from the Poles, Father! Oh no! I'm a great man for the Poles. I tell you, Father, if Martin Luther had only been a Pole, there wouldn't be a Protestant in the world today!"

Brotherhood. He went on, more personally. "And yourself, Father: did you have a nice ride today? Out there in the country?"

He had talked to Helen, then; I remembered that somewhere in our talk she had mentioned in passing that her father telephoned her every night. Presumably to keep his thumb on all the threads. Did he call John, I wondered? And with what results? But I said, "Yes, I hadn't been out there in years. It's very pretty; it used to be a favorite spot of mine. Although if it hadn't been for Helen I'm sure I'd never have thought of going out there again."

"She's a grand girl," he said approvingly. "She drives very fast, but a grand girl all the same. A bit independent, I s'pose, but not so bad as she used to be. I tell you, Father, there was the girl that would argue day and night with old Charlie once upon a time. Just like her dear ma did when *she* was young. But they grew out of it, the both of them. After a time. Oh yes. Yes they did."

There was a pause: was Charlie remembering ancient victories? Apparently, for he said buoyantly, "Well, we mustn't complain. That's the way the world goes. And ain't it nice, Father, you could have your little trip today? I tell you, we all ought to go out more than we do: that's what God gave us the outdoors for. Your poor pa had a great friend one time I never liked much named Jocko Kinsella that never went out of the house. He always said that with everybody spittin' and coughin' the way they did the whole outdoors was nothin' but germs. So he never went out. He died at the age of forty-two, and before he died he was laid out for months on a little cot, pale as a parsnip, and bein' fed through tubes out of a milk

[284]

bottle. Oh yes, the sun never got at Jocko. You got plenty of sunshine today, did you, Father?"

"Plenty of sunshine, Mr. Carmody."

"Ain't that grand! And fresh air and birds and trees?"

"All those too, Mr. Carmody."

"Ain't that lovely! Oh, I tell you, that makes me feel good, Father! Sunshine and fresh air: you can't do better than that if you're a king. It all goes to prove what the man once said, Father: *the best things in life are free!*"

There were moments when Charlie could be said to speak with a burning sincerity. But I wondered now, as I did so often during our apparently aimless talks, in which direction we were heading — in other words, what was the reason behind this particular call? And it was at this instant Charlie showed me he had not lost his ability to astonish, for he said simply, "Well, good night, Father. Sleep well. And say a prayer for Charlie."

Baffled, I wondered if by any chance he had forgotten what he had called for; I said, "Good night, Mr. Carmody. There was nothing special . . . ?"

"No no," he said. "Just a call to wish you good night, the way I used to do to your poor pa every now and again. Like a shake of hands, you know, between old pals. Good night, Father."

"Good night, Mr. Carmody."

And so the late night telephone conversation ended. Had he in fact ever called my father in this way? Never. Then why. . . ? But it was late, I was very tired, and all Charlie's doings were at least faintly mysterious; I think I was asleep inside of ten seconds after the final, hearty good night. . . .

III

9

CHRISTMAS CAME. It was my second Christmas in Saint Paul's; it was quite different from the first. Not that the first had been at all a hardship; far from that. In many ways it was the most peaceful Christmas I'd ever known. But there were a few difficulties, disappointments. I was completely alone, I was still new to the parish, unfamiliar with everything and everyone, and although I'd noted — noted! — the apathy, the lack of response, I think I hoped that somehow, on Christmas, the spirit of the day would do its work and there would be a bright reversal: no great revival, to be sure, but a certain sharpening of interest, or maybe just a few more people at Mass. A modest enough hope but, as it turned out, unfulfilled. Completely. So that was discouraging. I could of course find excuses; I even blamed the weather — I must say not without some justice. For on Christmas last year the weather was dreadful — in other words, we had had a white Christmas. Which is lovely in the country, yes, but in the city — especially in an old city, and in the oldest section of that old city — the snow is soiled almost before it hits the ground; the snowplows are few and come too late; the sidewalks become impassable, the streets a crisscross of frozen dirty ruts. Snow paralyzes this city, even the lightest fall, and last year there had been a blizzard. It began two days before Christmas and continued for a day and a half, tying us up completely; by itself it wasn't enough to keep people from the church, but it must have pared down our never-too-sturdy potential. Be that as it may, Christmas last year brought no throngs to the doors of Old Saint Paul's. I said Midnight Mass on Christmas Eve with Roy as my altar boy: were there thirty people in the whole church? I don't think so. . . .

But this year, as I say, there was a difference. I sang Midnight Mass assisted by Father Danowski; in place of Roy we had four altar boys; there was the choir — small, uncertain, but powerful — that Father Danowski had bulldozed into shape in preparation for the Bishop's visit some months before. And the church was now more than half full — I know there's a beguiling effect to sheer numbers, and that in themselves they mean very little, but all the same I was glad to see them there. And at all the other Masses on Christmas Day there seemed to be something of the same sort of lift, so that while there were still no crowds, and in comparison with other churches on this day our own attendance must have been pitifully small, nevertheless there were signs of gain, of at least a little progress. I felt pleased and, I suppose, a little proud. Proud of the parish, that is, not of myself; I had no reason for personal pride. I think this came home to me most clearly at one of Father Danowski's Masses on Christmas morning. I was standing unobserved in the rear of the church, looking around before going back to the rectory; my curate had come down from the altar and was now in the pulpit, delivering his Christmas sermon. . . .

". . . to imagine the emotions on that glorious morning so long ago. I beg of you, my beloved people, to try to conjure up in your minds the joyous feelings of that great occasion. Recall, I beseech you, your *own* most pleasant sentiments when, in the bosom of your own home, you have perhaps gazed fondly down upon a small crib, and have remarked proudly to your good spouse, 'Well, here is our tiny infant in his swaddling clothes. . . .' "

The style was familiar: it was vintage Danowski. And yet for once I didn't smile, because as I looked around the church and saw the people who had come here this morning, I knew that it all had very little to do with me, and the credit for whatever change there was belonged almost entirely to this broad, bustling, zealous, slightly ridiculous boy, of whom it was always so easy to make fun. . . .

And of course he himself was the greatest change of all. For me personally, that is. Life in the rectory with Father Danowski was a world away from life in the rectory alone: it was a totally different kind of experience. And a good experience — although one which, in the beginning, I never would have chosen for myself. Because I wasn't eager for change. I was alone in the parish, but I was never really lonely: at that time it seemed to me that the rectory was just about ideal for me. I was grateful for the peace, the solitude, the sense of complete separation from the kind of parish life I'd had before; I had asked for no curate because none seemed necessary, because I really didn't want one. And then came, not just a curate, but Father Danowski. He came bringing conversation, noise, a bulging mobility, and that complete portfolio of his astonishing mannerisms: comic enough, to be sure, but also — especially at first, in those early days when we were still strangers to each other — just a little maddening. So there was a breaking-in period; I had to get used to my curate; I had to get used, not only to Father Danowski, but to having once again a younger priest in the house and in my charge — a younger priest who must have had his own misgivings, since he could hardly have avoided knowing all about me before he came. But from the first day Father Danowski gave no sign of this at all, and it was I — hypersensitive, I suppose, by now out of the habit of daily association with the young, and inevitably less plastic as I grew older — who came close to explosion, who on several occasions nearly spoke cruelly to him, or cut him short, or took advantage of him in any of the usual ways so available to age, authority, position. But I never quite did this, partly because I'd remember just in time that he was so young and inexperienced and obviously well-intentioned, but mainly because . . . well, because he'd stop me himself. That is, he'd say something which would so annoy me that I'd be just on the point of coming down hard when he'd say something else which would instantly strike me as being so absurd — and not just what was said, but the whole combination: the air of portly solemnity, the biretta tilted oddly on the round young head, the boy's face saying the mighty words themselves: "It is my belief, Father, that our young people of today must be informed that Life is not a bowl of cherries!" — that even the possibility of rebuke would collapse, and I would have to turn away quickly to avoid hurting him with badly buried laughter. . . .

And so we got by the first few weeks, and as we did I found myself discovering the other qualities, less obvious, that he had brought with him to the rectory: his loyalty, his goodness, his sense of dedication. And his sheer *youth:* something which, originally, I'd rather dreaded — in the way that you do, sometimes, when you yourself are no longer young — but which I'd come to welcome. Because with all the banging and bumping and motions, it was a good thing: it opened the rectory up, it let in air. . . .

Not to mention his kindness. On this day, for example, I knew that he wanted badly to go home and have Christmas dinner with his family; earlier, he'd mentioned that this was always a great social occasion, with normally far-distant Danowskis coming in to swarm all over his father's house. He could have gone easily enough as far as any parish duties were concerned, for I planned to be on hand all day — the Carmodys were dining at Helen's; I had been invited, but had decided not to go — but when I told him this, and suggested that he might leave immediately after the last Mass, he refused, saying that he would prefer to dine in the rectory on Christmas, and he offered numerous elaborately worded justifications for this preference. And of course the simple truth was that he didn't want me to eat alone on Christmas Day. Which, considering the fact that I was fairly used to being alone, may have been unnecessary, or a little sentimental, but which was certainly kind, thoughtful, all the same.

And so he stayed — he insisted on it — and we had a good day. Before dinner we exchanged gifts — I gave him a breviary, he gave me a rosary — and examined some of those we had received from others. I had sent out no presents, but the Carmodys — or Helen and Charlie — had remembered me in characteristic ways: Helen lavishly, with a handsomely bound set of Newman; Charlie mysteriously, with a money belt. It seemed to me the most superfluous of gifts, but I think Father Danowski saw it as a happy portent: his eye fell upon it and gleamed. Better things to come . . . ?

I had given both Mrs. Addione and Roy money; not a great deal, I'm afraid, but at least something, and what they could best use. Mrs. Addione had cried; still crying, she had given me a pair of bulky knitted socks. Roy had not cried. He had mumbled, rather than proclaimed, his thanks, but I think he was pleased; at any rate the following morning he had come around with a gift for me, which I had opened immediately. It was a leather key case. It was not new.

"Roy looked all around," he explained. "You know what they got in those stores, Father? *Junk.* Roy said to the clerk, he said, 'You don't fob off no junk like that on Roy! Roy ain't going to give no cheap stuff to a priest what's as good to him as Father!' So then Roy said to himself, he said, 'Roy, ain't you got something at home Father would like? Something he couldn't buy in no store for no money?' And," he said, his voice rising dramatically, his eyes beginning to bulge, 'you know what happened, Father? Wham! It hit Roy right smack in the head what he could give! That special key case!"

The special key case was in my hand; I looked at it more clearly. It was rather more worn than it had at first appeared; there was a slight tear in the leather; once, long ago, there had been initials, but these were now indecipherable. Roy said, "See, Father; it's all broke in for you."

"Yes, so I see. Well, Roy, I thank you. I thank you very much." But I was disappointed; I had expected, not a more substantial gift, surely, but something more in keeping with Roy's wild powers: an inventive excuse, for example, for giving me no gift at all. Still, he was not finished; he said now, "You know who that key case belonged to, Father?"

I shook my head; he said casually, "That prince. The Duke of Windsor."

"The Duke of Windsor?"

He nodded. "That used to be the king one time. And got busted down. When he got himself married."

So I had my wish: these were new heights of fantasy, even for Roy. And I had my gift: a gift with a pedigree. It bulged in my hand; I said, "There seem to be some keys still in it."

"To the palace," he said knowledgeably. "And all them places. But they probably got all the locks changed by now." Then he said, "You wonder, Father, how Roy got ahold of a special key case like this?"

"Yes, I wonder that indeed."

But he gave me a crafty smile. "Don't ask Roy no questions, Father," he said, "and you won't get told no lies!"

On Christmas Day, before dinner, I showed the key case to Father Danowski and told him the explanation. He frowned. He had also received a pair of knitted socks: Mrs. Addione played no favorites. But with Roy he was far less satisfied. He said now, "He is a crazy person. The Duke of Windsor! Why, Father, look at these keys! They are quite ordinary. They are Woolworth keys!"

"You don't think I could get into the palace, then?"

He gave me a look. "Come come, Father! You are surely joking! It is my opinion that you do not believe this madman any more than I do. I tell you, Father, he gets worse with the passing of each day!" The period in which Father Danowski decided he understood Roy had come to an abrupt end some weeks ago; now he said, "For example, we have only to look at this present to *me!*"

And he produced a small, thick, squarish book with a bright blue cover; he thrust it at me and said, "Just have a look at that, if you will, Father!"

His tone was so indignant that I wondered what on earth Roy could have given him. Pornography of some sort? A scribble of scurrilities? But when I quickly flipped through the pages I found that, apart from a date on each, they were entirely blank. The offensive book was in fact nothing more than a diary. As I held it, my fingers suddenly felt sticky; Father Danowski said triumphantly, "You observe, Father, how the cheap dye of the cover comes off all over one's hands?"

I looked at my hands; they were quite blue. I agreed that I observed it.

"That is *one* thing," he said. "But it is not the main thing. Look at the book itself, Father: you see what it is?"

Had I missed something? I said, "It's a diary; is that particularly bad?"

"But," he said, *"it is for last year!"*

I looked again; so it was. Father Danowski stood, helplessly regarding his useless present. "What is the purpose behind it?" he asked. "What is the purpose to giving anyone a last year's diary? There is no purpose at all. That is why I say he is a crazy person. And you note, Father, the position in which I am placed. I cannot acknowledge such a gift. I cannot go up to him and say, 'Well, Roy, I must thank you for your nice present of a last year's diary!' No no, Father. That would be foolishness. I cannot do that." He brooded for a moment, then said, "You do not think it could be some form of affront? What we might term a calculated insult?"

I suggested that this was most unlikely, although to tell the truth I didn't think it was at all, and quite obviously neither did he. But he grew cheerier almost immediately, for he began to show me the gifts he had received from the various members of his family. These were mostly articles of clothing, a sedate and appropriately clerical collection, with the single exception of one spectacular garment. This was a billowing shirt with short sleeves: it was a dazzling red in color and was spotted with yellow palm trees. As we went in to dinner, Father Danowski held it up, rather tentatively, for my inspection.

"It is a sports shirt," he explained. "From my sister Stella."

"I see. You plan to wear it around the rectory?"

Father Danowski blushed. "No no, Father. It is what is called 'resort attire.' It is for use only when I go on my vacation. I do not know if I will wear it even then. It is somewhat vivid, as you see. And I do not wish to invite comment."

I said that I thought the shirt would be quite safe in such circumstances, that it would not be a source of diocesan scandal. We sat down to eat and I asked him about his sister. He had a large family, and spoke about them all, often and with affection, but I could never remember which one did what.

"Is Stella the teacher?"

"No no. That is Olga, my oldest sister. Stella is the physician. She is a graduate of The Arthur B. Morgan School of Podiatry. In Elizabeth, New Jersey, where she is at present a resident. She is a specialist," he said proudly, "in disorders of the foot."

So. We talked about different professions; Father Danowski spoke glowingly of several boys he had played with who had since grown up and done well, who were unquestionably on their way to fame and riches. I said, "You see what you missed by becoming a priest? You might have been a criminal lawyer. Or a tycoon." And then, remembering a conversation we had

had in this dining room weeks ago, I added, "Or an inventor. You might have invented a better Jello."

But he said, with great seriousness, "Oh no, Father. I never wanted to be anything but a priest."

I said, "Didn't you indeed?" Not because I didn't believe him — I think it would be impossible not to believe Father Danowski — but because I was curious: this was a subject we hadn't covered before or even touched upon. Which wasn't strange: the history of one's vocation is a private matter, after all, and not the sort of thing which is likely to turn up in rectory small talk. But now he had mentioned it, introducing a part of himself about which I knew next to nothing, and I said, "Not even when you were a little boy? Didn't you ever want to be a cowboy? Or a fireman? Or a burglar?" And then I remembered that these were the aspirations current in my own boyhood, and that by the time Father Danowski was a boy I had been a priest for many years. I would have to become more contemporary; I would have to update. I said, "Or a jet pilot?"

Had I updated too far? Yes, of course, but it made no difference, for he had been shaking his head stubbornly and continued to shake it now. "No. Never. Even when I was a small boy I had the desire to become a priest. It was quite well known, in fact. Sometimes the little children who went to school with me would make fun of this and would call me 'Father.' As a nickname. But I did not mind."

It was a scene I had no difficulty in imagining: the circle of waiting children in the morning schoolyard, the shrill voices raised in an onslaught of derision as in marched the stocky little "Father" Danowski, who had so solemnly confessed to them his extraordinary destiny. I said, "What about your family: your father and mother? Were they bothered at all by such an early decision?"

"To some extent, Father. I would say that it was perhaps my mother who at first approved far more than did my father.

[297]

Not that he is not an extremely religious person, with a great regard for the priesthood. But I believe it was in his mind for many years that I should follow in the footsteps of my older brother Teddy. Who has done so well."

"Teddy is the athlete?"

"So to speak, Father. That is to say, he was *formerly* an athlete. He is at present a professor. Of Physical Education. For some years now he has been a member of the faculty of Loyola College. *There* is a splendid school, Father."

Teddy the academician. I said, "But your father eventually came around?"

"Oh yes. There was never any great difficulty. He was aware of my deep respect for his wishes, but," he said simply, "after a time he realized that I would only become a priest. So he agreed. And my mother was most sympathetic from the beginning. She was a fountain of encouragement, Father. When I was a small child she would say to me, 'You must study your lessons harder than that, Stanley, if you wish to become a priest. They do not let dumb bunnies into the seminary, you know!' Dumb bunny," he said. "That was an expression my mother would use upon occasion."

"I see."

"To spur me on in my studies." He added, "You see, Father, I was not at all a bright boy."

Every once in a while, right in the midst of one of his most ornate and overblown flights, my curate will suddenly say something like this. I think he may be the only man I know who can do so completely without self-consciousness, guile, or calculation: it's as if a great child were talking. So that what comes out is not just another of those dreadful false apologies — "As you can see, Father, I'm really not a very interesting person"; "I'm afraid, Father, that I tell a story rather badly" — which whimper for effusive rebuttal, but a plain statement of fact, delivered with such candor, such astonishing simplicity, that I know at once that no soothing words are called for

[298]

and none are expected. Nevertheless, habit is strong, and so I said now, "I don't know that many of us could call ourselves exactly brilliant in the grades. You're probably being a little hard on yourself, don't you think?"

"Oh no, Father," he said. "I do not mean that I was a stupid boy, but I was not as quick to learn as most of the other children. Learning has always come hard to me. Even much later, in the seminary. There it was especially difficult. Not only because there were so many things to learn, but because they were all so important. If I was to be a priest."

And I was suddenly curious about this, too; I said, "Tell me about the seminary: did you like it there?"

"Oh yes. Yes indeed, Father. It was of course very hard for me, as I have just said, and sometimes the fellows who were there as my classmates would play pranks upon me. For example, Father, there is what is known as the 'apple pie bed.' In which the sheets are short. So that one is unable to retire properly. . . ."

"Yes, yes, I know." A question: Does my curate ever suspect that I am his fellow countryman? From time to time he courteously interprets for me American customs and traditions, much as if I were a visitor from some distant land and ancient times: a courier, perhaps, from the court of Kubla Khan. . . .

"I experienced this," he said, "quite regularly. Also, I would be sent upon artificial errands. For implements which did not exist. And then many times in the gymnasium after taking my shower I would go to put on my clothing again only to discover that someone had exchanged my trousers for the trousers of another person. A person," said Father Danowski delicately, "who was invariably much *smaller* than myself. So that there were these little things, Father. It was a form of teasing."

He said this without the slightest rancor, indeed with an air of great benignity, and I said, "It didn't bother you?" For I knew this "teasing" — just as I knew this seminary: it was the same one to which I had gone, so many years ago. By the time Father Danowski had arrived it would have changed, of course, but I think not greatly. The majority of the boys entering would still be happy there — as, certainly, I was — but there would be the exceptions. With some of these it would be a question of vocation: boys sometimes come into the seminary prematurely, without being at all sure that this is what they want to do; or sometimes, happy enough at first, they pick up scruples or doubts that can't be resolved, or else, now having sampled the beginnings of the priestly life, they tremble a little before its permanence, before the notion of being fixed to it forever. Whatever the reason, those who feel it are not happy in the seminary. Most of them — quite wisely — leave, but a few stay, and for these I find it impossible not to feel the greatest sympathy. Because they're doing a wrong thing and a terribly foolish thing, but leaving a seminary is not exactly like walking out of the training program of, say, an insurance company. When you decide to leave a seminary, you decide, not just to walk out of a way of life, but a way of life which you once thought would be your whole life — and this is no minor dislocation. At the moment you seem to break yourself apart, and it's not altogether surprising that at such a moment some poor fellows panic a little — and begin to think, too, of such side considerations as appearing on the streets of their home town again, this time as the ex-seminarian, the almost-priest. And so, out of indecision, or weakness, or the most unfounded optimism, or the awful, irrational doggedness that sometimes drives us along courses we know to be wrong, some stay, and some, even, are eventually ordained. It's a sad and dangerous business, and while, of course, one can't have the arrogance in such matters as to surely predict disaster, one can at least say that the outlook is forbidding, that the invitation to catastrophe is there. . . .

All this, however, is a far cry from Father Danowski: he was a stranger to all such agitation. But there's another kind of seminarian who has no vocational problem, no doubts, no desire to be anywhere but in that seminary, yet for whom life there can be a series of torments, simply because . . . well, because he's rather an odd stick, someone decidedly apart from the prescribed pattern of that remarkably homogeneous world: the boys' school. Because, after all, that's what a seminary is, especially in the early years; I've never observed that the emphasis on religious training did much to dim the sharp eye of youth for the slightly "different" member of its community, the one who parted from the understood norms, the one who — by being too polite, too studious, too eloquent, too devout, too stout, too *anything* — immediately and by common consent became the target for all fire, the butt of all the jokes. For this role my curate would seem to have been superbly qualified. Especially in this seminary, where the boys still came mainly from a middle-class, closely knit, Irish-American society, admittedly less inbred and parochial than in my time, but hardly so much so that they could have avoided converging in amazed and rather snobbish delight on the solid, formal, absurd, vulnerable figure of this heaven-sent Pole. He must have seemed too good to be true: certainly, he would have been one of the great victims. And it was for this reason that I asked him now if all the "pranks," the "teasing," hadn't bothered him, for the cumulative effect of such jokes has a way of becoming far more erosive than the jokesters — who, after all, are young rather than cruel — intend.

But he said immediately that it had not. "Because they did not mean any harm by it," he said. "They were all quite good fellows. It was a way of having fun for them. I myself was always of the opinion that it was quite a silly way to have fun. I would occasionally say to them, 'Well, fellows, what has all this skylarking accomplished for you? A little foolish merriment, yes, but have you added to your stature one cubit?' But even such a reprimand itself," he said regretfully, "they seemed to find uproarious. So that we did not see eye to eye, as it were. But it was never *unfriendly*, Father. Oh no. And besides, it did not really matter. Because I was so pleased to be there. Right where I had wanted to be from the time I was a small child!"

And I suppose that in a sense this is what we really mean when we talk about such things as a steadfastness of vocation, or a lifelong dedication, or even, more broadly, simply the love of God. In my curate this came all wrapped up in fairly outrageous trappings, but it was there, all the same, and there were those moments when it came through — and managed to put me to shame. . . .

He went on now to talk about his life in the seminary. His enjoyment of it had been complete, even though — or so I gathered — his studies had grown no easier. But on the other hand, the famous jokes had grown fewer. They had not disappeared entirely — this would have been asking too much, surely — but they had diminished as the years passed by and as, presumably, his classmates came to grow used to him, to know him, to be fond of him, and — in a peculiar and, I imagine, a reluctant way — to be impressed by him. For his part, clearly he had been fond of them; he had admired many of them; since leaving the seminary, he had kept in touch with them. His correspondence — which I think I've forgotten to mention until now — is heavy. He sends out letters daily, numerous letters, letters which — to judge at least by the weight of the envelopes — are lengthy, and letters which, moreover, are answered: replies pour in regularly from rectories all over the diocese. To someone like myself, who may write perhaps two or three personal letters a year — and receive as many — this exchange is staggering. . . .

"Oh yes, Father," he said now, "we had many bright fellows, some of them, I would say, even *brilliant*. And how well they have done in recent years! There is Father Tim Donahue, who only ten days ago was appointed by His Excellency as head of the Guild for the Blind. That is quite a post for such a young man to hold. And then there is Father Bart Cavanaugh, who for more than six months now has been the assistant editor of our splendid diocesan newspaper. You are undoubtedly familiar, Father, with his many editorial efforts?"

But I was undoubtedly not, for the fact was that I hadn't so much as looked at our splendid diocesan newspaper for — how long? Ten years? Twelve? I said, "Perhaps not entirely familiar. . . ."

"How penetrating they are!" he exclaimed. "And yet a child can understand them. Mark my words, Father, we will be hearing great things of Father Bart one day. But then I am almost forgetting to mention the classmate of mine who has become the most illustrious of us all. By reason of his innumerable television appearances. He is of course the celebrated Father Clement Cassidy."

Of whom of course I had not heard. My face must have showed this, for Father Danowski said quickly, "He is better known to some, perhaps, as The Whistling Priest."

The Whistling Priest. Really? A fact? A fact. I heard about him now. He was a young priest who appeared each Sunday night on a popular television program; he was sponsored by a bath mat. On this program he had one function: he whistled. Songs. In his selection of these songs he offered a shrewd change of pace; he "mixed them up"; there was something for everybody. Father Danowski explained this to me.

"He will whistle first, let us say, a grand old favorite song such as 'There Is a Long Long Trail A-Winding.' Then there will come a popular song of the moment such as 'How Much Is That Doggie in the Window?' And lastly," he said, "he will whistle, let us say, 'Ave Maria.'"

"I see. He always concludes on the spiritual note?"

"Oh yes. That is the whole idea."

"Does he do anything else? Such as say Mass, for example? Or hear a confession now and then? Of course I don't suppose his whistling really leaves him much spare time."

He stared at me. "Oh no, Father," he said reprovingly. "You

[303]

have quite misunderstood. No priest is more scrupulous about his duties than is Father Clement Cassidy. The whistling is all in *addition*. It is what we might term a supplement. It is a way of reaching those who might not otherwise be reached."

Another bridge to the unregenerate. This time the Bridge of Whistles. I said, "And these people your friend is whistling at: you feel they're being reached?"

"One can judge," he said, "only by the response. And the fan mail is *positively overwhelming*." His voice as he said this was awed and slow, but then after a moment he said, a trifle more sensibly, "Of course I realize that that does not prove everything. One perhaps cannot hope for a profound or permanent spiritual effect from merely a whistled hymn, but it is a beginning. Possibly it will prove to be nothing more than that, but even if it does, a road has at least been opened. And after all, Father, that is just what we are enjoined to do!" he said enthusiastically. "It is our task to open up the roads!"

All roads lead to Rome. So they do, or so I hope, but I have my doubts about the highway of The Whistling Priest: that is, I wouldn't think it led much of anywhere. I've always disliked and mistrusted this carnival shill approach to the Church — and yet heaven knows we see it often enough. Does it really work? I don't think so, but more than that I think it's all wrong. Because for one thing it's so unworthy. I don't mean by this that it's too informal, too much in the market place, too "popular"; I do mean, quite simply, that it's cheap. Obviously when you talk about such things as God, religion, the church, man's soul, to a great many different people, you must necessarily do so in a great many different ways and on a great many different levels. But none of these levels can be — or at least none of them should be — in any sense flashy or false or vulgar, because if they are — no matter what the apparent justification — you run the very serious risk of making God, religion, the church, and man's soul seem just a little bit of the same. It's all very well to suggest that this really doesn't

[304]

matter so much, that what does matter is that, as a result, the people come in, but I think that's a great mistake. I know they come in — and often in considerable numbers — in response to such techniques. That's not surprising. The gaudy, the meretricious, frequently have a powerful and immediate seductiveness: at a fair or a circus, the children invariably make a beeline for those horrible puffs of pink candy. But what is surprising is that we sometimes take comfort from this: I know priests, for example, who will point with great pride to statistics proving the value of such appeals. So many appeals, so many souls for God: Q.E.D. Of course what the statistics don't do so well is to measure the depth, the strength, and the duration of the faith of those who do so come in — or in other words, they tell you absolutely nothing about the only thing that counts. And — still more — while there are all sorts of statistics to tell you how many souls these tactics have brought in, there are no statistics at all to tell you how many they may have kept out. Who knows, for instance, who can even guess the number of those who, with every sympathy, with every good will, have tentatively approached the Church only to be repelled by vaudeville antics at their first point of contact? As I say, we have no statistics for that at all; if we had, they might not be so comforting. . . .

So then, these are my misgivings, not about Father Clement Cassidy himself — who most probably is a very decent young man, and whom in any case I suspect of being something less than this magically compelling Pied Piper of my curate's story — but about the kind of apostolic work he represents. Needless to say, they're misgivings my curate doesn't share; I don't think they even occur to him. In so many ways he's singularly young and unformed, and I'm apt to forget this — I think that, even as well as I know him, the layers of pomp sometimes throw me off a little. But I'm sharply reminded of it whenever his enthusiasm — so sudden and shapeless and without discipline — bubbles up through the pomp: then it's as if a sign had sprouted underneath his neck, reading BEWARE OF THE GROWING BOY. Would he recognize a difference, I wonder, between the approach of The Whistling Priest on the one hand and, say, that of the Curé d'Ars on the other? He might, if he were cornered and forced to think it out, but I'm sure his immediate reaction would be to establish them in a glorious and perfectly balanced equation: two men working away for the greater honor and glory of the Lord. Which wouldn't matter particularly if it were only The Case of The Whistling Priest, if it were simply Father Danowski being overexuberant about an old friend from seminary days. But of course it's more than that: it's a failure, apparently an inability — at least at present — to distinguish between the good and the dubious, all done in the name of God. All too obviously, he's not alone in this — it's the old problem of ends and means once again. Which can hardly be resolved by zeal alone: what's needed is judgment, taste, a sense of relative values, of some discrimination. This is where my curate must be reinforced and broadened. Here time can be of some help, but not, I think, of much, and the truth is, I suppose, that this shaping of my curate is really more or less up to me. Which is fair enough, and as it should be. Not only because he is a good lad, and because I am fond of him, but because I'm his pastor, and this is a part of the pastor's job. It's a part I've never been too successful with; my record as a guide for young curates is hardly a proud one. But perhaps with Father Danowski it's just possible that I might be able to do something that I should have done with the others, something that I never even began to do. . . .

If so, it's high time we got started — in fact, well past high time. But not necessarily on Christmas Day. Especially under the circumstances of my curate's being here; the firming hand could wait another day. And so I said nothing, and he continued to talk on, uninterrupted. He was never reticent, but today he was in a holiday mood, he was intentionally "keeping me company," and he talked more freely and more personally than at any time since he had come to Saint Paul's. He talked mostly about himself, with that odd mixture of self-satisfaction and completely unselfconscious simplicity, switching from one to the other without warning. He talked about the seminary, his childhood days with his family, and about his future: his hopes and aims for himself as a priest. They were good aims and modest aims: my curate had no dreams of personal glory. I listened — amused, touched, fascinated at moments — and in this way we passed the remainder of Christmas Day. Not an exciting day, and surely not the kind of day that most would regard as memorable. But it was for me. It was the best Christmas I'd had in years. . . .

In the evening, Father Danowski went off to spend an hour or so with his family. This was at my suggestion rather than his own, and at first he had objected, dutifully and with great formality.

"Oh no no, Father. It is most kind of you, but I will stay here. Why, I assure you, they do not even expect me! In answer to my parents' queries, I have acquainted them with my position. I have many times informed them that on Christmas Day above all other days, the proper place for a priest is in his rectory. . . ."

It was a little drama of renunciation: Father Danowski, turning his back on The World. But I insisted that he go. A generous gesture on my part? Not quite. It's true that I thought it both pointless and unkind to allow him to stay when I knew he was really aching to go — but it's also true that by now I was quite willing to be alone for a while. Which is to say nothing against my curate — except, possibly, that he's not as old as I am. And I'm grateful to him for making this day the kind of day it was — but the point is that I wished to remain grateful. This sometimes takes a little doing. Because inevitably the moment arrives when I realize with special acuteness that the middle-aged and the young belong to two different worlds, that they move at different speeds, and that their powers of endurance are far from the same; that moment, in short, when I realize that what I need more than anything else is time out: a breathing space in which to recover from Father Danowski's abundant, freely given companionship. Otherwise, I find, the mere *presence* of so much vitality, so much exuberance — even if it's just sitting there quietly, temporarily silent, for the moment doing nothing — can exhaust rather than enrich. And so, for the benefit of both of us, I try to keep some sort of balance, to avoid this overexposure. As my curate says, on Christmas Day above all other days. . . .

So he left for his family, and I was alone in the rectory. I sat by the front window of the little downstairs office-sitting room, looking out at the dark street. The newer lighting facilities, those tall slim stone pillars with their tubular white lights, are still only a myth in this part of the city; we have the stunted lamp posts of another era, and our light at night is soft, yellow, picturesque and insufficient. The street was deserted now, which is not uncommon, and Christmas of course would make no great difference: over here a holiday — even this holiday — is one more day. Indeed, tonight the street seemed even emptier than usual; after Father Danowski drove off there was not a sign of movement: not a car, not a man, not a cat or a dog. It was a cold, silent, windless night; against the street light opposite the rectory I saw a few slow flakes of snow, but these soon stopped and, looking up, I could see stars through gaps in the clouded sky. So this was good: we would have no storm. . . .

I sat there for a little while, comfortable, no more than pleasantly tired, with the evening still before me — I had no immediate duties, and bedtime was a couple of hours away. Suddenly, for no reason — or for none that was apparent to me — I decided to do a curious thing: I decided to take a tour. A complete tour: the church, the rectory, everything. From top to bottom. It would be more or less the same tour

I had taken with John when he had first come over to cast his cold eye on the parish — it was a tour I hadn't made since that day. But I made it now. Why? I don't know — an overseer's property survey at the end of the year? In the absence of something better to do? In any case, I started out, first going into the church, systematically and slowly walking up and down and across the familiar territory. This was what in better days had been known as The Basement Chapel and was now known simply as The Basement. It had been nothing more than a storeroom for years, or, more accurately — since we had little of value to store — a junk pile of odds and ends; lately, I knew, it had become a refuge for Roy, in flight from Father Danowski. Or from me. I hadn't been down here for a long time: I switched on the single light and saw the long, bare, dirty cellar, with its gloomy evidence of past and present. The past: a few old kneelers, an overturned pew, a confessional tilted to one side. The present: a worn, uncovered mattress which had been dragged in and propped against the confessional; on the floor around this rude couch was a vast litter of cigarette butts and grubby magazines: *Western Thrills, Jungle Terror, Space Kicks*. Roy's library. I found it all depressing beyond words. Not, certainly, because a poor fellow came down here to hide — but because the place he came to hide was once a place where people came to pray. And a disused church is not a sight to warm the heart. . . .

I went back into the rectory, and then through all the halls on all the floors, opening doors, entering all the abandoned rooms, meeting in each one the same combination of total emptiness, stale air, dust, and motionless dead cold. It was a melancholy journey, and before I was halfway through I found myself wondering why I had even begun. But I kept on, stubbornly, and each new step seemed to reveal the place under the light of an essential hopelessness. That is, all the unpleasant aspects of Old Saint Paul's that I'd come to terms with long ago, all the drawbacks I'd dismissed as being small and of no matter, now seemed to pounce out of these cold shadows to remind me with force and with contempt, that whatever I was doing here, whatever I could do here, was really all for nothing: the place was dying, dying, dying, and could not be saved. I think at this point I may even have begun to walk faster — acceleration to defeat depression? — a mindless maneuver which succeeded no better than such maneuvers usually do. A jeering and persuasive voice kept pace with me, suggesting that of course I knew all this to be true, that no matter what I said or felt or claimed to feel about this niche being the one that was just right for me, by every single action I revealed my own awareness of the farce. For example, even now: an aging priest walking by himself at night through long deserted rooms — was this the action of a pastor of a living church? Or the routine stumbling of a caretaker, the custodian of a ruin . . . ?

I finished my tour, and closed the door behind me; I stood at the top of the stairs looking down into that part of the rectory which we still use each day and which is the only place I know that I can call my home. I could not lose this sadness which had come upon me so suddenly; it seemed as though everything I did, every thought I seized, however eagerly, to bring me onto firmer, saner ground, was nothing but a detour back to where I started from: in such a mood all things support despair. I thought of the Christmas afternoon, so pleasantly spent with my curate: he, surely, was happy here. But then I took the next step and reminded myself that he was here at the beginning of his priestly life; I would be here at the end of mine. There was a difference. And then, one step more — memory cooperates obligingly in these circumstances — took me back to the time when I was my curate's age, when I had announced, as he had done today, my hopes and plans for the future. That is, I had announced some of them; the more ambitious ones I kept to myself. But even the humblest of these had not quite included anything like Old Saint Paul's, and now, looking around me, thirty years after that time of youthful, optimistic declaration, I thought: *So much for dreams come true.* . . .

So then, this is the way a happy day can end, dissolving in an instant into a wash of melancholy, which may be sentimental, false, absurd, and which in fact I know to be just that from the very moment it begins, but by which, all the same, I always seem to be engulfed. I say "always," but of course that's not quite true, because this queer, causeless sadness is not a regular thing with me — it comes very seldom, really, but when it does it comes with leaping unexpectedness, from nowhere with the speed of light: the blizzard from the blue sky on a day in early May. I don't know why it comes this way; I don't know why it comes at all. Because now, surely, I have no reason for sadness, but still, it comes, every once in a while, and I'm taken by surprise each time: I'm like a man who in one moment is boasting that he's never been in better health, and in the next is lying chilled and shaking in his bed — it's that sudden. I suppose there's an answer to this: it may simply be that the battle never really ends, and that we are never more vulnerable than at the precise moment when we feel ourselves least so; the defenses relax, and the enemy strikes. . . .

And yet there is a difference. I mean, between now and then: between these dark sweeps across the mind and those of years ago — and the difference is that these don't last. No matter how bleak the moment, there is somewhere in the background the whispered reassurance that it will pass — and this is something: an enormous something, in fact. Although not everything, because this gloom, this despondency is real enough while it lasts, and standing now at the top of the stairs, I did not feel like crying out for joy. In the last half hour everything had been touched with gray; I felt discouraged with myself and with the parish: I found myself wondering if John, that

[311]

completely unsentimental man, might not have been right after all: that the only solution to the problems of Old Saint Paul's lay in the bulldozer and the wrecking crew. . . .

Glum thoughts. But they came to an end quickly enough, and in a way I hadn't foreseen, for suddenly the telephone rang and kept ringing, and when — finally — I answered it, I heard news which took me from myself in seconds.

"Father? Father?" It was a woman's voice, urgent and even hysterical; it was a voice I was sure I'd never heard before until it said, "This is Mary! Mary Carmody! Is that you, Father Hugh? I want to talk to Father Hugh Kennedy!"

And I knew at once that something had happened to old Charlie — nothing else in the world could have stirred this plodding, monotonous, timid woman to such a frantic pitch. I said, "Mary, yes: what's wrong?"

"Daddy!" she cried. Needlessly. "Oh, it's terrible, terrible! I don't know what . . . can you come, Father? Now!"

She continued to talk but her voice tumbled off into a kind of sobbing unintelligibility, and I was no closer to what had happened; my single thought was: *Charlie's dead.* I felt sure of it; I said insistently, "Mary! Mary, listen to me: I'm coming. Right away. But try to tell me: what happened to him?" And then, because it was the question that had to be asked, I said, "How is he now?"

But once again what I was sure of turned out to be not so — for Charlie was at least alive. She said, still sobbing, but a little clearer, "He fell! He fell *over.* And I didn't know . . . they have him in bed now. The doctor came and . . . he asked for you! Twice! So come, Father! Please! Hurry!"

But *who* had asked for me twice? The doctor? Or Charlie? Not that it made any difference to my going — obviously, I'd go as quickly as I could in either case — but it might have told me a little bit more about Charlie, about how he was. Was he able to ask for anyone? Was he conscious? Was he in immediate danger? Was he in *any* danger? Or was Mary vastly exaggerating in her panic? These were all questions which came rushing up together in no sensible order, all following, I suppose, from that first question which had not yet been answered: *What had happened?* And I saw that it would not be answered now, for Mary, poor Mary, distracted with fright and grief and all the bewilderment of a new and awful responsibility, was barely coherent, and could only repeat over and over exactly what she had said at first. She began to sob again, in a strange way, like a little girl who was being punished for something she really hadn't done, and when I left her, after trying in the usual way and with the usual success to reassure her by telling her that it would be all right — without even knowing what "it" was — and promising that I'd be there in a matter of minutes, I could still hear the pathetic little gulping moans. More than most of us, Mary was not meant for crisis. . . .

And so I called Father Danowski's house immediately to summon him from his family party, to bring him back to cover the rectory while I was gone. As I dialed, a new set of questions began to arise, questions which were more orderly and practical. For example, I was going to Charlie, yes, but — where was he? Mary hadn't said; I hadn't asked. He had spent the day at Helen's — had whatever happened, happened there, or was he in his own home? Most probably the latter: that would explain why Mary had called rather than Helen. Then where was Helen now? And John? And Ted? Had they been reached? Were they on their way? And to *what*? And I thought of myself and why I was wanted. I thought — as a priest always does at a time like this — of the last rites, but if it were for this, then I was hardly the man. . . .

In the Danowski house the telephone was lifted; I could hear little giggles before a child's voice said, "Hello." There were more giggles; then the child's voice said clearly, "Coo coo on you!" There was a clattering in my ear, the child had hung up.

Exasperated, I dialed again, and the same voice said, "Hello."

I said, "Look —" but before I could say anything more a familiar voice broke in saying, "Good evening. This is Father Danowski speaking."

I said sharply, "Father —"

"Ah, Father!" he said, in surprise. I could hear him say, "Go along now, children. Otherwise I will not be a camel for you any more!" To me he said, "I fear the children were being somewhat naughty, Father. I reproved them by threatening not to participate further in their little games."

I said, "Listen to me, Father." And then I told him briefly what had happened: as much as I knew of it.

"Oh my!" he said. "Why that is dreadful. That poor old gentleman! I will of course come back at once."

"All right. I won't wait; I'll leave right away. I'm sorry to have to do this to you."

"Not at all, Father! Why, do not even think of that. And I hope that Mr. Carmody proves to be quite all right. To think of such a thing occurring," he said, "on such a happy Christmas Day!"

On such a happy Christmas Day. . . .

And so I left the rectory, driving swiftly out of the dark and silent parish, across the center of the city, shining with its Christmas lights, and into the older, more spacious residential section, hurrying to reach an old man who had so recently, so suddenly, and so vigorously become a part — and just how much of a part I don't think I realized until now — of my life. . . .

10

AT THIS HOUR of the night, Charlie's house was seldom at its most inviting: it was one of those old wooden houses so shaped and so situated that it seemed to double in size and to radiate a mysterious shuttered gloom as soon as darkness had fallen. There was sometimes a single light visible from the street: perhaps Mary, busy with some end-of-the-day household chore, or Charlie himself, walking — he once told me that he retired early, but woke often during the night — and reaching for the telephone. But tonight there were lights in many rooms, and cars were in the driveway: two of these cars told me that Helen and John had arrived. On the way over I'd convinced myself that neither of them would be here, that somehow Mary would have failed to reach them, and now that I saw they *were* here, I immediately — and irrationally — felt better, much better, as if their very presence were a sign that the tide had begun to turn. And in a different and more selfish way I also felt relieved: I hadn't really looked forward to dealing, alone, with Mary. But as it turned out, I wasn't even to see Mary for a while, for — I learned all this later — she *had* called both Helen and John, they *had* arrived before me, and with their coming Mary, no longer the sole keeper of a terrible charge, dissolved, and Helen led her, docile and weeping, up to her room. John had gone straight in to his father and was in there now, and I was met at the door by Frank O'Donnell. And so it was from a medical man that at last I heard the story.

"A coronary," he said. "About an hour ago."

"Severe?"

"Well, any coronary's severe. It's his first, so far as I know. Which is in his favor. Although at his age, of course. . . . Mmm."

"It happened here? In the house?"

"As soon as he got home, apparently. He'd been at our place all day, you know. I thought he seemed about as usual. A little tired when he left, maybe, but that was to be expected. He's eighty, after all. And it had been a busy day: he was thrown off his routine. No afternoon nap, for one thing. So that under the circumstances some fatigue was . . . however, there was nothing more than that. Which doesn't mean anything, of course. These things don't always give advance notice. Often they come on with no warning to speak of. . . ."

I said, cutting through, "And then what? After he left your house?"

"He came home with Mary. He drove, of course. Luckily nothing happened in the car. But when he got into the house he keeled over. Here, on the hall floor. He didn't black out, which was all to the good, because only Mary was here, and it's not easy to tell what she would have done on her own. All the best will in the world, of course, but the difficulty is that with someone like that you just can't . . . Mmm."

"Frank, I know Mary. I've known her all my life. What about *Charlie*?"

I spoke impatiently enough, but he didn't seem to mind. "Well, he more or less took charge. Lying there on the floor. He must have been in considerable pain, but he managed to get Mary to telephone the Clinic, and they got hold of young Jack King. They were fortunate on that one," he said thoughtfully, and added in explanation, "it being Christmas Day."

[316]

It was the note of the professional man, recognizing the odds against the securing of a colleague on Sundays, holidays, or after hours. I said, "He's their heart man?"

"One of them, yes. They have several new men up there. I don't know much about him but he's undoubtedly capable or he wouldn't be there. By and large they get the cream of the crop."

But it suddenly struck me as altogether incongruous that this man, who was himself so capable, who was by reputation one of our finest doctors, was now, at this moment of extreme emergency, standing outside rather than in the sickroom, casually telling me of the capabilities of somebody else. I said, "You haven't seen Charlie yet?"

He shook his head. "No. We got here just a couple of minutes before you did. By that time everything that could be done had been done. At a time like this nobody works any miracles. Any decent doctor knows what to do, and actually there isn't a great deal he can do. It's as important as anything else to keep the patient calm, quiet, free from agitation. Do you know how we sometimes do that, Hugh?"

I said — again, I'm afraid, impatiently — that I didn't, and he said, in a dry voice I'd never heard him use before, "We give him a doctor in whom he can feel some confidence. A good doctor."

And it was only then — I suppose because I'd never before thought much, really, about Frank and his feelings — that I realized he had been stung. I suddenly remembered the birthday dinner, with Charlie standing at the head of the table, loudly singing the praises of the "young lads" at the Clinic, all the while never quite looking in the direction of the son-in-law at whom, none too obliquely, he was aiming his shots. I had seen this performance only once, but the odds were that it had been repeated fairly often over the years in the family, among friends, before strangers: in making little points of this kind, Charlie did not avoid an audience. So that today, now,

[317]

what Frank felt for his father-in-law was probably something quite different and far less benign than the simple wry acceptance I had once imagined he felt. This was the first time I'd seen this bland, assured, self-contained man reveal anything so deep beneath the surface, and possibly he realized this and regretted it, for he said quickly, "However, as soon as we got here, I did have a word with Jack King."

"And . . . ?"

"Nothing definite. About what I expected. The infarction's there, plus the possibility of some failure. There seems to be a slight congestion . . . however, it's too early to tell very much."

"But it's definitely dangerous?"

"Oh yes. It's that all right."

"It could go either way?"

He nodded. "I think you could say that, Hugh."

"I see. What would *you* say?"

"Oh, about the same," he said easily. "About the same, Hugh. You see, there's really not much anyone else could say at this stage. There are so many factors involved . . . and then bear in mind that I haven't examined him myself. . . ."

But I cut in again, saying, "Frank. Come on. Don't play doctor with me now. I want to know. I'm a full-grown man; I promise you I won't break apart. And I'm not after a certified, foolproof prognosis; all I want is your guess. What about it?"

He hesitated, then said reluctantly, "Well, if it's a guess you want . . . and it's no more than that, remember. I could be all wrong. But purely as a guess . . . I'd have to say that I see little reason for optimism. *Very* little reason." He added, in quick warning, "Although this is for your ears alone, Hugh. I wouldn't want it passed along to Helen. Not yet. Because as I say, we can't be sure. I could be wrong. . . ."

It was hedged, guarded, characteristically qualified, but to me it had the ring of the irreversible verdict, and in this instant I became certain of what I had suspected before: Charlie was going to die. And with this certainty I felt something I hadn't felt since my father died. It wasn't the same thing — not the same thing at all, but there was a queer dull ache, and if you can feel darkness I felt a kind of darkness too, as if the edge of the approaching death had come up quietly and touched me. I don't want to overdramatize this, since every adult who's ever been told that someone close to him is about to die knows the feeling all too well, but I suddenly realized, just now, that with all my experience with death — all the sickrooms, the anointings, the last confessions — I had had very little *personal* experience with it. My mother's death I don't remember; I had mourned no aunts or uncles, sisters or brothers; a few friends had died, including one elderly priest I'd known since my earliest seminary days — a soft-voiced, charitable, holy old man whom I'd loved — but I hadn't been with them before they died, I hadn't been thinking especially of them, and by an odd and unhappy coincidence the death of each of them had occurred without my knowing of it, without my even hearing of it until some time later. So that over all the years it was really only once that I had looked at someone and known that he was going to die and suddenly felt that this death to be was also in a sense my own. And while of course I felt nothing so numbing or total or shattering as this now, nevertheless what I did feel was at least a shadow of it, and I knew that I would miss old Charlie, and that I would miss him badly. . . .

And Frank, who had been talking, suddenly said, "He'll be missed. A strange man, but he'll be missed."

It was a complacent statement of obituary and, suddenly angry, I said, "Tell me this, Frank: How much will he be missed by you?"

The question was not a polite one — from his point of view, not even a forgivable one — but if he was annoyed, or more than that, he didn't show it. His lips twitched slightly, and for an instant it occurred to me that he might even be about to *smile*, but instead he just stood there looking at me with no other change of his expression.

[319]

"Oh," he said, "I'll tell you what, Hugh: you asked me a moment ago to make a guess. So now I'll ask you to make one. I'll ask you to guess the answer to your own question. It shouldn't be too hard."

For the second time within minutes, then, I had been given a glimpse of a different Frank, a Frank who must seldom have been reached, a Frank who was somehow more *real* — and my immediate reaction was to wish for the return of the old familiar counterfeit: the bogus bedside manner seemed easier to take than this admitted indifference to a dying old man of whom I was fond. And yet my anger didn't grow; in fact it disappeared as suddenly as it had come, for in his voice there had been no satisfaction, no trace of gloating. He had spoken with a kind of regret, as if he wished that the truth weren't true, as if he were sorry that he couldn't be sorry, and, looking at him, I realized that I was in no position to pass judgment on him. Whatever his relationship with old Charlie had been, it had surely not been the casual and largely comic affair that I had known. And much as I had grown to enjoy Charlie, and anxious as I was about him now, I was forced to remember that there was a far less amusing side to him which I almost never saw, but which my father had known well — and I was forced to remember too, as I stared at Frank in this moment, that he had spent more than thirty years as an only and none-too-cherished son-in-law, and that for the sake of his wife he had undoubtedly put up with much. . . .

So that I couldn't really say anything, and fortunately there was no need to, for Helen now appeared at the top of the stairs and came down quickly towards us. At the same moment the door to Charlie's bedroom opened and John came out, followed by a stranger — the young doctor, I assumed. We all met at the foot of the stairs; Helen looked tired and worried, John taut and harassed — although perhaps no more so than usual. There were quick greetings; I was introduced to the doctor. And this young doctor was indeed young; to someone like myself who, I suppose, in spite of everything still cherishes an image of some legendary wise old family physician, he seemed almost dangerously so: a slender boy with a crew cut and an undergraduate face, who might have been about to raise his hand and ask his elders for permission to leave the room. Something of what I felt must have come through, for he said with a smile, "I'm a little older than I look, Father." Which was disconcerting, and of course I began to fumble with an apology, but he said pleasantly, "Oh, that's par for the course. It happens all the time." Then, speaking to all of us, he said, "He's sleeping now. At least for a little while." And, coming back to me: "He seems especially anxious to see you, Father. When he wakes, why don't you go in? I wouldn't stay too long; the nurse can tell you when it's time to go. But say hello, let him see you, have a few words. The main thing is to satisfy him without exciting him." He turned to Frank and said, "Wouldn't you say that's about the size of it?"

And I thought that in this turning to the older man there was something more than mere politeness; there was a deference, a genuine respect. Frank nodded and said, "No change?"

"No, none. *Status quo.* I'd like to have you take a look at him a little later, if you wouldn't mind."

Frank nodded again, and taking Helen's hand he said, "Is Mary all right?" And added, with a more evident concern, "Are *you* all right?"

"I'm fine," she said, as if it didn't matter. "And Mary's asleep now, too; whatever you gave her worked like a charm. I only hope she . . . could you get in touch with Dan?"

"No, not yet." He said, "That may take a little time. I called that last address, but he's not there any more. And no one seems to have any idea where he may have gone. Apparently he's traveling."

"We could send a wire to every race track in the South," John said bitterly. "That would get him soon enough."

Helen blinked in protest. "No, please," she said. "Not to-night, John. We have enough to do without . . . anyway, there must be *someone* who knows!"

Memory clicked, and I thought of Dan's hasty visit to me, and his mention of that mysterious figure of piety and finance. I said, "He once spoke about a Will Altgeld. . . ."

She said absently, "Yes, well, the trouble is that I don't think Dan's with him any more. That arrangement didn't seem to work out too well." It was not a great surprise. As if she were blushing herself for this shortage of information, she said, "It would help, wouldn't it, if I knew what my own brother was doing these days?"

Frank said, quickly and soothingly, "Now now. We'll find him. There are always ways of doing these things. The State Police, for example. They have their connections all over the country. We'll get working on them right away." He added, "I'll call General Collins personally."

I saw John stir at this — it was the kind of announcement which might well have been preceded by an important little cough — but he said nothing. And Helen seemed to accept it, for as Frank went to the telephone she called after him, "Yes, that's a good idea." But she said this as though she were thinking of something else; after a minute she said suddenly, "Julia. She'll have to be told."

John said impatiently, "But told *what*? That's the question, isn't it? I don't mind dragging Dan back from wherever he is — always granting that he's somewhere he *can* be dragged back from — but Julia's an old woman. And not very well. She can't just pick up and come all the way here on a moment's notice unless it's absolutely necessary. And that's just what we don't know." He turned to the young doctor and, with a certain air of challenge, said, "Do we?"

"No," the young doctor said. "No, Father, I'm afraid we don't. Not yet."

"Furthermore we all seem to be acting as though my father

were already *in extremis*. Why? I don't see the evidence for that at all." He spoke with a brisk querulousness which was almost professional: he might have been a colleague called in by lesser physicians to resolve their doubts about a difficult case. Sometimes priests who have spent much time near the sick or the dying fall into this habit — although here it may well have been something quite different: it may simply have been John trying to lift his sister's spirits. He said to the doctor, "For instance, you certainly wouldn't disallow the possibility of recovery?"

"Oh no. That wouldn't be a very sensible thing to do."

Which seemed to me less than positive encouragement, but John said, "There you are!" as if something had been settled. "You're moving much too fast, Helen. I'm against telling Julia anything. It's not necessary and could be fatal. As old as she is, she'd come on in five minutes, and what then? She'd stay here. Gloom and doom. Memories of Martin. She's not exactly a contribution to convalescence."

Helen didn't argue. All she said was, "Maybe you're right." But she said it without conviction, without attention, even, as if somehow what John had been saying was really irrelevant. I think she saw no period of convalescence; I think she saw only a grimmer outcome. She may have had one of those sudden, despairing intuitions which have nothing to do with reason; she may have seen through her husband's professional cover to the expert's calculations underneath. I don't know; however she had come to the conclusion it obviously preoccupied her now, and I don't think she was more than half aware of anything John or anyone else said to her. She walked slowly now across the hall and into the living room; we followed her. I hadn't been here since the birthday, and of course the changeless hallway was still the same: the carpet with its ancient stain, the untouched letters on the long table, the pointless bust of Daniel O'Connell. But in the living room there had been a change, for in the far corner stood a large Christmas tree,

[323]

reaching to the ceiling and loaded with tinsel and gay fragile bulbs: it gave the tall plain room a color and cheer it did not normally possess. Underneath this tree Christmas packages had been carefully spread out, and I saw with surprise that none of them had yet been opened, that all were still in their Christmas wrappings. When did Charlie open his presents? Did he postpone his delights each year, like a canny little boy husbanding his store of cookies until the other little boys had eaten all theirs? Probably; in any case it was sad to see them there now, and to wonder when they would be opened this year. And by whom. . . .

Helen had come over next to me; she said, "It's strange, isn't it? I mean, today of all days. . . . Did you know, Hugh, that you were the first one he asked for? Before any of us?"

This was unlikely; I said, "I'd doubt that. Was anyone sent for first, really? In the confusion? I'd imagine it was a situation where the names just came tumbling out, and that Mary was in a panic and called them any which way."

"No," she said. "It wasn't like that at all. There was no confusion. It was all very orderly. From what I could get out of Mary he was quite precise. He made her call the Clinic first, then he made her call you. After that he asked for us."

She said this unemotionally, and certainly with no suggestion of reproach towards me, but it was clear that this latest stroke of her father's had hurt her. Naturally enough: a dying man who knows that he's dying is rather apt to be guilty of a peculiar honesty, and I suppose she felt that the order of final invitation showed how her father really felt about those who should have been closest to him. And for just an instant — I'm almost ashamed to admit this — in this moment which above all others calls for an exercise of charity, and in which I really did think of Charlie with sorrow and a sense of personal loss, by some trick of the mind I found myself thinking also that it was not at all untypical of him that even his deathbed request should seem to contain a gratuitous slight to his family, and, in a flash of illumination, I wondered if perhaps, here and at last, we did not have the real explanation for his mysterious cultivation of me: that I was an instrument through which he could wound, a unique, manipulable figure in another of the little games he would play right up to the end. . . .

Which was hardly the charity the moment demanded, but which does show, I suppose, how ready we can be at any time to welcome and play with suspicion. And which shows, too, that even now my feelings towards old Charlie were not quite so noble or so simple as I had imagined them to be only a moment before. I wasn't proud of this; I was even less proud of it when, in the next moment, I reminded myself what I had done, almost by instinct, in the rectory in preparation for this visit, and remembered that there was, after all, another reason why Charlie might have sent for me. I said, "Wasn't it natural enough, Helen? If your father thought he was in any danger he'd certainly want to send for a priest right away. And which priest? Not John, surely. He wouldn't have his own son anoint him, or hear his confession. So he probably thought of me. . . ."

It was of course what had occurred to me — as it would have to any priest — before I left the rectory; I had brought the oils for anointing along with me. But Helen was shaking her head; she said, "No. He did ask for a priest, but not for John, and not for you, Hugh. He sent for one of the Franciscans out at the monastery on Indigo Road. I don't know which one; I don't know that he asked for any particular one. But one is coming; he'll be here at any minute. So you see, Hugh, it wasn't as a priest that he wanted you."

Then as what? But we didn't discuss this further now; it wasn't the time for speculating about motives, and in any case there were new arrivals. Ted and Anne came in, and almost at the same moment, Bucky and P. J. I assumed that the two old men had come together, but apparently this was not so, for Bucky, as he entered, was clearly out of sorts and was carrying

[325]

on a loud complaint that must have begun on the steps outside.

"So there you were!" he said. "There you were, P. J., in your nice warm car! And the daughter to drive you and bring you here! And not a thought of Bucky Heffernan! Not a thought of Bucky who called your house and got no answer!"

"I was out to the car, most likely," P. J. said, in his soft voice. "With the daughter. Tryin' to get it to go, d'ye see? Ye couldn't get so much as a whisper out of it. I dunno is it the spark plugs or maybe the batt'ry's all dried up. Anyways, we had to get a push from a policeman. The fat Cassidy lad. That used to be the schoolteacher but had to quit on account of the harelip. So they made a policeman out of him. Well there, Helen, how's Charlie?"

"A bad night for us all, Helen!" Bucky said loudly. Not to be outdone in solicitude? "Oh yes. No one denies that one. Sad news. I got here as soon as I could. I would have got here sooner but I missed my bus. The public can go to the devil on Sundays and holidays, that's the attitude of the bus company. There's a public utility for you! I missed the express at seven minutes past the hour, and when do you think the next one was? Twenty-three minutes past! And with a transfer at Carver Street at that! That's the kind of service the public gets these days. Some people," he said, "might have come by and picked me up. Some people with cars. I mention no names. But they didn't. So what did I have to do? I'll tell you what I had to do: *I had to call a taxicab.* That's what I had to do!"

"For the love of God, Bucky," P. J. said wearily. "Dry up for once in your life with your buses and your trolley cars and your taxicabs. Nobody gives a damn if you got here by elephant! You're here and that's that. Can we see Charlie, Helen? Is he all right?"

I saw Helen take both old men by the arm; it was a gesture which was surprisingly effective in calming the irascible Bucky, for he softened and listened quietly as she talked, presumably telling the two men just what had happened. As she talked I saw them interrupt her — pinning her down, I suppose. At a time like this, for old people the exact details become a matter of consuming importance. . . .

John had gone into a corner of the room with the young doctor, and for the moment I was alone. I looked around at the people standing in little groups in the living room and the hall, and once again the birthday party seemed to come back before me. Inevitably, because everyone here tonight had been a part of that earlier, happier gathering of Charlie's proclaimed "family and friends" — even the young doctor, although not himself present, had been there as a figure of eulogy. And suddenly I thought of another parallel, less obvious but far more startling than the first: were we all here now, just as on the birthday, at the urgent, personal request of our host? Was it old Charlie who had invited us to this as well? I think so. It was queer and macabre to imagine this ferociously determined little old man, stiff with pain and nearly breathless on his hall floor, doggedly gasping out a guest list to a terrified daughter at the telephone — yet this, or something very close to this, is what must have happened. And all of us had come; we were here and we were waiting for . . . what?

For what one usually waits for in these awful intervals: a word, a decision. One hopes in spite of all evidence for the good word, of course, but at the same time there's also this hoping for the word *as such*; at such moments the *definite* acquires an overpowering value. . . .

John came over to me and said crisply, "I've suggested the hospital. Without success. He prefers to leave things as they are for the time being. I'm not going to press the point; he's the doctor. And doctors are always right, aren't they?" He smiled without mirth. "Clerical levity. To lighten the difficult hour. You've heard about the Franciscan?"

"Yes. Helen said she didn't know who he was. He could be some friend of your father's, I suppose?"

"No no. I have no idea who he is, but I can promise you

one thing: when he comes he'll be a stranger to everyone. Including my father. That's why he was sent for. My father acknowledges the seal of confession, of course, but by nature he's a cautious man. He takes no chances. I know very well the way he'd think, the way he'd *have* to think: *Be careful. Don't lose your head. You want a priest now. All right. Call the priest but make sure he's a priest nobody knows. And make sure he doesn't know you.* That's what you call insurance, Hugh. In matters of faith my father is convinced but cagey. Therefore we get the anonymous Franciscan."

He spoke with all of his old sharpness on the old familiar theme. In this emergency his thoughts about his father must have undergone some change, some softening, but he gave no hint of this in any tenderness of speech. His clear, restless eye now surveyed the room, clicking across the company. "Everyone's here," he said. "He got them all. It's incredible. Think of *thinking* of that, even, at a time when. . . ." He shook his head in a weary, acid echo of the boyish bafflement of many years ago. "Poor Mary," he said. "She must have been put through the wringer. Just picture it, Hugh: sitting here playing switchboard operator for a man who's just been knocked flat on his back with a thrombosis!"

"Yes. Of course it may not have been too much fun for the man with the thrombosis, either."

He looked at me quickly, but said with surprising mildness, "No, I don't imagine it was. But I'll tell you something about the man with the thrombosis, Hugh. He's not going to die. I don't mean not ever; that's always been his opinion rather than mine. I mean right now. He's going to live. Whether you believe it or not."

And whether I believed it or not, it was perfectly clear that he did. It was astonishing, because he was not a man who dealt in prophecy — certainly not in optimistic prophecy. Yet his tone had been one of the most complete confidence and, puzzled, I said, "This is a new note for you, isn't it?"

[328]

"The crystal ball, you mean? It's not that entirely: I have some evidence to go on. The evidence in my *bones*. I know, I know," he said, one hand fluttering as if to ward off the objection which, I assume, I was now to have raised, "that's an even newer note, isn't it? Ouija board. The hag over the bubbling cauldron. All right. The point is that I do have this feeling about my father and what's fairly likely to happen now. Possibly because it's not quite without precedent; it's all happened before, you know. Or did you know?"

"No. No, I didn't." And I realized how little I knew of Charlie — nothing, really — from the time my father had stopped speaking of him, shortly before his own death, up to the time he had come sweeping in on me The notion of his having been seriously ill before — more than once? — had simply not occurred to me: the bounce, the vitality had been against it. I said, "Not the same thing, surely? Frank said this was the first cardiac. . . ."

"No, not cardiac. But critical all the same. Certified as such by the usual accredited physicians. Twice before we've had the sudden dramatic collapse, everyone summoned to the bedside, the touch-and-go situation. Everyone sat up nights on end, ran errands, said chain rosaries, coped with the nurses, coped with my father, tore their nerves to shreds. And in two weeks the moribund victim was out on the street, stomping his way across the city to corner some poor little wetback to remind him of the pleasant North American custom of paying the rent on time. Now, I'm not ungrateful for the speedy recuperation and I don't question the fact that he was really sick each time. But I'm also saying that my father is one of those really rare people who have a gift for magnification — do you know what I mean? Everything that happens to them seems to be bigger or better or sadder or worse than the same thing happening to anyone else. This isn't an accident with them; they work very hard at it. At least my father does; he always has. The result is that you look at him through the

[329]

multiple lens that he's set up for you. In sickness as in health. If he sprains his thumb you think his forearm should be in a cast. And a serious illness seems immensely more so because of the apparatus with which he surrounds it. It becomes a production, Hugh! Look at this tonight: not just a heart attack — which is bad enough, I agree — but a *super* heart attack, a heart attack plus. You can sense it in the room: the aura of drama. My father's the Belasco of the invalids. I tell you the whole production's been stage-managed by the central tragic figure. No, no, this current disaster is like all the others essentially, and do you know why? Because it has my father's stamp all over it. And death — the real thing — isn't quite that obliging, Hugh; it just doesn't let itself be stamped!"

The words were not loud — I doubt that they could have been heard by anyone in the room but myself — but they came out with great force, unhesitating conviction, and I was impressed and even cheered: the others could be wrong, after all! But this was a first reaction, an instinctive one, like the shout that goes up as soon as speech is over, but before reflection begins. And when, after a moment, I began to consider *what* he had said, I felt, not encouraged, but troubled and a little appalled. I suppose that without intending to I thought from the platform of my own feelings for my father at such a time, and so John's steady refusal to face what were, after all, the probabilities, seemed stubborn, unfeeling, even a little irrational. I said, "Does past performance mean so much in something like this? Does it mean anything? This is a heart attack, John. And your father is eighty-two."

"Eighty-one." It was an automatic correction, and it would have been impossible for him not to have made it: I had succumbed to the innocent propaganda. "Look," he said, with the same air of brusque authority, and then suddenly he stopped, and it seemed to me that he was considering whether to go on or not. When he did, there was a change in his voice; to my surprise I noted a certain awkwardness, embarrassment.

[330]

"It's difficult," he said. "As you say, these intuitions aren't really in my line. I've spent half my life flying away from old biddies, male and female, who insisted on telling me their private visions, and now I'm telling one myself. I guess that's what you'd have to call it, isn't it? A vision? Or, more kindly, a hunch? All right, Hugh, I have a hunch. And the hunch is that my father's death, when it finally comes, won't be anything like this at all. I think it will probably come very quietly and be over in an instant: quick, unrehearsed, unattended by a throng. No fuss, no fanfare, no fireworks. That's what I think the real thing will be like. That's my hunch. The Franciscan can come: that's all to the good. Naturally. But the Requiem Mass is far away. Or," he said, "so I think, Hugh. I really do!"

The conviction seemed no weaker than before — and the grounds for it no stronger — but there was a quality in it, almost of appeal, which was unusual for him, and I found myself thinking that what he said was not, after all, impossible. Medical experts, as all experts, make mistakes, and in a sense all things are possible — I am no foe of miracles. But to be possible is one thing, to be certain or even likely is quite another, and when I thought now of what Frank had said, or of the carefully neutral manner — never in my experience a harbinger of good news — of the young doctor, or simply of Charlie at eighty collapsing to the floor, then — well, then I could not share John's hunch. But I said only, "I wish you could pass on that confidence. I think Helen could use some."

"Yes. Of course that's a special situation. She's always been at a disadvantage with my father. I've often thought that it helped in dealing with him if you were either infinitely malleable or absolutely resistant. In other words, if you were Mary or me. But Helen was in the middle. On the one hand, she wasn't tough; on the other, she had a will of her own. That made it hard. So that whenever she did fight back — and she did, once or twice — it was apt to be a shattering experience for her. She had a strong sense of family, you know. She was appalled; I think she's still appalled. Or remorseful — the one leads to the other. I'm no authority on just what happened, or what was said." He added abruptly, "I've never inquired about these things. But it's my opinion that she'd have very little reason for remorse. Although that doesn't seem to be her opinion." He shrugged. "Well. Dan of course solved the problem by packing his suitcase. And picking up that blushing bride. By the way," he said, "that's true, isn't it? I mean, what you said about Dan? You really *don't* know where he is?"

"I? No. How should I know? And why would I keep it a secret if I did know?"

Again he shrugged. "He sometimes writes to people outside the family if he's in a jam. He usually suggests that they not tell us. On the grounds that he doesn't want to worry us needlessly." He smiled grimly. "Dan has quite a sense of humor. But I'd just as soon get to him before this lunatic charade of Frank's goes into operation. Imagine it: a nationwide dragnet! For Dan! And with squad cars, no less! The very thing he spends every waking moment trying to avoid. . . . Aha! Here we are!"

For the Franciscan had arrived. He must just now have come in, for he was standing near the front door, a few flakes of snow still clinging to his cowl. I had the impression — as useful and as relevant as such impressions usually are — of someone large and pale and somewhat in need of a shave. John went quickly to him; the Franciscan nodded a greeting and at the same time slightly lifted the small black valise he held in his hand, both the gesture and his silence showing that he was carrying with him the Blessed Sacrament. So then, Charlie was to receive the last rites in full: he would be anointed, he would make his confession, he would receive Holy Communion — the old ritual which sees us from this world. And as I watched the Franciscan go up the stairs, led by

Helen, who was holding the prescribed lighted candle, and followed by the young doctor, once more I was almost overcome by the special feeling of this moment, this profound and unique moment which is like no other in time, this moment which is suddenly stripped clean of everything that once seemed so important, and in which nothing now matters but the limitless mercy of God. . . .

They reached Charlie's bedroom and went in; a few minutes later Helen, the doctor, and a nurse came out. So Charlie was no longer asleep; he was awake and alone with the priest. Frank went up to join Helen and the other two outside the bedroom door; the rest of us remained where we were. This is a hard time, always, for those who are waiting — and it's harder, of course, the more intimately you're involved. Silence, I suppose, might be to some purpose at such a time, but in actual fact it's impossible: everyone feels compelled to say something — assurances, unconvincing optimism, leaden consolations. Whatever one says is likely to be fitful, forced, highly repetitive; everyone is aware of simply marking time; and I think that the only ones who behave without self-consciousness or a sense of inadequacy are those old campaigners who have been through it all so many times over the years — and, perhaps, are now so close to it themselves — that they seem able to abstract themselves from the essence of the situation, so to speak, and to see it instead in a social sense, as a kind of formal gathering with its own set of complicated and inflexible proprieties, with all of which they are exhaustively familiar, and over which they stand a jealous guard. Often, both in this parish and in Saint Stephen's, I'd seen this sort of thing in action, and so, while I wasn't actively expecting it now, I wasn't surprised when Bucky edged over to me and said in a low but sharply critical voice, "I take a poor view of that Franciscan, Father. A very poor view. A man as sick as Charlie has a right to a priest from his own parish. John should have

[333]

seen to that. That's the way it should be. A priest from the parish, not some Franciscan nobody knows!"

I explained that it was Charlie himself who had sent for the Franciscan, and Bucky frowned.

"I say nothing against Charlie," he said, "now of all times. But some people act as if they owned the Church. Some people not a million miles from here. I mention no names. Sick or well, they act that way. And rules are rules, Father. The parish within the Church, the man within the parish. We all know that. That's what history tells us. A man's got no right to jump out of his own parish!"

In the light of his impassioned plans for his own burial, this scrupulous regard for the niceties was something new. But now he shifted his grounds for complaint; he said, "What's more, the man needs a shave. There's no excuse for a scrubby-looking priest! What kind of a priest is it that hasn't the decency to shave himself when he comes to a man that could be dying?"

It was in a sense a just observation; the Franciscan, poor man — slovenly man? — was undoubtedly guilty; but there was the question of relevance. I said, "I don't think it matters too much right now, do you? And he was probably called in a great hurry. . . ."

"As were we all, Father!" Bucky said. "As were we all! And which of us is the only one that needs a shave? No no, Father. Be prepared! That's a motto for one and all. Priests included. Franciscans have got razors, the same as everybody else!"

"I don't like beards on a priest," P. J. said reflectively. "I'd be in a terrible fix if I was a Russian. They're the lads that don't shave. The priests, I mean. The only Russian priest I ever saw was a queer-lookin' feller with a beard down to his belly."

Bucky, momentarily diverted, said, "The Greeks as well. They're all what they call the Orthodox. They don't care how they look."

[334]

"I don't mind the Greeks so much," P. J. said. "Greeks are a very hairy people anyways."

"And Julia," Bucky said, returning to the point. "Has Julia been told, Father?"

I said that, as far as I knew, Julia had not been told; he made little clicking sounds of disapproval.

"That's a bad business," he said severely. "Julia not told! Julia would want to be told. She has a right to be told. The next of kin are *always* told. At a time like this! That's the custom the whole of the civilized world over! I never heard of not telling the next of kin!"

He was plainly outraged, although whether because of any affront to Julia or the alleged violation of protocol it was impossible to say. But his voice was growing louder by the second, and so I said quickly, "Most of the next of kin are already here, Mr. Heffernan. And I'm sure Mrs. Burke will be told as soon as it's necessary. . . ."

"They'll need to tell Julia nothin'," P. J. said, flatly and unexpectedly. "Julia will *know*. I never knew anyone could tell when people were sick or dyin' like Julia. She's like one of them big birds that flop around in the sky, way up over nothin' at all, but a thousand miles away some poor feller falls over in the sand for want of a drink of water and they know it the minute it happens. And off they go. While he's still wigglin'. Just like Julia. The time before Martin fin'lly died she was to Chicago or Texas or some such place and all of a sudden she got the feelin' that she'd best get home right away. So she did. Just in time to see them slidin' Martin into the patrol wagon that rushed him to the hospital. And she hadn't had a blessed word from anyone to tell her he had so much as a temp'rature. But there she was. Just in time."

For some reason this compliment to the powers of someone whose rights he had just been vigorously defending seemed to offend Bucky. "One moment, P. J.!" he said. "One moment there! There's no miracle in that. No miracle at all. Martin was

[335]

sick all the time. Everybody knew that. There wasn't a day he couldn't have gone down the skids!"

"But he didn't," P. J. said calmly. "Not till Julia got there. I tell you, if I was sick and lay in my bed and who did I see come into the room but Julia, I'd know what was what. Julia knows the times. I wouldn't be s'prised if she wasn't on the train this very minute. Or the bus. Julia's a great one for buses. You see more of the country that way." And then, in one of those always astonishing turns that old people can make, he came sharply back to the moment out of the wandering drifts of the past and said, "Poor Charlie. I wonder will he make it? I hope so. He's a queer, quarrelsome sort of a man, but I'd miss him. I'd miss seein' him around. You get used to a man, you know."

I had the feeling that now the soft voice was really addressed to no one but himself. He was an extremely detached old man, and I don't think I was ever so aware of that detachment as now — I mean, that as I listened to the gentle speech, and looked at the placid old face, so miraculously without a line, almost beautiful, I couldn't help but wonder — not too uncharitably, I hope — whether he would indeed miss Charlie as Charlie, or whether he would miss him rather as one more of the familiar, long-known objects which vanish, regrettably and one by one, from an old man's world. Probably a mixture of both — probably even a stronger dash of the second. Which is no attempt to pass judgment on him, certainly, and in any case it's no more than a guess. But to the very old, the death of someone, even the death of a close friend, must come with a different kind of impact, not necessarily stronger but with entirely different meanings and associations, than it does to those who are younger and whose horizons, though hardly boundless, are still far away. . . .

Ted and Anne had come close to us during the last part of this talk and stood listening quietly. What they heard could not have been encouraging, for Ted drew me to one side and

[336]

said, "I hadn't realized it was quite so decided about Grandpa, Father. Is it?"

Which was fair enough: the two old men — and, unwittingly, myself along with them — had been talking as if Charlie were in fact on the point of being buried. Guiltily I said, "No. No, it isn't, Ted. Nothing's decided at all. There's always a certain amount of pessimistic talk at a time like this; what you have to remember is that it really doesn't mean anything. It's amateur pessimism. The doctors are the only ones with information."

"We didn't have much chance to talk with them," he said. "We got here a little late, and then we were mostly with Mom — she was so upset. But I did get the impression that my dad was playing his cards pretty close to the vest. With doctors, that's not normally considered a good sign, is it? It always seemed to me more of a storm warning than anything else. At least with Dad."

So Frank, who had so firmly urged secrecy upon me, had so far been an open book to his own family: first Helen, now Ted. But I said carefully, "I don't know that in this case it's anything more than a sign of simple caution. Your father told me it was still too early to make any kind of definite prediction. The other doctor seemed to agree with that."

"Jack King," he said, nodding. "I went to school with him for a couple of years. He's bright enough."

Anne, who had joined us, said, "Is he the one who took care of Tony Murray?"

"No, that's his brother. That whole family's a nest of doctors. Jack's supposed to be the best, or so they say. Well then," he said to me, "we can't do much but wait it out, can we?"

"I think that's about all. We'll probably learn more when they see him again. After the priest comes out."

"It's a problem, isn't it?" he said. "I mean, the business of administering the last rites?"

"A problem in what way?"

"Well," he said, "I don't mean that it applies now, but isn't it conceivable that in a situation like this the priest might be in some danger of doing more harm than good?"

Anne said, "Psychologically, Father. In the effect he might have upon the patient."

She spoke with great earnestness, in the way pretty young women sometimes do when they wish to point out that they are not merely pretty young women. I had the feeling that she and Ted had just been discussing this subject and now presented a small, solid front. And I was a little surprised, not by the objection itself, which I'd heard often before, which I understood, and with which I had some sympathy, but by the fact that the objection had come in this setting and from such a quarter. Because surely old Charlie's grandson, Helen's son, should know. . . . I said, "You think the priest might frighten him to death?"

Anne said, "Well, no. . . ."

"Well, yes," Ted said, with a smile. "More or less that's what I do mean, Father. Let's say that a man is in a critical condition, that he doesn't know how critical it is, and that his doctor thinks it might do him harm if he did know. Well, suddenly that man opens his eyes and sees a priest bending over him, preparing to anoint him — that doesn't leave much room for doubt, would you say?"

"No, except that it really doesn't work out that way. That is, the priest doesn't come as quite this jack-in-the-box surprise. . . ."

"Yes, but occasionally he must come as a bit of a shock," he said. "You see what I'm driving at, Father?"

"Oh yes. I do indeed. It's not entirely a novel thesis, you know."

A dry comment? A little too dry for simple politeness? The long months of practice with Father Danowski resulting in the emergence of a well-known clerical type: the ironical elder? But he took it very nicely, smiling once more, an immediate

[338]

and friendly smile which gave a quick liveliness to his quiet and rather too controlled good looks; in such a moment I could see a great resemblance to his mother. He said, "No, I suppose not. It's something that occurred to me only now, but of course it must be an old story to you. You must have heard it hundreds of times before. And from experts at that."

It was polite, disarming, and only slightly increased my bad conscience. I said, "I think all I really wanted to say is that the priest's coming in to your grandfather isn't automatically a sign — to him or to any of us — that the worst is coming. In other words, Extreme Unction isn't necessarily one step before death. It's really more of a precaution — just in case. I've anointed many people who've got well afterwards. In most cases they'd have got well anyway, I imagine, Extreme Unction or no, but it *is* a sacrament, after all. With its own special graces. And you wouldn't exactly be called heretical if you thought it might occasionally help towards recovery."

Which was all good elementary catechism doctrine, something he must have known, indeed memorized, from his earliest days, and even as I talked I felt that this might all be faintly ridiculous, a bit like reminding him that an island is a body of land surrounded by water, or that π_r^2 equals circular girth. Yet as I watched him listening to me so politely, nodding in the most friendly fashion, what bothered me a bit was the lack, not of any impatience with what I said, but apparently of any recognition of it: I had the feeling that the pleasant smile and the courteous regard might have been given equally to a water dowser explaining the mysteries of his craft. What was missing was a certain *involvement*. At least this was the impression I got; it may have been unfair. In any case he didn't press the matter further; he said only, "I hope so, Father. Because there really isn't anyone quite like him around any more, is there?"

Admiration? Or a more detached observation? The curiosity I'd felt at the birthday dinner — about the kind of relationship that could possibly exist between two such vastly separated figures as old Charlie and his grandson — came back to me now, and I wondered in just what way he saw his grandfather as unique. I said, "No, he's pretty much all by himself. There are Bucky and P. J., of course, and then there are a few more of the old-timers still living over here whom you may not know. But I don't think any one of them is quite like your grandfather."

Which was true enough, heaven knows. He said thoughtfully, "You know, I really don't know him terribly well. I didn't see very much of him when I was a boy. You know how he is: he's not the kind of man who plays with children. And then I was away at school so much when I got older, so that it's only recently — since Anne and I were married, in fact — that I've come to know him at all. Now he drops in on us every now and then; Anne's turned out to be a great favorite of his."

She said fondly, "He tells these stories about the old days, you know, and about some of the things he used to do. To get ahead, you know: all about evictions and cutthroat competition and all sorts of things the government puts you in prison for today. Some of them are absolutely *blood-curdling*, Father; you'd be appalled if you believed them!"

This had a peculiar ring: it sounded as if Charlie, ordinarily the most circumspect of men in talking about his business dealings, had — for whatever reason of his own — been guilty of a surprising candor in his conversations with the young. Safely enough, apparently; I said, "But you don't believe them?"

"Oh, I think it's mostly just a huge tease," she said, with a wonderful, fresh, careless assurance. "I think he has great fun telling me all these things and pretending he's some sort of medieval *ogre*; I can see him watching me out of the corner of his eye when he talks. He enjoys shocking me, you know.

Except that he doesn't, really, because I think that underneath it all he's nothing but an old sweetie."

An old sweetie. Mr. Grumpy, forever concealing his inner twinkle. It's great to be young. And innocent. . . .

"As to being close to him," Ted said, "I'm not, but I'm pretty sure not many people are. Wouldn't you agree?"

"Yes, I think so. Your grandfather never really went in for confidants."

"The odd thing is, though," he said, "that in one peculiar way I may be closer to him than Uncle John is, or Uncle Dan, or even Mom. That is, I can talk to him more easily. Without suspecting that he has something up his sleeve. Do you know what I mean, Father? Because I always get the feeling that none of them — his own children, I mean — can say so much as 'Good morning' to him without wondering if and when he's going to lower the boom."

"Yes, I know. Although don't forget that they have a certain amount of history on their side: he has been known to lower a boom or two in his day."

He laughed, quietly, affectionately. "So I understand. I sit in on those stories, too."

"And believe? Or disbelieve?"

"Am I like Anne, you mean?" he said, with a smile. "Well, not quite like Anne. For one thing, I don't think he's much of a tease. I'll tell you how I feel when I listen to him talk, Father. I feel just the way I did when I was a boy and used to listen to football games on Saturday afternoons. There was an announcer who used to broadcast most of the games — I don't remember his name now — and I used to love to listen to him because he made everything so exciting and dramatic and colorful. Well, when you read the papers the next morning you discovered that almost everything he'd said was wrong, that as a factual, detailed account of what was happening on the field the whole thing was a fraud. But that didn't matter when you were listening because he gave you such a sense of scene, of atmosphere. That's the way I feel about Grandpa. Most of what he says is exaggeration, I don't believe the details, but all the color and excitement is there, and I can even believe that maybe they did play fairly rough in those good old days."

"They did. They did indeed. And when your grandfather started to play he had nothing; before too long he was a millionaire. He didn't do that exactly by turning the other cheek; quite a few of his fellow players have every reason to remember your grandfather vividly. I wouldn't dismiss too much of what he told you as exaggeration."

It was a curious way to defend a dying man: to insist that he was at least as bad as he claimed to be. Yet it seemed as though I'd somehow been pushed into the position, that what was important was that I should establish that Charlie, whatever else he was, was at least a *reality*, not just a caricature of his own imagination, some sort of Pickwickian rogue, quaint and entirely fictional. . . .

"Growing up," Ted said, "I used to hear — or overhear, really — from different ones in the family how formidable he was. But the thing is, Father, that he's never seemed formidable to me. Maybe it's because I'm his grandson instead of his son. That makes a difference, I know: not quite so many battle-grounds to share."

It was a shrewd comment from an intelligent young man; I remembered that Helen had once said something very much the same. He added, "Or maybe it's just as he grew older he grew more benign. That's what's supposed to happen, isn't it?"

Which was not so shrewd; I said, "So they say. I haven't found it to be particularly true."

"Well," he said, "once upon a time there must have been something there that made everybody jump. All I know is that I've never seen him as the terror or the tyrant or the man to beware. And lately, as I say, I've seen him more than ever.

[342]

Since about the time I told him I was going to run for Congress."

I hadn't mentioned his political plans; in fact I had forgotten all about them, and now I asked him if everything seemed to be going well.

"No complaints," he said. "Or no serious ones, anyway. I'm working at it a little harder than I expected, and seeing a lot of people I wouldn't otherwise see. It's dull and routine, in a way, but it's new and exciting, too. And Anne's a great help."

She said, "I go around pouring tea. At different women's clubs. It's all organized: we have 'Tea for Ted' parties. It sounds awful, I know, and actually it *is* pretty awful, but everybody says it gets votes. And that's what's important."

And once more earnestness settled down upon the pretty face. Ted said, "Speaking of seeing people, Father, I'll be dropping over to see you one day soon, if I may. Officially. Your parish is in my district, you know."

I didn't know, and I couldn't for the life of me see how a talk with me — official or otherwise — could have any bearing on his campaign, but of course he was welcome, and I told him to come ahead, at any time. Then, because I wanted to get back to Charlie, I said, "Tell me about your grandfather: does he seem interested in your running for office? Does he talk much to you about it?"

"All the time," he said. "He's interested, all right. I get the political history of the city every time we get together. Or *a* political history of the city: it's made up mostly of people with names like Big Thumb Connerty and Jumbo Riley and Snake Devlin. Was there *really* a Snake Devlin, I wonder? Did you ever hear of him, Father?"

"Vaguely. But tell me, in your talks together, doesn't he sometimes give you a few tips that might be of some help? He knows the city pretty well, you know: I'd think that at least some of what he tells you might come in extremely handy."

[343]

"Well, not really," he said. "That is, it's all wonderful stuff to listen to, of course, but it's not the kind of thing you could use in a campaign today. And I don't even think he seriously intends it to be used. I think he comes over so often and talks the way he does because he likes to feel busy, and this gives him the illusion of still being in the thick of things, of keeping right up to the minute. We usually have people in these nights — mostly some of our friends who are working on the campaign — and they're fascinated by him. They've never seen anything like him before; even sometimes when he goes on a little too long they seem to think he's great. So that he's happy about it, Father, and so are we. It all works out well for everyone."

I had a vivid and not particularly pleasant picture of this scene: Charlie, capering about among the amused young, the comic relief from all serious business who sometimes stayed on too long. I have no doubt that this boy meant to be tolerant, kind, but I found myself wondering which was kinder, really: Bucky and P. J. discussing the sick Charlie as if he had in fact just died, or Ted discussing him as if, from the point of view of any consequence, he had really died thirty years ago . . . ?

But there was movement now at the top of the stairs; the door to Charlie's room opened and I saw the Franciscan come out. Helen came down the stairs to see him out; the two doctors went into the bedroom. Ted said, "Well, that's that. Now let's hope that Dad and Jack King can bring us some good news." And then he said, "Incidentally, Father, there's something you can settle for us. About the priest — what kind is he? I mean, from which order?"

It was an extraordinary question — at least so it seemed to me, and for a moment I thought he was joking, but apparently not; both he and his wife were obviously waiting for an answer. I said, "He's a Franciscan," and almost added the "of course"; as it was I couldn't have been able entirely to keep the surprise from my voice. But this went unobserved, for Anne simply said, "There, you see, I told you!"

And she said it with a kind of triumph, as if she had solved a peculiarly baffling problem against all reasonable expectations. Ted said, "One up for you. Except that you weren't any too sure of it yourself, remember." He smiled at me again, the pleasant, intelligent smile, and said, "We more or less boxed the compass on this, trying to guess which order he belonged to. Anne finally settled on the Franciscans; I thought it might have been the Carthusians."

The Carthusians. He might as well have said "the Eskimos" — there were approximately as many of each in this part of the world, and each was equally likely to be summoned on an errand of this kind. I felt disconcerted and somewhat embarrassed, in the way you do when, occasionally, you come upon a totally unexpected gap in someone's knowledge — a gap you simply feel has no right to be there. Not that a Franciscan is so absolutely unmistakable, but it would never have occurred to me that anyone here, in this room, would not have known one when he saw one. The older people, certainly, would have known in a glance. But Ted had not known; he had even come through with the absurd "Carthusians"; and this, coupled with his earlier observations about the last rites, made me wonder now if he were not far from the older generations in more ways than I had at first suspected.

The Franciscan left the house, nodding to me as he went; Helen came over to us and said to me, "He wants to see you, Hugh. That's the last thing he said to the priest. I guess you ought to go up."

I said, "Come along?"

She shook her head. "I think he wants to see you alone. I know he does. Go ahead, Hugh; I'll be along later."

And so I went. Uneasily, for Helen's sadness — in not being able to go herself, in seeing an outsider, even me, called in by her father before any of his own children — was achingly clear; old Charlie remained a peculiar and a hard parent to the end. And yet there was nothing I could do about it — other than to continue up the stairs. As I walked I could see Bucky and P. J. staring up at me from below, P. J.'s expression as calm as ever, but Bucky's one of renewed outrage. I gathered that I was usurping still another prerogative: I was taking the turn that could have been his. . . .

At the door I was met by Frank and the young doctor. Before I even asked the question the young doctor was ready with the answer: he said, "No great change; he's about the same. But he's wide awake now, and he's quiet. And he keeps asking for you, Father. It might be best if you didn't stay more than a few minutes. And keep everything pitched on a low key; go very easy with him."

I don't know what he imagined I had proposed to do: Indian wrestle? Conduct a debate? But I promised that my visit would be both decorous and brief; then, at last, I entered Charlie's room.

At one time or another — mostly when I was a small boy — I had been all over this house, but I had never been in this room before: the intrepid adventurers of childhood had not quite dared to cross this frontier. The room was spacious, high-ceilinged; facing north, and with large windows, it must have been, under ordinary circumstances, easily the lightest and airiest room in the house. But now it was a sickroom, unmistakably so: the instant I went in I felt the smothered stillness, the peculiar *fragility* of the atmosphere, the sense of mysterious suspension, as though in this room everything we mean by life had suddenly paused and was now waiting — watchful, motionless, with one foot poised in the air — for the solemn, stupendous, unprecedented decision to come. . . .

The room was dimly lit: a single table lamp had been turned on; that was all. I saw, first, the nurse: a plump woman in white, bending over the bed, expertly fluffing a pillow.

She moved away from the bed — and then I saw Charlie. He was lying not quite flat, for his head and the upper part of his body had been lifted a bit by pillows: even this slight elevation gave him a deceptively convalescent appearance, as if, after a long illness, he had now progressed to the point where he could begin to sit up in bed. He had evidently heard my step, or else the nurse had said something to him, for he turned his head to me and said, loudly and clearly, "Hello there, Father."

And when I heard him and saw his face I felt a new twist of pain — not because he looked ravaged or ill, but precisely because he looked so well. There was not a visible trace of the damage that had been done. The old kewpie-doll face with its crown of white hair was exactly the same as it had been on that bounding day of the birthday party and every day since; the dusty voice seemed not a bit weaker. I shouldn't have been surprised at this, of course; over the years I've been often enough in these final moments where the truly desperately ill looked so fit that I've sometimes wondered whether some wild diagnostic mistake had not been made — the layman's eye is a bad guide in these matters. So then I suppose I should have been prepared for at least the possibility of this with Charlie, but somehow I was not, and the conjunction of the unchanged façade with the violent fact beneath seemed a cruel and unnecessary trick. I went to his bed and took his hand; I said, "Hello, Mr. Carmody."

"Merry Christmas," he said. Ironically, rather than bitterly, and I knew I should have ready some apposite, evasive response, some cheery bedside lie designed to "kid" him out of his mood: *You look right as rain, Mr. Carmody; you'll be on your feet again in a week* or *You gave us all a scare this time, Mr. Carmody!* As if the danger, although certainly grave enough, were now past. I have no contempt for such jolly untruths; they do no harm and sometimes, I think, can even do good. I know priests who can deliver them with ease and apparent convictions; I can't, and often wish I could. As now, for instance, but instead I merely held on to his hand and said nothing, and suddenly he said, "What time is it, Father?"

I told him and he nodded, apparently satisfied. "That's all right, then," he said. "A man likes to know the time. I asked the doctor and he told me but you can't depend on that. Those fellers tell a man that's sick so many lies they get in the habit. Did he talk to you, Father? Did he tell you about me?"

"Yes. He told me all about it, Mr. Carmody."

"And did he tell you I was goin' to die?"

There was a disapproving movement from the nurse's chair at this; I said quickly, "No, he didn't tell me that. In fact what he told me was nothing like that at all."

"Well," he said, "then he told one more lie. Because I am."

It was a flat statement of fact. By now I could see that the signs I had not noticed at first were nevertheless there: the surface was not quite the same. There was a dullness in the blue eyes — fatigue, I suppose — and his voice, which at first had seemed so unaltered, was slower, and in this more extended speech I could catch a touch of breathlessness and a faint, peculiar bubbling sound which seemed to underlie the words: I was reminded that Frank had suggested the presence of congestion. As if to emphasize this point now Charlie coughed, wetly, and I said, "Easy, Mr. Carmody. Don't try to talk too much."

"I want to talk," he said stubbornly. "I *got* to talk. I got somethin' to say. That's why I got you in here, Father. I got somethin' to say to you." His head nudged in the direction of the seated nurse; he added meaningfully, "Alone."

The nurse heard this, for at once she gave me a quick, competent, slightly conspiratorial smile: we both recognized, it seemed to say, the impossible whims of the severely ill. However, she did not move, and Charlie turned towards her and said, "Nurse, I'm goin' to talk with Father now. By myself. We'll call you when you're wanted."

[348]

She smiled again and said, "Now, Mr. Carmody, you know very well the doctor wouldn't want —"

The tone was kittenish; it did not please Charlie. "Get out!" he said, loudly and angrily. "Now!"

The nurse jumped to her feet, alarmed, both by the words and by the fact that Charlie was struggling to lift himself in bed. I put my hand on his shoulder and said, "It's all right, Mr. Carmody. It's all right." To the nurse I said, "I think you'd better go. It will be easier on everyone. Under the circumstances. And tell the doctor why; I'm sure he'll understand."

She hesitated for a moment, but then she left, glaring hard at Charlie as she did so. I could sympathize a little with her: she would keep an uneasy vigil with this patient. . . .

Charlie sank back on his pillows. "By God," he said wearily, "if they don't kill you one way, they try another. And get paid like queens for doin' it." He closed his eyes, and his breathing came faster; clearly, even the slight exertion had been too much for him. It was alarming enough so that I thought of bringing the doctor back in, but I hesitated, and after a moment the breathing seemed to slow down, became more normal, and as it did Charlie opened his eyes. "Ah," he sighed, "I tell you, Father, there's damn little steam in the boiler these days. I dunno could I even blow my nose without restin' up for a week."

And my mind popped back to my father, saying in a puzzled voice, "I've no more strength than a chicken. I don't dare blink my eyes for fear it will tire me out. . . ."

Charlie motioned with a hand toward the nurse's chair. "Pull that thing over here and sit down next the bed, Father. So's I won't have to talk loud."

I brought the chair over and sat down; he said, "I had the priest, Father. I got the whole works."

"Yes, I know. I saw him come in."

"A Franciscan," he said. "I picked him out myself. Nobody knows that feller." It was a small victory, of the little bonus variety which usually gave him such pleasure, but which did not seem to please him now. At any rate he did not linger over it; he said, "So there it is, Father: the slate's all wiped off. I told him all my sins: the whole lot. And he gave me Holy Communion. So now I'm ready, Father. I'm all set to go. Just the way I always wanted to. In the state of grace."

But he spoke with great glumness, and for a moment I was tempted to try encouragement, to remind him as I had reminded Ted, that recovery was by no means impossible, that death did not inflexibly follow the administering of the last rites. But I didn't do this. Charlie was not Ted, and moreover, it would have been to no purpose. Whatever Charlie wanted from me now — and just what he wanted was, as always, a mystery — it was nothing on this level of consolation. For when people come unwillingly and grimly to this conclusion, when their minds are made up that they are soon to die, then the usual reassurances are of no value at all; it's not like telling a child that the pain will go away. Very often what you say is not even heard, even though it may appear to be acknowledged, for the dying can often talk to you and yet at the same time seem somehow in communion only with themselves, peculiarly abstracted from your presence. As Charlie was now. His head did not move on the pillow, but his eyes had begun to shift about the room, looking up and down, at the walls, at the ceiling, pausing every now and then to focus, with an odd expression almost of disbelief, on some familiar point of reference which he must have seen every day of his life, but which now seemed to strike him as something new and strange.

I heard him talking — and certainly he wasn't talking to me. "I dunno," he muttered. "I dunno at all." Then there was more silence, and the eyes continued to rove, and then he said, "It don't seem right. It ain't *fair*. What's the reason? Who knows that one? On top of the world one day, and then the next, nothin'. . . ."

They were private ruminations, but he had not forgotten me,

for although he still stared at some remote point in the dim room, he said suddenly, "Priests are the ones that see people dyin'. You've seen your share, I s'pose, Father?"

It was not the line of talk I would have chosen, but then, it was not mine to choose. I said, "Yes. . . ."

"And anointed them? With the oils?"

"Yes. Often, that is."

"And heard their confession? And gave them Holy Communion?"

Or, in other words, had I done to them exactly what had been done to him? It was as if, before talking to me seriously, he wished to establish my experience, my qualifications. I said, "All of that, Mr. Carmody."

"And," he said, "and then, Father? After all of that: what was it happened next?"

It was an opportunity to say what I'd already decided there was no point in saying. "Different things. Quite a few of them got better, in fact; they're still around today."

But as I had expected, Charlie was having none of this oblique encouragement; he was shaking his head before I was halfway through. "No, no," he said impatiently. "That ain't what I mean. That ain't what I want to know. What I want to know is this: did any of them ever *want* to go? Did any of them ever say to you, 'I got no more sins on my soul, Father, so now I'm ready and willin' and waitin' to go?' Did any of them ever say that to you?"

The old question of the last reluctance; I said truthfully, "Not very many, Mr. Carmody. A few, perhaps, said something like that. . . ."

"Then they were damn fools," he said bleakly. "Or else they were lyin'. No matter what anybody tells you, Father, I'm tellin' you that." He closed his eyes once more and was silent; after a while he opened them and said again, "What time is it, Father?"

It's the great small question at such moments: in a single

[351]

hour it may be asked over and over and over again — I think for no other reason than that in such a room, in this queer, half-lit, floating atmosphere of waking and sleeping and waking again, all the normal measurements of time are blurred or disappear, and so time itself becomes of the greatest importance: it has to be pinned down. And so I told him and he nodded with the same apparent satisfaction as before, and repeated the words he had said before: "A man likes to know the time. . . ."

There was more silence. Then he said suddenly and loudly, "I hate to go. I hate it like the devil. They talk about dyin' happy: it's all bunk. There's no such thing as dyin' happy. Don't b'lieve them when they tell you that one, Father. They talk about heaven. All right: I got nothin' against that. I know there's a heaven and I hope to God I wind up there, but the thing is this, Father: who wants to wind up there *now*? I got my plans all made; I still got things to do. How can a man die happy if he's got things like that on his mind? How can a man do that? All right, I'll go because I got to go, and I hope I have good luck wherever I go, but I tell you this, Father: I'd a damn sight rather stay here. Where I know what's what."

It was hardly the faith that moves mountains, but it wasn't unusual, either. Or unnatural: most of us will die a little less than heroes or saints. I said, dutifully if not too hopefully, "All this talk of going: I hear it from you, Mr. Carmody, but not from your doctor. . . ."

He paid no attention to this. Instead, he shifted his head so that now he looked directly at me, and then he said, very slowly, "And I'll tell you somethin' else, Father. How can a man die happy if he knows that when he goes he won't be missed by a single livin' soul? Not one!"

And I find it difficult, now, to describe what I felt when I heard him say this, and when I saw his face when he said it. I was accustomed by now to the bursts of self-pity, the little swoops into pathos which were always accompanied by the

[352]

sharp cock of the inner eye to see how you were taking it. But this was something else; this was far different. There was no sentimentality here at all: this was Charlie as I'd never seen him, without a mask of any kind, uttering at the end a cold, dry, naked cry — a cry that was unexpected, bitter, and dangerous. I said sharply, "Listen to me, Mr. Carmody: you're wrong, you're mistaken. There's no question of being forgotten here. You're not a lonely forsaken figure with no one around you; you're a man with a family and good friends —"

"No," he said stubbornly. "Stop. You listen to me, Father. I'd listen to you if it was somethin' you know more about than me, but you don't know more about *me* than I do, and that's the only one I'm talkin' about now. Because it's me that's dyin', Father, and I got somethin' to say to you. So for the love of God just let me say it and don't start arguin' with me now. I ain't got the *time*. So listen, Father!"

It was the white face and the short gasping breath which reminded, as fully as the words did, that he was indeed a man who might be dying, and that if so he was talking far too much, and that surely I had no business to make matters worse by struggling with him. But of course it wasn't as simple as that, for I was a priest, after all: I couldn't let this old man die in despair. The last sacrament had been given, but agitation and a kind of misery remained: I wanted to help, but I knew that nothing I could say would break through. I could only listen, and hope that out of the words might come some easing of his mind, some thin possibility that I could reach and calm him. . . .

I touched his shoulder and said, "It's all right, Mr. Carmody. You tell me: I'll listen. But take it easy; don't strain; there's no hurry. Just go as slowly as you can and I'll be here as long as you want me. And I won't fight you."

"All right," he said. "All right." And then he was quiet for a little while, with his eyes closed again, as if he were gathering up all his forces, and once more I thought that it might be

[353]

prudent to have the doctor in here, within arm's reach. Just in case. But it was a foolish thought: nothing would have infuriated Charlie more than the entrance of the doctor or anyone else at this point: he would have fumed, and he would have told me nothing. So I sat, waiting, and as I waited I felt Charlie's hand reach out and grasp mine and hold it tightly. I couldn't help thinking that it must have been one of the most uncharacteristic gestures of his long and unconfiding life. . . .

"I won't be missed," he said flatly. "I tell you that because it's true. I made my confession and I won't get a chance to make another one, so I wouldn't tell lies after that. I'll tell the truth, Father. I'll tell you somethin' I never told you or anybody else before. And that is that everythin' I told you about me bein' so popular and havin' a lot of friends and people wantin' to be like me is all bunk. It ain't true. Not a word of it. I go around the city day by day, doin' different things, payin' bills, sittin' on boards with top men, collectin' rents from little nobodies, meetin' them all from the highest to the lowest, and I might say a few words to them and they might say a few words to me. Sometimes the words ain't so bad; sometimes we even have a little laugh. Ain't that nice, Father? But it don't mean a thing. Not a damn thing. Because I know what they're thinkin', and what they been thinkin' for years. When I walk away from them down the street, every last one of them says to himself, 'There he goes. One of these days he'll go for good and won't come back, and when he does it'll be hip hip hooray and goodbye and good riddance from me.' I know that's what they think and I know that's what they say. And I'm tellin' you the truth now, Father: there's not a man in the city today that's more hated then me."

It was awful to listen to, awful because it was coming from a dying man, awful because it was coming with such conviction. Stripped of all hypocrisy or falseness, it was impossible to dismiss or discount; listening to him I had only the impression of a terrible sincerity. He spoke with none of the old ebullience;

in fact he spoke with no emotion at all. His words came one after another in a slow, cold procession, and all the time he talked he kept his eyes directly on mine, as if this were in some way helping him to drill his words home. I had said that I wouldn't interrupt, but of course I couldn't help it against this; I put my free hand up to stop him but he shook his head vigorously and began to cough.

"No," he gasped, after he had finished coughing. "No no. Listen like you promised. I ain't done yet." There was another pause; then he went on. "I say they hate me and they do. I s'pose they got their reasons. I been a hard man in lots of ways all my life. Some of the things I done I ain't too proud of. I'm even sorry for them now; I told the Franciscan that. But by God, Father, life around here was tough. I came out of nothin'; you know that. My pa laid pipe in this city twelve hours a day and got paid a dollar for doin' it; we didn't any of us starve but we came damn close to it. And when I was on my way up, d'ye know how many around here gave me a break? Not a soul. Not a livin' soul. But I got up there all the same, and once I did I gave them no more breaks than they gave me. That ain't what the catechism tells us, is it, Father? But it's the way I done it. The only way I knew how. And maybe it was bad and I'm not sayin' it wasn't, but I dunno was it so much worse than what most others were doin'. Oh, I might of give it an extra little twist here or there, the way you have to do sometimes, but I swear to God I never thought it was anythin' dreadful. Like a monster or somethin'. It was more like a kind of a game you knew how to win at better than the other feller. Well, all right. And then one day you're walkin' down the street, doin' what you got to do, and you begin to see little looks in eyes you ain't meant to see, and you begin to hear little whispers behind your back you ain't meant to hear, and people seem to be gettin' out of your way as you come along, almost like they were duckin' you. So you watch out more and more and pretty soon you come to see there's damn little else but the looks and the whispers and the duckin'. And pretty soon you come to know what you don't tell anybody but yourself — and it's damn hard to even do that. You come to know that nobody, not a single soul, wants you anywheres around. They can't do anythin' about it; they *got* to have you; you got the money, the houses they live in; but they don't want you, and way down deep you know that when the day comes you won't be around any more, that's the day they'll all of them give three cheers. So you know that, Father. All of a sudden you know there's somethin' about you that people hate more than they do about anybody else. You don't know exactly why but they do. And what d'ye do about it? I'll tell you what you do: you do nothin'. What can you do? Jump around sayin' 'Free rents for everybody'? Give picnics and lollipops for every kid in the city? Hand over shares of stock you won fair and square? I couldn't do anythin' like that, Father. There's somethin' in me wouldn't let me. And even if it would I wouldn't do it. They'd only hate you for that too, and say you were gettin' soft in the head at last and laugh at you. So I did nothin' except go right on doin' what I was doin' already. And they kept on hatin' me for it. And I knew it. I never let on to anyone I did, but I knew it all right. I knew it for years." And for the first time he took his eyes from mine and stared out, straight ahead — at what, I don't know. After an interval he said, "It don't make no difference. I never set out to be the most popular man on the block, anyways. I had other things to do. All the same, a man don't like to be hated. That's only human." And then, coming back to me, he said, "Are you followin' me in this, Father?"

"I'm following you, Mr. Carmody." Not that this was hard to do, for the story wasn't complicated: it was all too simple and clear and sad. Sad because so much of it, I suspected, was true; sad because it showed what Charlie realized about himself; sadder still because it showed what he did not. And I suppose that now, despite all instructions, I should have made a fresh try at consolation, but I didn't — not yet. I simply sat there, waiting for the rest to come, and suddenly Charlie began to cough again: a series of heavy, watery coughs which shook his body and left his eyes streaming. I pressed his hand and said, "Easy now. Don't push yourself. Just take your time." Although even as I said this I wondered — as he had earlier — just how much time might be left. The performance would have been a brutal drain on anyone, and poor Charlie had few reserves to spare. . . .

"There's the family," he said at last. "Family and friends." It was the jubilant phrase of the birthday — not so jubilant now. "They don't hate me. But which one of them would miss me? Not a one. They don't care. They don't give a damn."

I said quickly, "No, you're wrong there, Mr. Carmody. You're all wrong. They do care. They're here tonight because they care."

"No," he said. "It's you that's wrong, Father. I know them all, a whole lot longer and better than you. I s'pose Mary's the one would miss me the most. But there's nothin' she don't miss. She's a good girl but she's a simple girl. She feels bad for everythin'. She cries just the same for people that get sick or pets that lose their fur or trees that get chopped down or blankets the moths get at. When I go I'll get her tears all right. But it won't mean no more than a little girl cryin' 'Boo hoo hoo, my dolly's lost her shoe.' It don't go no deeper than that with Mary. But she'll cry. As will Dan. Dan that was always a silly boy and now he's a silly man with his silly new wife that laughs all the time and that's older than him. And when I go he'll get down on his knees and cry like a baby. Because he'll miss me? No. He'll cry because when I go the bank is closed. That's what I mean to Dan. And that's what he means to me. Nothin' more."

The bleakness was not fading; it was growing with every

[357]

sentence, and I gave his hand a little shake. To twitch him out of despondency? I said, "You're forgetting something, Mr. Carmody. . . ."

But he was not listening. He said, "And John. John with the brains. He's a boy that never gave me a day's worry. And that never gave me a day's love. Cold as an icicle. He got away from home as soon as he could and stayed away as long as he could. Now he's back and not a half a mile from the house and the only time I see him is of a Sunday if I go to see him say his Mass in church. No, he never missed me alive, and he won't miss me dead. You can count on that one. And there's Helen."

And at this point he paused. Not, now, to cough or to catch his breath, but apparently to consider what he was about to say. It was as though with the mention of Helen's name he had reached a natural dividing line, and would now have to proceed in an altogether different direction. A hopeful sign? Possibly; I pressed the point. "And Helen? What about Helen, Mr. Carmody?"

"Helen," he said again, and from the dead flatness of the tone I knew that I had been wrong, and that we had not changed directions at all. "Helen. A good wife. A good mother. And the only one of all my children that ever said she hated me."

And this was so unexpected that I had nothing to say. But Charlie now expected something, clearly; he was staring at me, waiting for comment. After a moment I said, "Think what you're saying. You *know* that Helen doesn't hate you. And never did. . . ."

"She said so," he said. "And meant so. At the time. She was livin' at home then, out of college a while, and one night she was standin' at the foot of the stairs, arguin' with me. Like she used to do. God knows why. I might of been a bit strict with the girl, but 'twas all for her own good. All of a sudden she turned on me with her eyes all mad and yelled, 'I hate you! I hate you more than anyone I know!' And d'ye know what I

[358]

said to that, Father? Nothin'. I said nothin'. I just stood there for a bit, lookin' at her, and then I went away. And I never said nothin' about it to this day. To her or anybody else. But that's what she said to me that night." There was another pause before he said. "That's all long ago now."

But not long enough ago to be forgotten by Charlie. Or by Helen: I remembered now the autumn afternoon in the clearing and the story she had been about to tell. Clearly this was at least a part of it; the rest wasn't hard to imagine: I had a fair idea of what Charlie's being "a bit strict" implied, and of how Helen must have felt, coming home to discover, for the first time as a young woman, the full weight of her father's restrictive thumb. Had Charlie at this stage decided he needed two Marys rather than one? Had he tried to beat Helen down? It didn't matter now, but I could imagine the growing bitterness and the final explosion. And I could also imagine the consequence of that explosion: the shock, not only to Charlie, but to Helen as well. For it would have been a great shock to her, brought up as she had been in a firm tradition of filial respect, to find that this tough, awesome, supposedly invulnerable parent could in fact be badly wounded with a word — and that the word had been delivered by her. I think something like this can last for a very long time. It had with Helen; it had with Charlie. I said now, "Whatever she said, she was very young at the time. And the young say things they don't mean. And you of all people know that your daughter does not hate you."

"I know that," he said. "Like I said, it's all long ago now. She don't hate me any more. But she don't care, either. No more than the rest. I know Helen. And I know when I go she'll feel bad. But not for me. She'll feel bad because she *don't* feel bad for me. That's the way Helen is. It's a nice way to be, no doubt, but it don't do me no good. And then," he said, "there's Ted. My own grandson. The only one I got. I never had a cross word with the boy. And I never had a sensible one. He's a smart, p'lite lad, nice and neat with the tight suit and the narrow shoulders with no paddin', and he always listens with a smile, but he pays no mind at all. I'm his grandfather, but when I talk to the boy I might as well be the end coon in Freddy McCarthy's Minstrels. He's a quiet boy and has lots of thoughts, but there ain't any of them for me. They're all for himself. I'm a tough man, Father, and John's a cold one, but with all the nice manners and the soft voice Ted just startin' out is tougher and colder than the both of us put together. There's the lad knows what he wants. And let's see anyone stop him from gettin' it. And when I go I s'pose he will miss part of me. He'll miss my vote. But he won't miss me."

It was a surprisingly harsh — and, surely, unwarranted? — judgment on his grandson, and I wondered why. Simply the old, raging at being treated half humorously by the young? But now Charlie burst into another spasm of coughs, which were about as severe as those that had gone before: no worse, but still alarming. He recovered in the same manner, and when he had he said, "That leaves who? Bucky and P. J.? They're old men like me, Father, and no matter what they tell you, old men don't miss nobody. When you're old and someone else that's old dies you might say out loud, 'Ain't that a shame!' but what you say to yourself is, 'One more gone, and the next one might be me.' That's what you say, and that's what P. J. and Bucky'll say when I go. And why not? I knew them all my life, and there ain't a week goes by I don't see them to talk to, but I dunno are we such pals. I dunno if they even like me much. Or if I like them. You can't tell sometimes. I dunno if it's any more than that we all grew up together in the same place and now we're the only ones left. So we got to talk to each other; there ain't nobody else. It's a kind of a habit. And when a habit like that is broke, Father, you don't feel bad. You might feel a bit different for a while, but it don't last long. And it don't mean nothin'. Nothin' at all."

It was a desolate reading of an old association, as desolate as anything he had said so far. He closed his eyes now, but he had not quite finished; he said slowly, "So there you have it, Father. The whole list, right down the line. And when I go they'll have the wake, they'll come to the church with their black dresses and their black neckties, they'll hear the Mass that's said for me, and they'll see me wheeled away and dropped down into the ground. And some of them will bawl like little babies. But when it's all over, which of them will remember for more than a minute and a half? And which of them will really give a damn? You know the answer to that just like I do, Father. Not a one. Not a one, not a one, not a one. Not a single blessed one."

It was a tolling close to the long lament. And now it was my turn — not that I'd been waiting for it. What could I possibly say that would move or change this old man — this old man for whom, as he lay there, frail and helpless and unhappy, I felt such pity and pain? Because he had some of it right, but he had so much more of it wrong; it would take a miracle to set him straight, and I had no miracles up my sleeve. Still, I had to say something, not only because he had sent for me and was now waiting, but because I had no choice: I couldn't let him go like this. And so, with no time for argument or even reassurance, and indeed with very little talent for either, I made no moves in this direction; instead, I talked to him directly and with no evasion about the only thing that mattered.

"But it's not important, Mr. Carmody. I mean, how popular you are or were, or how much loved, or how long you'll be remembered. It's nice if you were liked and not so nice if you weren't, but it couldn't matter less now. It's all in the past, it's all *happened*, and now nothing is important to you but what's going to happen."

"Not a hell of a lot," he said morosely. "How much can happen to a man that's got no more than a couple of puffs of wind left? And you know that's all I got; I can tell by the way you're talkin'."

I said, "I don't know if it is or it isn't. But even that's not

[361]

important, because a couple of puffs of wind is long enough for you to lose something. Listen to me, Mr. Carmody. Just for a minute. We both believe in the same things. We both believe that if a man is very ill and is anointed and makes a good confession and receives Communion, then in a sense he's ready to die. He may not want to die, he almost certainly doesn't, but at least he's been prepared: he's in the state of grace. But there's a danger here, and that is that somehow he'll fall out of the state of grace. Because even if you're flat on your back with only a couple of puffs left, you can still sin because you can still *think*. And if, for example, you begin to think of all the things that have been done against you, all the slights and offenses and injuries, and of all the people who you think were guilty of them, very often these thoughts lead to resentment, to anger, even to hatred — and this is a sin, Mr. Carmody. A grave sin: a sin against charity. Or else there's the sin of despair. Which is the greatest sin of all, because it means that in the end you've given up, that you no longer trust in the love and the mercy of God. It seems to me that the first step towards such despair can be the feeling that slowly you've been abandoned by everybody, that no one around you cares; from this it's quite possible to go on to the feeling that you're absolutely alone, that you've even been forgotten by God. And these are sins, Mr. Carmody, just as surely as drunkenness or murder or robbing a bank are. And they're peculiarly dangerous sins because the temptation to them can come at just such a moment as this — they're the sins to which someone who's sick or dying is peculiarly vulnerable. Even if he's received the last rites. The thing to remember is that even though you may be in the state of grace, you can still lose it, and if you do, there simply may be no time left to get it back. And if that's so, of course, when you die you die not in the state of grace, but you die badly; with an offense against God on your soul. I'm saying all this to you now because you told me you were dying. If you are, or if you think you are, then, Mr. Carmody, be careful. Because the danger is here. It never lets up, it never stops. And you can lose so much so easily. So in God's name, Mr. Carmody, be very very careful!"

And this, more or less, was what I wanted to say, and I said it, not with any great eloquence, but as well as I could. He listened with his eyes on mine all the way, but long before I finished I saw that somehow I was disappointing him, that what I had to offer was not what he wanted to hear, and as I neared the end he began to shake his head with a great vigor, and the pressure on my hand tightened.

"No, no!" he said, and he said it with a kind of violence. "No no no! I know all that. It's true enough, but what's it got to do with *me*? You don't get what I'm sayin', Father. You're not on the bull's-eye at all. Who's givin' up on God? Not me! Why would I give up on God? Who else would pull me through? Don't tell me to trust in God. I do I do I do! Who else would I trust? I know He'll take care of me. I always knew it. I know when I die He'll take care of me. He's got to. I dunno how but He will. If there's anyone will do the right thing by Charlie, it's God. And more than the right thing. That's what I need, Father: not the right thing, but *more* than the right thing. A special break. That's what I need from God. And that's what He'll give me. Or else I'm a goner. A goner! A goner!"

The last words were almost a scream; he had become greatly excited and tried once more to sit straight up in bed, to *thrust* himself at me. But once more the coughing intervened, and now at least it had the effect of calming him, for when the fit was over he was back against the pillows, his body slack and boneless, all fight gone. He blinked a bit, then said weakly, "You tell me not to hate people. Who do I hate? Dan? Helen? John? My own children? No. I don't. I swear to God I don't. I dunno what I feel towards them, but I don't hate them. I may say hard things about them sometimes, but afterwards, when I stop and think it over, I ain't even mad at them. They don't love me, none of them, and that ain't easy. But I ain't a dunce; I know it ain't all their fault. I even know whose fault it mostly is. I dunno why. I dunno what I done wrong. Maybe I was too tough or mean or tricky with them. I dunno. For a hell of a while I thought nothin' about it, except that kids were like that, always fightin' their dad. But when a man winds up with none of his own children even *likin'* him, and he knows it, and when he knows too that his own wife didn't speak ten words to him — except in front of company and the children — for the two years before she died, well, then. . . ."

His voice faded off, and again he looked away from me and stared straight out into the room; after a time he looked back at me and said, "So what does a man do? Does he change? How? That ain't so easy, Father. People get used to you the way you are. How do you change without makin' a clown of yourself? And without givin' up everythin' you worked hard to get? And what do you change *to?* I dunno. I s'pose I could of done it easy enough at that. If I wanted to. But it was too late, and then every time I might of they did some damn thing that made me mad. So I never did. And now maybe I wish I did. But I didn't. So there we are, Father. That's why I don't hate my kids. Because I can't. I wish they were different to me. I s'pose I wish I was different to them. But they ain't and I ain't. And that's why I say I won't be missed by them when I go. And that's why I called you over here tonight, Father."

And into the old blue eyes there now came a look which was unmistakable but which, in this particular setting, must surely have been rare: it was a look of genuine *imploring.* Directed at me. And then I knew my function, or thought I did: I was to be the mourner, the only one who would miss him when he died. I thought sadly how pitful all this was: this poor old man, shouting *"Mea culpa!"* at the end, but closing the door on even the possibility of love from those around him, and reaching out, in a kind of final desperate panic, to me. I could have told him — once again — that he was wrong, that there were those in his family who cared deeply, but what was the use of that? At this stage it would be like telling him he could fly unaided to the stars. It was better to tell him the one thing he would take in, the one thing he seemed to want to hear: that I, at least, would miss him very much. And I was just about to do this when he said, "Oh yes, I thought a lot about it durin' the last year or so. I thought a lot about dyin'. The way you do when you get to be as old as me." A faintly cunning expression crossed his face; he said, "I'll tell you a little secret, Father. About how old I am. I ain't eighty-two like I said on the birthday. I'm only eighty-one."

What a confidence. At what a time. But I said that I had been fooled and he smiled feebly. "Eighty-one," he said, with a touch of the old satisfaction at the successful small coup. "But what I do is, I tell them all I'm eighty-two. It's a kind of fun I have. You'll tell no one?"

"I'll tell no one, Mr. Carmody."

But then he remembered, and satisfaction vanished. He said, "It don't matter. It don't mean nothin' now. Anyways, I been thinkin' about it. And about the people that might of missed me. There was only one, Father. Out of the whole bunch, there was only one." And then came an unexpected identification; he said, "Your pa."

So Charlie was retaining his capacity to astonish until the end. To astonish and to deflate, for when I heard him say this I suddenly felt — what a thing to admit! — a certain childish, pouting disappointment: he hadn't wanted me at all! So much for the lone consoler. He was reaching instead for my father: it was a long reach. And, for Charlie of all people, clearly an impossible one. . . .

But he thought otherwise. "And he ain't around no more," he said. "Your pa. There was the man I liked. He was a queer man in lots of ways and no damn good at all at business and sometimes he made me mad he was so stubborn, but I'll tell you this: he was the kind of a man you like to be liked by. But did he like you or didn't he? That's what a man never knew about your pa. Oh, he was a grand talker and he'd always give you the nice quiet smile, but what was he really thinkin'? Underneath? That's what was hard to tell about your pa. Even for somebody like me that knew him all his life. He wasn't the kind of a man that would come right out and say, 'I like Charlie Carmody.' And to tell you the God's honest truth I never thought much about it one way or the other until maybe a year or so ago. When I started thinkin' about all this stuff. And I started askin' myself which one of all the people I knew in my whole life would I like most to say about me, 'Charlie's a fine feller,' or 'They come no better than Charlie,' or maybe just, 'Charlie's the man I'd hate to see go.' And there was only one. Your pa. Dave Kennedy. And o' course I never myself heard him say anythin' like that because that wasn't his way. But I think he might of felt it all the same. You couldn't get it out of him with a crowbar, but I always had the feelin' that deep down he thought I wasn't such a bad feller, that he even might of liked me a lot. That's what I guessed, anyways. But guessin' on a thing like that ain't good enough, Father. Not when a man's as near the end of the line as me. Then's when a man wants to *know*. That's when a man wants to make *sure*. And how could I make sure? Could I walk up to your pa on the street and say, 'For the love of God, Dave, d'ye like me or not? Tell me once and for all: I got to know!' Could I ask him that? I could not. Because he wasn't around to be asked no more. He was dead. Years ago. So who could I ask? And then, Father, I remembered you. One night lyin' in my bed I remembered you. And I said to myself, 'By God, he'd know. If there's one man in the city today would know to the last inch what Dave Kennedy felt about every man jack around here, it's Father. And nobody else.' So," he said simply, "I looked you up."

And there it was, as simple as that: he had "looked me up" — and now at last I knew why. The mystery was solved. The great game of What-Was-Charlie-Up-To was over, and all my suspicions and speculations — and John's as well — had been

ingenious, shrewdly reasoned, and completely wrong. For what
Charlie had been up to all along was nothing more than a pat
on the back. A special pat on the back, to be sure: a pat on the
back from my dead father. Passed on by the one possible mid-
dleman. Somehow, in the end, this was what had come to matter to him, and in one way I understood this easily, for I'd seen
it before: old men who by some sudden flash of honest light
are shaken from their self-regard, who in this instant see themselves as unloved, friendless, and alone, sometimes claw desperately through the past to find someone, anyone, who has ever
said a few words in their favor — even the most casual phrase,
said by chance and without thought, can at such a time be
made to swell and glow. So, as I say, in general it was understandable enough, but in this case, in these particular circumstances . . . poor Charlie! To have fixed on my father, of all
unlikely people! And to have gone on with me for so long,
week after week, month after month, working so hard — softening me up? — shouting and bouncing about and talking
entertainingly and endlessly: so much effort and so many
words, and yet not once able to bring himself to ask the one
question he really *ached* to ask — I suppose because at bottom
he feared what the answer might be. It must have seemed
advisable not to chance it just yet, to let it alone for the moment, and maybe tomorrow or the next day . . . but now he
had run out of tomorrows, there was no more time with which
to play, and now he had to ask the question or never ask it at
all. And I would have to answer . . . how? Because of course
the words he wanted so badly to hear had not been spoken.
My father had discussed Charlie with me a thousand times; for
long periods he seemed, indeed, to discuss nothing else; in a
sense Charlie had been the great conversation piece of his life.
Yet in all the talk, in all those innumerable stories, never once
had I heard him say anything in which Charlie could rejoice —
or even take comfort — now. Not once. . . .

And yet this was all he wanted: it was so pathetic it was

close to being unbearable. The pressure on my hand, which had tightened a few minutes before, grew even tighter; it pulled my eyes down to a face which was not at all like the cocky, buoyant, old-rogue's face which I had known ever since I had known Charlie. It was suddenly a strange face, strange and small and very old, anxious, and with a peculiar kind of frightened tightness about it, as if it were waiting, and waiting eagerly, for what was to come, but at the same time were not at all sure that what was to come would not turn out to be a savage blow. So this was Charlie, then, at the end, dying not as people do in romances or in edifying manuals, not nobly or serenely, not in peace or dignity, but as people all too often and sadly and humanly do in life: trembling and apprehensive, their minds and imaginations hypnotized before a pinpoint of irrelevant concern. . . .

Charlie coughed again, but now for the first time he did not wait for the coughing to stop. There was a new sense of urgency now: willfully, with great effort, breathing hard, he began to talk through the coughs. "So, Father," he gasped, "you *got* to tell me. What did he say? He must of said somethin'. He must of told you about me. Different times. Maybe when he was dyin'? When you were in there with him, all alone? Did he say anythin' then? He must of, Father! I know he must of! Then's the time he would!"

And I thought: one more bad guess. Poor Charlie, not trusting my unsupported memory, was helping it along; he was giving me a lift, suggesting possibilities. And what a possibility he had suggested! For it brought me back to my father on his deathbed, and to his last words on the subject of his old obsession: "Charlie Carmody: as fine a man as ever robbed the helpless. . . ."

And it was as I was remembering this that Charlie presented his last demand. He had managed to push himself up into a sitting position; he leaned forward now so that suddenly the eager, fearful face was just inches from mine and, although he must have been very weak, I felt a quick pain from the pressure of his hand. And then he shouted — it was *really* a shout, *"Did . . . he . . . like . . . me?"*

And what could I say? I said the only thing that it was possible to say and still remain a human being. I said, "Yes. Yes, he did, Mr. Carmody. He liked you very much, and he spoke of you often. And when he was dying, he spoke of you with . . . special affection."

I saw his eyes change, and felt his hand loosen and his whole body ease; I heard the whispered, *"Aaahhhh!"* — it was the loudest whisper I had ever heard. Then, very slowly, he subsided, almost melted, back into his pillows and lay there, his eyes closed, but conscious, awake, obviously listening. And he continued to listen as I continued to lie. . . .

I talked, not for very long — three of four minutes at the outside — but long enough to supply a small series of quiet, complimentary anecdotes, meditative tributes of a kind my father might conceivably have delivered — although not of course to Charlie. Once or twice I was sure that I was being heavy-handed, that I was going a little too far for belief, but apparently not: it was all done in a fair parody of my father's style, and in any case Charlie was not now disposed to be critical. He listened. He listened without a word, his head occasionally dipping in what I took to be acknowledgment that he heard. He gave no other sign, certainly none of great joy or even of satisfaction, but he was breathing it in deeply, storing up the words, and his face was now calm and completely free of that strange wild tautness — I think he was content. And I talked on. . . .

". . . once said to me, 'When Charlie was growing up he was a wildcat. He'd tackle anyone three times his weight. And win. He was a great scrapper. People might have said he was a quarreling man, but I don't know about that: I always liked the way he stuck up for his rights. . . .'

". . . remember him saying, 'Tom Cleary said to me one

time that Charlie had a rat's nose for the dollar. Well, when you say that about a man, nine times out of ten it means that what you're really saying is that he's smarter than you are, and you're sore as a pup that he is. And Charlie's a good bit smarter than Tom, and a whole lot smarter than most. . . .'

". . . one afternoon in the country, riding around, and suddenly, for no particular reason, he said, 'I was thinking the other night: if ever a man got into a scrape, a bad one, you know, and needed somebody to help get him get out, he could do worse than have Charlie beside him on the step. . . .'"

And so I went on, inventing niches for Charlie in the hallway of my father's esteem. I don't lie well, or comfortably, but for some strange reason the stories seemed to come almost by themselves, and they were obviously what he wanted to hear. So I was pleased at that, and yet I couldn't help but feel uneasiness, too. Not because I was putting impossible words into my father's mouth — this was a mild enough misrepresentation, which could do him or his memory no harm. But as I looked at Charlie and saw him so weak, so passive, so stripped of all the apparatus of his normal scepticism, so trustingly defenseless against each of these barely plausible tales, I couldn't avoid the thought that it was somehow *unfair*: that while it undoubtedly was all for his benefit, at the same time it was a little like taking advantage of the credulity of a child. But more important than this, I think that at such a moment you're apt to feel — at least, I am — some doubt, some disquiet about these deathbed fictions in themselves. You're apt to feel that there's something just a little shabby and undignified and wrong about them, no matter how well-intentioned they are. What it boils down to, I suppose, is that you feel that a man who is dying and who is listening to what may be the last words that will ever be spoken to him is entitled to hear, not just a few more of the old duplicities, but now, of all times, the *truth*: you feel that should be his right, simply for having been a man. This, as I say, is a feeling I've often had, and I had it now, but there was also a stronger and blunter consideration: that we are what we are, not what we might or should be, and that for most of us the uncushioned truth at such a moment would be a cruel and perhaps unbearable burden — because it came too late to help. There are those times when simple compassion demands evasion. . . .

And I did what I did from compassion, yes — as anyone would have done — but not from compassion alone. I did it also as a form of payment in return. For I owed Charlie something. I don't think that at this point — especially at this point — I had many illusions about him. He was an old man who had spent a great part of his eighty years in winning the suspicion and distrust and outright enmity of many who had come to know him. He had behaved with trickery and meanness to those who had most right to claim affection from him: he had been a hard father to his children and, by his own admission, a husband whose wife had finally refused even to address him. In no sense had he been a man who was much loved, and the absence of this love was hardly undeserved. I knew all this was true. But there was more than this. Once again, now, something my father had said came back to me — something he had really said, that is, not something I had invented for him. One day, years ago, he had been talking as he often did of people I never knew particularly well — if at all — but with whom he had grown up.

"Sonny Garrahan," he had said slowly. "Nobody had a good word for Sonny. He wasn't the kind of a man you could like. Drunk half the time and mean as a panther the rest, with a nasty tongue, and with half a dozen kids by two different women. A bad sort altogether. I never had much to do with him or gave him more than a hello. But when your mother died, a week later there was a knock on the door and when I answered it who was on the front steps but Sonny. 'I just wanted to tell you I was sorry,' he said. And then he went off before I could say a word to him. Well, a thing like that makes

[371]

a difference. I don't mean to say I sat right down and wrote a letter to Rome to start a drive for Sonny the Saint. It's as well I didn't; two weeks later he was hauled in for nearly clubbing one of the wives — or whatever you'd call the poor things — to death with a crutch. That he'd stolen. God knows why he'd steal a crutch: the man never even limped. But as I was saying, it made all the difference, of course. The way it had to. If a man blows up city hall and half the police force too, but the day before he did it he helped your ma across the street, well, in a way, you know, you hate to see him locked up. You know he should be and all, or else the city would soon be nothing but matchsticks, but all the same, you don't like to see it. Because everybody else is thinking of the one thing that happened. But the other thing happened to you."

And of course it was the "other thing" that had happened to me with Charlie. I now knew all — or, at least, a good deal — about what he had done to others, but I also knew what he had done for me. Unasked, he had come into my life bringing a richness and color and gaiety that hadn't been there for a very long time. Until then I hadn't thought much about it, but I suppose I'd missed it a little all along. Not that I'd been dissatisfied with Old Saint Paul's — I was far too grateful to it for that — and if Charlie had never come along I'm sure I would have passed these last few months just exactly as I had passed the months that had gone before: quietly, uneventfully, but contentedly. So that Charlie hadn't saved me from despair or redeemed my life or done anything dramatic or crucial — my crisis had been passed some time ago, and with no reference to Charlie at all. But what he had done was to provide something *extra*: one more of the little bonuses, you might say — except that this time, surprisingly, he had chosen to give rather than receive. He had brought a flash of brightness, an odd, bumpy, full-blown boisterousness into the calm gray days — he had, for example, made me laugh. I'm not suggesting that the pre-Charlie life in Saint Paul's had been dour or unrelievedly

somber; for some time there'd been the sources of quiet amusement — there was Roy; there was, after all, Father Danowski —
but until Charlie came I don't think I'd laughed out loud —
really *laughed*, I mean — in years. Which isn't everything, of
course, or even from a pastor's point of view, very much — the
"laugh meter" is not a prescribed piece of rectory equipment.
Still, it was something — and something for which I was grateful. But more than this, on quite another level, there was the
fact that Charlie had brought with him warm recollections of
my father and the world in which they both lived — a past, a
part of history, of which I'd always been fond, and of which in
recent years I'd had so few reminders. And finally — and most
important of all — it was Charlie who, through the birthday
dinner, had brought me back to face another past: my own. It
was he who, in a way, had forced me to do what I should have
done long before, but which I had failed to do through ti-
midity and shame. And now it was done. . . .

So then, this is what Charlie had brought to me. The question of motive arises, of course, and I can hardly say now that it
was an act of disinterested kindness. But it was kind just the
same — kindness crept in, if you will; quite apart from the end
he had always had in view, I really think he enjoyed his performance, and I know that I did. And so for all his faults and
misdemeanors and sins — which, in any case, he had now confessed, and which were far out of my jurisdiction — I could
only say that what I felt for him, in addition to both affection
and pity, was gratitude, a sense of debt. He had given me
much, and now I was paying him back: not in full or in kind,
but as best I could.

He continued to listen to me closely but passively, saying not
a word, his eyes remaining closed, his expression unchanged.
When I finished he still said nothing, and for a few seconds
there was a silence in the room; it was a silence in which at
first I heard absolutely nothing, and then, gradually, I picked
out a single sound: a strange, rapid sound, with a regular push-

[373]

pull beat; it was the sound of Charlie's hampered breathing. I sat there in the dim light, now listening myself, hearing only this harsh and fuzzy and rather awful proof that Charlie was still alive. He gave no other sign of consciousness, and I wondered if he were waiting for me to go on, if he understood that I had finished — or if, now, he were able to understand anything at all. Suddenly and irrelevantly I realized that I had been in this room now for a very long time, and all the while Helen, John, the doctors and the others had been outside, waiting. And I thought again how extraordinary and how sad it was: this double visit of the priests, and so far not a single member of the family. . . .

Charlie said suddenly, "Well. That's it."

His eyes had opened, but his look was now drowsy and withdrawn, and his speech was thicker. The signs of sedation? Or of something more serious? I said, "That's it, Mr. Carmody."

He said, "It's all true?"

"All true."

He nodded. "I always liked your pa," he said. Then: "What time is it, Father?"

I told him, and there was another nod, although I don't think that the passing of the hours and minutes now really meant anything to him, for he simply said again, "I always liked your pa." He said it slowly, more to himself than to me, and with an evident satisfaction, as if he were congratulating himself on at least one piece of affection that had not been illplaced. He blinked, and then the old blue eyes were full on me again, and in them I thought I saw a hint of . . . what? Impatience? Suddenly he said, "Well, goodbye, Father."

It was the dismissal. And a fairly abrupt dismissal, after all that had happened. For a moment — quite absurdly — I felt stung, hurt. I had expected something different: a warmer and more gradual tailing off, words of regret and appreciation, a lingering farewell expressing mutual regard. Which was fine but foolish: I had been in too many sickrooms for that. Old

[374]

people in any case are apt to get past the little amenities, and when they're sick and tired, they can be with you one moment and not even near you the next: suddenly they want to stop talking, to stop listening; they want to be alone, they don't want to be bothered. And, after all, I had finished what I had to say; old Charlie had what he had wanted for so long. It was time to go. I rose and held his hand; I said, "Goodbye, Mr. Carmody."

He said, absently and faintly, "Thanks for your trouble."

"It was no trouble. No trouble at all." I added, "I'll be in to see you soon."

An occupational fault: the note of cheer, trooping in at the end. As soon as I'd said it I felt the false heartiness; I expected a protest but none came: Charlie seemed caught up completely in his own thoughts, and his lips were moving soundlessly. I was still there, but I might just as well be gone. And so I took one more look at him — at old Charlie, this frail, subsiding echo of the rip-roaring little figure who had so churned up and warmed my days — and I felt still one more pang; then I said a quick and silent prayer, and then I left the room. And this was the way I said goodbye to Charlie. . . .

Outside, everyone had gathered on the landing at the top of the stairs, just a few steps from the bedroom. As I came out the nurse, glaring at me, went in; I caught Helen's anxious eye, but it was the young doctor who spoke first. "A long visit, Father," he said.

It was a reproof; he was not pleased. I couldn't blame him; the conflict is an old one. I saw Frank looking professional but neutral: he had been through it all before, but this was not his problem now. I said, "Yes, I know. I'm sorry. There wasn't a great deal I could do about it. It just took that long."

The young doctor nodded agreeably enough, but said nothing. He moved quickly towards the bedroom, saying to the others, "I'll just go in and see how everything shapes up before we do anything more." He looked questioningly at Frank,

[375]

and Frank, walking more slowly, followed him into the bedroom.

I went towards Helen and John; before I reached them Bucky plucked at my sleeve. "There's a young lad needs a lesson, Father!" he said indignantly. "A little respect for the cloth! That's what that lad needs!"

It was a defense which wasn't particularly welcome at the moment. I said, "No, he's all right, Mr. Heffernan. He has a hard job." And I went to move on, but Bucky still held me.

"And Charlie?" he asked. "Is he all right, would you say? Did he know you? Is he breathing nice and easy? That's the thing that counts, Father! At a time like this it's the nice and easy breathing that matters! I have the word of the very top doctors on that one! I have the word of Dan Doyle!"

I said yes, yes, he was, it did, is that so? — and then I pulled myself away. Impolitely, I'm afraid, since nothing was clearer than that Bucky had more — much more — to say. But I wanted to see Helen and John before either of them went in to their father; I wanted to give them some explanation — a partial one, necessarily — of why their father had been so eager to send for me: I thought it might help. As I came up to them Helen said quickly, "Well? What do you think, Hugh? How did he seem?"

A natural question — *the* natural question, I suppose, but the only answer I could give was a really meaningless one: the layman's prognosis. And so I said, "You know how much my medical opinion is worth. But certainly he seemed no worse than I'd expected. Weak, of course, but still, he managed to talk a lot. Continuously, in fact. And vigorously, for the most part; he was clear as a bell. . . ."

"There you are," John said briskly. "Continuous, vigorous, clear as a bell — how does this square with a dying man? No no no!" A shade more gently he said, "You see how it is? You're chewing yourself up needlessly. You always do. This is something we've been through before. It's no more than that!"

He was persisting in this queer and, to my mind, groundless optimism; I hadn't intended to fortify it. It was an approach he'd probably been pressing on Helen, for she said, in a sudden, exasperated rush of words, "These bright and happy visions — from a man who never otherwise sees a silver lining anywhere! Well, I can't see it here; I'm simply not that sanguine." She shook her head and said to me in a quieter voice, "Anyway . . . was he in any kind of spirits at all?" She hesitated before adding, "Did he say anything? In particular, I mean? Or want anything?"

And I knew she said this with an effort, that it was both painful and humiliating for her to have to ask. I said, "Let me tell you what he wanted, mainly. He wanted to talk about the past — about my father, really. It was the kind of nostalgia that old men sometimes have: suddenly they want to talk about the old days and old friends, and nothing else is important. Well, I was the link, apparently, because of my father. So we talked, and he reminisced and asked me questions about my father. It was almost all in the past. An odd sort of thing to do, I suppose, at a time like this, but it's what he wanted to do. And I think once he did it he felt satisfied. At least he seemed easy in his mind when I left him."

A lot of words to convey what was, at best, a partial truth, and I wondered if it were at all convincing. John said nothing, but I saw the scepticism in his eyes. Helen said doubtfully, "Yes, I guess so. . . ." And what she would have gone on to say I don't know, for now Frank appeared from the bedroom and signaled to her; they were going in. . . .

Helen took my hand and said, "All right, Hugh. Will we see you when we come out?"

But I was not going to stay. I said, "I think I'll go back to the rectory. I'll be there if you want me at all."

"All right," she said again. "And thanks. Thanks for everything."

Although what there was to thank me for was hard to say. I

said goodbye to her and to John, and made a little sign of goodbye to all the rest, and then as they went in to Charlie's bedroom, I went down the stairs.

But I had gone only three or four steps when someone tapped me on the shoulder; I turned and it was Ted.

"I just wanted to say goodbye from both of us," he said. "And to remind you that I'll be over to see you one of these days. If I may."

Which wasn't at all a strange thing to say, certainly, although the timing was a bit peculiar. But I said yes, of course, any time, and he smiled at me again with the sudden, attractive young smile, and then hurried back up the stairs to rejoin Anne, who was waiting for him at the bedroom door. And I continued down the rest of the stairs, a little puzzled by this odd farewell touch, and thinking of Ted and of his grandfather's curiously harsh judgment of him. . . .

No one was in the hall when I came down, and I stayed there for a minute, looking around at all the familiar objects, the marks of Charlie's long tenancy. I felt suddenly that I was not unobserved: I looked up and saw, ducking back through a door at the kitchen end of the hall, the face of Agnes, the old Carmody maid. And I wondered what she felt, now, about the approaching death of the man she had served for so long. Was there affection here . . . ?

I looked up the length of the stairs to the bedroom door; it was closed. Here in the hall it was still, very still. I looked around me once more, slowly, completely, and then I left the house and went back to my rectory. And this was the end of Christmas Day. . . .

IV

11

NO NEWS of Charlie came that night. Helen telephoned late the next morning to say that there had been no change; what this meant, if anything, she had been unable to learn. The young doctor had been carefully noncommittal; so had Frank.

"He simply says that it's too early to tell. That it's still a 'fluid situation,' whatever that means. Or no, of course I know what it means, but it gets a bit irritating when you've heard it a few times." She said, "Do I sound bitchy, Hugh?"

"No. A little tired, maybe. . . ."

She sighed. "Yes, well, I'm that, all right. But I shouldn't complain; so is Frank. And he's been very good, very kind . . . it's only that sometime you'd like to *know*. But nobody knows, so you can't. Of course John finds it all encouraging. I must say I don't. In fact early this morning I called Julia; I thought she ought to be told. She's coming on. Tomorrow. And then, late last night, after you'd gone, they finally got hold of Dan."

"Ah. Where was he?"

She gave a short despairing laugh. "It's almost too good to be true," she said. "He was in Las Vegas. I mean, if you were writing a farce, that's where you'd put him. And that's where he was. Anyway, he's coming on too, although heaven knows when he'll get here."

I went back to Charlie. "When you went in to see your father last night — did you have a chance to talk to him?"

Her voice changed. "Yes, we all did. Not long, you know, because he really was so tired, but long enough to see that he was . . . different. He was quiet and peaceful and reasonable and . . . well, he was just *nice*. It was heartbreaking, really. I don't think I've ever seen him like that before; not quite in that way. And it wasn't just that he was tired; it was something else. I think you were right, Hugh, when you said his mind was easy. I thought so, too. And that was good."

We talked some more, and before she hung up she said she'd call me every morning — or the instant anything happened. She added, "Although I'll probably see you before I call you. I imagine Daddy will be shouting for you the minute he wakes up."

But Charlie did not shout for me. For the next three days my only contact with him was through Helen's morning report. Each report showed apparent slight improvement — that is, Charlie was at least holding his own, and each day in which he did so was one more day in his favor. And while neither the young doctor nor Frank held out more than the most modest hopes — the "fluid situation," they made clear, remained exactly that, still, from both came the cautious admission that Charlie had done somewhat better than expected, that the odds for his recovery had mounted slightly. And so by the third morning I could tell from Helen's voice — rather than from anything she had to say — that the small and not quite positive evidence had made itself felt, and that in spite of her first convictions, she had begun to hope a little.

During these three days I thought often of going over to Charlie's, just to pay a quick call, to see for myself how he was doing — possibly to have a word with the doctor. But I didn't. Not because Charlie hadn't specifically asked for me — that wasn't important: I haven't much of that kind of vanity — but because, now, I really had no function there, and I suspected that one more visitor at this point might simply be one more complication. I had gathered from Helen that there was now some crowding and confusion at Charlie's house. There were the nurses, of course, and more doctors had come in as consultants; Julia and Dan had arrived and both were staying in the house. And while Mary was on her feet again she seemed bewildered and certainly incapable of coping with her expanded household, and Helen had moved in and temporarily taken charge. So that to drop in, even if only for a few minutes, might only add to the chaos; I thought it more sensible to depend upon the daily bulletins.

There was another reason: suddenly we had entered one of our rare busy periods in Saint Paul's. The week between Christmas and New Year's is normally an active one, and this year, in addition, we ran into a series of emergencies which kept both Father Danowski and myself on the move. None of these was really serious, except one, and this was the death, two days after Christmas, of the old man who for so long had been coming into the church and staying for hours on end, sometimes prowling about, sometimes standing for a long time as still as one of the statues, sometimes kneeling with his head lost in his hands, and almost always muttering what I suppose may have been prayers. It was Roy who found him. Early in the afternoon he had gone into the church with his broom; reluctantly, as always, he had been pushing it up the center aisle when he saw, seated in the last pew, the old man. Roy, who on occupational grounds dislikes all visitors to the church, was of course not fond of this constant guest; besides, I think he feared him. In any case — as he later told me — he was pushing his broom up the aisle towards the rear of the church when he noticed that the old man's eyes were wide and fixed upon him; uneasily, he continued, and then, just as he came opposite the pew, the old man pitched to the side and toppled out into the aisle, his hand flopping across Roy's shoe as he fell. Roy had run screaming from the church; it was a little while before I could get from him the story of what had happened. When I did I sent for a doctor, but it was too late; the old man was dead and, moreover, had been dead for about two hours when Roy found him. This was a piece of news which at first brought great relief to Roy, for I'm sure the poor fellow thought he might somehow be implicated: he had a deep suspicion of the police and kept on babbling to me that he had done no more than *look* at him. Later, however, when he learned that there was no question of any danger to himself, his old manner returned, and this look became subject to another interpretation; weeks afterward I overheard him discussing it with Father Danowski. As usual in his conversations with Roy, my curate was not entirely comfortable.

"Come come, Roy!" he said nervously. "That is not quite normal talk. We do not live in medieval times these days. We do not believe that we can look at a man and he dies. That is nonsensical, Roy. That is *weird*. If you go around talking like that, do you know what people will say of you? They will say, 'Why, Roy is quite a foolish person!' Do you wish people to say this of you, Roy?"

"Only," said Roy, darkly stubborn, "it happened to Roy *before*. Two times!"

And while normally I let Roy go on in this free-wheeling style, now I surprised him — and myself — by stepping in and cutting off the talk sharply: I suppose because it was about this old man whom I had never really met, but who had come to be a part of my life here as pastor, and who, in a curious way, had even come to be for me a kind of symbol of the parish itself. I tried, now, to find out something more about him, but with little more success than before. His name did turn up — from an old envelope and an even older card in his pocket; on the back of the card had been scrawled, "Camp is nice. I am fine. Billy"; it was Nicholas Aswell. Which surprised me; vaguely, and for no good reason, I'd imagined him to be an Italian. He had no money with him, no other identification;

from another pocket had come another piece of paper, and that was all. It was a torn piece of wrapping paper, on which had been written — recently — in large shaky letters, SACRED HEART OF JESUS I LOVE YOU. And that was everything I knew about Nicholas Aswell. I said his Mass for him and buried him two days after he died. It was a small, sad, silent funeral; those present were the undertaker, Father Danowski, and myself. . . .

So then, death — or the hint of death — seemed all at once to surround me at this time. Which, among other things, was a mark that I was growing old, for when you're young death is an isolated event, surprising by its rarity. But later, death comes in sudden clusters, and there are intervals when every aging man looks around him bewildered, as if he were the one witness to some unpatterned cataclysm. Not that anything as total as this was happening to me, but still, the atmosphere of death was present, and I was aware of it, whichever way I moved. I think I must have showed this in some fashion, for my curate now began a campaign to cheer me up. I hadn't said much about old Charlie to him, but I'd said enough, evidently, for him to deduce that recovery was improbable; as a consequence, our dinner table now rang each night with inspirational anecdotes, each one dealing with a miracle of returned health. . . .

". . . cannot recall, Father, if I have spoken to you of my mother's Uncle Teddy? For whom my brother Teddy the athlete was named? It is a most amazing story. He was an extremely robust person, capable of lifting great weights. Well, suddenly a mysterious stomach ailment quite robbed him of his appetite and he began to lose his strength. He was taken to doctors. To *specialists*. All pronounced him incurable. It was pitiful to see him, Father, all skin and bones as he was. But Uncle Teddy would not give up. He said to my mother, 'Well, Stasia, I will tell you one thing: I am not going to die. I am going to get *well!*' And suddenly, one day, his appetite returned to him. He began to grow in strength. The doctors, Father, were *confounded.* . . ."

[385]

". . . I can remember my father's account of a particular friend of his from the old country That is Poland, Father. Here was a man who had a disease of the bones. A famous physician said of him to my father, 'Well, Casimir, I have sad news for you. Your old friend will not survive this year. His bones are turning to jelly, Casimir; they will not support his bulk.' My father was greatly disturbed to hear of this, Father. To say nothing of his friend. But here is what is truly remarkable. At the end of that year, my father's friend had not only survived: *his good health had been completely restored.* Why was this, you may ask? Was this pure determination, too? Or was it perhaps that his lifelong devotion to Saint Joseph, for which he was well known. . . ."

There were more stories. All proved that Father Danowski, if not always credible, was at least unfailingly kind.

During this time, too, Ted kept his promise: he came over to see me. He came late one afternoon, just as I was returning from a sick call. I was surprised. Even though he had made rather a point of wanting to come, I'd put this down mainly to politeness, and in any case I had hardly expected to see him so soon. But here he was, and I asked him at once about his grandfather. He answered that he had seen him only an hour or two before, and that he seemed pretty much the same.

"Which, as I understand it, isn't bad," he said. "They don't seem to be looking for dramatic improvements. Apparently if he can keep this — what would you call it? Stability? — for the next few days, then he may be on his way out of the woods. So I think we're all a little more optimistic than we were. I know I am. And so is Anne."

And then, as most visitors to this rectory soon enough do, he stepped back and looked around at his immediate surroundings. As I think I've indicated, this isn't an inspection that permits any great variety of response; it's mostly a matter of the concealment of dismay. But all he said was, "Do you like it here, Father?"

[386]

He sounded genuinely curious — curious and interested, rather than merely puzzled, and when I said that I did, he nodded and said reflectively, "Yes. Well, I can see that."

I didn't know whether he could or he couldn't — I rather thought he couldn't — but at least it wasn't the standard reply. I suggested to him now that he might like to look around a bit more — although heaven knows why I make this suggestion, almost automatically, to all visitors who come here: it must be the last thing they want to do! He couldn't have been eager, but he agreed instantly, and we set off around the rectory and the church. He asked few questions, but none were pointless, all were intelligent, and by the time we returned to the rectory we were talking rather freely about the makeup of the parish itself: not Saint Paul's as it used to be, but Saint Paul's as it is today.

"It's a mixed bag, isn't it?" he said.

"Oh, completely. Italian, Spanish, Portuguese, Syrian, Puerto Rican, Chinese — we have a little bit of everything. Including home-grown stock. And the balance is always shifting."

"Yes, but there must be quite a few who don't shift. For example, the other day I was looking over the voting lists, and this section has a fairly heavy registration. Which means that you must have a decent proportion of more or less permanent residents."

"We have. After all, it isn't like some sort of detention station where immigrants come for a few days and then leave. With all our floaters, we still have large numbers of people who've been living here for some time. They probably came originally because housing was cheap, or because they had friends or relatives here. But then they sank down roots, you know, the way people do: they got jobs, children came along, and pretty soon it was home. The children won't stay, of course. They'll leave for something better, one by one, as soon as they can, but when they go some new group will come in, and the whole process will start all over again. But all this takes time, naturally, and this means that in spite of all the shifting we always have a reasonably steady core of families."

"Mostly Catholic?" he asked.

"I'd say so, yes. Nominally, at least. It's sometimes a little hard to tell; our figures aren't quite as exact as they are in some of the other parishes."

"And do they come to Mass? Regularly, I mean?"

"They do pretty well. They could do better, but then we all could do that. And then they're apt to have special problems; it isn't always easy for them. No, on the whole they don't do badly at all."

The pastor rising to the defense of his parish — although no attack had been made. He said, suddenly and thoughtfully, "Do you know what I'd like to do, Father? I'd like to come over here some Sunday and meet them. I thought I could talk to them as they came out of Mass: introduce myself, tell them what I was running for. I could even break the ice, I imagine, by doing something like passing the basket at the collection at Mass — just so they'd have the feeling that I wasn't coming up cold to them on the church steps." And then he smiled with that quick, frank boyishness which had so surprised me that night at his grandfather's: the suggestion of great openness and charm breaking across the reserved young face. He said, "Do you think there'd be any objection to that, Father?"

So there it was, all at once spelled out before me: the reason he had come here today. I felt a quick dig of disappointment, and along with this I felt annoyance, too. The annoyance was at myself, for obviously I should have known what was coming: you can't be a parish priest for thirty years without developing some sort of nose for little propositions of this kind. I suppose I might have sniffed this one out earlier, except that it hadn't occurred to me to connect Ted with anything of the sort — and this for no other reason, I think, than that he was Helen's son, and I had known him since he was a little boy. Which, as a reason, is hardly unassailable: little boys grow up. And of

[388]

course it's foolish to expect or predict too much or, indeed, anything at all, on such faint and ancient clues, yet all the same when I heard him now I felt this sharp disappointment, and for a moment I didn't say anything at all. And then I said, "I think there'd be an objection, Ted. From me. I don't think it would be a very good idea."

A curious expression appeared on his face: just what it suggested I didn't know — except that I was sure he hadn't expected a refusal. But it was gone in an instant, and he said quietly, "I'm sorry, Father. I didn't mean to offend you."

I said, truthfully enough, "I'm not offended, Ted —"

"I didn't even mean to surprise you," he said. "But I guess I did, didn't I?"

"Yes, I think you probably did that. . . ."

He said, with what seemed a genuine curiosity, "Why, Father? Was it such an unusual suggestion?"

"No. At least I've heard it before. And of course in this city of all places it has all kinds of historic parallels. But . . . did you ever hear of a man called Jigger Toomey?"

He shook his head and said, "He sounds like someone my grandfather would have known."

"He would have known him very well. When I was growing up in Saint Raymond's it was hard not to know Jigger. He was a politician, although purely on the local level: the kind of man who's always running for the City Council. I don't remember how successful he was; I have the impression that he lost just about as often as he won. But what I do remember is what you might call his campaign style. It consisted largely of being in church. For the weeks directly preceding the election, that is; the rest of the year he wasn't quite so scrupulous. But for these weeks he was in church every morning, and on Sundays he could usually be seen at two or three of the Masses, bustling about, helping old ladies down the aisle, ushering people to their seats. And, of course, praying. Loudly. All in all, he was a conspicuous figure. Which, naturally, was

[389]

the whole point. And in case anyone missed the point, he occasionally placed little campaign ads in the newspapers, listing his qualifications for public office. One of these seemed to be that he was a former altar boy."

He smiled slightly. "I see. And am I the Jigger of today?"

"No, I wasn't trying to push this into an exact equation. Although you might like to know that Jigger was always fond of passing the basket at collections: it was a valued part of his technique. What I'm saying is that this is an old story here: this using of church premises and services for what is really — no matter what you call it — a kind of political rally. But the fact that it's old doesn't necessarily make it any more acceptable. Even though I know very well that some of the priests wink at it or even — in the case of a few of them — seem to encourage it. But I'm not inclined to do that, Ted. I can't. In spite of the fact that I'm glad you're running, and that I'd very much like to see you win."

He said, "Is it the church and state business that bothers you? I mean, you think that what I'm suggesting may be . . . what? Slightly unconstitutional?"

Slightly unconstitutional. Would this boy be scandalized to learn that this aspect of the problem wouldn't have occurred to me in a thousand years? It was disquieting; here we were, two men talking about the same thing, and yet not really talking about the same thing at all — it was as if an artist and a starving man were discussing The Banana. I said, "No, I'm apt not to think of something like this in political terms. I was really thinking that it might be a little cynical."

"Cynical?"

I think he was genuinely surprised — at least his expression seemed to show that the notion hadn't occurred to him. I said, "Well, I think you might have some trouble defending it as entirely sincere. For example, I don't imagine you really plan to come over to Saint Paul's to attend Mass and help out in small ways on very many Sundays *after* the election, do you?"

"Oh," he said, and again he smiled slightly. "I see what you mean. No, probably not. But I wouldn't think that was especially cynical. I mean, it seems to me that you have to look at the *reason* for it. If I come over here on a Sunday, I'm not out to deceive or trick or harm anyone. If I come over here it's because . . . well, it's because I want to win an election, yes" — and here he smiled once more, not slightly this time, but with that sudden warm burst which I'd found so engaging — "but I want to do something a little more than that, I think. Do you know the man I'm running against?"

"Yes: Arthur Sullivan. I've known him for years. He's not much: one of the old hacks."

"Yes, but an entrenched old hack," he said. "That makes a difference. He's incompetent and lazy and as corrupt as they come, but he's in there. And he's been giving these people the worst representation imaginable for years. Well, I'd like to do something about that. But you see my problem: it's my first time out and I'm simply not well known. Up to a point, I suppose, there's a certain advantage in that — there's such a thing as being *too* well known; I keep hoping that will catch up with my opponent before he's through — but on the other hand, elections aren't often won by anonymous candidates. So what I have to do is plain: I have to get known. I have to meet as many people as possible, and since I haven't got much time, that means I have to meet them *en masse*. I have to go to all the places they normally get together. That's the way it's done, Father."

A Child's Primer of Political Tactics — did I deserve this? But as a declaration of purpose it was simple, manly, straightforward — and irrelevant. I mean, irrelevant to the point I was trying to raise. I wondered if, really, he grasped that point at all? Or if, indeed, he grasped it quite well, but preferred to put it to one side as unimportant? Or inconvenient? This was a possibility, maybe more than that — but I simply couldn't tell. I said, "Of course it always comes down to a question of ends and means, doesn't it? And I don't think this is really a permissible means. I sympathize with what you want: heaven knows I have no love for Arthur Sullivan. But the Mass isn't quite the same as the regular monthly meeting of the Parent-Teacher's Association, is it? It's a prayer, after all; you can't *use* it for anything else. And even to be there — to be seen, as a candidate — would be using it. No, I'm afraid I'm against it, Ted."

Which was a simple statement of fact, yet I suppose it must have seemed to him . . . what? Pompous? Holier than thou? Or simply naïve? But he smiled, as brightly, as attractively, as instantly as before, and said, "All right, Father. I won't press you. I know you would if you could. And I can see your side of it." He added thoughtfully, "Although I guess I probably don't see it as being quite as serious as you do."

And was there any point in saying, now, that to me that was the only side worth seeing seriously at all? No. None. So we talked a bit more, pleasantly enough but to no particular point, and then he was on his way — intending, he said, to look in on his grandfather before he went home. None too happily, I watched him go — I had the feeling that I'd handled this exchange rather badly, that it could have been done less bluntly and with less suspicion, with much more kindness and finesse. And I also had the feeling, now stronger than ever, that this boy was separated, not only from Charlie and his world, but from me and mine, by a distance incalculably vast — and that this was, at least in part, our fault. . . .

The next day, I heard from Helen as usual: her father was about the same — still no marked change. So then, Charlie was at the very least living out the Old Year, for this was the last day of December. It was also the day on which, almost a week after the attack had occurred, I finally went over — unbidden — to see him.

I did not see him. I arrived at the Carmody house to be greeted by Dan — and greeted effusively. I had the immediate impression that he would have been equally delighted by any interruption of routine — that this steady vigil had in all probability come to seem slightly monotonous to so highly mobile a man.

"Come in, come in, come in," he said, almost pulling me into the hall. "It's great to see you, Hugh. Great. That's the trouble with the way we live today: all over the place and we never get a chance to see old friends. Half the time we don't even know where they are. Isn't that so? How are you, anyway?"

I told him, and asked about his father.

"He's sleeping," he said. "He just dropped off a couple of minutes ago. Plenty of rest: that's the best thing in the world for him. And Helen and Mary are off downtown on some errand: you just missed them. So I'm here alone, holding the fort. Along with Aunt Julia. She's here, of course. Somewhere upstairs. Do you want to see her, Hugh?"

I said quickly that I wouldn't think of disturbing her, and he seemed relieved. "Because she's probably taking a nap, too. And even if she weren't, you don't know how she'd be. She's a peculiar woman, Hugh. Not," he said hurriedly, "that she isn't a *fine* woman. She is. They don't come any better than Aunt Julia. But she's peculiar. Nothing really serious, of course. I don't mean she's at all *off*, or anything like that. Far from it. But all the same . . . do you know her very well, Hugh?"

"No, hardly at all. . . ."

"She has this way of looking at you," he said. "She's always had it, I guess, but I haven't seen her very much in the last few years, so I'd more or less forgotten about it. But she just looks at you, you know, with this mournful stare she has, and she doesn't say anything. Not a word. She can do this for quite a long time. You'd be surprised how long, actually. And then all of a sudden she'll sigh and say something like, 'It's God's will.' Or 'What's to be, will be.' Or 'One by one.' That's

[393]

all. Nothing else. And then she'll look at you again. I tell you, Hugh, you get a funny feeling when this happens day after day. I don't know how to describe it, but you do. Do you know what I mean?"

"Yes. I do indeed."

"Of course she belongs to an older generation. She's not like you and me, Hugh. She's a fatalist. A pessimist. Now, I'm not. I can't afford to be. Not in my work." He did not define this further; he said, "I don't say there's always a silver lining, but there usually is. I *know*. I haven't always been successful, Hugh. No matter what you may have heard. I've had my share of hard knocks. I've been in bad scrapes in my time. Some of them may even have been my own fault. Partly. But the point is no matter how bad they were, they usually came out all right in the end. Take this business with Dad. I tell you, Hugh, it hit me hard. I was out West when they reached me — did you hear about that, by the way?"

I said prudently, "No. . . ."

"This whole new field is opening up out there," he said vaguely. "I'd like to talk to you about it some day, Hugh. But anyway, when I heard the news about Dad it nearly knocked me over. I felt awful. And when I hopped on the plane and got here and saw Dad and saw how gloomy everybody was, I felt *whipped*, Hugh. Whipped. But then," he said, "I started to look on the bright side. I couldn't help it, Hugh. I always do. Take my word for it, nothing's as bad as it seems at first. There's usually a way out. The great thing is to look for it."

It was, recognizably, the voice of experience. Dan's whole life in a sense had been a broken-field run: a series of desperate sprints from one "bad scrape" to another, yet here he was in his early fifties, a little worn around the edges, but still dapper, still undaunted, still unimprisoned. And still optimistic. . . .

"And look at the way it worked out!" he said. "One week ago Dad was in the grave, and look at him today! Just look

[394]

at him, Hugh. Oh, I don't say he's made a complete recovery or anything like it yet, but he's on the way, he's on the way. Picking up a bit every day. Slow and steady, but coming right along, Hugh. Coming right along. He won't want all of us hanging around here too much longer. As a matter of fact," he said, his tone perceptibly brightening, "I expect to be moving along any day now myself."

I said, "Ah . . . ?"

"Oh yes. I've got to get back, Hugh. You know how it is when you're getting something started. You take your eyes off it for five minutes and before you know it the nickel and dime men have moved in. To tell you the truth, Hugh, I'd like to have a word with you on that very thing. I'm in a position to let you in. . . ."

And then, suddenly, his voice fell off, and I saw that he looked slightly embarrassed. I think that he had completely forgotten his visit to me in the rectory, and that it was only at this moment that it came back to him. All of it: Old Saint Paul's, with its shabby buildings, its deficit, its pastor with no bank account. A dim prospect. The dimmest. He cleared his throat and said uneasily, "Well, anyway, that's something we can talk about later. There's no hurry on that, is there?" He went on, rapidly. "Yes, I'll be glad to get back, Hugh. Wild horses couldn't have kept me away from here, of course, in an emergency like this, but now that it's about over I'm anxious to get back. Just between ourselves, Hugh," he said confidentially, "I get restless. It's not quite my speed here. It never has been. You know that. East is east, I imagine. And all the rest of it. And then on top of that there's Flo. I don't mind telling you I miss her, Hugh. I wouldn't say that to everyone, but I do."

I said, "I'd think you could say that, Dan. It's allowable for a man to miss his wife."

"No, but at my age, Hugh. I'm not a chicken any longer. For that matter, neither is Flo. Actually, she's a little older than I am, although you'd never guess it. But she is. Just a shade. But she's the one for me, Hugh. You were right."

"*I* was right?"

"Dead right," he said. "Isn't it funny? Everyone's always giving me advice and I can never remember any of it, but I remember what you said. Every word. 'Cut it out, Dan,' you said. Nicely, you know, but firmly. 'This isn't getting you anywhere. Cut out all this playing around. Cut out running from pillar to post. Life is more than a merry-go-round. Settle down, Dan. It's high time you found yourself some good steady woman and settled down!' "

Better to marry than burn? These extraordinary memories, all of them embarrassing, all of them nonexistent in fact: how did he dredge them up? I said, "Dan —"

"So I did," he said. "And I've never regretted it. Not for a second. Do you know what she's given me, Hugh? Something I never had before." He paused dramatically, then said, "*Permanence.*"

Permanence. I thought of Las Vegas. And all I could say was, "That's fine. I —"

"I'll tell you about Flo, Hugh," he said, with great earnestness. "Do you know what she is? She's a sport. A great sport. Always ready for anything. I can come in to her in the middle of the night and wake her out of a sound sleep to tell her we have to get moving — you know how it is in business sometimes, Hugh: getting the jump on the other fellow means everything — and I tell you, she'll be ready and in that car before I am! And if somewhere along the line I might make a little mistake or two — and that happens, Hugh, that happens: we're all only human — well, she doesn't *harp* on it. She's not always *at* me. No, it's over and done with, and that's that with Flo. It's on to the next town, and keep smiling. And you know, Hugh, that's just the way I am myself. That's probably why we get along so well together. Plus the fact," he said simply, "that I *like* her. And she likes me. Is that a funny thing for a married man to say, Hugh? About his own wife? I guess it is. But anyway, it's true. And I can tell you this: it's a great thing to know!"

Or, if not a great one, at least a good one — and perhaps not altogether so common as is sometimes supposed. It was a touching statement, and for the first time I saw Dan in a somewhat different light: with all his fears and frauds and perpetual escapes, he was an oddly contented man. The preposterous alliance of middle-aged people, at which there had been so much wincing and laughter, was perhaps not so preposterous after all — and the "permanence" at which I had so easily lifted an eyebrow might in a sense indeed be there. What anyone else needs or wants most, or who can supply it — that's a very hard thing to know. I had a sudden picture of Dan, now, riding through the night in one of his jaunty, semi-owned cars, whistling, perhaps glancing back occasionally over his shoulder, while beside him sat Flo, the good sport, laughing, ready for anything. As, indeed, she might well have to be. . . .

But all this was a great deal about Dan and very little about old Charlie — whom, after all, I had come here to see. And whom, apparently, I was not to see — not, that is, if his nap had begun only shortly before my arrival. And since it was also unlikely that I would see Helen — for, as it turned out, Dan wasn't quite sure where she had gone, and had only the vaguest notion as to when she would return — there seemed little point in remaining; I decided to go back to Saint Paul's. At this Dan protested, strongly and — I think — sincerely: he was anxious for company, the alien ear. But steadily and politely — I hope — I made my way to the door, and it was only when I was actually on the front steps that he made his suggestion.

"I'll tell you what, Hugh," he said. "Why don't you drop over to see John? It's only a few blocks, and I know he's in now. He'd be tickled to death to see you. And then, when you've finished, you could come back here for a few minutes before going home. By that time everybody will be back. Or awake."

It was a good suggestion and an obvious one — although it hadn't occurred to me. I hadn't seen John since the night of his father's attack; I hadn't visited Saint Raymond's since long before I'd left the city. And here I was in the neighborhood with a little time to spare . . . and suddenly I felt a great longing to see, once more, this rectory where I had been so happy for so long. So I agreed that I would come back, and then I left Charlie's house and drove away down the short distance to Saint Raymond's.

It was unchanged. Or so it seemed to me, anyway, as I walked up the neat series of flagstones which bisected the front lawn — that lawn which somehow managed to look trim and precise and well tended, even in these dead months of winter. It seemed, in this moment of approach, so unchanged that I might have been coming home, fifteen or twenty years before. Inside, of course, the changes began. They began with the housekeeper. She was new; she had not seen me before; she had undoubtedly never heard of me; identification was required. And when she went to notify John, and I began to poke around a bit while waiting, to peer into and examine some of the old familiar first-floor rooms, I saw at once that they were not so familiar any more. The marks of the new pastor were all around. The old décor was for the most part gone; paint had been applied; the heavy, cumbersome, comfortable interior had been made leaner and brighter and whiter: John had a swift contemporary eye for light and cleanness of line. And yet the curious thing was that although these changes had been made, and although I don't think that in this first brief inspection there were really half a dozen objects — a bench, a *Pietá*, a curving sweep of stairs — at which I could look and say with satisfaction, "This was here when I was here," still, I had no feeling of *strangeness*. The new broom had swept clean, yes, but with all the sweeping some-

[398]

how this house remained recognizable and the same. The process had not been one of obliteration; the signature of the old Monsignor and his regime had mysteriously and in some measure survived; and, suddenly and queerly, I felt a sharp sense of *belonging* in this place: a sense of belonging so powerful that it stopped me, stock-still, and I just stood there in the center of a room, like some poor idiot deprived of the powers of speech or thought or motion, stupefied and blinking — and almost bursting with happiness. And this is the way I must have been when John came down the stairs.

"Ah," he said briskly. "Good. I wondered when you'd finally get over here. Well, how does it look? Different?"

"Different," I agreed. "But not altogether; something of the old place comes through."

"I'm working on that," he said sardonically. "But it takes time." Then he said, "Look, I know you gave me the total tour of your establishment, but do you mind if I don't do the same for you today? I've got workmen all over the house, and there's something going on in the church. What, I don't know; there's always something going on here. We ought to put up a sign: We Never Close. And then there's some sort of bazaar or food sale in the parish hall. Home-baked goodies from the ladies of the parish. Brownies and layer cakes: they buy them from each other. God knows why. So let's just go up to my quarters. It's the only place we'll have any quiet. Besides," he said, "for some reason I'm a little tired today."

It was a most unusual admission for him, and he seemed to make it with reluctance. Yet he didn't look especially tired; he looked exactly as always. I said, "Yes, sure." And then, carefully, because I remembered that on the only previous occasion he had spoken of his health he had been rather prickly, I said, "Occupational fatigue?"

"I've been a bit off my feed," he said shortly. "That's all. It's probably the prospect of another glorious winter to be spent in my beloved homeland. Come on, let's go up."

[399]

We went up the stairs to the second floor; it was a passage which revealed changes every foot of the way, and yet the essential sameness was inescapable. At least to me. Maybe it really wasn't there; maybe this was nothing more than the strength of memory overcoming reality — but I don't think so. It was there. We passed the door of the long common room: I could see, inside, a young priest whom I did not know seated in an armchair I did not recognize, watching a Popeye cartoon on television. All changes. And yet not out of place, not disconcerting: it was a question of atmosphere. Of warmth. Of home. . . .

We went into the pastor's quarters: a suite of two rooms at the front of the house. And, ironically, it was only here, in this space where the old Monsignor had spent so many of his moments, that no trace of him remained: here, in these personal, private rooms, where perhaps John's determination to close out the past had been just a bit stronger, the transformation was complete. But oddly — or not so oddly, I suppose — this didn't seem to matter to me now. I had little sense of attachment to these rooms; I had in fact rarely been in them. The Monsignor had believed in keeping this preserve to himself; young curates came only when bidden, and that was not often. What vague memories I had of this area were memories of a kind of semidarkness, vast furniture, and impossible crowding: the Monsignor kept here the great quantities of extraordinary bric-a-brac with which, for some queer reason, he preferred to be surrounded. These possessions were both devotional and otherwise — I have, for example, one specific recollection of a huge gun, a blunderbuss, really, which he had hung on one of the walls. A gun! Why? The Monsignor had never volunteered an explanation and I, of course, had never asked. And I remember now another specific — and exotic — note: there had always been a small blue tin box in the center of the dressing table. It was indispensable to the Monsignor, who neither smoked nor drank. But who did take snuff. . . .

All this, every hint of it, was gone. These rooms were now white and spare and surgically clean. On one of the gleaming walls, directly over his bed, was a crucifix. On the opposite wall, at a point not far from where the blunderbuss had ruled, hung a good-sized Rouault. It was genuine: I remembered when he'd bought it, years ago. It must have been one of the very few times when I suddenly became conscious of the fact that, although John and I had been boys together, and although we now were priests together, in our financial circumstances we were hardly in the same universe. He was, after all — although I never thought of him as such — a rich man's son: one of the few priests I knew who was privately well-to-do.

Which was just something I was reminded of at the sight of the picture as we entered the room. He went in first and, making straight for a chair, sat down quickly. And this again was unusual with him: normally, while others were seating themselves, he stood or strode restlessly around. So that he was certainly tired — for all his offhand talk about the activities of the parish, he was in fact a hard-working pastor who kept his eye on all details: his duties here during the busy Christmas season, plus the demands made because of Charlie's illness, may have been very hard on him — and I was suddenly conscience-stricken at having chosen today for my call. But there was little I could do about it now, and when he spoke it was with his old crisp alertness. "Well? Have you been over paying your respects to the well-known convalescent?"

"Not quite." I told him about my attempted visit to his father, concluding with a report of Dan's optimism; I added, "Which would seem to be pretty well shared by now, I gather."

"The foregone conclusion," he said. "People always pretend to hate to say, 'I told you so.' I haven't any objection at all. Look: about Dan. What did he say again? That he was pulling out soon?"

I repeated what Dan had said; he nodded grimly. "Another

foregone conclusion. Dan doesn't waste any time. Open the door a crack and he's out in the yard and over the fence. A responsibility to Dan is nothing more than a starting block. He uses it to help him get away. Fast. And he's been getting away for the last forty years." And then he said, "Not that I'm blaming him, especially."

It was an odd twist, a kind of fraternal tolerance I hadn't expected — or heard before — from him. It surprised me, and I suppose this showed, for he said, with the familiar fierce politeness, "Softening up, you think? Old age working away on me? Like a meat tenderizer? The enzyme of advancing years?"

I said, "No. I was just thinking that earlier this afternoon I found myself revising my own opinion of Dan a bit."

"Well, there you have it all over me," he said. "Because that's not what I was doing at all. My opinion of Dan has remained constant for a very long time. All I said was that I don't blame him *especially*. Or principally. That doesn't mean I'm giving him three cheers. Of course I blame him. No adult can behave the way he does and escape blame: he's a responsible human being with presumably some control over his actions. He's not a child. Or a piece of putty. But on the other hand, in the beginning — and later on as well — there were many things that could have been done for him and simply weren't. In the way of encouragement. Or direction. Or just reasonable, human talk. But there was none of that. Not for any of us, but chiefly not for Dan. Who needed it most. No, I don't at all admire Dan or his way of life, but it isn't all his fault. Not by a long shot."

He spoke bitterly, and from both the words and the tone it was obvious that we had come back to Charlie. I said nothing; after a moment he said, "This must be the way monomania starts. I've sung this song so many times I'm a bore, and now I'm singing it again. But I've been thinking a lot about it lately. Because of my father being sick, and the whole family

[402]

being here together. As well as," he said brusquely, "for other reasons. Anyway, I've been reviewing our family history, Hugh. It hasn't been exactly an enchanted journey down memory lane. You know a good bit of it. Naturally. But close as you were to us when we were children, you still knew our house from the outside only. You didn't live in it day after day. I did. Mary did. Helen did. And Dan did."

He was talking rapidly and with his accustomed lack of filial regard, but now I noticed a difference. He was covering all the old ground, of course, but before, these onslaughts had usually been delivered with a peculiar kind of vigorous, slashing ferocity which — for some reason I find hard to explain — somehow diminished their effect. It wasn't that he wasn't serious; you felt the genuine irritation there, but you felt also that it was just a bit of a performance, and that he was actually enjoying the sparks. But now there were no sparks; the liveliness had gone. It had been succeeded by a blunt, unanimated melancholy which was not only new but was distressing. And whose cause I didn't know: was it simply that everything had become concentrated and so gained strength by being brought together in the tiny world of Charlie's sickroom? Whatever the reason, I wanted to stop him, or at least divert him — but to divert anyone at such a moment and in such a mood is not easy; it's perhaps impossible. It was he who had used the word "monomania." . . .

He said, "Of course when you're children you never know anything. You think that everything that happens is the normal way of the world. Even my father. Not that I ever considered him the model parent — good God, no child could be quite that childish! — but it wasn't until years later, until long after I'd been ordained, in fact, that I even began to realize just how much he'd been responsible for. In a word, misery. Sustained misery. Without intervals. He could keep it up, you see; he could pour it on; he had *reserves* of misery. You think I'm being harsh."

[403]

Which I did — and he knew it. So was there any point in telling him this once more? I said, "I'll tell you what I do think: I think there are subjects we agree on more."

Routine and feeble; he said at once, "Yes. So do I. But how about indulging me in this one? Just for a few minutes? I've got something I want to get off my chest. And you're elected. Not just because you're here but because I can't think of anyone else I'd talk this way to." It was a compliment — although one not to be accepted altogether easily. One hand gestured with a kind of angry helplessness, and he said, "The whole thing is so full of misconceptions . . . do you remember Father Gilroy, for instance? Father Timothy Gilroy? The one with that empty smile and that queer, creeping shuffle?"

"Yes, of course." In defense of old Father Gilroy I said, "He was a good enough old man."

"He was a good enough old halfwit," he said morosely. "He was the dumbest priest I've ever met. And think of the territory *that* covers. One day in the seminary he cornered me and started to tell me about my father. By way of a short — or not so short — sermon on the sins of the father: drunkenness, adultery, failure to provide for one's family. He knew fathers like that, he said. But do you know what made the world all right again? He also knew my father. And do you know how he referred to him? As 'The Example.' I guess he was at that — at least of what old Gilroy was talking about. My father didn't drink, much less get drunk; I don't think he ever looked at a woman besides my mother; and all of us ate three good meals a day and had no holes in our shoes. He had all the domestic virtues, you see. Except that it was hell on earth to live with him."

"And yet you did," I said. "So was it really as bad as all that? All of you lived with him, and for quite some time."

"Well, what did you want us to do?" he said wearily. "Join the Foreign Legion? We had no great choice, especially while my mother was alive. He was at his best with my mother. He

[404]

must have invented a hundred different ways of plaguing her, humiliating her — no day was complete without its little dig. We'd have chicken for dinner, for example; in advance, my father would rejoice over this, and begin to talk about how hungry he was, and how roast chicken had always been his favorite. Then we'd sit down at the table, the chicken would be produced, and my father would smile and say 'Ah!' and 'My my my!' — anticipatory delight, you see: the build-up — and then he'd take a bite of the chicken. Just one bite. No more. And then, gently, and with that look on his face — good God in heaven, that look! — of having been disappointed again, of having been betrayed in his own home once more by those, to whom, of course, he'd given everything, he'd begin to talk. And talk and talk and talk. And my mother would say nothing. I think in the beginning that she did, but the years with my father, for some inconceivable reason, seemed to have done something to her spirit. She couldn't quite bring herself to accept him as the quaint, comic, picturesque figure he was sometimes alleged to be. So towards the end she didn't say a word. Oh, it was all very effective, Hugh; my father was a skillful man. And the result is that today, whenever I see one of our respected colleagues step into the pulpit to declaim against the destroyers of the home — the drunks, the adulterers, the improvidents — I always have the feeling that it's misdirected energy, that he ought instead to be talking about the *real* destroyers of the home. The people who do more harm, day in and day out, in their own unspectacular way, than all the others put together. The people who push the roast chicken away, Hugh. The people like my father!"

I listened to this in silence and in pain — pain not for Charlie, asleep in the afternoon just a few short blocks away, but pain for John, because I heard his voice shake, and for the first time I realized — so tardily! — that this was not more of the same, and that this was not still the boy, the young priest, speaking of his father in fitful exasperation. Thirty years had gone by, and this was a different man, saying something far more grievous: vexation had hardened into something else. And as, dumbly, I realized this, I found myself staring at his face as if I expected to *see* something different, some sign of the change that had been worked, but all I saw was the John I'd always known — a little thinner, a little whiter, a little older, but not much, not much at all — and suddenly I felt the pain expand, and I had the sense that I had lost something, and so had he, and that both of us had lost it forever. Instinctively I reached out and touched his arm; I said, "Don't. You do yourself great harm. . . ."

He didn't hear me; I don't think he felt my touch. "And then my mother died," he said. "And who's to say that was a misfortune? For her, that is. For us . . . well, of course, now my father thought of us. Not that we'd been ignored before, but now we got what you might call the full benefit of his attention. So Dan . . . well, I've said enough about Dan; there's no point in going over that again. But Mary was something else. She was the answer to all my father's prayers. He could grind her down, bit by bit, to just the size and shape required; no one could have been more grindable than Mary. The result was that in no time at all my father had a new pet: a nice, docile, hard-working, talking cow. One talking cow would seem to be enough for anyone, but my father is a greedy man, Hugh; he wanted two. And there he ran into trouble. Because the second was supposed to be Helen, and she didn't want to be a cow at all. She fought back and eventually she got out of it. But the way she got out was through a marriage that she never really wanted to a man she never really loved. So you could say my father won that one, too."

And this last struck a special chord in me, because it was Helen, and because I knew by now — and probably had known from the instant I first saw her again at Charlie's party, months ago — that here too, everything had not gone well.

[406]

Nothing about her suggested the tragic figure, she didn't radiate mournfulness — far from that, but all the same I knew at once some element of happiness was missing. The edge of sadness was visible; it was clear that she hadn't found . . . what? What we all hoped to find, I suppose: at one time or another we're all optimists. In any case, she hadn't found it in her marriage — or so I suspected, and now to have this confirmed by John, who knew his sister so well, was hardly the best news of the day. Yet even as I heard it — this confirmation — I began to wonder about it: about how firm it was, how sure. Like everything else John had said so far, it undoubtedly held some truth, but there was a queer lopsidedness about it: a wildness, a disproportion. It was the talk of a man with an obsession: the swift, pared logic flowing from some impossibly simple premise. And this forced me away from Helen's problem, back to the more immediate one of John. I said, "You don't believe it yourself. It's not a picture, warts and all; it's a picture with nothing but warts. You don't allow him anything. It's pure monster — sitting back pulling the strings, chuckling and rubbing his hands while all the puppets dance. It's a little more complicated than that, isn't it? You can't just point your finger and say, 'See who's responsible for everything!'"

He shrugged. "I don't say he's responsible for everything. For example, I don't say he's responsible for *me*. Or the way I've evolved or developed. As it's turned out, my own life isn't much of a model for all priests everywhere — or even for any priest anywhere — but whatever it is, it's mine. Freely chosen. My father had nothing to do with what I became. Not that he didn't try; it's just that with me he wasn't successful. Helen married Frank to get out of the house, and Dan did what he did for the same reason. But I didn't. I never thought of the seminary as an escape hatch, or an answer to my father."

He said this with an air of challenge, almost of defiance, as if he expected me to question or rebut it; a little surprised, I said, "No, of course not. It wouldn't have occurred to me that you did."

Which was perfectly true, for I knew John. And I knew him, and remembered very well, when we had gone into the seminary together. He looked at me now, and then shrugged again. "Well," he said, "you're a charitable man, Hugh. Because it must have occurred to a great many people. Including me, from time to time." He was silent, and then, after a moment, he repeated slowly, "Including me."

And so I knew that he was thinking, not of his father now, but of himself — which seemed to bring him no particular comfort. For all his sharpness towards others, his occasional arrogance, he was in a sense a genuinely humble man. That is, I think he actually did what so many are alleged to do: I think he often took a hard, objective look at himself, and then decided he was not pleased with what he saw. I say "I think," because in this matter I could only observe and guess: he volunteered nothing. Ready enough to parade his annoyances and irritations, he shrank from giving personal revelations even more than from receiving them; about himself and his thoughts he was not a communicative man. He was a very private man — perhaps the most private I've ever known. And, inevitably, as he grew older he became more so: isolation enveloped him as, I suppose, it did me — although for rather different reasons. But even so, there were moments — fairly rare, to be sure — when I suddenly felt that his isolation had been shaken, that the shell had cracked slightly and temporarily, that he was willing, and might even have felt a necessity, to open up, to talk a bit on an extraordinary — for him — level. Not in order to invite sympathy or understanding, but simply, for a few seconds, to have a little human give-and-take. And it seemed to me that now one of those moments had arrived; I said, "It's still the same, then? No better? No growth of . . . what? *Rapport?*"

He didn't answer immediately. Then he shrugged again and said, "No growth. Of any kind. Unless you mean a growth of discontent, which must be mutual by now. Although I see no sign of it on their part; they keep coming. They won't quit. Every day I get up, I walk across to the church, I say Mass — and that's the end of the day for me. Because then they begin to come in. Good God in heaven, how can people *talk* so much? It's endless, Hugh. Endless, endless, endless. My day is spent in listening to one continuous supplicating whine. I know everything they're going to say before they open their mouths: over and over again, the same troubles I've heard for thirty years, the same complaints, the same banalities, the same gossip, the same trivialities, and if you're foolish enough to respond, to actually offer the advice they claim they need so badly, they almost go crazy with impatience. Because you've interrupted them; they haven't finished complaining: 'Yes yes, Father, that's true, that's very true, but there's one thing more, there's one thing more I've got to tell you. . . .' There's always one thing more. Every day. The same old whimpers and whispers and groans and tears from people who can't manage their own lives and who can hardly wait to bolt down their breakfasts before rushing up to the rectory to tell me they can't. And it's all nonsense; it means nothing. I'm a priest, not a wastebasket. These people who every morning sing to themselves, 'Pack up your troubles in your old kit bag and take them up to Father' — I want them for once, just once, to stay at home. Or at least to stop talking. To *shut up*. That's all. Just for a while. Because I'm tired, Hugh. Dead tired. Worn thin. It can't go on this way."

And again I was bothered by a difference: in the old tirades there was never the slightest doubt that he was fully in command of himself and everything he was saying; now, I wasn't sure. These words, all delivered in this new, almost toneless voice, had a tumbling, desperate quality . . . and moreover, what they were saying was slightly unreal. Most pastors, most priests — as I've said — have their nuisance parishioners, and John — as I've said also — for some reason always seemed to have more than his share. But no priest, not even John in Saint Raymond's, is quite this beleaguered, and the exaggeration, which once would have had its comic side, now, in this context, held no comedy at all. It was an extremely serious and delicate business; I said, picking my way, "I think that Saint Raymond's must have changed a good deal since my time. I never knew any priest over here to be so wildly in demand. Petitioners storming the doors, panting to get at you: is that a fact? Are there really so many of them?"

I wasn't at all sure that this was the right tone: I didn't even know exactly what I was aiming for. Was I trying to "jolly" him out of it — to provoke that traditional sign of the return to Common Sense: the slightly shamefaced grin? This did not happen. To my great surprise there was an even more complete about-face: he collapsed suddenly into acquiescence. "No," he said quietly. "No, I suppose not. Probably no more than there always were. What's different, Hugh, is that there *seem* to be more. And I mind them more. So that's just as bad as if they were really there, isn't it?" He looked at me soberly and said, "You used to be a man who took a drink now and then. I mention this only for analogy: you know how it is, sometimes, with drinkers. They go along for years and gradually they discover that they can't take as much as they once could. It's a question of tolerance. Well, that's the way it is with me and my parishioners. My tolerance is lower. Not that it ever was high, but now it barely exists. If I'm with them, listening to them, or if I even think I'm going to have to listen to them, I feel as if someone were standing behind me, turning a key in my back, tighter and tighter, and that in one more second, with one more turn, the spring will break — and so will I. And all I want to do is run, to get away from them as fast as I can, to get back to —" He stopped here, cutting himself off sharply, and then he said, "I almost said, 'back to my work.' And then what would you have said, Hugh? That listening to these people *is* my work? Would you have said something like that?"

I nodded. "Something like that, I'm afraid. If I'd said anything at all, that is."

"Well, you'd have been right," he said. "I won't argue with you there. It's all fairly elementary pastoral theology, isn't it? We all know what we're supposed to do: the shepherd-flock relationship. But, Hugh, what if the shepherd knows all this, what if he understands exactly what his duties are, what if he realizes that in a very special way this flock is his responsibility and nobody's but his, and that it is in fact the only reason he's where he is and what he is — what if he knows all this and tells himself all this at half-past seven every morning, just after he's finished saying Mass, just after thirty minutes of proclaiming — quite honestly, he thinks at the time — his own love of God, and what if he comes out of the side door of the church with every good intention in the world and suddenly he meets that flock in person? What if, then and there, he sees some old biddy streaking down the street towards him, her jaws already working, or he sees some poor old slob with his hat in his hand hanging around, waiting, outside the rectory door — what if the shepherd sees this and suddenly his stomach turns and all he can feel for his beloved flock is a total, overwhelming disgust! Not apathy, not indifference, but disgust. Disgust for the whole whispering, confiding, sordid, sniveling lot! That's what the truth is, Hugh! It's not simply, as my father has so pleasantly broadcast to anyone who would listen, that I'm a 'cold proposition'; it's more than coldness now. It's that I can no longer stand the sight of them! They make me *sick!*"

And as he said this he actually shuddered, physically, and his voice rose, and I felt an instant and great alarm — God forgive me, but I wondered at that moment if he were quite sane. But he calmed down immediately and said with a tight

[411]

smile, "Well. It's quite a spectacle, isn't it? All this bitter grousing about being battered to death by people with their problems — and now I batter you with mine. What for I don't know: I'm sorry."

"No no," I said. "I'm glad you did." Which wasn't true, which wasn't true at all: who could be glad to hear anything like this? I didn't even remotely know what to do, where to begin — for what John was doing was asking for help. John, of all people! And from me. Of all people. I said, "You know, it's possible you may be reading into this something that isn't there. I don't mean that it isn't serious; obviously it's that, no matter what it is. But this disgust for people: is that really it? Or is it just your old dislike of this city, this parish, as places? You don't want to be here; you never did. So that couldn't this disgust for all parishioners really be nothing more than this feeling you have against being here? Wouldn't things look entirely different in another parish? Away from here? Transfers can be arranged, you know. . . ."

But it was a simple explanation which I didn't really believe; we were in darker waters than this. He thought so too; he said, "No. That's no answer. The proof is that pretty much the same thing took place in Deerford. The idyllic Deerford I've told you so much about: where by my own report I was so content. It's not true. I wasn't. It was smaller than this, and I didn't know anybody, but in the end I felt the same . . . distaste. It was better than this; perhaps anything would be better than this. But it's not a matter of location. What we're really talking about here isn't anything like that. What we're really talking about is simply this: misanthropy. Isn't that what it is? Pure and simple? What else could you call it? I wouldn't know; I've run out of euphemisms. So there's a question, Hugh: Can a priest be a misanthrope? Can he? And still function? I'll put the question another way: Can a priest who says he loves God really love God — and still throw man away? How's that for a question, Hugh? And if your answer is

[412]

the same as mine, then, what does that priest do? What do *I* do?"

There was a long silence then. He had finished talking, and I — I had nothing to say. Or rather, nothing I could say. I don't remember now what I thought, or if I thought anything at all in any rational, consecutive way: even in the silence it seemed to me that his words were still pounding on, each one as shocking, as totally unexpected, as tragic as the one before. And when I finally did speak, it was like some buried, blinded animal clawing aimlessly away, hoping somehow to get through to open air: I said, "I don't know about . . . you say it's misanthropy, but that's . . . very rare, surely. Maybe a change . . . would a change help? Not to another parish; I mean away from parish work entirely for a while. I know it's a little late in the day, but possibly a monastery . . . I mean, that might be an answer. . . ."

He just looked at me. "Good God," he said. "A monastery. Don't you think I thought of that? Months ago?"

"And . . . ?"

"And," he said bitterly, "I went to your friend the Bishop. To get the necessary permission. But I didn't have your good fortune with His Excellency, Hugh. He refused. In that charming stolid way of his, he refused. And so I came back here. Right here."

And suddenly he got to his feet, but when I went to move too, he said, "No. Stay there, Hugh. Please. I just have to leave for a minute. I'll be right back. Stay right there."

He went swiftly into the small bathroom adjoining his bedroom, closing the door behind him, and I wondered again if he were ill. Acutely, that is: physically. It was what I had suspected when I first came in here with him, but that seemed a long time ago — and now I knew that if indeed he *were* ill in this way, it was only one of his troubles, and possibly even the least of them. And so I sat there, just as he'd asked me to, and waited for him to come out. I tried to think carefully, to plan step by step, but the steps collapsed, and all I could see was the image of John, facing me across the room — that terrible side-by-side, before-and-after image: at one moment as strong, confident, driving and unshatterable as always, and then suddenly there he was, strange, stripped, defenseless and — the last word I would ever have dreamed of applying to John Carmody — *pathetic*. More helpless and hopeless and pathetic than I had ever been — or so, in that moment, I felt; because to have it happen to me was one thing, to have it happen to him was . . . unimaginable. And yet it *had* happened, and I sat here, my eyes on the bathroom door, my mind unable to touch the future at all, racing over and over again through a scene not five minutes old, which had ended with that agonizing cry: "What do I do?" And I am no man of strength or resource or ready solution; my story is not that of someone who has helped, but of someone who has *been* helped; and so as I had done for myself so often, I closed my eyes and said a prayer for John. For my dear old friend. . . .

He came out of the bathroom and walked to his chair quickly; I had the impression that he couldn't wait to get to it, that his hands were almost reaching towards it as he walked. He sank down with a long grunting sigh; I said anxiously, "All right? Can I do anything?"

He waved me off impatiently. "No. A little nausea, that's all. I said I've been off my feed. I'll live; it's not important." And then he said, "And neither is all this I've been telling you. I don't know why I . . . good *God*, how I hate this sobbing into other peoples' laps! Anyway, do me a favor and forget it. It doesn't mean a thing."

So then, by now he had had time to think it over, and I could imagine with no trouble at all the appalled look on his face when, suddenly, he realized just how much of himself he had disclosed to someone else — and worse than that, that he had asked for *help*. Poor John: he'd had no experience in this kind of humbling, naked arena which isn't quite so rare to

[414]

most of us — and now, obviously, he had decided that the way out was to pretend that it had all been a mistake, something not worth bothering about: not a serious problem; in fact, not a problem at all. And this seemed to me most unwise; I said, "No, wait. Don't do this. It does mean something. You know that just as —"

"It means nothing," he said, almost angrily. "Be your age. Because that's what it is: age. Or largely so. It happens to all of us. We're not as resilient, we get tired more easily, we say things. . . . I talked like an imbecile. Is it such an unprecedented spiritual crisis when a middle-aged priest occasionally gets tired of his parish? In God's name, who doesn't now and then? Don't you?"

"Yes. Although I didn't know we were talking about 'now and then. . . .'"

He didn't comment on this; he said, "All those people in Old Saint Paul's: you're their pastor. Don't you ever get tired of *them*? The talk, the nonsense, the sheer *abrasiveness*? Don't you ever look down at their faces and suddenly want to head for the hills? Any hills?"

I said again, "Yes. Of course. But —"

"But," he said swiftly, "they don't *disgust* you: is that what you were going to say? Is that the difference? Well, let me tell you about that difference, Hugh: it may not be so much of a difference after all. It may even be the difference between the boy who said he hated oatmeal and the boy who said he didn't — and then one day it turned out that the second boy had a great advantage: he'd never eaten any. So how highly would you rate his considered opinion, Hugh? Without knowledge, without intimacy, without any of the familiarity which is the well-known breeding ground et cetera? And at least I'm intimate enough, familiar enough with my own people over here. I may not want to be, but I am. I can't help it. I'm with them all the time; I can't get away from them. So I know them. Good God, how I know them! From the ground up.

[415]

That's the solid base for my feelings about them. I *know* them. I'm *with* them. Whereas. . . ."

Whereas. He let it stop there; completion was hardly necessary. It had become all too clear that he had determined to get farther from himself by driving in on me; it was a shift which I found uncomfortable. I said, "What? Ignorance is bliss? You mean that I don't know mine . . . ?"

"Well, do you?" he said, with a crisp reasonableness. "Do you know them? Are you ever with them? All those Syrians and Greeks and Portuguese and whatever else you've got over there: how much time do you spend with them in the course of the week? I appreciate the fact that in a place like that they don't rush you the way they do over here, but — do you rush them? At all? Ever? Or do you keep away from them except for doing what you absolutely have to? Do you know what goes on in their houses? Do you even know their names? Or do you let that Polish comedian you've got in the house with you take care of that end of it?"

It was a sharp, savage attack: far sharper and more savage than any I'd expected — but then of course I hadn't expected to be attacked at all. Out of the blue he had turned the tables completely, the counsellor had become the victim, and for a moment I don't think I really took in what was happening because, absurdly, I actually opened my mouth to begin a defense of Father Danowski — and then it dawned on me that it wasn't he who needed the defending. As for John, he seemed revived: he was bending forward in his chair, so close to me that we were almost touching, and he was talking with all of his old harsh force. It was a recovery for which I did not now feel grateful. I sat staring at him: wordless, gaping — and hurt. The attack had been more than sharp; it had been shrewd, knowing: he had his father's gift for striking, hard and at once, at the vulnerable spot. And it was not over, for he went on talking now with what seemed to me to be almost a kind of joy, conducting all by himself an exuberant dialogue, anticipating the questions I might ask, supplying the answers, explaining, wrapping it all up. . . .

"We were talking about me, not you, Hugh? Is that it? But it's the same thing; it all ties in. I don't want to be here: all right. But look at yourself in Saint Paul's: do you really want to be there? Come clean, Hugh. Do you? Of course you don't. I spotted that the first day I went over to see you. In five minutes. Is it even a parish to you? I doubt it? You're just there. Like a chaplain in a rest home. Ready to be consulted if the occasion arises. But as far as actually going out on your own into those salami-cured tenements, as far as actually bringing anything *to* them, as far as actually working to make your parish any kind of living, breathing spiritual community — well, how about that, Hugh? Yet isn't that just what we were enjoined to do? Most solemnly? Years ago? All of us? And how many of us are doing it today? Am I? We know the answer to that, don't we? And are *you?* Don't we know the answer to that one, too? Don't we, Hugh? I think we do!"

Two old friends at twilight. . . .

And I think what hurt most at this pont was not what he said but the peculiar air of *triumph* with which he said it: as if all this were a demonstration of logic, nothing more, and that the only thing that mattered was the skill of the professor. He seemed entranced by his own performance: each question, each accusation, really, was flung out like a jubilant challenge — an invitation to rebut it if I dared. And I didn't rebut it — any of it. I didn't because I was still too surprised, too stunned, to make any kind of effective response. But more than that, I didn't because . . . well, because I *couldn't.* For how do you in any honesty rebut a charge when you know — and have known, really, for some time, even though you may have tried very hard not to know — that, quite simply, it's true . . . ?

He said, "It's a haven. That's what Saint Paul's is for you. Not a parish but a haven. A nice quiet recovery room. For someone who's licked a Problem. And you've done that all

[417]

right, Hugh. I don't take that away from you for a minute. But how much does that mean to the faithful flock of Old Saint Paul's? You don't drink any more — but how much good does that do *them*? And how much good do *you* do them? Sitting up in a bedroom reading Newman and being grateful to God that You Have Come Through is all very well, but what's it got to do with running a parish? But then of course you can't run a parish if you don't think of it as being really a parish at all, can you? Isn't that so, Hugh? And what kind of parish have you if your church is shopworn and obsolete and falling apart at the seams, and all you ever see in it is a few hundred strangers who look like extras in an Italian movie and who eat funny food and who plant fig trees in the back yard? That's not a real parish at all, is it? We all know what a real parish is. A real parish is an old-time parish. One with a fine, big, old-fashioned, well-kept church with — and here's the important things — lots of Irish to put inside it! People like ourselves, Hugh. The kind of people you grew up with; the kind of people you like; the kind of people you *understand*: comic, picturesque, a little sharp in the tongue at times, maybe, but decent, God-fearing, generous, and devout. The kind of people who can sing 'Ave Maria' inside the church, but can give you a chorus of 'There's a Little Devil Dancing in Your Laughing Irish Eyes' on the way home. Those are the people the Church was really meant for, wouldn't you say, Hugh? The kind of people we all remember. Or think we do. Isn't that what a real parish is? And isn't that really," he said, his tone suddenly dropping the heavy irony, and becoming one of somber, straightforward accusation, "isn't that really the one kind of parish you want? Don't answer because I know the answer: I know *you*, Hugh. And I knew what you wanted that day I saw you at my father's birthday party — just as I knew it today when you walked into the rectory. It stands out, it *shines* out, all over you: you want to come back, you're homesick. And homesick for what? I'll tell you

[418]

for what: a dream, a never-never land. You're a sentimental man, Hugh: a romantic. Whether you know it or not, you live in the past: you feed on memories. You think of the world as it was — or as you think it was — before anything happened to you: before your father died, before you drank. The pre-catastrophic world of Father Hugh Kennedy — the happy time. To which, one day, you hope to return. You do want to come back, don't you, Hugh? It's impossible, but you want to do it anyway. You want to come back here, to Saint Raymond's, to Saint Stephen's, to anywhere — so long as you're with your own. Back to where everybody in the parish says 'Hello there, Father!' and you won't be lonely any more. Back to where they all stop on the street for a friendly word because after all you're one of them, they know you, and they knew your father before you. Back to the old crowd, Hugh: back to the Backbone of the Church. Isn't that what they're called? Or is it only what they call themselves? I've forgotten, and it's no matter anyway. My own feelings towards that famous Backbone are well enough known; there's no need for one more sneer from a disaffected pastor. But disaffected or not, at least I don't see them through a ridiculous puddle of moonbeams, and if I'm all wrong as a priest for wanting to get away from them as fast as I can, is it any less wrong for a priest to want to be with them so much that he dreams his hours away thinking only of The Great Day When? And meanwhile neglecting his present parishioners, not even knowing who they are and not wanting to know? Isn't there an extraordinary snobbism here — and isn't the priest who's guilty of it in some danger of confusing that celebrated Backbone with the whole blessed Church? We were talking a minute ago about the differences between us, Hugh, but I'll tell you what the real difference is. It's that I may have turned my back on my parish, but you've never even turned your face on yours. You don't even know it's there. And so what does it all boil down to? Just this: that you don't do your job, either. Only

[419]

you don't do yours in a slightly different way. That's all."

And it was all. His eyes dropped from mine, and he looked straight down at the floor, his hands folded, his job done. It was absolutely still in the room: I sat there, looking at the top of his bent head, not really seeing anything at all. Then at last I said, with great bitterness, "Do you want congratulations? On knowing me so well? I think perhaps a medal should be struck off for you, John. In tribute to your special powers. With a little motto reading: 'He saw his friends as they really were — and hastened to make them ashamed!' "

For several seconds he didn't answer, but continued to stare downward. Suddenly he spoke — to the floor, to himself, but certainly not to me, for his voice was too low for me to hear clearly what he was saying: it sounded as if he were whispering, rapidly and over and over again, the single phrase, "Oh God!" Then this stopped, and he shook his head briskly — and then he looked up at me.

"I'll give you a different one, Hugh," he said. "One that might serve as an epitaph. 'Here lies John Carmody, parish priest. All his life he envied happiness — and snapped like a dog at his friends who found it.' Don't you think that sums it up? I do. I think that sums it up just fine." He looked down at the floor again for a moment; then he shrugged and said simply, "I'm sorry. It doesn't do much good to say that, does it? I don't imagine it ever really does: a few soft words tacked on after the kick has been delivered. But anyway, I do say it. I *am* sorry, Hugh. I'm desperately sorry!"

It was true enough. I could tell it, not so much from the words, but from his eyes, because I could see the anguish in them: the rare, real anguish that can sweep across a face and tear it apart. And I knew it was there because of what he had said, or done, to me — and I knew that never in all his life could he have expected to do this, or have wanted to. And yet he had, lashing out from the dark spring of his own desperation: misery screaming for company, and not caring how it got it. And so, still angry and hurt, I looked at him now, looking directly into his eyes, seeing the pain, and watching it swell and deepen until finally there came a moment when it seemed as if the eyes and everything around them had vanished, and I was looking at nothing but the pain. It was a strange sensation: I felt as if another kind of vision entirely had taken over, through which I saw John, not as he had been for a few awful minutes in a rectory room, but as he had been at other times, as he had been, in fact, all the rest of his days to me. And it seemed, then, that whatever had been said in these last minutes, it wasn't so earth-shaking after all, that it even was . . . I almost said that it even was *forgotten*, blotted out, but of course this wasn't quite true, and I don't suppose it ever would be: we have a way of hanging on to our moments of humiliation, as if they were prizes. But at least it no longer filled the horizon, and at least the anger and the bitterness were gone; I reached out and took his hand, just as — incongruously, this now occurred to me — a few days ago I had taken his father's, and said, "No bones broken, John. It's no more than the old story of the truth hurting a bit. . . ."

"Even when it's not the truth," he said. "It was all sleight-of-hand: a little bit of the truth made to look like the whole. You *do* cast that look back on the good green fields, and I don't imagine you're really a driving dynamo in Saint Paul's. But that's just a part of the picture — the part you yourself feel a little guilty about. The complete picture is something very different — naturally I didn't give that to you, because it wouldn't have helped my case at all. What I was trying to do was equate us as parish priests. Unhappily, the equation can't be made. I wish it could. But it can't. And I know it. Because in one of us, despite everything, the *goodness* comes through. Whereas in the other. . . ." He rose quickly and began to walk across the room; I thought at first he was returning to the bathroom, but he was only walking — walking and brooding. I was extremely uncomfortable; again, I didn't know what to say. Suddenly he stopped, as though a decision had been made; he said, "You reach a point where more words don't help anything; you stall in them and sink deeper. We've said enough for one day, Hugh — I've said far too much. Maybe we can pick this up again sometime later; it might be a good idea. I don't know. But for now, let's call it a day." He looked at his watch and said decisively, "Besides, I have Benediction in ten minutes."

Back to work. And I knew — or felt — that unsettling as all this had been to me, it had been far more so to him, and now, suddenly, he wanted nothing more than to bring it to a close. So this was how my visit — and this strange, disturbing talk — ended. There was no more to be said. John walked with me down to the rectory door: on this return trip I turned no slow inspecting gaze around the familiar scene. It was a quick walk and a silent one, and between us there was, not a frostiness, but a restraint — the restraint that follows when too much has been said. At the door we said goodbye; he hesitated and said, "Again, I'm . . . sorry. For all the world I wouldn't have. . . ." Then he said, loudly and abruptly, "Anyway: no hard feelings? Really?"

I said, truthfully, that there were none. I added — and here I too was hesitant, "About your own . . . difficulty. It's not insoluble, you know."

Although, certainly, I had no idea what the solution could be. And he wasn't disposed to go into it further; he said quickly, "We'll see. We'll see." There was an awkward interval, as though each of us were waiting for the other to go off first. He said, "Well . . . we'll be in touch."

"Yes . . . I'll give you a ring in the next day or so."

"Do that," he said. "Do that." And then he looked at me with an odd, almost an embarrassed smile, and said, of all things, "Thanks." With that there was a short, hasty movement of his hand which I suppose was a wave, and the rectory door closed.

It was a queer and, to me, an affecting farewell. I got into the car and drove off, back towards Old Saint Paul's, and I must have been halfway there before I remembered that this wasn't what I had intended at all, that I had promised Dan that I would return to Charlie's. But it was late now; I had gone too far to turn back and drive all the way there; in any case they would soon be sitting down to dinner; everybody (including the mournful Julia) would be there; at the end of the day visitors to Charlie might not be encouraged; I was expected back at the rectory — in short, I did not want to go. . . .

And so I continued to Saint Paul's.

I must have been poor company at supper that night; still, I doubt that this was noticed. Father Danowski, seldom silent at the table, was tonight more eloquent than usual. He had had an active day in the parish, making his rounds at the end of the year. He was full of gossip and small scraps of information, and dutifully and happily he passed these on to me. . . .

". . . to my utter astonishment that a small crisis was brewing in, of all places, the Elias family! And he is normally the quietest of men. Perhaps you recall him, Father? In the gasoline station at the corner of Camber Street? A very small person? It is rumored that in days gone by he was a most successful jockey. . . .

". . . little Maria Serafin is recovering quite nicely. You remember, Father, the incident of the tiny turkey bone? Which lodged in her throat on Christmas Day . . . ?

". . . how good it was to learn the news of young Sandy Guglielmo! It appears that at *any moment now* he may receive word of his appointment to the United States Military Academy. At West Point, New York. You of course know Sandy, Father. He is not only the somewhat older brother of one of our altar boys, little Sal Guglielmo, but he is, moreover, related by marriage to our own Mrs. Addione. . . ."

And so on. Tonight I didn't really pay much attention to him, or hear much of what he was saying, but occasional

[423]

snatches kept leaking through, and gradually — and disquiet-ingly — I became aware of what was a persistent narrative trick of my curate's. His stories were all about Saint Paul's and our parishioners, and yet as he talked to me he took great care to equip each figure with a suitable phrase of identification — as if he were telling the stories to a newcomer, a stranger who could not otherwise hope to follow the plot. I hadn't noticed this in him before, but it now occurred to me that of course he must have been doing it for some time — probably, in fact, since he had first come here and had begun these enthusiastic nightly reports on the people he had encountered during the day, and had found, to his surprise, that the names he assumed would be knowingly received instead drew only blanks: the inquiring look, the murmured "Ah!", the polite uncompre-hending nod. And so, little by little, perhaps even uncon-sciously, he had begun to provide a scorecard so that the pastor of the parish could stay somewhere close to the game. It was only tonight that I realized just what he was doing — and I wouldn't have realized it now except for the severe prelimi-naries of this afternoon. In all innocence, my curate was con-firming what — by now — hardly needed confirmation. It was not the most consoling table talk.

But in any case there was no time now for consolation — or for any such luxury. Tomorrow was New Year's Day, the Feast of the Circumcision of Our Lord, and after supper I went immediately into the church to hear confessions. On this last night of the year the confessionals are always crowded — even here in Saint Paul's. The slate is being wiped clean — and sometimes, for the priest, this is tedious and unusually trivial. One can discern, at this time, the impulse of an office-party New Year's Resolution: so much of it is small, negative, not quite serious, like a child solemnly parroting that it will abandon jelly beans as of Jan. 1. Yet these are adults . . . and they take up so much time. On the other hand, I suppose there is at least this desire for a fresh start — which is by no means contemptible. Then too, there are those others whose problems are not at all trivial, but are severe and complicated and often of long standing. They come also on this last night — they take time, but they *need* time: that's the difference. And of course you don't mind giving it to them: that's what you're there for. All the same, it can be tiring, it can even be exhausting: if you've been a priest as long as I have, you hear nothing new, but the old is quite enough — after a few hours of being buffeted by voices whispering alternately the nonsensical, the sordid, and — more rarely but still there — the genuinely evil, you feel beaten, drained dry. . . .

And on this New Year's Eve it was a few hours: a few hard hours. When I left the confessional, in fact, I had only a short time before preparing for Mass. This year, for the first time, we were to have a midnight Mass — just as we'd had on Christmas Eve. I sang it; Father Danowski assisted; there was our new, determined choir. The people came, perhaps not quite in the same numbers as on Christmas Eve, but still, they came. And since I'd been so busy that I really had had no time to think in any full or undistracted way about myself, it wasn't until I went into the pulpit to deliver my sermon and looked down through the half light of the gloomy church at those who had come, and saw them looking up at me, that John's words came pouring back, unsparing and all at once — and while I continued to talk now, I did so with the greatest difficulty. It's perhaps some measure of the standard set by my sermons that no one seemed to notice. . . .

After Mass, alone in my room, saying my prayers before going to bed, I prayed for John. Too much had happened too quickly for me to think with any exactness or clarity about him — and I was too closely involved for detachment. But obviously he was in a most serious predicament, one in which no priest would want to find himself: the kind of predicament from which escape would seem to depend upon either a great change in himself or great help from the outside. The first was unlikely: unlikely enough for anyone in middle age, and much more so for anyone of John's rigidity; the second . . . well, this was unlikely, too. For from whom could such help come? From the Bishop? Whom John distrusted in any case — and whose actions in this one were surely hard to understand? From some doctor? Whom — and this had of course occurred to me since our conversation — he might indeed need to see, but almost certainly would not? From his family? Obviously not — he had respect only for Helen, and she had no influence over him. From his friends? But these were few now; he had been a lone wolf too long; the only one left, I suppose, was me. And I was someone who was willing enough, heaven knows, but who had neither knowledge nor technique to offer. Who had, in fact, only his sympathy and affection and — his prayers. And so, tonight, I prayed for John. . . .

I didn't pray well. I meant to, I tried to, but my platform was too shaky: my prayers were meant for John, but I kept crowding in. John had said this afternoon that I was a man who lived in the past, and I suppose that this was true: in any case it was the past which bubbled up now, exploding softly through the stream of prayer. My attention fluttered; my old habit of going back in review took over. Yet tonight there was a difference: the past that now came up before me was not the old past, the past of my boyhood, of my father, of the seminary and Saint Raymond's and Saint Stephen's and The Cenacle. It was the recent past, the past of Old Saint Paul's, the past that I hadn't thought of as a past at all — or as a present or a future either, if it comes to that. John had been mortifyingly right: Saint Paul's for me had never really been considered a part of my working life as a priest at all. I lived here in a kind of suspension: I *did* look upon it as a place to which I had come after a crisis; it *was* a recovery room. In which I had been recovering now for more than a year and a half, and doing nothing more than that. Nothing, that is, beyond the absolute minimum required of me as a priest. I don't think I intended this, or that I did it deliberately, but somehow, easily and lazily, I'd slipped into regarding Saint Paul's as being something of an *interval:* a way-station for me, in which my function was to mark time — and wait. Wait for what? Again John had been right. I suppose that in the back of my mind was always the idea that this was a period of probation which would one day end, and that then I would go back and finish my life as a priest in some parish very like the one in which I began. Even if I didn't acknowledge it, this was really what I wanted: to go back to the place I loved, to the people among whom I belonged. And what's wrong with this — except everything? Because, if you're a priest, to speak of *belonging* in this way makes no sense at all: it's as if, having been formally consecrated to God, you confront Him with a condition of employment: "I love You and will serve You to the best of my ability — provided, of course, that You don't take me out of my yard. . . ."

It makes no sense — but the fact was that I had been taken out of my yard, I wanted to go back, and meanwhile — was I doing more than merely marking time? In my own favor, I could at least say this: that towards the people of Saint Paul's I'd always behaved well, I'd never hurt them or scandalized them, I'd always treated them with decency and kindness. So then, this was something — although not much. For decency and kindness can be overrated: many an ante-bellum plantation owner gave that to his slaves — his one small fault was that he didn't regard them as human beings like himself. Or in other words, his one fault was that he failed to give them what they deserved, and never once saw them for what they were — and that being so, did all the rest matter at all . . . ?

So with me in Saint Paul's. I haven't given them what they deserve, and have never once seen them for what they are — John's way of saying the same thing was that I'd never turned my face on my parish. I had been looking ahead to . . . what?

[427]

To the time when — to use a worn campaign phrase — I'd be back with the first-class citizens again? So John had said, and even though he'd hurried to cushion his indictment in the end, the truth of it remained. It was a truth I should have faced up to long ago, but I'd smothered it, hadn't admitted it, and drifted along lazily, on the whole pleasantly, with a whole part of my being numbed and no longer in use: a semi-pastor, a half-priest. And half a priest is better than none? I'm not so sure. . . .

In any case, I could never again not think about it, or not admit it, after this afternoon. And I thought of it now, to-night, which is why John got such intermittent attention in my prayers. Even the thought of his problem seemed to bring my own to the surface, and somehow I couldn't discipline my mind to separate the two. So side by side they rode together, as I knelt there; they tumbled and twisted uneasily in and out of each other until, at last, I went to bed. I lay there in the darkness, still thinking, but aware now of my own fatigue, and feeling sleep already beginning to come on. And then, in what must have been the fading seconds of wakefulness, I suddenly thought: Charlie! I had forgotten him. Completely. This little old man, whose living or dying had been the great issue of the week, who had been almost the sole object of my prayers at the beginning and end of each day, had now, in an instant, been pushed from my mind so thoroughly that I hadn't even given him a thought — let alone a prayer. So much for the capacity of the pastor of Old Saint Paul's to handle multiple burdens. Guiltily, before sleep came, I did attend, however briefly, to Charlie, and in this way I closed out the day. . . .

But not quite closed it out. Because suddenly, as it had a week ago, the telephone by my bed rang. I woke, reached for it, and mumbled fuzzily, "Yes? Yes?"

And it was Helen's voice which woke me completely, saying, "Hugh? Are you there, Hugh? Is that you?"

Her voice was quiet, controlled, but filled with tears — so I

[428]

knew what had happened. Poor Charlie. Poor old Charlie. I said, "Helen: bad news?"

Stupidly — for would she have called at four o'clock in the morning for anything else? "Bad news," she said. And then her voice was no longer so controlled; it broke as she said, "Oh Hugh, Hugh! Dreadful, *dreadful* news! Horrible news!"

And what can you say? No word or phrase in the language of man is any good at a time like this. You fall back on clichés as much as anything else; at least they've stood the test of time. I said, "Ah, Helen. I . . . don't know what to say to you. He was a good old man. . . ."

Was he? It didn't matter. I'd intended it only as one of those things you say because it's supposed to help, but here, instead of that, it produced an extraordinary reaction. For she gasped; loudly. I could hear it; I said, "Helen?"

And she said, in a rush, "Oh my God! You don't *understand*. Hugh! It's not Daddy. It's *John*." And then, as if to point up what as of this instant needed no pointing up at all, she sobbed, "*John is dead!*"

John is dead. . . .

And I sat there on the edge of the bed, the telephone in my hand, and I heard Helen sob again, and then she left the phone and was succeeded by Frank. He talked to me; I talked to him. We both I think talked calmly; I don't know. I don't remember what either of us said; I don't remember feeling pain or shock or anything at all. And to this day I don't remember dressing and rushing out of the rectory and driving to the hospital where John had been taken to die. I did it, but I don't remember it. What happened afterwards, I remember perfectly. But there is a gap in my life — a gap of perhaps an hour or a little less, a gap in which my mind and memory came to a halt and sheer instinct took over, a gap which began with three stupefying, incomprehensible, awful words: John is dead. . . .

[429]

12

I T WAS FRANK who, later, in the hospital and in his own way, told me what had happened.

"Duodenal ulcer. Hemorrhage," he said. "And probably nothing new with him. This must have been going on . . . mmm. I'm trying to get in touch with his doctor out in Deerford now; he's the only one who'd have the history. Under normal circumstances I might have known. Or I might have guessed from something he said or did. But he never let on. To anyone. Not even to Helen. You didn't know, I suppose?"

"No." Then, wearily rather than impatiently, for I don't think I had the energy or the will for impatience, I said, "Frank, do me a favor. John is dead: tell me how he died. That's all."

He looked at me curiously, as if I were not well myself — but he told me. Shortly after two o'clock in the morning, the young curate who had the bedroom next to John's had been awakened by a loud noise; he thought he heard someone call. He got up and walked out into the hall; John's door was open. Looking in, he saw John on the floor in his pajamas; there was blood, a great deal of blood; John, barely conscious, was trying to raise his head. The curate had rushed in; John, unable to speak, had pointed to the telephone and then had fainted.

"The curate had the brains to call the hospital," Frank said, "and they sent an ambulance and got him here in jig time. They're fast workers over here when they have to be. They transfused him, but by then it was too late. He'd lost an enormous quantity of blood. As a matter of fact it had probably been happening most of yesterday. You saw him then, didn't you, Hugh?"

"Yes. . . ."

"Did he seem tired, washed out? Unusually so?"

And I thought of the white face, the confession of being "off his feed," the collapse into the chair; I said, "Yes. Yes, he did. . . ."

"Well, there you are. Undoubtedly there'd been bleeding throughout the day, little by little. And then finally this massive hemorrhage. . . ." He shook his head and said regretfully, "It was so careless. He must have noticed it. And known what it was. He should have gone to bed, called a doctor. Instead of which he probably did a full day's work. Running around, agitating himself." He said thoughtfully, "He could have been a secret worrier. It's hard to tell. I didn't really know him well at all. Not nearly as well as you did, Hugh."

It was almost more than I could bear. I said, "Where's Helen, Frank? Is she here?"

"No. I made her go home. Right after she telephoned to you, in fact. This place wasn't doing her any good." A worried look appeared on the handsome, rather complacent face, and the husband replaced the cool physician; he said, "I don't know what this will do to her, Hugh. She thought the sun rose and set on him. She's a very strong woman, as you know, but sometimes these completely unexpected things . . . I just don't know. Anyway," he said, "she's gone home. And so have the others; they couldn't be of any help here. I'm the only one left."

I said, "What about Charlie? He hasn't been told?"

"No. There's no point in asking for trouble. It might have a very bad effect on him. We can tell him later, when he's

[431]

stronger. . . ." He looked around the bleak official room where he had met me and said, "Well . . . I guess that's about it. I should be getting a move on. To see how Helen's doing." He hesitated, then said, "Would you like to come along, Hugh?"

I said, "No. But thanks, Frank. I think what I'd like to do is to see John. Can that be arranged?"

It could be arranged. And so I went down, with Frank and a hospital attendant, to an even bleaker and colder room, and there I saw John. My old friend. . . .

I stayed there . . . not long. I knelt by his dead body; I rose and stood looking down at him for a moment, at his face which was tranquil now and still oddly young, still with surprising hints in it of the boy I had known and played with every day, fifty years ago. Then I touched his forehead lightly with my hand — and then I left him. . . .

Frank and I walked to the front door of the hospital together. We said goodbye and as we did, he repeated his invitation, but again I thanked him and declined. And so, he went home to Helen. And I went home.

John was buried on a Thursday, two days after his death. The wake was held in the rectory, and it was a large one. Predictably so: he had been the pastor of the parish, the Carmodys were without doubt its best-known and wealthiest family, and moreover, John, although hardly a man to encourage the warmth and affection of the crowd, had enjoyed the popularity that remote men sometimes mysteriously win — perhaps because of their very remoteness. In any case, he was waked, there were great quantities of flowers and wreaths, people crowded to the doors, and on the first night I went, rather late, and it was there that I saw Helen. She was pale, subdued, and sad-eyed, and yet she seemed to carry herself well; Frank, in his worry, had underestimated her; she was — as he had also said — a strong woman. We met for only a moment as I came into the room; she pressed my hand, but before

[432]

we had a chance to say more than a few words to each other she was drawn away by a family group whom I recognized as distant Carmody relatives; as she went she made a sign which I took to mean that she would come back and we would talk a little later.

I went up to the coffin and saw John; it wasn't a pleasant sight. These undertakers have a way of counterfeiting life, of investing a dead man with an indecent, shut-eyed, chalky charm — it's awful. So I said a prayer quickly and left him for now, pulling over to a side of the room where I stood by myself. Not for long; Bucky and P. J. detached themselves from the room and came over to express their regrets in their respective ways.

P. J. said softly, "Oh my my, Father. A young feller like that." He said it with sorrow but without surprise. I think perhaps nothing could have surprised this very old man by now.

And Bucky said, "One week ago today, Father! One week ago today! I talked with him myself! Standing right here on the church steps! And do you know what we talked about? I'll tell you what we talked about: we talked about burying *me*. And now look!" He waggled his head and said sepulchrally, "*We never know!*"

Conversation piece: the enigma of it all. . . .

Different members of the family came over: Dan, Julia, Ted and Anne. As I remember it, we said what is usually said — originality plays no great part in such occasions. We stood together for a while, an uncomfortable band, each feeling that something more should be done or at least said — and doing or saying nothing. Although Julia, I think, was exempted from this: frailer and more mournful than ever, perhaps not entirely here, she had no visible self-consciousness; she swept the room with slow, sidelong, peculiarly satisfied glances; once she muttered, loudly and cryptically, "It's all the same!" And I wondered if she knew, really, that it was her nephew who was dead, or if by this time life had become for her one long

[433]

continuum of death which had begun with poor thin Martin? Dan, on the other hand, obviously had been badly shaken by his brother's death; the event must have set his mind working along an unfamiliar and unwelcome groove; for the first time, this jaunty man looked old. He told me, twice, that he had sent for Flo and hoped that she would get here soon. As for Ted and Anne, I had the feeling that they were somehow out of it — that both had, in this small group, the uneasiness of strangers. Strangers to John, for one thing: Ted could not have known his uncle well, and Anne, of course, could have known him as someone seen occasionally on the altar, and very infrequently at family gatherings. But also, strangers to this special world: the world of the wake, which was so natural to the rest of us, but which was disappearing every day, and which, to youngsters like these two, must already have seemed baffling, primitive, a queer survival of another time. . . .

I said to Ted, "Your mother: how is she?"

"Much better now," he said. "Right after Uncle John died, and up until this afternoon, in fact, she was in pretty bad shape. It scared me a little: I'd never seen her like that before. You know, she usually doesn't let on when anything goes wrong, no matter what it is, but I guess this was just too much. She cried: she didn't stop, Father. I know Dad was alarmed. But then this afternoon she came out of it, and now she seems fine. Not *fine*, maybe, but all right. She just snapped back. Like that." I heard the admiration in his voice; after a pause he said, "She takes after Grandfather. You knew he's been declared out of danger?"

I didn't know; he said, "According to Jack King. So that's pretty official. They all feel he's turned the corner. It's strange, isn't it? I mean, that it should happen now, of all times?"

I suppose it was — although would my father perhaps have said it was inevitable? I said, "You haven't told him about John?"

"No, not yet. Although I don't know how much longer we

[434]

can hold out. Aunt Mary's at home with him now, and she's not very good at keeping things from him. And of course she's upset, too, so anything could happen. . . . Mom is all for telling him. She said so tonight. She seems to think he should be told. Of course she knows him so much better than I do, but still . . . what do you think, Father?"

I gave some sort of answer, but what really struck me now was not the question, but the ease and the naturalness with which Charlie's name had slipped into the conversation, and threatened — even here, even under these circumstances — to become its center, as it had in so many conversations of the past. I remembered, suddenly, something my father had once said on this very theme. . . .

"Charlie has a trick that's worth more than a mountain of gold: he knows how to keep people talking about him. He doesn't care much what they say, so long as they mention the name. It's the kind of thing he works at night and day. He has it all figured out, don't you see, that if he keeps at it long enough, people will do it out of habit, and there'll come a day when if they don't mention Charlie's name they'll all start to sweat and think maybe they're not even talking at all. Oh yes, it's a great trick, and there's none better at it than Charlie. . . ."

He had had fabulous success, certainly, with my father, and scarcely less with his own family — including his grandson now. But I didn't join in; I had shifted slightly so that I was once more facing the front of the room, facing the coffin, and this brought me sharply away from Charlie, and away from Ted, too, and I thought now of John, and of all the things we'd done together, so long ago and not so very far from here. It's funny the way you can skip the years, as I did now, and suddenly see only a wide-eyed child caught up in the excitement of chasing down an escaped white rabbit with frightened pink eyes — or see the same child running across the fields, his shirt bulging with its load of pears, hastily and illicitly picked,

[435]

all but inedible — yet we ate them all. Seeing only this, then, instead of an aging, unhappy, isolated priest — it was, of course, living in the past again: would he have disapproved . . . ?

So I continued to think about John, and as I stood there I was joined by two other priests: they were curates here at Saint Raymond's. I hadn't met them before, but they seemed to know me; they were pleasant, alert young men, and we talked briefly — if not very personally — about the man who had been their pastor. It was evident at once that both men felt that they hadn't really known him at all; from what they said I gathered that he had been perfectly decent to them, but distant: there had been no mixing. On the whole; he had been to them an efficient man, a fair man — and a mystery. Which was about what I would have imagined. . . .

They left; other people began to come over. These came, not warily, exactly, but slowly, hesitantly, and this was not surprising: I was known to them, but it had been a long time, after all, so much had happened, and what did one say to a priest, anyway, in closing such an intermission? But they came, in little groups of two and three. I suppose at one time I had known all of them, but now there were some I would never have remembered — just as there were others I could never have forgotten. It was good to see them again; they were people with whom I had spent much of my life, and spent it most congenially; a few of them had known my father well. We talked about John, carefully, with a rather stylized sadness, and then — as often happens at wakes — the talk broadened; a word, a sentence, the mention of a name opened the way to reminiscence, and soon they were plunging into old times, and I listened, warmed by the talk, not at all realizing how effortlessly I had slipped away from what was before my mind and eyes — until suddenly a chance word brought me back with a snap. This, as I say, happens at wakes:

this changing of focus, this ebb and flow of attention. I don't think it's a bad thing, necessarily, and I've seen times when it's been valuable rather than anything else: it's a way, I suppose, of handling death, of taking it in. Yet even so, whenever it happens to me it always shames me a little, and tonight it did more than that, for this time it was John who was dead: I might have been expected to keep a slightly firmer watch. Especially since diversion had come from, of all places, the very quarter he had warned me so savagely against. . . .

It was near the end of the evening now, and time for the rosary. We all knelt and recited it together; after this, the people began to go home. I hadn't yet talked with Helen, but when I looked for her I saw that she was in one of the side rooms, surrounded by a small, eager group of those who had probably come early but still had something to say — every wake has this irreducible core of professional mourners. And it occurred to me now that, badly as I wanted to talk to her, it would be no kindness to do so, to force her to talk still more after this day of shock and brutal exhaustion. Surely the kindness would be to leave her alone, to postpone the meeting, to let her go home with her husband, to give her the chance, at least, for rest. And so I left without seeing her. As I went out, Dan caught me by the arm; he said again, "It's awful, isn't it?"

"Yes. It's awful, Dan."

"It makes you think, Hugh. It makes you think." Perking up, he said, "I told you I've sent for Flo? She may get here in the morning."

"That's fine, Dan."

"Although," he explained, "it may not be until the afternoon. We don't know yet; it depends on the connections. But with any luck, she'll be here in the morning!"

Which, of course, would solve everything. Although, I suppose, it probably would come very close to doing that for Dan. I said good night to him, but he followed me halfway down

[437]

the walk; it was clear that he had no desire to go back inside. As I drove off he was still standing on the walk, looking after me, alone. . . .

On the next afternoon, the priests of the diocese — or those who were to be there — gathered in the rectory; we chanted the Office of the Dead, and bore John's body to the church. There, before the main altar, it stayed all night. Late in the afternoon I went back to my own parish, but at night I returned and, kneeling in the sanctuary, I stayed there a good part of the night, too. It wasn't much to do, but it was all I could do. . . .

The funeral was held the next morning. The church was packed; shortly before Mass there was an unexpected development when the Bishop appeared, unannounced — and this, of course, brought back old thoughts and wonderings: I was no closer than ever to understanding his action towards John. The Mass was celebrated by the senior curate, a man of my own age; after Mass there was the absolution; and then we went to the cemetery. Snow was on the ground; it had had to be cleared away for the grave, and a large pile of it had been pushed over to one side, mixed with the fresh earth. The grave had been blessed; the coffin was lowered; the short litany was repeated; holy water was sprinkled upon the coffin; and then there was the final prayer:

". . . may Thy mercy unite him to the choirs of angels . . . may his soul and all the souls of the faithful departed rest in peace. Amen."

So I said goodbye to John. And now, for the first time since his death, for the first time, indeed, since I could remember, I wept. . . .

That night, in the rectory, Father Danowski said, "I met him only the day he came here, so of course I did not know him well. But he was most obviously a very remarkable person!"

I said, not really listening to him, "Yes. He was remarkable in many ways."

[438]

Father Danowski cleared his throat; he said importantly, "An aristocrat down to his finger tips!"

And this brought me sharply out of abstraction: it never fails. Even after all these months, my curate's special magic works. I looked at him and said, "What?"

The round young head nodded. Sagely. "One could not help observing it immediately. In the way that he carried himself. What a *pride* he took in being a priest, Father! And what an example to those of us who occasionally forget what it is we represent, and become slack or boisterous or go about in clothing that is not neat. A priest like Father John Carmody, Father, is a lesson to us all!"

A lesson to us all. And I wondered what Father John Carmody would have found to say to this. . . .

It was three days later, on the Sunday following the funeral, that finally I saw and talked to Helen. She came over to Saint Paul's after the last Mass; I saw the car drive up just as I was leaving the church. She was alone; I hadn't expected her. She still looked tired, but she had improved since the night of the wake. I took her into the office-reception room, and she said, sitting down, "So here we are. It's not much like we thought it would be even a week ago, is it? John dead, and Daddy getting better by the minute. Is there an answer to that, Hugh? If there is, you don't happen to have it handy, do you?"

I said, "No special answer. Just the one you already know. Sometimes it doesn't seem to help much, does it?"

"No," she said. "Sometimes it doesn't. Right now, for instance, the thought that it's all a part of the Grand Design which we below can't even hope to know — that's not really flooding me with comfort. I think I'd like to see through a glass not-quite-so-darkly. . . ." She sighed and said, "I'm just talking. It's been a bad time. . . . I loved John, Hugh. He was a grand boy, wasn't he?"

[439]

Did we all think of John in that past, then? All of us who had loved him? I said, "Yes, he was. Grand."

"He changed such a lot, I guess. It wasn't that he soured; it was more that he *froze*. I noticed it — you couldn't help noticing it — but I never paid too much attention to it because he never froze towards *me*. Or you, did he?"

"No. No, he never froze towards me."

She wanted to talk about him. "You saw him that afternoon: how was he? Did he seem at all . . . happy?"

I hesitated, and then I saw her looking at me; I said, "Not very."

"No," she said. "Although I don't know what would have made him happy, do you? I don't know what he really wanted. Unless it was to be alone. I once told him that: I told him that he ought to be stationed on some mountaintop, saying Mass on Sundays for total strangers who came up in buses and went away without saying a word the instant Mass was over. Do you know what he said? He said he wished to God I'd been a bishop. But we talked about all this once before, didn't we? What about your talk with him, Hugh? Was it a good talk?"

"I don't know that you could call it a good talk. In a way it was a very painful talk. For both of us. But in another way . . . do you remember, Helen, how we used to talk about doing favors for each other? All sizes: small, medium, large, enormous? Well, John did one for me that day."

"Did he?" she said. Then, like a little girl, she said, "Which size: enormous?"

I nodded, and she said, "I'm glad. I wonder what it could have been? Don't worry, I'm not going to ask you. But that's something, isn't it, if a man can do someone an enormous favor on the very day he dies? That counts, doesn't it?"

I agreed. It counts, it counts, it counts indeed. . . .

She said, "I was thinking about him last night when I went

[440]

in to see Daddy. That makes everything a little harder, you see, with Daddy not knowing."

Which was a small surprise; I said, "I thought he'd know by now. Ted said you were going to tell him."

"I was. But then Frank, and Dr. King, too, said I shouldn't for a while so — I didn't. Except that I think now that I should have; it's just going to be harder than ever. Anyway, he hasn't been told, and he's feeling better, and he's sitting up in bed, and of course he knows that John hasn't been around to see him. So that's rather awful at times: he has quite a lot to say about ungrateful children. He was going on and on last night, and that's when I began to think of the two of them together. They never got along, you know. Not even from the beginning. And naturally in the beginning it was all Daddy's fault: he knew that there was something . . . *resistant* about John which he couldn't do much with, no matter how hard he tried. So he made life fairly disagreeable for him — in fact, he was just plain mean to him. And John always had a good memory; he never forgot. And he wasn't the most forgiving man in the world, so that later when Daddy tried — and he *did* try, in his own way, a couple of times — to make amends, or at least to put things on a little better footing between them, there was nothing doing. John wouldn't give an inch. Did you know about that, Hugh?"

"No. But then, it's not something I would know about."

"Unless you'd heard it from John. But he wouldn't have been likely to tell you that because I don't think he really understood. Understood Daddy, I mean. You see, that was a strange thing about John: he was wonderfully intelligent, and I adored him, but he just wasn't much good about *people*. About what they were really like, or why they did certain things. He wasn't very interested in them to begin with, and I guess you have to be that if you're going to find out anything about them. But he'd just make a snap judgment, an impatient simplification, and that would be it: he just wouldn't go beyond it. I don't think he really *got* many people at all."

I said, "I don't know about that. He got me pretty well."

"Did he? Well, I can believe that. I don't exactly know why, except that you were always a special case with him. But he never got Daddy. He got half of him or maybe two-thirds — but he didn't understand him. He didn't understand, for instance, that Daddy was proud of him. And he was. He was much prouder of John than of any of us. But you had to know *Daddy* to know that — and John never did. And if you did know it you made a few allowances — which John never made. That's why he used to get so upset with me — because he could never understand why I defended Daddy, or took his side. He used to say that I had less reason than anybody to do so. You see, he blamed Daddy for my — in this talk of yours, Hugh, did he tell you about Daddy and me?"

I said, perhaps too quickly, "We talked about everything under the sun. . . ."

"It's all right," she said. "I know he never would have said a word to anyone but you. And I don't mind your knowing, Hugh: I almost told you myself, that day in the clearing. Remember?"

"Yes. I remember."

"Well," she said, "getting back to John: he always blamed Daddy for my marriage to Frank. Not that he thought Frank was Daddy's choice, but he thought I married Frank simply to get out of the house. I tried to tell him nothing was that simple, that he was wrong, but I didn't have much luck. And of course it was true — as I told you — that life around the house was pretty miserable in those days; I won't go into details now, either, but Daddy wasn't an easy man to live with. So there's no use pretending that wasn't a factor; it was. But there were . . . other factors. Frank wasn't unattractive, you know, by any means; in our little set he was considered quite a catch. I wasn't wildly in love with him; I've never been. He

[442]

knows that. But I liked him very much, I liked him enough to marry him, and I don't think it's worked out so badly. John's trouble was that he couldn't stand him: he thought he was dull and pompous and uninteresting. Well, he's *not* the kind of man a girl wants to run off and go dancing with until four o'clock in the morning, and he's *not* the kind of man who knows about existentialist poets or even what opens on Broadway next Thursday night. But he's been a good husband for me; he understands me, and he's kind and decent and generous — and I know he loves me. And we had Ted — and now we have the grandchildren. So I get my moments of discontent and unhappiness like everyone else, but life has been all right for me, Hugh; I don't complain. It hasn't been bad; I'm not a woman trapped in calamity."

I said, "You don't have to persuade me. I never thought of you as that, certainly."

"Didn't you? No, I don't suppose you did, Hugh. But John always did. I couldn't persuade him of anything else. And of course there was always one person he blamed, and that was Daddy. And when I'd tell him that this just wasn't so, that I was an adult, responsible for my own decisions, and that beyond all that Daddy simply *wasn't* this monster, without a redeeming quality, that along with all the mean and petty things he'd done, he'd done some rather nice ones, too — well, when I'd tell him this he'd close his eyes in that pained way, you know, and act as if I'd said I'd seen elves on the front lawn that morning." She sighed again, and said, "Poor John. Poor, dear John. I know the reason for it: he thought I'd been treated badly. And he really did have a great affection for me. He didn't have it for many people, did he? He had it for you, and for me — and not many others. And maybe when you don't spread your affection — or love — over more than one or two people, it gets concentrated, and the people you do give it to you're likely to put on some kind of pedestal. Or think they're more than they are. That could happen, don't you think? Anyway, he thought that when I married, I should get — I don't know *what* he thought I should get. Not Frank, obviously. But I think he had these golden, impossible dreams for me . . . which was nice and wonderful and all very much as if we were all children in the fields again playing King of the Castle, but not really very realistic for a grown-up girl who was looking around and ready to be married. It's funny, but I don't know anyone who took more pride in calling himself a realist than John, and yet was less of one when it came to something like that. He didn't even sense that all those wonderful possibilities might just not be there."

"And yet a lot of them must have been," I said. "For you, I mean. Because I remember you, Helen. I remember you very well as you were then. I wouldn't think the possibilities were limited at all."

And she looked at me in the strangest way. "Wouldn't you, Hugh?" she said. "You're a gallant man. But you're wrong; there were . . . limitations. Things I had no control over; things I just couldn't do anything about. Although later, sometimes, I wondered if . . . for instance, Hugh," she said, "and just for instance: did it ever even enter your mind that you might marry me?"

All my life, it seems to me, people have had a way of coming at me with questions which I never expect at all. And, heaven knows, I hadn't expected this one now, and yet somehow it was different, because as soon as she asked it I felt in a curious way as if I had been expecting it. Did I blush, I wonder, like a schoolboy: all Adam's apple and big raw knuckles? I don't know; I felt shy, embarrassed in a way I hadn't felt for . . . how long? She must have seen it, for she gave a faint and rather sad smile and said, "Come on, Hugh. It was a long time ago. Did it?"

I nodded. "It did. Often. It was a very attractive notion."

"Was it? I'm glad. Whatever happened to it, by the way?"

And I didn't say anything. Awkwardly, I spread my hands apart and just sat there, helplessly, as if to say that here I was, as I was — and that was what happened to it. . . .

She gave the same smile again and said, "A more attractive notion came along?"

I said, "A different notion came along. I don't know that I had much choice. This just seemed to be what was right. For me, anyway."

"And no regrets?" she said. "Ever?"

I said, truthfully, "No. Never." But this was a kind of talk in which I was unskilled; I was clumsy, even impolite. I said, "That's not what a gallant man says, is it?"

"Oh," she said, "there are better things than gallantry." She stood now and said, "We talk about Daddy and about ourselves . . . but I guess it's all related to John. Anyway I'll miss him, Hugh. Dreadfully. And I know you will, too. Say a prayer for him now and then."

"I will, yes. . . ."

"And come to see Daddy. Come to see *us*. Will you?"

I promised that I would. And she left. It had been a strange visit, one which I was glad had taken place, and yet a little sorry, too. Because somehow, although nothing had been said about this, there was a certain *final* quality to it: that is, I felt that simply by being talked about, simply by being this much better defined, another part of my life had somehow come to a close — or at least, that it would not be returned to often again. . . .

After this, days and weeks went by before I saw any of the Carmodys. For the first time I began to move about in my parish, to call on people, to extend a few of the parish services — in short, to take charge, to do my job. I did this because . . . well, because I had to, now, and I did it with a few misgivings. It had been so long, and then I remembered that I also wondered — absurdly — how my curate would accept this retarded plunge into activity. But I needn't have wondered; he was delighted, if astonished.

"Why, Father," he exclaimed, "if I may say so, you have of late become a very *whirlpool* of energies! In sheer speed of foot alone I find I am hard put to keep up with you!"

Jocosity. The twinkle in my curate's eye at such a moment must be seen to be believed. I said, "It's the winter months. They've put ginger in my step."

"Aha ha ha, Father," he said. Tolerantly. "But how good it is to see everything humming so briskly along! Mark my words, Father, do you know what I predict we may soon expect among the parishioners of Old Saint Paul's? We may expect mighty *changes!*"

The great expectations of Father Danowski. The mighty changes, of course, did not take place — or if they did they remained invisible to me. Which was natural enough: the parish would go on as before, since a slight increase in the zeal of one man produces no miracles — unless the one man is himself one of the extraordinary few who can and do change history. But nothing like that was involved here. I did my work, time went by, and in the rectory each night Father Danowski continued to smile and talk exuberantly of the glories to come. . . .

In all this time I had not seen or heard from Charlie. I'd heard about him: a few weeks after she had come to the rectory, Helen had telephoned to ask me to dinner. I couldn't go — I didn't go, but out of the call had come the information that Charlie had recovered to a degree remarkable for such an old man. It was probable that he would never again enter into work with all of his old bounce and vigor, but he was up and around, already taking short walks; the doctors were surprised and pleased. I asked how he had taken the news of John's death; Helen said that he had taken it very quietly, and for a long time he had simply not mentioned John's name at all.

Recently, however, he had begun to speak of him again, and — curiously — in much the same ungentle way he had spoken of him when he was alive.

"And I'm not crazy about *that*," she had said, "but it's not the easiest thing to stop; sickness hasn't really made Daddy much more *tractable.* . . . Hugh, why don't you go over and look in on him? I know he'd love to see you."

But I was not so sure. Charlie in his convalescence had not sent for me, and I thought I knew the reason why. It wasn't merely that he'd gotten what he wanted from me — although that was undoubtedly a part of it. But more important, I think, was the fact that he had talked too much to me. In a panic, lying on what he considered to be his deathbed, he had talked for once in his life without pretense, and had given me his real evaluation of himself. Now, the danger past, he must have regretted it deeply. Possibly he thought that if we met again I might return to the subject; possibly it was simply that I *knew* — and that was enough. In any case, from that time on, old Charlie had kept his distance. . . .

Then, one day, I met him. It was a day in early April, a warm and windless day with plenty of sunshine: a fine day at the beginning of spring. I had been on a sick call in one of the tenement buildings on the edge of the slum; I came out of the dark hall, blinking into the sunlight of the street — and the first thing I saw was Charlie. He was standing on the sidewalk about three houses away. He seemed to be examining with some care the house in front of which he stood, and he was heavily wrapped up to the point of almost being disguised, but it was unmistakably Charlie. He looked up and I think he saw me just a second or so after I'd seen him — I think we were equally startled. I waved; after only the briefest of hesitations he called out, "Well well, Father! Ain't this grand? Ain't this a surprise? I tell you, Father, you're a sight for sore eyes!"

And the old voice sounded exactly the same. I went down the steps and over towards him, and it was when I got close I

[447]

saw that he looked smaller and older. We shook hands; I said, "You look fine, Mr. Carmody."

"I'm thin as a snake," he said. "They got me on a diet. I get nothin' at all to eat nowadays. D'ye like salt on your food, Father?"

I said that I liked salt, yes. . . .

"Salt is grand," he said. "Salt is lovely. I dunno is there anythin' I like better than salt when it comes to makin' things tasty. And now they say I can't have none. 'No salt, Charlie!' they say. 'Not a speck. Else you'll keel over into the bread puddin' one day.' That's hard on a man, Father. I tell you, it's lucky I had lots of practice all my life. Goin' without things."

I passed this by; I said, "I'm surprised to see you all the way over here. You didn't walk?"

"No no," he said. "I ain't quite up to that, Father. I will be, but I ain't yet. I'm all right on the straight, but on the hills I get out of puff. So Mary drives me around to different places I want to go. Then she goes off somewheres, maybe lookin' in store windows, and then she comes back in the car to pick me up." He looked up and down the street. "She'll be along here any minute now," he said, "unless she's got in an accident. She's a damn bad driver."

But what I was wondering was why, of all locations, this should be one of the places Charlie wanted to see. His next words were a clue.

"D'ye know this buildin', Father?" he asked, pointing to the one he had been staring at. "There's a fine old place."

I knew this fine old place. It was very much like its neighbors: run down, in need of repairs for twenty years. I said, "One of yours, Mr. Carmody?"

"That and the two next to it," he said with satisfaction. "They don't put buildin's up like that today, Father. Today they're all stuck together with thumbtacks and liberry paste:

[448]

a man that owns one is halfway to the poorhouse before a year is up. But buildin's like these here go on forever; you never need to touch them. A prince could live in them and be happy." He looked fondly up and down the desolate façade. "Oh, I tell you, nothin' makes me feel better than to come over here every once in a while and take a look at them. Oh yes." And then he said, "And yourself, Father? You're feelin' good?"

"Yes, fine, Mr. Carmody."

"Ain't that grand!" Suddenly he switched; he said, "They tell me you were with John the day he died?"

"Yes. The afternoon before. . . ."

"A stubborn boy," he said. "A stubborn boy that never listened to his pa. And now . . . well, well. . . ."

It wasn't an especially sympathetic or paternal comment, and as he said it I saw him flick a glance at me. To see how I was taking it? I think so; I think Charlie was out to prove something to me, in much the same way that old men will sometimes desperately display their scrawny biceps, to argue that ancient glories still remain. But I said nothing, and now he began to look impatiently up and down the street once more, and this time he saw what he was looking for. "Aha!" he said. Relieved? "Here she comes now!"

Around the corner, three blocks away, and just barely nosing along, came the vast old Carmody car. What was remarkable, I suppose, was not that Mary drove badly, but that she drove at all: as far as I knew, this was a skill acquired only since her father's heart attack. The car crept towards us, hugging the right curb.

"Mother of God, she'll get here day after tomorrow!" he growled. "What's the point to havin' a big lovely car like that if you drive it like a go-cart?" He turned to me and stuck out his hand in farewell. "Well, Father, we'll have to be gettin' together with each other one of these days."

I said that we would, we would indeed. . . .

[449]

He said, "I dunno, when was it we had our last good chat? It must of been when I was flat on my back. Did we have a chat then, Father?"

So this was the way it was to be. I said, "Yes, we had a long chat, Mr. Carmody."

He seemed thunderstruck. "Is that a fact! A long chat! It's the damnedest thing, Father, I don't remember half what went on while I was lyin' there. People comin' and goin' all the time. . . . I remember you comin' in one time and tellin' me nice things your pa said about me. Oh my, Father, I tell you that cheered me up. But I don't remember a blessed thing else we talked about. I don't s'pose you do?"

I said, "As I say, it was a long talk. It covered a lot of ground. . . ."

"I don't remember none of it," he said. "Ain't that funny, Father? A man with a mem'ry like mine? Although it's prob'ly just as well: they tell me I made no sense at all. I said to the doctors only a week ago, I said, 'Well, doctors, I s'pose I must of said some queer, crazy stuff whilst I was sick in bed, back there?' 'You did, Mr. Carmody,' they said to me. 'You did. But we paid it no mind. We pay no mind to what any man says when he's out of his head.' And I said to them, 'Are you tellin' me, doctors, that I was so sick I was drove loony? And nothin' I said was true?' "

But at this point the car pulled up beside us, the old-fashioned fenders hanging over the curb so that they nearly brushed against us. "Easy, easy!" Charlie cried angrily. "Are you tryin' to run over your father? In God's name, girl, easy!"

The car shuddered, then was silent. Mary, still gripping the wheel fiercely, gave me a frightened smile.

"Say hello to Father, here!" Charlie commanded. She did, and I greeted her; Charlie, opening the door, put one foot in the car and then said to me, "So I said to them, 'And nothin' I said was true?' And d'ye know what they said to me, Father? I'll tell you what they said. They said, 'No, Mr. Carmody,

[450]

nothin' at all. Not so much as a word!' *That's* what they said to me!" He shook his head incredulously, as if unable to believe it himself. "Well," he said, getting in the car, "that's the way it goes, Father. We mustn't complain. Goodbye now. We'll see each other one day."

I said, "Goodbye, Mr. Carmody." And I also said goodbye to Mary, but I doubt if she heard this, because at that moment Charlie turned to her and said irascibly, "All right, all right!"

And the car started off, bucking badly. Through the window I could see Charlie in a pantomime of shouted complaint; the car moved forward down the street, more rapidly now, with Mary presumably goaded into greater temerity. It had gone perhaps thirty or forty yards when suddenly Charlie rolled down his window and poked his head out; he was looking back at me.

"Not so much as a word!" he bawled. "*Not a single blessed word!*"

And then, at the corner of the first side street, the huge car slowed and swung into a great, sweeping, painful arc to the right. Like some enormous river beast, uneasy in an alien element, it moved clumsily ahead, and in a moment it was out of sight. I did not think that I would see it often again. . . .

April passed, then May, and then, in the middle of June, the Bishop came to call. It was not an official visit; he came without notice, and he came, I remember, on a day when the heat and humidity of the summer had begun to make itself felt. He came at a time when Father Danowski was out, Roy was somewhere in the basement of the church, and Mrs. Addione had left for the day. So that I was alone in the rectory, and suddenly the Bishop appeared at the door. He nodded and said simply, "You're not busy, Father?"

I was not busy. We went into the house, and as we crossed into the office he stopped and said, "It's cool in here. The

[451]

thick walls. . . . When I was a young priest I spent a year or so in the desert country. It was blazing every day. For weeks on end. But we lived in an old adobe structure and we were reasonably comfortable. The same principle, I would imagine . . . you find this bearable right through the summer?"

I said that we did; it was one of the virtues of the building. I wondered, irrelevantly, what he had been doing in the desert country, why he had gone out there as a young priest: the missions? And then I remembered that of course he *was* a Westerner — and I remembered too the outside heat; I said, "Can I get you anything, Bishop?"

He shook his head and sat down. "I came up here this morning for a funeral," he said. "A man named McCartney died. I didn't know him. I don't think many people did. He was a man who kept to himself. He lived alone; apparently he'd made some money in textiles. The first Christmas I was here he sent me a check for ten thousand dollars, with a note asking me to use it for the blind children. And every Christmas since I've had a check for the same amount. For the same purpose. I've never heard from him at any other time, and he's never asked me for anything." He paused now, and in that curious way he had of seeming to speak really to himself, he said, "It's not unprecedented, of course. There's a great fundamental generosity. . . ."

It called for no comment; I made none. After a moment the heavy face seemed to turn out to me again; he said, "Your parish: what's it like these days, Father?"

I said, "About the same, I'd say. We don't change much. There's been no falling off, at least. And I think there's been some improvement. More of them seem to be coming to church, and we've been able to get around and see them a little more often. Then, because he deserved mention, certainly, if anyone ever did, I said, "My curate's been of great help. He's a hard worker. And a good priest."

The Bishop said, "The Polish boy. Yes. He's very young,

[452]

isn't he? Still, that's not a crime. And there's plenty of time.
. . ." Then he said abruptly, "And you, Father?"

"I'm doing well. Saint Paul's has been good for me — and
good to me. I have no complaints, Bishop."

The Bishop said simply, "Nor have I." It was the closest he
had ever come to a positive compliment; I felt suddenly and
childishly pleased. There was another of the long pauses which,
as much as any of the words he used, seemed to form a part
of his conversation. Then he said, "After the funeral I stopped
for a short time at Saint Raymond's. You were a close friend
of Father Carmody's?"

And I remembered now what of course I should have remembered at once: that the last time I had seen him had been
on the day of John's burial. I said, "Yes. He was my closest
friend."

"These deaths," he said slowly. "Here in the diocese we've
lost three priests in the last six months. None of them old
men. All your age and mine. I knew Father Walker fairly well.
And Father Byrne was with me at the Cathedral." Then he
said to me, "Tell me about Father Carmody."

In a few well-chosen words? I said uncomfortably, "It's a
rather long story, Your Excellency. . . ."

But he said only, "I have time."

And so I told him about John. It was a John he could never
have known, because it was John as he was to me — and, for
the most part, John as he was when he was younger. For once
the excursion into the past served some good purpose, because
I wanted the Bishop to glimpse, at least, a little of the happier
side of someone he must have known only as a rather forbidding and difficult subordinate. I said nothing, of course,
about the private problem that had harassed him at the end,
and I said almost nothing, indeed, about these later days,
his time at Saint Raymond's.

The Bishop listened quietly: with a strange absolute physical stillness. When I finished there was a silence; then he

[453]

said, "I brought him back to Saint Raymond's. It may not have been a wise assignment. I don't know. But it's not always. . . ." He did not complete the sentence; after a moment he said, "Your priest who becomes a recluse for no apparent reason: this happens, sometimes. I don't know why. Disappointment. Boredom. Pride, perhaps. And for some there seems to be a special temptation: one towards loneliness. . . ." He fell silent, looking at the wall opposite him with that familiar, steady, self-communicating gaze which seemed to go with the private voice. "It's always a problem. The parish can become a formula; the priest can become . . . a number of things. To some extent this was happening in Deerford. That was why I brought Father Carmody back here. It was possible that Saint Raymond's was a parish in which, for obvious reasons, he might find it hard to . . . calcify. And he was a gifted priest; I thought the two might help each other." There was silence again for a few seconds before he said, "They didn't. And yet I . . . does this distress you, Father?"

It did, of course . . . oddly, it was the mention of Deerford which struck with sudden pain, because it brought back John's voice bleakly reciting the truth of his failure in that parish which he had so long proclaimed as his ideal. I said, "A little. . . ." And then I asked the question which, I suppose, I had no right to ask, but which had puzzled me ever since that last afternoon with John; I said, "The monastery, Bishop: what was wrong with that as an answer?"

He showed no surprise at my knowing about this. He said, "It was no answer at all. It was an . . . evasion. The monastic life is a specific calling; it's not an escape hatch. Father Carmody knew this. So do you, Father. So do I. You go into a monastery because you want to be nearer to God. Not because you feel a revulsion towards people. It's a question of motive. It was my opinion that Father Carmody didn't really want to go to anything; he wanted to get away from something. It didn't make much sense; it was even slightly . . . frivolous.

Like these restless people who suddenly jump on boats or planes: they think that by sailing or flying two thousand miles they'll get away from their troubles. I'm not at all sure about these matters, but I think that Father Carmody wouldn't have gotten away from anything. It was . . . all wrong. And so I refused him, Father. I couldn't do anything else."

I said nothing; I suppose he was right. I thought of poor John with his wall around him, a little more added to it each year, and so really alone that even those who loved him never had a hint of the crisis that threatened him or the sickness that killed him. And all I could say was, "I miss him. And I have great reason to be grateful to him. . . ."

I don't say these things well; it sounded dramatic, a little false —everything I meant it not to sound. But the Bishop said only, "That helps." And then he added cryptically, "It may even be enough." He got to his feet and said, "I must go."

I walked with him to the door; as I opened it he said, "One thing more, Father. I'm pleased with . . . everything."

So this was good; I thanked him. He said slowly, "And yet . . . I may take you away from here."

He stood by the door, one hand touching it: he seemed to be watching me, listening. And when he said these words I must have stopped dead still. It was one of those moments filled with silence, and then against this backdrop of the absence of noise, the small, distant, irrelevant sounds came swimming by, brushing the silence without disturbing it: the sounds of the street blown in through the partly open door, Roy, who must have left his hideout in the basement, whistling faintly and monotonously from somewhere in the back part of the rectory. In the strange stillness I heard all this, and then I said, "Yes, Bishop. . . ."

"There's a vacancy," he said. "You know what it is. So far I've appointed no successor to Father Carmody. Now I'm going to have to. Soon. The parish needs a permanent pastor. I was thinking of you, Father."

[455]

So here it was. After all the months. And the funny thing about it was that as often as I'd imagined this scene — and I think I began to imagine it, really, from the very first day I came to Saint Paul's — rehearsing all possible details with that queer mixture of reluctance and pleasure, conducting long and even rather subtle debates with myself about what I might say and what I might not say, what in all decency and fairness I could do and what in the same decency and fairness I could not do, carefully balancing what was now against what just possibly could be — the funny thing about all this was that now that the scene was actually *here*, it didn't matter at all. I mean, all the rehearsals, the debates, the balancings just didn't count; they were out of date. Because now there was no longer a decision to be made; that decision had been made already, five months ago. On, of all days, New Year's Day. So that despite my superior comments on New Year's Resolutions, I suppose I now had one of my own. . . . But the Bishop was waiting for an answer, and now I knew that Saint Raymond's was mine if I wanted it. And I *did* want it: heaven knows, I wanted it as badly as ever. I think I wanted it even more because . . . well, because now I knew that I couldn't take it. I said, "It's . . . kind of you, Bishop. . . ."

He shook his head. "No. It's a good parish, but I think it could be better. I think you might help to make it so." And then he looked at me in exactly the way he had on that day in his office years ago, the day he had told me he was sending me to The Cenacle; in the same courteous, level, uninflected voice, he asked the identical question, "Does it appeal to you, Father?"

I fumbled a bit; I knew what he was offering me and I knew what I had to do, but I didn't want to do it rudely. I said, "I was just thinking . . . have I the choice?"

He nodded. "Yes. I won't transfer you against your wishes. I think you deserve that. But I should tell you this: if you stay in Saint Paul's, you'll stay in a Saint Paul's which won't . . .

change. I have no plans for rebuilding or renovating. I can't. It's impractical; it's in fact economically impossible. I'll continue to maintain it. As long as I live it will always be here. It's my guess that it will last a little longer than both of us, but not much longer than that. Meanwhile, it will just . . . be. And that's your future in Saint Paul's, Father."

I said, "I think . . . if I could . . . I might like to stay."

There were no frowns. And no cheers, certainly. The heavy face was as impassive as ever; he said, "All right. I'll decide on Saint Raymond's later. But . . . this is yours, Father."

It was done, then. I thanked him, and then I said, "You're not offended, Bishop?"

He smiled faintly. "No," he said. "I'm not offended, Father. I'm not offended at all." He put out his hand and said, "Goodbye. My blessing."

And so I said goodbye to him at the door. He walked down to the waiting car; the chauffeur sprang out and ushered him in. He looked through the window again; there was just a brief nod; and then he was off, down the hot summer street. . . .

So I was alone again. It was hardly the first time I'd been alone in this rectory — but now there was a difference. This was the first time I'd ever stood, all alone, in the silence of this old building filled with little but the echoes of a past which was over before my own began, and looked around me, and slowly realized, at last, that this was mine and would be mine: that it was my home for the rest of my life. And with this at first I felt a touch of regret, an edge of sadness: I knew that as long as I lived in Old Saint Paul's it would never mean to me what Saint Stephen's and Saint Raymond's had meant — that it could never grip my heart and affections in the same way. And then, out of nowhere, a single question came before me: *Was it ever intended to?* It was a simple question, but one I'd never asked myself before. I had no direct answer, but possibly the question itself was enough, for slowly another feeling came in, rising over regret, a feeling which swelled until it was almost . . . what? Joy? Maybe that's too strong a word at this point, but it grew and grew until I felt it so strongly that I could feel nothing else: an awareness, an *assurance* that while something was over forever, something else had just begun — and that if the new might not seem the equal of the old, that might be because the two were not to be compared. The new was something of another kind, something I had never known before. And at this moment, here in the rectory hallway, I stood aching with excitement, for suddenly it seemed to me that something might be ahead which grew out of the past, yes, but was totally different, with its own labors and rewards, that it might be deeper and fuller and more meaningful than anything in the past, and that as a priest in Old Saint Paul's, working day by day in this parish I had really been shamed into choosing by the scornful words of a dying friend, I might, through the parish and its people, find my way not again to the simple engagement of the heart and affections, but to the Richness, the Mercy, the immeasurable Love of God. . . .

And then the feeling passed, swiftly, leaving me still standing here in the hallway, almost gasping, as if I'd suddenly exhaled some time ago, and hadn't quite been able to catch my breath again. All this could have lasted no more than a moment or two, and what it meant, or if it meant anything at all, I couldn't say. And yet I think it did. . . . I walked into the office and sat down at my desk; I felt, now, a little shaken . . . but strangely hopeful. And strangely happy. . . .

I sat there for some time, thinking. I sat there until Father Danowski came back, some time later. He was excited; a neighbor had told him that the Bishop's car had been parked outside, that the Bishop had been seen on his way inside.

"How I wish I could have been present to see him once again!" he said regretfully. "My admiration for our Bishop, Father, knows no bounds!"

He stood before me, obviously waiting — presumably for

[458]

news of the visit. But I nodded and said nothing; presently he said, with a great elaborateness, "Might I inquire, Father, if perhaps the Bishop had some special purpose to his visit? I do not wish to pry, of course," he said hastily, "but possibly he had something especial in view? With regard to the parish?"

I said, "No. No, I'm afraid not. Nothing especial at all."

Suddenly he smiled at me, wisely. "Ah ha ha ha, Father," he said. "He may have *said* nothing. But you know and I know, Father, that a busy person such as His Excellency does not make a visit like this with *nothing in mind*. That is not the way bishops are, Father. I am of course not a professional prophet, but I think you will find that one day, before very long, His Excellency will announce *certain plans* relating to Old Saint Paul's. You are too modest to proclaim this, Father, but our parish has of late been moving ahead by leaps and bounds! In my experience, this is not the sort of thing which is ignored in diocesan headquarters. I think that very soon now we may expect to see a vast improvement in our physical surroundings. Oh yes, Father, Old Saint Paul's is quite definitely on the way back up! Mark my words!"

And for just one moment I was tempted to tell him the truth — I thought it might be a kindness. But then I didn't, because it wouldn't have been. For, as the Bishop had said, Father Danowski is still very young. He's a priest who is, in his way, just beginning. And in a few years now he will leave Saint Paul's and will go to another parish. I think he won't like to go, and I think that he'll always remember Saint Paul's — but after a few years he won't remember it with quite the same intensity, and gradually, as he moves along, Saint Paul's will necessarily become less and less a part of his life. Whereas as I move along, it will remain all of mine. So that the situations are hardly the same — and why down a hope or burst a bubble now, when in the end it won't even matter at all? So I said only, "We'll see. We'll see. . . ."

"And *soon*," he said positively. "Unless I am quite wrong,

[459]

Father, we shall see very soon! And now I must go up to my room and tidy up a bit. I have a few small chores to perform before supper."

He started off up the stairs; when he had nearly reached the top he turned and called down to me.

"Mark my words, Father," he said joyously. "Great things are in store!"

Great things are in store. He bounded happily up the rest of the stairs and disappeared into his bedroom, whistling. I watched him go with amusement, with affection — and with gratitude. And then I left the office and the rectory, and went over into the church to say my prayers. . . .